THE WORLD ACCORDING TO VICE

EDITED BY
Andy Capper, James Knight and Bruno Bayley

EDITOR IN CHIEF VICE GLOBAL
Jesse Pearson

DESIGNER
Stacy Wakefield

EDITORIAL ASSISTANCE
Piers Martin
John McDonnell
Alex Miller

CHAPTER ILLUSTRATIONS
Johnny Ryan

VICE FOUNDERS
Suroosh Alvi
Shane Smith

VICE MEDIA GROUP EU CEO
Andrew Creighton

THANKS TO
Alen Zukanovic at Inkubator

THE WORLD

ACCORDING

TO

VICE

THE WORLD ACCORDING TO VICE

Published by Canongate Books in 2010

1

Copyright © Vice UK Ltd, 2010

First published in Great Britain in 2010
by Canongate Books, 14 High Street,
Edinburgh EH1 1TE

British Library Cataloguing-in-Publication Data
A catalogue record for this book is available on
request from the British Library

ISBN 9781 1 84767 969 7

Printed and bound in Spain by mccgraphics

www.viceland.com
www.meetatthegate.com

CONTENTS

INTRODUCTION
By Andy Capper and Jesse Pearson

9

THE STATE WE'RE IN
13

DISPATCHES FROM A WORLD OF VICE
53

VBS, OR THE REVOLUTION WILL BE TELEVISED (JUST NOT ON TELEVISION)
119

(DON'T) TRY THIS AT HOME
131

PHOTOJOURNALISM
159

INTERROGATIONS
221

INTRODUCTION

THIS IS A CONVERSATION BETWEEN ANDY CAPPER, BRITISH EDITOR OF VICE, AND JESSE PEARSON, THE EDITOR IN CHIEF OF VICE GLOBAL, WHO IS AMERICAN.

Andy Capper: Jesse, we have to do a thing where we talk about the last eight years of *Vice* magazine being in Britain.

Jesse Pearson: Why?

AC: We're doing a book with Canongate that's apparently going to open us up to a "whole new audience". I'm very excited about that.

JP: Hmm.

AC: Please?

JP: What is it that you want to say?

AC: Well, this book is for a Brit audience and we are here to talk about yours and my experience of how the British *Vice* started and how the special relationship worked and survived against the ridiculous odds; and I guess how the start of British *Vice* and then *Vice* EU coincided with the start of both our careers as editors here.

JP: So this is for the kind of audience that likes Ant and Dec...

AC: Yes, that is correct. You seem to have your finger on the pulse of Britain.

JP: I like British people. I think they have the best sense of humour in the world, apart from New York City Jewish people. Russians come third. But I think Brits are too fond of making lists and doing weird awards things. Like the whole Christmas number one thing—to me that's insane.

AC: You should have been there when it was East 17 vs Oasis. It was one of the cultural highpoints of the last 100 years of Britain.

JP: I also like the way British people get weepy and have sing-alongs while drunk, because I do that too and I also like their attitude with regards to partying, which is pretty much Friday from 5 PM until Sunday, or rather Monday, at 4 AM, going for it.

AC: It's more like Thursday from noon. One of the first stories we did together was when I was sent to Paris for the weekend to meet the *sapeurs*. I wrote the article and people seemed to like it but I was not actually sure if I found any *sapeurs*.

JP: There was also a grime article pretty much every month.

AC: We were the only people who wrote about it in such detail aside from *Grime Monthly* or whatever. We did those articles 'cos that scene at the time was like a young, black version of *Eastenders*, with all the gossip and chit-chat and "incidents", which were turned from people quarrelling violently at pirate radio stations to shootings, stabbings and jail sentences. And now, some of those kids from that scene are Britain's biggest pop stars—Dizzee, Tinchy, Wiley. It's nuts.

Let's give people some more history. What was *Vice* like eight years ago, before the British office opened and you and I became the editors?

JP: People liked it in the main because of the DOs & DON'Ts, I mean, it was great because it was like nothing else. The focus of the magazine was more on retardation in general, but that's what attracted me to it.

AC: It started as a reaction against the tail end of the 90s, which was a time when a lot of people were being overly pious about things, I feel.

JP: It was the funniest magazine around. And, yes, coming out of the liberal arts education prison I had been in for five years before, it was very refreshing. My college was one big, long take-back-the-night rally. I had to constantly be getting talked to about how insensitive I was, so *Vice* appealed to me for sure.

AC: Those sensitive types are like the self-proclaimed "socialists" who've never had to be poor or work a hard job but have rehearsed polemics about workers' rights. Not that workers shouldn't have rights, but essentially the people who yell about them the loudest generally have no idea what the fuck they are talking about.

JP: It's easy to say you dig blue-collar people if your family is not blue-collar. But I have to admit I mostly read the D&Ds and the guides to funny shit. I was into more sophisticated things such as *i-D* and *Sleazenation*, you know, timeless things like that.

AC: Where I grew up in Southport, which borders on being a hick town, I honestly didn't know what *i-D*

was about. As a kid, I didn't understand the concept of "fashion magazine".

JP: Oh, well, re: *i-D* et al, to be honest, I started looking at them for tits because there was no "alt porn" back then. Those were the best places to see the nude boobs of the sorts of girls I liked.

AC: We shouldn't talk about other people, it's a bad vibe. Looking back over the glorious career you've had as the main editor, and from which period most of this book comes from, which would you say were your favourite issues?

JP: My second issue was the Special Issue. It was the first time the majority of an issue was given over to one group of people.

AC: What was the thinking behind that—giving over the issue to a small group of people rather than "check out the world through our gay magazine lens" like a lot of other people do?

JP: It started to become clear to me that to do themes like we were doing, we needed to go all the way and get every single page of the magazine in line with the theme, and so we had a run of issues where every single page was dedicated to one theme.

AC: That's kind of where that "immersionism journalism" started that I always talk about when other people interview me about what *Vice* is. And I guess that style of journalism became our hallmark, right?

JP: Well, I have to say, we acted like we invented that and we 100 percent did not. Ever hear of a guy named George Orwell?

AC: The name rings a bell. Is that the guy who wrote *The Da Vinci Code*?

JP: Yes, that's correct.

AC: Yeah, we definitely didn't invent immersionism

in any way at all but it became what we did.

JP: The whole thing from our perspective was to let the subjects tell as much of the story as possible. There were obvious ones like the Poverty Issue and the Mentally Ill Issue, all of which involved me going and staying with the people in the mag and you and other editors doing the same.

And then the Cops Issue came out which was a classic. For a magazine like *Vice* to come out with an issue all about our respect for cops was pretty good. The thing about cops, or one of the things we wanted to get across, is how insanely funny they can be, and who has better stories than cops?

Soldiers and ER doctors I guess can compete, but not many other professions.

AC: I guess VBS started out of that immersionism journalism thing. Remember when that started? It was when Spike [Jonze] said to Shane [Smith, *Vice* CEO], "Why don't you film your articles?" But let's just talk about the magazine here. There's a whole section about VBS later in the book.

JP: Yeah, well, immersionism started to turn into a bit of a crutch for the magazine and I think it's important to keep changing things up and so we stopped doing as much.

AC: We started doing longer interviews, like huge interviews with people. But that in itself was also a kind of immersionism.

JP: Yeah, but they weren't just interviews like: "Let's ask the guy from a band what inspired his stupid shitty boring new record". I think that the interview is one of the best and most maltreated formats there is. It's direct in the same way immersionism is, if it's done right.

AC: It was a natural extension of what we were doing. My favourite interview, but also possibly my hardest and worst interview, was with Shane Mac-Gowan.

JP: Yeah, Mumbles MacGowan. I wish that one were longer.

AC: It was four hours of transcription and the time we spent with him was amazing, but we only got 800 words of understandable stuff. And Shane is so far the only celeb we've put on the cover non-ironically.

For those who are new to *Vice*—such as the person who has just had this book bought for them for Christmas and is thinking, "What is this shit?"—why did we never put celebs on the cover?

JP: Because people only put celebrities on the covers to sell magazines, and we don't care about selling magazines.

I think that our Fiction Issues were a big step for the magazine.

AC: How did that change people's perceptions of *Vice,* do you think?

JP: It made them think we were even more pretentious than they did before.

AC: Haha. Why did people think we were pretentious anyway?

JP: It's probably because they didn't actually read the magazine. Instead they listened to what other people had to say about it — "hipster, etc, etc".

AC: There is currently an advert on British TV based on "how many hipsters can you fit in a car" or something and one of them is carrying an issue of *Vice*.

JP: Good, good.

AC: It's basically God saying to us both, "The last eight years of your life? With all that stuff you did? This is what it boils down to: two seconds in an unfunny advert for a shitty car."

JP: You could look it at that way, I suppose…

THE STATE WE'RE IN

Buried in among the important world news about celebrities falling out of nightclubs and criticising each other on Twitter, there are also less important things like war, famine, terrorism, aggressive dictatorships and global economic meltdown to report on. Additionally, there are extremely pressing news stories about sex, drugs and what it's like to live with a dog on a string for a week. In this section we attempt to tackle it all.

BABES OF THE BNP

BY GAVIN HAYNES | ILLUSTRATION BY DANIEL DAVID FREEMAN

Published July 2009

You no longer need to be a hatchet-faced National Front refugee to join the whites-only club. The fascist menace no longer wears jackboots. It no longer flags down the number 25 bus with a hearty "Sieg heil". Nope, ours is a new, gentler, more airbrushed age. Feminism's here, so now girls can dig race-hate too. As the BNP's attempts to reposition itself as a mainstream party have advanced its perimeter far beyond the usual crewcuts 'n' tats brigade, we spoke to three of the more acceptable new faces of the unacceptable. What a bunch of hotties! Phwoar! Makes you aroused to be British.

REBECCA EDWARDS, MANCHESTER

Vice: How old are you?
Rebecca: 23.

What do you do for a living?
I'm a full-time mum.

What first attracted you to the BNP?
My husband. He's been in the army for 12 years, and when I met him four years ago, he actually told me about the BNP and what they were doing. And from then on, I started to support them.

Are most of your friends BNP?
Yeah. Not particularly the people in our area, but our friends are.

When people say the BNP is a fascist party, what do you think?
Fascist—I don't understand that word.

Think of Nazi Germany, or 1930s Italy.
I can't even remember when that happened really, but I'm against them anyway.

You're against who?
The Germans. I know that sounds evil... I was brought up that way.

But not the Nazis?
No, I don't agree with that at all.

What's the best thing about living in Britain today?
I hate Britain, and I want to move to Spain in the next couple of years, 'cos our country's not England anymore. It's very rare for English people to live here anymore. When I went to Lanzarote, I felt more English there than I do here, and that's no exaggeration.

But won't you then be an immigrant too?
Yeah, but the answer to that is I would go over to their country and respect their country. I wouldn't go over there and try and do suicidal bombs [*sic*]. The immigrants that come over to this country should be making this a good country and proud of it and helping this country, but most of them don't.

What do you think symbolises Britain best?
Well, I used to know Britain as strong, and over the past couple of years, I don't know if I've grown up, but I've seen it going soft. The memory I have is the war, and how we fighted [*sic*] all the people in WWI and WWII, and it makes me proud to be British.

Fish or chips?
Fish.

Alan Carr or Jimmy Carr?
Alan.

David Mellor or David Beckham?
Beckham.

Jesus Jones or Jesus Christ?
Jesus Christ.

Hieronymus Bosch or a Bosch electric sander?

I don't know them, I'll just put the second one.

Plato or Playdough?
Playdough.

Towel or rag?
Towel.

Morrissey or Eric Clapton?
Morrissey.

Nick Nolte or Nick Griffin?
Nick Griffin.

In terms of the BNP's repatriation policy on immigration, if you had to choose, who would you repatriate first, Dizzee Rascal or Tinchy Stryder?
The second one, because I've never heard of him and I like Dizzee Rascal.

Which do you dislike more: Muslims or Jews?
Muslims.

Do you think Nick Griffin is actually gay, or is that just a vicious rumour?
No. I think it's a vicious rumour.

Have you seen him in the flesh? He's quite mincey.
I've only seen him on the news. I really like him.

Do you think the anti-BNP movements are too overtly black?
Not really.

As a hypothetical solution to the immigration problem, what about dividing Britain down the middle, and using the left half for immigrants, and the right half for everyone else.
Sorry, I don't get that. Am I'm being really thick? No. I don't think so.

What if immigrants could prove their usefulness—shouldn't they then be allowed to stay? For instance, if they began life here with a six-month

period of forced labour, perhaps spent making shoes for the rest of the population in a giant shoe factory in the East Midlands?

No. They shouldn't come to Britain at all in the first place.

What about people who've grown up in Britain from a very young age, but aren't, as the BNP would term it, "ethnically British"? When you repatriated them, don't you think the BNP should first give them intensive lessons in speaking, for example, the Ghanaian language, and learning the skills of an agriculturally based society?

No. I don't think so. Just send them back. I know that sounds really evil...

OK, what if Ghana, or wherever, decrees that these immigrants are now Britain's responsibilty—that they no longer have the right to live in Ghana. Do you think war with Ghana would be justified to force the issue, or would you simply propose a system of gradually raised trade sanctions, possibly with the aid of a UN mandate?

I wouldn't do the war, 'cos I'm against war. Er, the other one...

Carol Thatcher—hero or villain?
Hero.

Al Jolson—hero or villain?
I don't know who he is. Um, hero.

Mother Teresa—hero or villain.
Hero.

Hitler—hero or villian?
Villain.

Ant and Dec—heroes or villains?
Heroes.

Finally, has anything amusing ever happened to you in connection with spoons?
Spoons? No. I don't follow.

JO BELL, NEWCASTLE

Vice: How old are you?
Jo: 19

What do you do for a living?
I haven't got a job at the moment. I used to work in a call centre for TalkTalk. It was fun, but we got retrenched.

What attracted you to the BNP?
I just liked what they were saying. I think they're talking the truth, standing up for what they believe in, not just saying what they think people want to hear.

Are most of your friends BNP?
Some of them are. I kind of got into it through my friend Danny. He's really racist. Everyone calls him "Nazi Danny". He started telling me about them, and it made a lot of sense.

When people say the BNP is a fascist party, what do you think?
Some people don't understand what the BNP is about. I've had rows with people—not fights, just big arguments. I probably am a bit racist, mind.

What, to you, symbolises Britain best?
Um, I'd say maybe St George's flag, partly because my favourite film is *This Is England*—it's about skinheads, but they're not really racist, because one of them is a black kid. They turn on him in the end, but because he was one of the gang they're not really racist. They just believe in what they believe in.

Fish or chips?
Chips.

Alan Carr or Jimmy Carr?
Alan.

Princess Di or Jade Goody?
Jade.

Ant or Dec?
Dec.

Brown shirt or black shirt?
Black.

Bird in the hand or two in the bush?
Two in the bush.

Fred West or Stephen Fry?
Stephen Fry.

Morrissey or Eric Clapton?
Morrissey.

What do you think the BNP could do to improve its appeal to minority voters?
A lot of people have got an opinion against the BNP that they're racists or bullies. I don't think the BNP are a mainstream party that everyone should follow. I think they believe what they believe. I think if we came across more to the people, because I've spoken to people before, and they've been like, "Well, what is the BNP?" and they couldn't even say what BNP stood for. A lot of people don't really know much about it unless you're quite racist or quite nationalist. So if they could explain themselves to people more clearly, a lot more people would listen.

Do you think Nick Griffin has concentrated his manifesto enough on the problem of falling house prices?
Not really, but I don't think anyone is. I don't think there's anything that can really be done about it.

In terms of the BNP's repatriation policy on immigration, if you had to choose, who would you repatriate first, Dizzee Rascal or Tinchy Stryder?
Dizzee Rascal. I know this is gonna sound horrible, because he's the one who's the most, like… because my problem is that when immigrants come over to this country, they try and bring in their own churches and languages. And I think he expresses himself more as like an African or whatever he is, whereas Tinchy Stryder is more American. That's the difference.

Which do you dislike more, Muslims or Hindus?
Muslims. They're the ones who've got the most attention, they're the ones who are kicking off about things the most. They're more in the public eye as troublemakers.

If, as a hypothetical solution to the problem of immigration, we turned over one city to immigrants and made them all live there in a sort of ghetto, what city would you choose?
Birmingham, because it's full of them anyway.

What if immigrants could prove their usefulness—should they then be allowed to stay? For instance, by selecting only immigrants who were extremely good-looking?
No. I just don't think there should be any. You see, just because they're black, I haven't got a problem with that. If they've lived in the country for a long time and they're working, and say they're a doctor or they're actually doing something. It's when they're getting benefits that I have a problem, 'cos there's plenty of people in our country who need our money and plenty of people who are British who are homeless, and they are just being given our money.

Is the problem one of culture, not ethnicity? For instance, would you be prepared to accept Muslims in your community if they all converted to Christianity, took part in maypole ceremonies on St George's day, took elocution lessons and dressed solely in Harris Tweed?
You mean if they weren't trying to imply their own religion [sic] and if they acted like us? Well, I wouldn't have as much of a problem. There's a school in our town, and everyone jokes about it, like it's spot-the-white-kid school. In the town now, they've got a religious school, and they've got lots of prayers in Arabic on the wall, and I think that's

just totally wrong. Yeah, they should learn our language. I find it really insulting. Like, in the call centre, people would ring up, and you'd ask to speak to the account holder and they'd go, "The account holder doesn't speak English." It used to really, really annoy us.

Peter Andre—hero or villain?
Aw, hero.

Jeremy Clarkson—hero or villain?
Hero.

Enoch Powell—hero or villain?
Hero.

Nelson Mandela—hero or villain?
Villain.

Finally, has anything amusing ever happened to you in connection with spoons?
Spoons? As in, like, a spoon? I don't think so.

HELEN RIDDELL, NEWCASTLE

Vice: How old are you?
Helen: 19. Wait, no, 18. 19 next month.

What do you do for a living?
I'm a kitchen assistant at the minute.

What first attracted you to the BNP?
I don't know. I couldn't really actually tell you. There were a couple of the sentences I agreed with. Basically about how immigrants are coming and taking people's jobs and that.

Are most of your friends BNP?
Some of them are.

And your parents?
No. What are they? I think Liberal Democrat. I dunno.

Are there any BNP policies you disagree with?
Not so far, no, 'cos I'm still in the middle of looking up all that about it at the moment.

When people say the BNP is a fascist party, what do you think?
Yes, in some ways it is. But there we are. It's a hard decision. There's some things I think are good and some things I think are bad, so it's a hard decision to make, but it was the one party I felt closer to than any of the other parties.

Is there a big anti-BNP movement up in Newcastle? Do you get a lot of stick?
Not really.

Do you have arguments about it with people?
Sometimes, yeah. But not like heated arguments.

Fish or chips?
Fish.

Alan Carr or Jimmy Carr?
Alan.

Princess Di or Jade Goody?
Di.

Blair or Brown?
Brown.

Michael Jackson or Tim Westwood?
Michael Jackson.

Peter Andre or Stephen Hawking?
Peter Andre.

What do you think the BNP could do to improve its appeal to gay voters?
Erm, ooh, I don't know. I haven't a clue.

In terms of the BNP's repatriation policy on immigration, if you had to choose, who would you repatriate first, Dizzee Rascal or Tinchy Stryder?

Tinchy Stryder, 'cos he's not very well known. Dizzee Rascal's more of a worldwide-known icon.

What should we do with Lenny Henry?
I don't even know who that is, sorry.

Which do you dislike more, Muslims or black people?
Muslims. I've never seen any advertisements about blacks who come here and don't work. It's more the Muslims, 'cos basically that's what I object to. My mum split up with my dad a couple of years ago, and she was going to get a flat off the council, and the first question they asked her on the form was "Are you an immigrant?" I don't agree with that, you see, so that's where it started from.

So you agree with the BNP's send-'em-back policies?
Yeah.

But would it be possible to maybe come to a compromise with a noble race like the Chinese? Perhaps keep them on as a sort of servant class?
Yeah. I wouldn't mind them if they actually worked and didn't take all of our jobs, basically. I wouldn't mind them if they contributed something to this country.

What nationality would you most like to keep in the UK?
African, because my nana's African. She was a white African from somewhere next to Cape Town. She moved back here in 1987 or something. My grand-dad was in the RAF over there and she came back with him.

So what nationality would you most like to be waited-on by as a servant class?
Oh God, there's a few. There's a couple I would, but I can't really pinpoint one.

Go on.
I don't know. Chinese maybe?

Sure thing. What ethnicity would you most like to make love to?
Oh God, British.

Other than that?
Say... black?

What if immigrants only asked to be allowed into the country on condition they had been sterilised, so that they couldn't create any children to further burden the state? Would that be a potential solution?
Um, yeah, I think so.

Let's try a word association game. Just say the first word that comes into your head.
OK.

Golly.
Wally.

Rag.
Rug.

Goose.
Duck.

Oswald.
Place.

Concentration.
Head.

Bunny.
Rabbit.

Finally, has anything amusing ever happened to you in connection with spoons?
Spoons? Erm, no.

By the way, we got back in touch with Rebecca Edwards a couple of weeks later. She wasn't too happy.

BLOOD ON THE TERRACES

**HOOLIGANISM IS BACK, AND IT'S BETTER THAN EVER | BY FOREST GATE PHIL
ILLUSTRATION BY PADDY JONES**

Published March 2004

From Glasgow to Derby to Leeds to Wales and back up again, every week of my life I've travelled the country on trains and coaches looking for other gangs of like-minded young men to punch, kick, and stab. I'm violent. I know it's wrong, and on the one hand, I want people to know the truth about how bad things are getting with hooliganism. But when I get my fist into some poor bastard's face, I think, "Aw fuck it, this is war!"

Being a respected member of West Ham United's Inter City Firm for more than 20 years has given me the opportunity to experience the amazing diversity of the British Isles in all kinds of exciting situations. Sadly, our firm is nowhere near as strong as it used to be. We had ten years in the Premiership, where clubs don't have the same level of enthusiasm for hooliganism as the lower First Division clubs. This is mainly because there's less bitterness and desperation among the Premiership fans and the clubs can afford to spend more money on security measures. I'm sad to say it, but the Premiership makes you soft.

Now that we've been relegated to the good old First Division, it's nice to see so many old faces come out of the woodwork. We're starting to get a new firm together, and we're slowly but surely getting back to our best. A lot of young lads are starting to get into hooliganism again, so that's helped us out as well. Young men are attracted to it now that rave culture has died and cocaine is back. Happy pills killed things a bit, but Charlie keeps you on your toes. Believe me, there's a lot of coke going around on the trains and coaches when the football fans travel to games. A lot of people aren't drinking—they're just doing coke, so they're all hyper and ready to murder.

The Old Bill, the government, and the FA are suppressing information about the new surge in hooliganism because if the public knew how many lads were travelling up and down every weekend to bash each other in, then they'd want something done about it. That would mean money would have to come out of the pockets of the players and the TV companies, and that's never going to happen. In my opinion, hooliganism is just going to grow and grow all around the country until people start getting killed again. That's the beauty of this whole resurgence, really: things have become way more violent than they ever were but nobody dares report on it. If the television crews capture a row, we smash their cameras and batter the crew into the ground. If anyone asks the teams or anyone else with a financial interest, the company line is, "Everything's fine." The truth is, everything is not fine. It's covered in blood. And you don't even know how far we're willing to take this.

The UK is trying get the Olympics in 2012, and the bid for European championships also. News that young lads are cutting each other up every weekend and that pubs are being wrecked all the time wouldn't go down very well with the Olympics committee. So nobody's going to find out. Right? I said nobody's going to find out, right?

This magazine can run whatever it wants, because it's not like it's going to change the state of UK football violence. The important news sources—the mainstream media and the like—are the ones that drive the revenue of the football industry, and they will tell you that hooliganism died with all-seater stadiums. I am happy to say that's total and utter bollocks. It's just as bad as it ever was. And judging by some of these new lads, things are much, much worse (or better—I don't even know anymore).

MILLWALL

Because we came down to the First Division, our firm is like the fucking Man United of the hooligan league. Millwall's been anticipating us coming down to the First Division for years, because to scalp an ICF is the best you can do. We're the most glamorous, good-looking football fans in the world.

Last time we got the train to London Bridge, there was Old Bill fucking everywhere. We hardly got a chance. I think all the Bushwackers were still wincing from the last time we paid them a visit. The next time we play them, I fully expect there to be murder.

CARDIFF

Last time we played Cardiff, in the early 80s, we kicked the fuck out of them, cut them to pieces. They was all big men, but we was all like 16 and 17. We cut them to fucking pieces with Stanley knives. All their big blokes had never had a fucking kicking before, but they did this time and it was from a load of little Herberts from Canning Town.

At Upton Park in the early 80s, we got in the away end and stuck out like sore thumbs, all casual, dressed up to the nines. They were in big boots and donkey jackets, but we still kicked the fuck out of them.

LEEDS

The first time I went to Leeds, we got bushwacked by the Leeds Service Crew. About a hundred of us chased some of their boys into a car park, but what we didn't realise is that there were a hundred of them waiting for us there. They were everywhere. It was proper *Zulu*. Everywhere you looked, there was a geezer with a lump of wood, a brick, a blade, or something. Fuck, it was scary, but one of the big boys steamed into them, a gap opened up, and we had it on our toes.

SOUTHAMPTON

I lost our mob and I was wandering around on my own. But I heard an Old Bill car fly by, so I followed that, walked round the corner, and there was a geezer who'd been hit so hard that his eye had popped out and it was resting on his cheek. He was covered in claret and that, and there was a couple of screaming girls around him and his fucking eye was on his fucking cheek. It just made me feel sick.

ARSENAL

We always used to give Arsenal a slap, and in the old days it would go off anywhere. Once, we were at a disco in Camden and we got spotted by a load of Gooners. I glassed this geezer pretty bad. I got a pint glass in the bloke's face—it was fucking horrible.

TOTTENHAM

Everyone thinks our main rivals are Millwall, but over the last 15 years it's been Tottenham. They're the closest team to us. And whenever we go to visit them it's always a lovely day out.

We meet their firm at Liverpool Street, bash 'em, and go up to Northumberland Park to mob 'em up again. We generally walk up the ground, take the pub near the ground, go in the ground, take the piss out of them, and get home in time to watch *Casualty* on TV.

BRADFORD CITY

These Northern cunts were quite a force to be reckoned with in the 80s, but I can't say they've ever made a show with us. They turned over Cardiff late last season and always have a tear-up with other Yorkshire clubs, like Sheffield and Leeds, so I suppose they've got something about them.

WOLVERHAMPTON WANDERERS

They're so shit they don't belong in the Premiership, but they've had a well-respected mob called the Subway Crew for years. We had it with them in the cup last week, there were loads of blades everywhere and we were throwing bottles and bricks over the fat blue line (aka the Old Bill). Traditionally, Wolves are some of the worst dressers in the country. I had to go to court up there once, and me and my mates were approached by some oik who asked us if we were solicitors—as if they'd never seen a defendant dressed in a suit. Actually, that reminds me of one my favourite jokes: What do you call a scouser in a suit? The defendant. What do you call a scouser in a three-bedroom house? A burglar.

NORWICH CITY

The Tractor Boys have never had a proper firm, but I have had the honour of being run by their mob. Me and four mates drove up there and I had to get back early for a do. As we left the ground, about five or six nippers started mouthing off on the other side of the road. We just give 'em the "fuck off" mugs, but one ran over and kicked a mate up the arse, so we chased them up the hill, where about 50 of their mates swarmed us. There was a quick turnaround as I watched my mates in the distance. I stopped up against a wall and they came in round me so we could all discuss the merits of the 4-4-2 system. I explained as there were only four of us, we weren't "football" or a firm, and this confused the bumpkins. Hooligan law states that you can't lay into anybody else if they're not up for it, so we got away.

SUITING UP, CRUSTING DOWN

YUPPIES VS PUNKS FOR A WORKING WEEK

Published June 2009

Recently London was tousled by a series of riots led by outraged anarchists who were probably just really bored. As usual, it looked like a good time. But it also made us wonder who really has the superior lifestyle: hand-to-mouth agitators or the city-boy capitalists they abhor? So we assigned one staff writer to pose as a punk and another as a plutocrat to investigate. Here's what happened.

CITY-BOY DIARY

BY BRUNO BAILEY, PHOTOS BY JAMIE LEE CURTIS TAETE AND JUSTIN MULCAHY

MONDAY

I usually walk to work, but my new suede brogues (£150 from Men's Traditional Shoes in Camberwell) aren't meant for the trudging peasantry. The nearest appropriate transportation was the Underground. It was jam-packed with hundreds of stressed-out, grumpy city workers and the waft of coffee mixed with expensive colognes and rancid morning farts made me want to vomit.

Looking around at my fellow travellers I suddenly realised my beard was déclassé. When I arrived at my destination, Liverpool Street Station, the heartland of London's bankers, I booked myself in for a wet shave.

At lunchtime I went to All Bar One, an appropriately soulless chain of gastropubs that serves sausage and mash for £10 a go and pints for £3.50. I overheard one of the suited fellows next to me refer to the waitress as a "right spastic cunt", which was a lovely way to start my meal. Eventually I sauntered back to the office but, being disinclined to work, I went home early and puffed a cigar in the garden. So far, being a city boy was simply wonderful.

TUESDAY

My face was still sore from the shave. Sure, I'd taken the piss a bit with my productivity on Monday, but today I was determined to work at the computer for a few hours. My duties consisted of cruising various social-networking sites before an early lunch.

Canary Wharf is the towering hub of British and European finance. Feeling important, I headed over to have an overpriced club sandwich (£9) al fresco, right at the foot of One Canada Square, the epicentre of this glorious monument to success.

The gorgeous stench of billions of pounds wafted around me as I sat picking bacon fat from my teeth and smoking Montecristo Number Four cigars. A fellow capitalist grimaced at me for blowing fine Cuban tobacco smoke onto his eggs Benedict. I thought I was doing him a favour.

To satisfy the hunger for culture that comes with being a master of the universe, I booked a ticket to the Royal Opera House to see Wagner's *Lohengrin*. I sipped on a few brandies at a nearby pub before puffing another cigar on the steps of the opera house.

My ticket came with a glass of champagne that I slurped down in the foyer. As I looked for my seat, I realised that I had booked a standing-room ticket to a production that lasted nearly five hours. This was clearly a touch of idiocy left over from my poorer days. After fidgeting for three torturous hours and being frowned at by the elderly couple in front of me, I left on the verge of tears. Pretending to be filthy rich was beginning to wear on me.

WEDNESDAY

Somehow I had neglected to secure appropriate lodging. After surveying my humble residence, I decided my windfall of make-believe success allowed for a viewing of an obscenely expensive apartment near Canary Wharf. I felt a bit guilty about leading the estate agent on, so I lied and said I was waiting for my fiancée (who worked in a renowned Spanish art gallery) to accept my marriage proposal before I could really consider buying the place. Shaking my low-class scruples was proving

---

CITY-BOY CRITERIA

1. Drink champagne and brandy and smoke cigars every night
2. Dress like Charlie Sheen in Wall Street
3. Travel by tube or black cab—no walking allowed
4. Eat only sushi, dim sum, or food from gastropubs
5. Frequent central London strip clubs
6. Read the entire Financial Times *every day—even the bits that look like binary code*
7. Pretend to be stinking rich at all times

more difficult than I'd thought—and it was getting embarrassing. I left in shame with some paperwork.

But soon a reliable source informed me that after a hard day of wiping their bottoms with £50 notes atop platinum-plated shitters, many city boys retire to vast, vapid bars on the edges of the Square Mile, London's old financial hub, to watch sport. So off I went to watch football at the Barracuda Bar on Houndsditch.

As I strolled purposefully, some bike couriers near Aldgate looked at me like I was off to sell shares of a company that makes tainted baby food to rich, trusting widows. And I soon learned that the Barracuda is a South African bar. By halftime it was too much to bear.

THURSDAY

Today I realised that since I've been dressing up like a fop, I haven't taken the time to enjoy music—not on my iPod, not at work, not even at home. I hadn't even noticed. My theory is that this suit is sapping my ability to feel joy.

By early afternoon I needed a good meal, and being a modern man of means I opted for the exotic and worldly delicacy known as Oriental fusion. I thought it would be prudent to bone up on my "Eastern culture" now that the Chinese are set to rule the world. I know this because the articles in my new daily read, the *Financial Times*, have been hinting at it quite a lot.

By the time I had finished my lunch it was about 4 PM, and I contemplated heading back to work. But I was pooped. Instead I went to a fancy bar to relax, sip on a couple Rémy Martins, and enjoy a choice variety of D'Angelo tracks. I can't drink too much brandy—it makes me gag—so I switched to whiskey, which makes me retch slightly less.

No one spoke to me, even though I was wearing the right stuff. I think I might have been missing the lingo. I found myself contemplating the logistics of jamming a portfolio of mergers and acquisitions up one of their arses.

The truly prosperous must be in tip-top condition so they don't tire from fucking over as many proles as possible. With this in mind, I trotted along to an upmarket gym for a game of squash. I was feeling pretty sozzled, but no one likes a quitter, so I staggered through 45 minutes of painful degradation.

I tried to smoke another cigar after the match to regain some poise, but it made my oesophagus feel as if I'd been fellating exhaust pipes all day. I went home drunk, unwell, and unhappy.

FRIDAY

This morning I felt like a gold-leafed piece of shit. My diet of overrich food, cigars, brandy, and beer top-ups was clearly taking its toll. In an attempt to repair my discouraged body, I ordered some sushi for lunch. I ate it on the street, which was not very dignified, but I had a cigar for dessert. This time it got my head straight.

Disappointed with my lunch, I went to the city boy's favourite retreat—the titty bar. Talking to girls makes me nervous, so strip clubs are something I have studiously avoided until now. But being an abuser of the weak and a champion of the commercial means paying to look at a vagina (and maybe even a butthole) or two on a Friday afternoon.

The Griffin is one of those pound-in-a-pint-glass sorts of places. Mixed in wonderfully among the motocross and snowboarding displayed on numerous massive screens via obscure Sky channels, surprisingly attractive girls disrobed to a Nickelback soundtrack. During one awkward silence I heard the blokes next to me say, "As far as sports go later in life, cricket really is the only option." Unless it was a metaphor I didn't catch, these guys didn't have much use for naked woman gyrating to awful music. Turns out I didn't either, so I went home and felt relief wash over me like a bucket of cheap lager.

Now that my time as a city boy was over, I loosened my cotton yoke and tended to my blisters, all the while gorging on free-trade biscuits and tofu. Being a capitalist pig is far too much work.

ANARCHIST DIARY

BY JAMES KNIGHT, PHOTOS BY JAMIE LEE CURTIS TAETE AND MICHAEL OTERO

MONDAY

Everyone knows that no true anarchist would live in a place where you pay for things like hot water, electricity, and slaves of the state to come and take away the bins. Accordingly, my home for the week was a squat off Walworth Road in south London. I'd given myself a budget of £5 to last the five days, so for lodging, free had to trump comfort.

After settling into my bed on the floor and washing my face in a pool of stagnant water that had been in the sink for nearly 24 hours, I decided I needed a style update. It was an easy decision: LA posi-crust-hardcore punk from when more than ten people cared about Final Conflict.

I left the squat and lurked around a branch of the corporate pharmacy chain Boots awaiting an opportunity to nick some green hair dye. Boots supports vivisection. It is also fine with squirting shampoo into bunnies' eyes and making them wear lipstick on their skin and electrodes on their brains. I had absolutely no qualms about stealing from this outhouse of the bourgeoisie.

Of course, I had to have a mohawk. But the only implement we could find at the squat to shear my hair was a pair of blunt stationery scissors. This gave me an appropriately DIY (that is, awful-looking) appearance.

Punks don't care much about things like health and safety and hygiene, so bleach was applied directly to the remaining strip of hair by my new squat girlfriend, Karley. The only precaution she took was wearing a mangy goalkeeper's glove during the application process. It was all satisfactorily punk.

While the bleach settled I learned a new skill: sewing. No self-respecting crusty leaves home without a Los Crudos patch, and I made an adequate attempt at affixing some flair to an old denim jacket with cut-off sleeves.

Washing the toxic chemicals from my hair in the freezing shower was uncomfortable, but I kept up the don't-give-a-shit pretence until the dye was splooged all over my noggin and I realised that my forehead was rapidly turning green.

TUESDAY

Luckily the dye didn't stick to my skin like it stuck to my hair. It was like a rather punk tuft of grass had sprouted out of my skull. Night one in the squat had involved surprisingly little debauchery: my squat-mates had a TV and watched politicians spewing their filthy lies through the corporate media machine on *News at Ten*. I drowned out the elitist bullshit with a scratched copy of Conflict's *The Ungovernable Force* on a record player from the 1960s that somebody had brought back from Berlin.

Aside from waking up on the floor and feeling like I'd never be able to walk again, it was quite a letdown. There was no all-night weed smoking or heated political discussion. There wasn't even a police siege.

To amend matters I decided to pack up my sleeping bag and have a drink at the Foundry—a bar-art space-slop-house for Spanish cycle couriers with tribal tattoos and the single-dread-lock-that-looks-like-a-turd-log-jutting-from-the-back-of-the-head hairstyle. Surely I'd find like-minded souls here? The answer was no. But there was an organic ale that tasted of mud and parsnips.

After stealing six cans of cider from a nearby newsagent, I walked across Hackney Downs and went to borrow my friend's dog, which was overly pleased to have someone with Astro-turf for hair to play with. When we got back to the squat he savaged my mobile bed in excitement.

Factory-manufactured dog leads are tools of op-pression, so I lassoed the mutt with my belt and headed out wandering. It was pretty fun watching people cross the street with looks of total panic on their faces, but the police car trailing me all the way back across the river to South London was not so enjoyable.

ANARCHIST CRITERIA:

1. Don't engage with the system in any way—no mobile phones, bank cards, or public transportation
2. Live in a squat
3. Hang out with a dog
4. Don't pay for food
5. Look like a member of Extreme Noise Ter-ror (or at least Doom)
6. Make some new crusty friends
7. Attend at least one punk show

WEDNESDAY

Forty-eight hours in, it was time for a celebration. My squat buddies told me that they were up for par-tying so I went down to the local off-license booze store and discovered how punks can afford to get drunk: three litres of White Ace cost only £3. In a flush of excitement, I spent £9 of my new friends' money on nine litres of the stuff and retired to the squat.

I can now confirm that, cou-pled with the occasional bump of ketamine, drinking several White Aces leads to an almost lysergic experience. This is especially true if the person hasn't eaten for two days because all his money went to rotting his guts with cider that even street-sleepers wouldn't touch.

Fuzzy headed, I collapsed in a cor-ner and woke up intermittently to throw up into a shopping bag riddled with holes. The upshot was that the vomit had leaked all over my t-shirt and increased the authenticity of my getup. When I finally awoke I felt like someone had kicked my head in. My t-shirt for the week was saturated with a nice coat of bile, and I had un-explained cuts all over my forehead. Now I was finally getting somewhere! The taste of freedom was sour and painful but intensely liberating.

THURSDAY

I haven't eaten anything since Mon-day. I slept most of the day to try and kill the hunger pains but was jostled awake by my new squat buddies, Lauren and Kerri. They told me about some bins behind the local Marks & Spencer, in Elephant & Castle, that were a gold mine for just-out-of-date food. We headed over to see what the trash was serving for dinner.

Kerri was pretty optimistic after previous raids had yielded untold gourmet wonders. She brought along one of those shopping trolleys that your great-

aunt Edna might use. Everyone was in high spirits. As we rounded the back of M&S, disaster struck: a huge security fence had been erected around our expired morsels.

Like good crusties, we pulled the fence apart so Kerri could slip inside. After a root around in the huge bins, our worst fears came true: we had been beaten to the punch by fellow freegans. All that was left were some chocolate éclairs. My stomach was eating its own lining at this point so I started stuffing my face. Each slightly sweaty, turd-shaped dough popsicle tasted better than the last.

FRIDAY

After a week of drinking cider and sleeping on floors, I decided it was time to get back to nature. I'd heard that West Coast power-violence veterans Capitalist Casualties were playing at crust hangout the Grosvenor in Stockwell, so I decided to spend some time in a park close to the venue before catching the show.

I felt inexplicably uncomfortable and decided a couple cans of Special Brew would make everything a little better. As I sank my second I realised that in the same way Rastafarianism legitimises smoking

weed everywhere you go, being a crusty punk is just a big excuse to be a functioning (or at least semifunctioning) alcoholic.

Capitalist Casualties missed their plane. Very punk. Concertgoers were pretty sad, but there was a real sense of community and beery commiseration all round. I left feeling good about anarchy in general.

I might not have slept very well this week, and I never really ate, but drinking my body weight in cider and palling around with a few slightly smelly instigators is still preferred to mingling with the odious suited hordes that come spilling out of All Bar One every night.

In conclusion: being a champagne-swilling millionaire who shits on the weak and downtrodden while raking in profits culled from the genocidal rape of the earth causes heartburn and makes you miserable as sin.

By contrast, people who lie in the gutter begging for change while drinking a rusty old can of Special Brew as a dog dribbles on their filth-encrusted combat trousers are happy, morally praiseworthy humans. We cannot recommend becoming one highly enough!

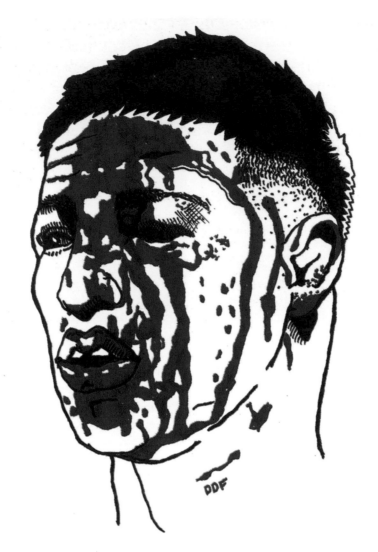

THE GLASSING CAPITAL OF THE WORLD

BY ANDY CAPPER | ILLUSTRATION BY DANIEL DAVID FREEMAN

Published February 2010

Drunk British people love smashing things into each other's face so much that somebody has invented a new pint glass that won't break even if you plunge it into some poor cunt's face at 2 AM in the street outside a bar where you can get triple shots of spirits for £5. How much do Brits like me love casual acts of extreme violence? Well, here's something to take into account: there are 87,000 deliberate glassings a year in the UK, which is roughly 4,000 more glassings than America has gunshots, both intentional AND accidental.

If any non-Brits out there are shaking their heads in belief about the veracity of our barbarism, you can come out with me on a night out in any town or city you choose to name and see for yourselves why this happens.

I was glassed/bottled once a year for three years running. The first happened in Southport because I was wearing a long scarf. The third time was for accidentally spraying somebody with beer in the Old Blue Last. The second, and worst, was on Charing Cross Road in London by a guy who attempted to smash a bottle on the wall three times to stab me. I laughed at him but then he smashed the beer bottle in my face and ran off while his girlfriend cried: "Oh my gawwwwd. What 'ave you done!" I put my hand to my head and felt a four-inch flap of skin come lose from my head.

But as I lay in hospital with my face turned to sliced ham, the whole vibe was very much, "Oh well, no big deal." I didn't want to press charges. The police didn't really care, the ambulance guys were like: "Ugh, whatever," and the people in A&E were like: "Take a seat over there please, dickhead, and please stop breathing booze on me."

If you're a dedicated British drinker who doesn't restrict himself to drinking in the same safe gentrified hipster bars every night, then being attacked with some kind of weapon is not just something you need to be mildly worried about. It's something that you must accept as normality.

Why? There are so many reasons. Most bars close before 2 AM and so the pressure to drink as much as you possibly can means people get as hammered as they possibly can in the shortest possible time. The feelings of injustice and frustration when they're turfed out of the club make hammered people feel angry and so they take it out on other hammered people's faces.

Often the attacks take place in the queues for kebabs or taxis and may involve matters of the heart such as competing males who wish to claim the rights to finger a slapper around the back of the butcher's. Girls and men mix illegal muscle-building steroids with cheap cocaine, even cheaper ecstasy, 15 lagers, and 40 percent alcohol that's coloured bright blue. This cocktail of fun releases a chemical in the brain called Imgonnaglassyershyafuckingtwatyercunt.

There are also sociological reasons, like high unemployment, poor prospects, bad housing, and the fact that hard-working, decent foreign people with good family structures are doing the jobs that fat, alcoholic, lazy British people cannot be arsed doing any more.

Britain used to be great at public disorder for political/protest reasons—see Toxteth, Brixton, Broadwater farm, the miners' strikes, and the poll tax riots. Now nobody except students can be bothered to turn up in groups to throw rocks at the establishment.

Instead we channel our anger into fighting each other in the street after drinking away any semblance of self-worth or identity or hope of getting up in the morning to go to a job interview in a shitty chain bar that's identical to thousands of others up and down the country.

Lock us up and throw away the key because we can start a fight with our own mothers, even if our mothers aren't even in the same room as us, and we are asleep, writhing fitfully in nightmarish sleep, slipping and sliding in a pool of puke, shit, blood and kebab meat. RULE BRITANNIA!

BOLLOCKS TO THE HIPPOCRATIC OATH

HEARING VOICES | BY DR MONA MOORE | ILLUSTRATION BY DANIEL DAVID FREEMAN

Published August 2009

I was having a moment of self-loathing on the tube yesterday as I recalled a particularly drunken misadventure and, without meaning to, I groaned and hit myself in the head a few times with my book, saying: "Idiot, idiot, idiot." Everyone on the tube turned and stared. I realised that must be what it's like to be mad. The voice in your head becomes so overwhelming that it requires action.

I was thinking about insanity after a 30-year-old lady came into A&E last week covered from head to toe in her own shit. She was clearly psychotic. We had to sedate her to clean her up because every time we tried to wipe any of it away she would flail and scream, agonised. She was very attached to it. Still a little stinky, she was inconsolable about no longer being covered in her own faeces in the examination. Eventually, we learnt what had happened. Her husband had died six weeks previously, launching her into a psychotic episode where the voices in her head convinced her that her husband was not dead but inside of her. She desperately tried not to shit, becoming toxically constipated, but eventually her bowels would explode in protest, so she would scoop it up and smear it over her body trying to preserve every last pellet of her husband. It was utterly tragic and part of me wished that we had scraped her shit into a little jar to take home with her.

One in a hundred people will have an episode of schizophrenia—you see people walking around with earmuffs in summer or headphones unplugged and often these are coping mechanisms. Auditory hallucinations are very persistent, like small children, so telling them to be quiet or threatening them just doesn't work. It is like your inner monologue, the wanky one that insists you're a twat, becomes self-sufficient—it no longer needs you to exist and, like a coke-fuelled motor-mouthed rant, it goes on interminably. Only you hear it as a constant outside noise.

I once sat in on a hearing-voices class where people are encouraged to articulate their voices, talk back and negotiate with them. A pretty 20-something girl had thought her Co-op was compelling her to buy things she had no use for, and she couldn't walk within 100 metres of the entrance. A Nigerian man's voices were personified by a 6ft blonde transsexual and an angry midget who would constantly argue in his head. And one old lady believed her husband worked for the secret service. They had kidnapped her and planted a chip in her brain, which made her act out their will.

They all agreed the best coping mechanism was using a mobile phone. They held it to their ear when they had the urge to talk to their voices so people didn't think they were insane. Many of them had learnt to live successfully alongside their voices—the aim of the classes. The pretty 20-something girl even said she had a new voice, who sounded like a younger version of herself, except incredibly witty, and she enjoyed their conversations.

The funny thing is psych consultants are all a bit nuts too. They like to provoke patients and get their voices to act up in an attempt to prove to them they are not real. I sat in on a psych consultation with a 45-year-old who had been suffering for four years.

The doctor asked, "So, where is your voice now?"

Perfectly sane, the patient replied, "He's in that chair," pointing to a very empty chair in the corner.

So the psych doctor stood up, walked over to the chair and sat in it, saying smugly, "So, where is your voice now?"

The patient looked at him, and replied, "He's in the corner and he's telling me you're a fucking cunt." It made me think that sometimes I would quite like a voice which I could blame for calling people a cunt.

HIGH SPY

**SMOKE POT WITH ME AND YOU'RE FIRED | AS TOLD TO EUGENE ROBINSON
PHOTO BY KATIE MURRAY**

Published April 2004

Hello! I'm a cold-hearted, misanthropic drug addict, and if you work in any small-to-medium-to-huge-size company it's very likely you spend each day alongside somebody like me.

Last year, the US Department of Justice announced that nearly one million individuals become victims of violent crime—mostly committed by people under the influence of drugs and alcohol—while working. When bosses and shareholders and presidents heard this, they hired undercover agents to weed out the miscreants. In short, I am a fucking narc and I work for a corporation that rents me and my fellow narcs out to your bosses for the sole purpose of getting you fired.

I'm just like any other employee. I've worked warehouses, stockrooms, mailrooms, wherever. A lot of these places just have guys doing the same old stupid shit: taking long lunch breaks and stealing office supplies. But I'm always under pressure to produce results.

That's where I got the idea of essentially entrapping people. "Hey, buddy, you want to get high?"—that sort of thing. Mostly I'll get my victims high on weed, but if I really take a dislike to somebody, I'll get some rock, stand near where I know there's a camera, and get them fucking annihilated like Pookie in New *Jack City*. The bosses tip me off whenever there's a mandatory drug test coming, so usually I strike right before it's piss-cup day.

Guilt? Ehhh, maybe a little. Not much, though. I only get minimum wage, but I'm on the so-called management track and am officially sanctioned to get high all day. Fucking unbelievable, no? They hire undercover drug addicts so they can fire their employees who get high a little bit, so their companies look better if the cops or government ever take a peek.

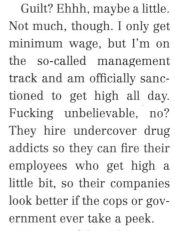

Because of the risky nature of the job and the constant threat of being exposed and having the shit kicked out of me, I move around a lot. That doesn't bother me, though. The more I learn about people and their motivation to make money by toeing the line and sucking the man's dick, the more I want to take them down. In fact, whenever I get somebody fired, I feel great about it. There's always someone else ready to fill their job anyway. It's sort of like natural selection. Shit, someone's coming… I have to go.

CUT THE SHIT

HOW PURE ARE STREET DRUGS? | BY ANN HIGGINS

Published May 2005

I bought cocaine, heroin, crack, weed and ecstasy and had them forensically analysed by a chemist at MIT because I thought they would all turn out to be poison. Guess what? Drug dealers don't cut drugs with cement and ground glass. They barely even cut drugs at all, because they don't need to. Relax, I'll explain later.

The samples were analysed by a PhD chemist at MIT (we can't say his name or he'll get fired) using acid/base extraction, proton nuclear magnetic resonance (NMR), and thin-layer chromatography. Acid-base extraction is the method used to isolate the chemicals. Once they're isolated, the NMR machine is what you use to analyse and identify stuff. Basically, the kind of NMR done here tells you about the hydrogen atoms in the molecules in the drugs. So it's like, the spectrum of heroin has 20 lines in it, all at different positions and heights, and you basically look for that particular set of lines. If you see another set of lines, you go, "Oops, there's something else besides heroin in here." Finally, thin-layer chromatography is a quick method that tells you how many components there are in a mixture. The MIT guy says it's "like that experiment you did when you were a kid (if you were a geek) where you put ink on a paper towel and, when the water diffused up the paper towel, all the colours separated." It tells you how many components are in a mixture but not what they are. That's what the NMR is for. Still confused? Show this to a smart guy and have him explain it more.

COCAINE

The cocaine was the first sample to come back from the lab. It was 98 percent pure. When everyone was done high-fiving, we started to wonder what was going on. According to the movies and *NYPD Blue*, you can only get cocaine like that from pharmacies. Street cocaine is basically poison, right? It's all strychnine and gasoline and nail polish remover or something.

I was not going to go buy 50 more samples of coke, because that would be a waste of money and drugs, but there's this guy named Peter Cohen who did his thesis on just that. Actually, his work is even better than that, because he not only analysed 50 samples of cocaine, he also interviewed the 50 cokeheads who had bought the samples. So he got the perception and the reality, see. He asked the cokeheads whether they thought their coke was pure, and 80 percent of them said no. Of those, 75 percent thought their stuff was adulterated with speed. They also commonly figured their drugs were diluted with ground glass, Drano, laxatives, and dirt. Cohen took samples from these cokeheads to the lab. The average purity was 65.1 percent. Second of all, the coke samples Cohen had were cut with speed, Daro, vitamin C, caffeine, sugar, nicotinamide, lidocaine, mannitol, and sodium bicarbonate. Daro is an anti-headache powder. Nicotinamide is vitamin B. Lidocaine is a topical anaesthetic. Mannitol is the sugar they put in diabetic candy. Sodium bicarbonate is baking soda. These are all innocuous things that bulk the drug out—most evidence of dangerous cutting agents is anecdotal. There's no glass in your coke, you fucking psycho.

I guess that doesn't mean that drugs are never cut with poison. The Drug Prevention Network of the Americas reports on a gang in Dublin that cuts coke with Phenacetin, a carcinogen that causes cancerous tumors in urinary tracts and nasal passages. Of male rats. There are a hundred million stories like that, and they get picked up eagerly by anti-drug sites, druggies, and editors who want sensational copy because that is the world we live in.

Findings: Most coke is way over 60 percent pure, and our coke is especially good. Thank you, Rico.

HEROIN

Our sample was 60 percent heroin, 20 percent acetaminophen, 10 percent caffeine, and 10 percent unidentiflable chemicals. Even though that sounds like a lot of additives, it's about right. New York heroin is 63.3 percent pure on average. Oh, forget the whole idea about heroin being cut with Drano. Heroin is most often cut with acetaminophen, caffeine, malitol, diazepam, methaqualone, or phenobarbital. Diazepam is a sedative hypnotic. Methaqualone is Quaaludes. Phenobarbital is a sedative used to stop seizures and treat insomnia. See, they just cut it with stuff that makes you sleepy but doesn't cost as much or cause as much hassle to get as dope. That's all. If you want some better shit, move to London. Ross Coomber of the University of Greenwich analysed 228 samples of heroin and found that 44 percent of them weren't cut with anything at all. The rest were cut with the same stuff as above. Coomber did another study where he gathered information from 17 heroin dealers at varying points in the chain of distribution. He asked them if they adulterated (that is the word for adding other drugs to) or diluted (that is the word for adding inert substances to) the drugs they sold. Eleven said that they never adulterated/diluted at all, four adulterated/diluted only sometimes, and only one (dealing four to five ounces a month) said he always diluted the heroin (with glucose, by around 10 to 20 percent). Asshole.

Findings: Heroin is a little more cut than coke, but ours is average. And dealers don't want to poison their customers. It's bad business, and if you're dead you can't buy any more smack from them. The most important finding to us in this section was this great new dealer who got us a bundle of smack, delivered to our door in 20 minutes in the middle of the workday. Too bad we're in recovery.

CRACK

Our crack, purchased from some human garbage in Bushwick, was about 95 percent pure, and the impurities were likely by-products of the synthesis, not contaminants. That means they weren't added after the crack became crack. Rather, they were a part of how the crack came to be. Crack is actually one of the purest drugs you can buy, usually about 85 to 95 percent, because it gets washed with solvent before or after heating. Just because of the way it's made (by "freebasing" it—or removing the active chemicals from cocaine from their base), you can get high-purity crack from only moderately pure coke.

Findings: Crack is a good bet. If you think your coke guy is stomping on your shit at all, cook it up and you'll take out all the dirt.

WEED

So according to an article published in the *New York Times* in April 2004, "Law enforcement officials said they are also seeing more examples of marijuana laced with other drugs, like cocaine, a narcotic; LSD, a hallucinogen; and PCP, a hallucinogen also known as angel dust." Our sample didn't have coke or heroin or PCP or anything in it. It was just normal. Sucks.

Now read that *New York Times* quote again. "Law enforcement officials"? I like cops and I trust them to protect me from getting raped. Journalists are liars though. Why would police give quotes about drugs and not give their names? Is this a top-secret thing that the "law enforcement officials" are afraid to go on record about? Seriously, there are a million alarmist accounts of PCP-dipped weed being sold as regular weed (just google it), but not one systematic analysis to back up the claim. Just look at the slang terms for weed laced with other drugs and the whole thing starts to seem like a priest dreamed it up: "Boat, Loveboat, Chips, Donk, Lovelies, Love Leaf, Woolies, Zoom, Caviar, Champagne, Cocoa Puff, Gremmies." What? Reporters are pussies that barely know what drugs are, so if they talk about the pervasiveness of embalming-fluid-dipped pot you're not going to ever find any evidence of them actually finding some. Hence quotes like, "Finding embalming fluid to buy on the street is not easy because most street drug dealers make more money selling individual joints soaked with embalming fluid for about $10 to $20. However, *if* found on the street to purchase, a two-ounce sample of embalming fluid costs about $50." Oh really?

Findings: PCP-soaked marijuana that is sold as PCP-soaked marijuana doesn't actually have PCP in it most of the time. There is no evidence at all I can find that marijuana sold as marijuana is soaked in PCP. However, if you want to deck your weed out, sprinkle some coke on it. It's called a snowcap and it gets you laced.

ECSTASY

Our sample was pure MDMA. Once again, that's because we have good dealers. We all know that E is often cut with dope, because we've all seen those little brown freckles in pills that we've taken. That's heroin, stupid. So while E can be dirty, it is not as dirty as a 1993 *Time Out* magazine article, "Bitter Pills", made it out to be. In that article, it was reported that E dealers spike tablets and capsules with heroin, LSD, rat poison and crushed glass. That story was repeated all over. Stephen Beard of the Newham Drugs Advice Project was the source for all this, and he said he got his info from a single dealer. This single supposed dealer said he made fake ecstasy by crushing light bulbs. The word for that is "hearsay". There was no supporting evidence such as lab tests or reports from doctors who had treated users. Oh, but again, it does happen that there is poison. In London, in 2000, there was an unmarked, half-scored, yellow-flecked tablet that was 8 mg of strychnine. The lethal dose of strychnine is 10 mg.

The verdict: It's not hard to get good shit. Drug dealers figure, I can sit here trying to figure out how to dilute this shit or I can get it on the street and paid for as soon as possible. If my shit is too pure—great. All that means is I'll have a reputation as Bobby PurePants and more people will want to buy from me.

Additional reporting by Gideon Yago

EASTERN PROMISE

MUSLIMS SERVE UP THE BEST CRACK IN LONDON | BY ANDY CAPPER
PHOTO BY ALEX STURROCK

Published February 2006

Britain's cocaine intake has skyrocketed since Oasis made every idiot in dear old Blighty want a bit of the blow. That's why the quality's gone down. Dealers now sell it to marketing girls at mobile-phone companies or 15-year-old middle-class car thieves up to 30 times a day. The real junkies, aka their best customers, can't get high from the shit that these amateurs are willing to buy. Hence, crack cocaine use has risen 87 percent in the last three years. You heard me right. It's the fault of Oasis that London is now full of blue-lipped crack fiends.

More crack buyers means more crack dealers. The crack-dealing chain was once made up almost exclusively of Yardies, scousers, and East End gangsters. But recently, fundamentalist Muslim gangs, some of whom employ children as young as two years old, are strong-arming their way into the business.

These are the cheery fellows who buy war-atrocity videos and feel empathy for the people who blew working-class folks to little pieces with bombs made out of Jean-Paul Gaultier cologne (they chose it because it comes in metal cans and when it explodes, the shrapnel darts out of the bomb like an X-Men weapon).

Yardie crack dealers did things the old way. They'd get boys to come around to their scary house, which always smelled like someone stuffed an old sock with cheese, and they'd give them baggies of crack to sell. However, the dealers were always nervous going to pick up their wares because a lot of the time those houses were being stalked. The constant ragga parties and prostitutes knocking on the door at 7:30 AM were sort of a giveaway.

The Muslim crack-dealer gangs are a lot more savvy, and they're undercutting the Yardies and making the crack trade their own. In east London there's a place called Brick Lane. It's often referred to as Curry Mile. An Indian feast there costs almost nothing, and you can't help but think, "How can they afford to employ all these people and maintain the rent money?" The answer is because they're stealing the crack-dealer runners away from the Yardies by giving them drug pouches like the picture you see here, and even occasionally performing fellatio on them! There's almost no chance of getting arrested when you're buying a samosa from a Brick Lane curry house. Not even if the samosa is stuffed with 35 bags of crack and heroin. The police are so nervous about descending on Muslims (hence the July 7 bombings) that crack dealers are getting all their shit from them. Peace!

It costs about £250 for a crack dealer to buy a samosa or onion bhaji stuffed with white and brown. They can make a £200 profit on that. Can you blame them?

The 15-year-old Muslim who sold us this samosa told us, "The Koran forbids lots of things. If you are a Westerner that's all you see—the restrictions on women and the strict rules about diet. Westerners can't comprehend the code because it's been so misrepresented by the media. In reality, the Koran is the most honest guide to life you could ever have. It's forbidden to lie, but if you are lying to combat infidels then lying is OK. In the same way, we look at the way we are profiting from this trade and at the same time, poisoning weak infidels and ultimately destroying their lives, and we are thankful to God. It's perfect. We like it because we consider it jihad and they like it because they are tripping their fucking balls off." Hey-ooooh!

This story was printed in our Lies Issue and is a big fat lie. Did you really think that crack was getting sold in samosas?"

Worst omelette ever. Thanks, rimonabant. Photo by Maggie Lee

NEW FRONTIERS OF SOBRIETY

BEING ANTI-HIGH FEELS ANTI-GOOD | BY HAMILTON MORRIS

Published August 2009

Newton's third law of motion states that for every action there is an equal and opposite reaction. In particle physics we learn that for all matter there can be antimatter of opposite charge. But what about drugs? Is there an anti-weed, an anti-heroin, or an anti-beer? Pharmacologically speaking, the answer is yes.

Scientists can identify regions of the brain stimulated by a given drug and then create an anti-drug with the opposite mechanism of action. Substances that do the opposite of common recreational drugs are useful in overdoses but rarely become recreational drugs in their own right for the simple reason that they make you feel totally and completely miserable. I decided to systematically test three of the most powerful anti-highs over the course of one week. Here are my results:

ANTI-WEED
RIMONABANT: DOSE: 60 MG

It has long been known that smoking weed gives people the munchies, so logically it should follow that deactivating the receptors in the brain responsible for getting high would give you anti-munchies. Pharmaceutical researchers tested a drug called rimonabant with just such an action and found that it was incredibly effective. The drug was approved in Europe and appeared to be one of the best weight-loss drugs in history. Rimonabant is inexpensive, effective, and totally non-addictive. Unfortunately, in addition to giving users anti-munchies it was found to have a prominent side effect called anti-happiness, aka suicidal depression. In the months following the drug's clinical trials, there were over 70 patients displaying signs of suicidality, two completed suicides, a host of seizures, precipitated multiple sclerosis, domestic abuse, and a man who strangled his daughter.

When you smoke weed, it stimulates parts of your brain called cannabinoid receptors. This may seem obvious, but our brain has these receptors for reasons other than getting stoned. Our cannabinoid receptors have an array of crucial regulatory functions in the unstoned brain. We depend on a cocktail of natural weedlike chemicals called endocannabinoids to regulate inflammation, appetite, and maintain some semblance of emotional stability. When you take rimonabant, not only is it impossible for you to get stoned on weed, it's also impossible for your body to feel its natural endocannabinoids. I have heard more than one stoner speculate about a future where the government requires rimonabant implants at birth to prevent the population from "ex-panding their minds". Unlikely, but one must wonder what it would feel like to live in such a world!

Since normal drugs are generally taken socially at night, I decide to do my anti-high experiments first thing in the morning and alone. But I'm curious about how my friend Sam would respond to rimonabant so I persuade him to try it with me. Sam has smoked weed all day, every day, for the last five years. When I suggest he take a pill that would make it impossible for him to get high for at least 24 hours, he is not too keen on the idea. But after asking about 50 or 60 times and offering to buy him weed in return, he cautiously accepts my offer.

Both Sam and I take a whopping dose of rimonabant three times higher than the maximum dose prescribed for weight loss. After swallowing the pills, Sam goes out to meet his weed dealer in Manhattan. A half hour later, he texts me to say he's having an attack of "explosive diarrhoea". I'm also feeling the onset as a subtle but persistent anxiety. Sam comes back to my apartment and shakily loads a pipe. He takes a deep hit, waits, and shakes his head, saying he feels "absolutely nothing".

We decide to go out and get some food at a Polish diner. Upon walking into the restaurant we realise that our waiter is an incredibly slow guy we've had in the past who never refills the small water glasses. Both of us tense up. I order an egg-white omelette and Sam interrupts me to say, "What are you talking about? You want the whole egg. Why would you just want the whites?"

"I usually get egg whites. They're good. Is there something wrong with that?"

Sam turns to the waiter. "He wants the whole egg."

I look down and see that my hands are trembling. I remember reading studies that suggest rimonabant

I am the least high person in the universe. Photo by Maggie Lee

lowers the seizure threshold. I don't mention this to Sam. My omelette arrives and I start to feel nauseated the moment I look at it. The omelette is made with a sickeningly orange American cheese. I might actually vomit. Sam has a healthy appetite. In the past I have seen him eat a whole chicken down to the skeleton, but on rimonabant he picks at his omelette for a few minutes before loudly protesting, "If someone does not get this omelette away from me I'm going to vomit… I'm going to fucking vomit and then I'm going to die!"

We leave the diner and anxiously walk down St Mark's. I stop inside a bong store and touch my fingers to the glass like a peasant outside a department store on Christmas. I have never felt so un-high in my life. I must admit that my thinking is unusually clear and I could see a lower dose of rimonabant being helpful when studying for a test—well, it *could* if it didn't make me feel like I was about to simultaneously cry, puke, and have a seizure. The fact that this is a widely prescribed drug is unbelievable. The idea of taking this daily is insane. It would be less than a week before I killed someone.

In the late afternoon I try smoking some weed. I take a deep hit, feel a transient sensation of threshold stonededness, and then whatever it was passes in less than five minutes. Sam is not willing to let the rimonabant win, and throughout the day he continuously attempts to get high, taking hit after hit after hit

from an aluminium cigarette. Around midnight, I hear him take a deep toke, sigh, and scream, "Damn it!"

ANTI-LSD: RISPERIDONE
DOSE: 4 MG

Psychedelics like LSD were used in many early models of psychosis. Even today, the majority of scientific literature refers to psychedelic drugs as "psychotomimetics", meaning drugs that mimic psychosis. Much psychedelic research has to be done under the guise of studying schizophrenia or related disorders. There is obviously a difference between schizophrenia and tripping on LSD, but the idea is that if drugs could be developed that did the opposite of LSD, they would be effective treatments for psychotic disorders. Antipsychotic drugs work by blocking the stimulation of dopamine and serotonin receptors, which are targeted by practically every enjoyable drug in the world from methamphetamine to cocaine to LSD. When the serotonin and dopamine receptors are blocked it effectively turns you into a zombie. Maybe you know a girl who takes Seroquel or you took it yourself once. It's not fun. Just keeping your eyes open is an enormous struggle. Although, if you're a paranoid schizophrenic, antipsychotics can chemically dull you enough to keep you from acting on violent impulses. They are also useful for aborting a "bad trip", and unlike Xanax or Valium, which only calm you down but don't

At the Chinatown needle exchange, where I am apparently a regular. Photo by Jess Williamson

actually stop you from tripping, antipsychotics stop the trip dead in its tracks.

Before getting out of bed I take 4 mg of risperidone, a dose high enough to make a 300-pound homicidal maniac slumber peacefully. I get up and go out to get some vegetable juice. I walk down to the East River and look out across the water. After ten minutes I'm starting to feel sedated. I lie down in the grass. It starts to rain so I get up again; this time my entire body feels leaden. I have to think about picking up each leg as I walk. Pick up leg. I'm getting really wet and I don't know if I will make it home. Pick up leg. A cop car drives by and slows down as it passes me. I feel painfully awkward because I know that I'm walking in slow motion through the rain without an umbrella, but I can't move any faster. The cop car speeds off.

Pick up leg. I'm a pharmaceutical masochist. Curiosity—the things you've made me do! I'm the least high person on the planet. In the history of humans no one has been less high than me. I take a Ritalin and it does nothing; I might as well have dropped it down the sewer. Pick up leg. A ten-year-old on Grand Street says that I'm "walking like a fag", to which I respond, "What's up." I stumble into my apartment building and crawl up the stairs. I crawl to my door, crawl inside, and pass out on the floor into the deepest, blackest, most deathlike sleep I have ever experienced. I wake up eight hours later feeling like I just had a successful lobotomy.

ANTI-HEROIN: NALTREXONE
DOSE: 200 MG

There are drugs called opioid antagonists, which do the opposite of recreational opioids like heroin. When paramedics treat heroin overdoses, they inject an opioid antagonist called naloxone into the body. On a molecular level, naloxone races into your brain, jumps ahead of the heroin molecules occupying your opioid receptors, and pushes them aside. Once the naloxone molecules are in place, the heroin can no longer suppress your breathing and the overdosee rapidly regains consciousness. Naloxone has saved countless lives.

Researchers realised they could use a similar opioid antagonist called naltrexone to stop junkies from feeling the effects of heroin. A device was developed that is surgically implanted under the skin and releases a continuous supply of naltrexone into the body for several months at a time. Although some addicts have benefited from naltrexone implants, the results are usually disastrous. When you give a junkie naltrexone it not only prevents them from feeling heroin, it causes them to go into instantaneous accelerated withdrawal, exponentially worse than natural opiate withdrawal. Some people have killed themselves to escape the pain after getting naltrexone implants; others perform home surgery and cut the implants out of their body.

In the same way that rimonabant blocks endocannabinoids, naltrexone blocks natural opioids called endorphins. Endorphins are pleasure chemicals commonly associated with sex and exercise, but more importantly they are regulatory factors in our daily mood and immune function. Even if you're not a junkie, taking an opioid antagonist has a profound effect on your neurochemistry. For that reason, naltrexone has been shown to be an effective treatment for paedophilia and kleptomania. The natural opioid release from acting on these compulsions is blocked, so fondling a child or stealing an iPod loses its euphoric rush.

I decide to take a dose of naltrexone four times higher than the daily dose used to treat opioid dependence. After taking the pills, I get on the train to Manhattan. I'm sort of giddy. I can't quite describe the feeling but it's not necessarily bad. The best anti-high thus far. I get off at Canal Street and I'm filled with tension amid all the shouting, sweaty, glistening tourists. At the same time I have this strange sensory enhancement that is not totally unpleasant. Vaguely erotic. I can feel each and every hair on my scrotum moving as I walk. Since I went to the bong store on rimonabant, I think it would only be appropriate for me to go to the needle exchange today. I walk inside and I'm immediately depressed and confused by my decision. As I'm filling out forms to get my needles, the woman looks at me and says my name is already in the computer—what? This twilight-zone moment makes me incredibly tense and paranoid. Why am I in the computer at the needle exchange? Why am I at the needle exchange? Why am I on naltrexone? I walk outside holding a paper bag full of needles and bleach and feel like I'm about to cry.

I'm totally absorbed in frantic and confused thoughts. I wish I understood addiction. I have read so many books, known so many addicts, but nothing makes sense to me. I don't want to say addiction is a disease, because diseases are excuses. Diseases are permission slips for being sick. If I'm addicted to Valium, that's a conscious choice I make each time I swallow a Valium tablet. But how can I say that? I feel guilty. I'm so confused. Thomas Szasz said, "If the desire to read *Ulysses* cannot be cured with an anti-*Ulysses* pill, then neither can the desire to use alcohol, heroin, or any other drug or food be cured by counterdrugs." But is he right? My trance is broken when someone offers me a flyer for "mad mojitos".

I get on the train to Union Square and find myself spontaneously breaking into song, then running full speed until I lose my breath. After running, my body is assaulted with sharp aches and pains. Is this what it feels like to be old? I almost step on a sparrow pecking at a muffin crumb and scream at the top of my lungs. Wow, am I on edge! When you meet new people, instead of shaking hands, both parties should scream at the top of their lungs. That would be the custom in a naltrexone alternate universe. As the day wears on, my muscles are starting to freeze up into terrible wooden knots. All my internal organs have been replaced with beef jerky. I have to keep stretching—continuously—to avoid hardening into a solid block of wood. I can't wait for this sensation to pass. O sobriety, how I long for thee!

CONCLUSION

There are so many anti-highs I have neglected to experience, but some are seriously dangerous. Drugs with the opposite action of ketamine are potent neurotoxins, and drugs that do the opposite of alcohol and benzodiazepines are known to cause seizures. Scientists are still mapping the gelatinous landscape of our brains, and as new drugs are discovered, new anti-drugs will also be found. Who knows what kind of chemical misery the future might hold! Although I must admit, after a week of enduring these anti-highs I feel incredible. The neurochemical floodgates have opened and there is unimaginable rebound euphoria. All night I walk down the street, peaceful and optimistic, ready to high-five strangers. Ready to high-five the moon! Hey moon, what up!

All that is loved is loved by contrast. We love intoxication because we know sobriety; to love sobriety we should know anti-intoxication. We can't know the high without the low, and after a week of getting low I'm feeling pretty high. I think the only thing we have to fear is the middle.

DRUG REPORT: LEGAL COCAINE!!!

INTERVIEW BY JAMES KNIGHT | ILLUSTRATION BY PADDY JONES

Published April 2009

Mephedrone is a drug that you can buy on the internet that's been described as a cross between cocaine and MDMA. It's been doing the rounds in gay clubs for a while, but now it's crossing over into straight places. It's not been illegalised yet and, as it only costs £60 for six grams, we had one of our writers get some and made him go on a bit of a bender with it. The interview you read below was done two days after doing the first line and was conducted about three hours after the hallucinations and panic attacks had subsided.

Vice: So where did you get it from?
Guy Who Took It: Some website that's like an on-line version of one of those stalls at a festival that sells wizard hats and poppers and glow-in-the-dark aliens. It was 60 quid for six grams in a big baggie and it looked alright. It didn't look too bad at all.

What was it like compared to coke?
It stings your nose quite bad. And it's quite thick so it gets stuck up there. So when you're talking to people

you sound like Ringo. Which is unfortunate because I was talking a lot.

So it's like coke. You just get all angsty and talk too much?
Kinda, but not really. It's got mild hallucinogenic qualities. It made my eyes wobble around. Things would get blobby. My eyelids would start fluttering and I found myself staring at things and noticing floppy waves of heatwaves coming off them. There

was none of the intensity of E or MDMA hallucinations though. The last time I did MDMA I did a cough sweet-sized lump and melted into a puddle in the street. My girlfriend had to come and pick me up.

Where were you when you did the mephedrone?
It was a classic way to do drugs: a crappy fashion party with free booze and loads of annoying people.

Great. And you were there talking like Ringo, and seeing heatwaves?
Yeah, and I was giving it to anybody I knew telling them how great it was because this was the first hour of taking it. I'm cringing now thinking about it.

Ouch.
Yeah, but that was the good part of the experience.

What was the bad part?
It went downhill about an hour after the first bump. Because I had this stuff in my pocket and I felt compelled to give it to people I'd never met before and, of course, to do as much of it as possible. And so you end up going to different locations, people's houses that you normally would never go to.

How much of the six grams did you manage to plough through?
I did all of it. Sniffing and coughing it down, all the time sounding like Ringo. And then I did that thing where you drink anything with even a hint of booze in it. Like other people's half-drunk alcopops, red and white wine mixed together in a mug, then vodka and warm diet lemonade in a paper cup. I also remember a tiny sip of straight whiskey out of the bottle that had some cigarette ash in it.

Mmmm.
I'd done all six grams by about 6 AM. Plus a gram of illegal cocaine that felt amazing in comparison.

How did you and your nose feel the next day?
Really, really terrible. It was the classic combination of sadness and fear, but feeling even more cheap and dirty than after doing proper cocaine. I guess that's what you pay for with coke: a rarefied sense of suicidal depression and shame. There was a big lump of stuff all still stuck up there, merged into one mess of crap, and ear, nose, and throat pain. My mouth is killing me.

I have to say it doesn't sound THAT bad.
There was also a totally paralysing mania. I felt totally insane. I remember just standing in my front room staring at the blinds on my windows and peering between them. They had heatwaves coming out of them. And I was terrified of every car that came past. Each one of them sounded like it was a bunch of people coming to visit me and tell me about all the bad things I'd done in my life, or kill me or something.

Eek.
Being on your own in an empty house intensifies all the bad stuff. And it got worse when I looked it up on Wikipedia. There was all the boring stuff about the different scientific compounds it was made out of, but what really stuck with me was the bit where it read "DEATHS" and had things like: "The 18-year-old and some friends took the substance in combination with cannabis on Friday, December 12. An ambulance was soon called to Bandhagen after the girl went into convulsions and turned blue in the face."

Imagine dying and being left there looking like an asphyxiated Smurf. What effect did the Wikipedia thing have on you?
Panic, regret, shame, fear. I chain-smoked. I don't normally smoke. There was a mild fear of death, but the sadness was so intense it negated the fear.

What did you learn from your mephedrone experience?
I haven't really touched drugs for months and months because I had a wee problem with a couple of things a few years ago. And I guess this seven-gram bender was a way of reminding myself about how grim the world of free booze, shitty uppers and bad people is. It's one of the reasons I got addicted to drugs in the first place. I'm never going back there. That's my excuse anyway. Can I go home now?

THE VICE GUIDE TO UNIVERSITY

BY ANDY CAPPER | ILLUSTRATION BY DANIEL DAVID FREEMAN

Published March 2010

ACADEMIC SUCCESS

Don't worry so much. The most common mark is between 50 and 65 percent. Nobody gets As except weird brainiacs or Asian people. This looks great on graduation day but understand that they have endured years of overbearing parents, endless maths tests and "educational toys" for Christmas presents. For the men, when they get to 32, they spend thousands on rare Stars Wars figures because they never had them when they were young. The women? It usually manifests itself in a huge dildo collection, prostitution, madness, suicide, or becoming a sexually voracious, piss-drinking slattern. Good six-month-girlfriend material if you can handle the suicide attempts.

BED SHEETS

A lot of students, especially the boys, are little wimps struggling to understand life away from the comfort of mummy's bosom. This is why they don't wash their bed sheets for a whole year. They sleep on gallons of dried cum, piss, vomit, spilled beer and tiny particles of Original Doritos. This is how they get "freshers' flu". It's because they can't take care of themselves. They invented a thing called the internet a while ago and if you type in www.google.com and enter "healthy diet" you can probably stop all this happening. Also, don't be scared of the laundrette. Just ask the immigrant lady how to work it. Or do a service wash. It's more expensive but time-wise it's a lot more economical.

COCAINE

University is probably the first place you'll encounter cocaine, and unless you've got wealthy folks, shelling out £50 on a gram of chalk dust as and when will be beyond the reach of most, which means you'll have to borrow off your friends until your next student loan payment and they will end up hating you. This isn't much of a loss as coke is completely overrated anyway. The exception is at parties where really drunk people with jobs, who like hanging around you because it makes them feel "young again", start racking up lines for you. In this case, you know what to do. Remember though, no bumps after 4:30 AM as 99 percent of the time nothing good is going to happen after that time in the morning.

DEBT

Hahahaha. This is why smart people never go to university. Even if you're thriftier than an edgy trust fund graphic designer whose parents just died in a head-on car crash, you can expect to be in AT LEAST £30,000 worth of solid gold debt by the time you graduate. If you can get your parents to pay your rent you'll still be about £20,000 in the red. Unless you're a millionaire and can afford to have that debt hanging over you for about 40 years, ask yourself this question: is that three-year course in 3D digital design really worth the effort? What are you going to be qualified for? Being an intern at a computer games magazine while all your friends who fucked their exams up are making £45,000 a year selling mobile phones?

EGGS

As well as noodles and spaghetti, eggs are all that you'll be eating for the next three years. You can't make them in the microwave but you can throw them around your halls when you're drunk (hilarious). These are the basis of the classic student dish: Spanish omelette. Boys who think they're classy invite girls over to their house and give them £6 wine and a Spanish omelette when they want to impress them. Most of the time the girl is thinking: "He promised me a 'chilled cordon bleu sesh' and he's serving me an omelette with potatoes in it."

FRIENDS

As much as you want to be the moody outsider Ian Curtis guy, you're going to need friends to get you through all this shit. If you're shy, have a few drinks, then be loud and gregarious at as many parties as possible. Eventually something will fall in your lap. People will spread the word that you're funny at parties and you'll get invited back. Eventually you'll have so many potential friends that you'll have to go through the editing process.

GAYS

University is where a large majority of people experience their first dabblings in the exciting world of homosexuality. The best thing to do is to experiment as freely as possible, but be careful—don't bow to peer pressure. The Gay and Lesbian Societies are huge in all the universities but that doesn't mean they're not annoying self-satisfied pricks who have swallowed so much mid-90s liberal dogma that having a conversation with them is like talking to an insane 90-year-old woman. It's barely-remembered catchphrases and blank expressions the whole time.

They're the ones self-righteously handing out sexual advice leaflets and free condoms while you're waiting to get your lunch. Like anybody who's old enough to go to university doesn't know how to avoid sexual diseases and buy their own condoms anyway. And sorry, men who like dressing up in women's clothes do not qualify as a social group. It's a sexual foible. Should we have support groups, pamphlets and long public meetings about empowering people who buy underwear three sizes too small or people who like fat hairy Greek taxi drivers who ladle dollops of yoghurt on their gigantic hairy balls while they're waiting to pick up a fare?

HALLS

More rules. Don't eat other people's yoghurts. Or any of their food. Conversely, if somebody steals your food from the fridge, don't leave gay little outraged notes for them in the fridge. Track the fucker down and confront them directly. Poke them in the eyes and kick them in the crotch.

Also, don't set the fire alarms off at two in the morning. What are you, 11 years old? Most importantly, don't have sex with the people you live with unless you're going to marry them. University is a chance to get laid as many times as possible with as many different people as possible. Leave commitment until your 30s.

INSANITY

Year two affects some people like a mini mid-life crisis. There's the realisation that you've pissed away your first year and that now, all of a sudden, you've got to start getting yourself together or the whole thing will be a gigantic waste. This is where the weak-minded and the druggies start to wobble and develop signs of madness—like not coming out of their rooms for days, cutting themselves, crying out of context, etc. These people need your help. Talk to them honestly about how much they're fucking themselves up and if, after six months, they show no signs of responding, then force them to quit university, rethink everything and go back to real life. Unless they're setting fire to your house or killing animals, DO NOT take them near any on-campus psychiatric units. If you get detained, you are fucked forever. Remember Angelina Jolie in *Girl, Interrupted*? The reality is a million times worse. You'll be plunged into a twilight world of really strong sedatives, cigarette-smoke-filled dayrooms, constant yelling, farting, puking, crying, and people who are 30 years older than you waking you up in the middle of the night crying and asking to borrow your clothes. Flirting with heroin and burglary is less risky than flirting with the mental health system. You have no fucking idea.

JOBS

Unless you're a leech with rich, misguided parents, you have to get a job at uni. It keeps you in touch with the real world outside student life and gives you a sense of perspective in between the all-night wine drinking and three-hour lectures about social media trend predicting. FACT: If you have a job, an internship or work experience while at university, the chances of you getting a job when you leave are quadrupled.

KNOWLEDGE

The pursuit of this is the main reason you're at university. Just a reminder. Like we said before, it's costing you at least £30,000.

LECTURERS

Lecture theatres are designed along classic panopticon lines, which means the teacher standing in front of you can see everything you do—even if you can't see them properly. So while you are busy drawing embarrassing caricatures of them in unflattering positions with farm animals, they can see. Texting a friend? They can see. It really is in your best interests to turn up, look interested, take notes, laugh at their jokes and, if you see them out, buy them drinks. If they like you, you'll get a better mark.

MEDIA STUDENTS

They have courses where you can learn how to be a TV presenter, but the people who teach you how to do it are failed TV presenters who wear cancer wigs in bed. The people who teach you how to be a journalist are bitter hacks from the local paper who became alcoholics and couldn't cope on the news desk any more. If you want a job in the media, the key is to have ideas and to be prepared to work for free in shitty offices for months. People think working in the media is a carousel of comfort, huge pay cheques and glamour. Fact is, 98 percent of media shitworkers experience that kind of thing once every three years. One of the only valid things that the

first-year feminists talk about is that media is still TOTALLY DOMINATED by rich white fat guys who like booze, whores, coke and paying their employees shit. You can forget waltzing through the doors with your piece of shit media studies degree and requesting a job starting at £40,000. It won't happen.

NEWSPAPERS

Fuck those catamites who still walk around the campus with the *Guardian* or the *Daily Telegraph* poking out of their bag as a way of announcing to the world that "I'm clever and open-minded". They are the worst. Fundamentally, there is no difference between that person and a working-class moron wearing a fake Gucci cap. They're both walking around with a bogus status symbol trying to accumulate some identity.

Relying on a newspaper for your news is near useless anyway. People who work at daily newspapers don't have time to get their facts entirely accurate. They just get a big whiteboard and write words like "racist", "celebrity", "cocaine", "paedophile" and "football" and create stories around them. Make sure you get a fast internet connection from your university and read as many different news sources as possible. That way you can form your own opinion about things. Again, make it easier for yourself.

FRESHERS' WEEK

The week leading up to the start of the first term used to involve avoiding all scheduled activities and signing up for classes quickly so you could get the hell out of there and go record shopping. Freshers' week today is like a crazy carnival, where first years flaunt their new Supré outfits and everyone seems blind to the fact that it's essentially a marketing exercise for banks and soft drink companies attempting to win over all the international and country students.

POLITICAL SOCIETIES

A total waste of time. Run by boorish losers with

dogma breath. Take a course in political science or read some books if you're that arsed.

QUITTING

If you're spending more time in bars than in lectures and tutorials, you should do this.

RATS

These are what you get if you live near a pub or a restaurant and never clean the kitchen or living room. They may be a source of amusement for a while and the Crispin Glovers among you might protest that they're living beings with as much right to life as humans, but bear in mind these fuckers carry myriad diseases that can kill you. If you let them live they will breed and then you will be charged about £300 by a pest control service who will douse your house with poison. Maybe they'll kill some of the rats but they won't stop the stench of their decomposing bodies that'll start coming through your floorboards for the next nine months. Suuur-WEET!

SOAP OPERAS

No time for these either. If you get to a point where you can remember watching *Neighbours* twice a day more than five times in two weeks then you're probably fucked.

TATTOOS

Go nuts. Traditional is always best though. No Chinese tummy tattoos for girls. No logo of any band unless it's Crass, Eyehategod, Black Flag, Misfits or Motörhead. Bands like that designed their logos so they'd look good as tattoos. No graffiti tattoos. No mystic symbols. A red devil on the arse of a drunken 35-year-old swinger mum of three is a million times better than getting an AK-47 on your leg because you're trying to divert attention away from the fact that you're the biggest fucking dweeb in the world.

VENEREAL DISEASE

Register with a doctor. Like all the things we're saying here, just be smart and don't be scared of life. A wart on your penis or vagina can be cleared up in five minutes. Just next time be more careful. However, AIDS can be a bit more difficult to cure.

WIM WENDERS

You're probably going to have to sit through one of his films during your time here.

XANAX

If you find an American exchange student, make friends with them. They will have Xanax. Also ask them about Oxycodone, Percocet or Vicodin (overrated). Google them. Erowid.org is a good resource for drugs information.

YELLOW SKIN

If you have this you're either Oriental or you have jaundice. Eat some fruit and vegetables. Peel it, put it in your mouth, chew and swallow. There you go, little baby!

ZERO

Ending up £30,000 in debt, failing your exams and endless feelings of guilt and regret just so you could be lazy, play computer games and network with other drunk losers is just fucking stupid. If you're unsure about university then fucking quit straight away. Save yourself the fucking bother. If you're not serious about using university as a way to better yourself and instead treat the next three years as a gay social club then you should be gassed. They send videos of people like you to the Muslims around the world. They watch them in between the footage of the World Trade Center and the London bombings. They're laughing at you, you white privileged lazy piece of shit. You are the reason that World War 3 is happening.

DISPATCHES FROM A WORLD OF VICE

We now have offices and correspondents in over 30 countries across the world. If there is an anarchist riot in Athens, a retro t-shirt trend in Liberia, or a woman in Brazil who happens to have the most famous fat arse in the world, then we have people well-placed to cover it quickly at first hand. Between the magazine, VBS and the viceland.com blog, we've always been at the forefront of the news that matters the most.

THE 2010 GLOBAL FEAR LEAGUE

BY OSCAR RICKETT | ILLUSTRATION BY PADDY JONES

Published January 2010

We used to live in a world of butterflies, bonfires and boating. Now we live in a world of dead butterflies, bonfires of dead bodies, and boats filled with pirates. We are all on our way out in a body bag marked "fucked", in an ambulance of dread driven by a Muslim extremist called Hussein. Oh, and Hussein is from Yemen now, not Afghanistan, and definitely not Iraq. Where is that country anyway? Who the fuck knows or cares anymore. Get with the times, Mr 2006! So, before we're all slaughtered in the street, I thought I'd let you know who's likely to be doing the slaughtering.

IRAN

The situation: The guys in charge want to groom their massive beards, enrich some uranium and deny the Holocaust. The rest of the country wants to watch *Cheers*, wear Bart Simpson t-shirts and listen to Bruce Springsteen while employing a straightforward Ronald Reagan-style interpretation of The Boss which ignores any criticism of America that may or may not be found in the lyrics. Also, they want to get drunk.

Islam factor: Fucking high.

Danger rating: Shit's gonna get nuclear.

UNITED KINGDOM

The situation: Provided no one reverses time and uncolonises the world without severing it into an endless number of discordant, senseless states, each one threatening the existence of the last, then the UK shouldn't be a problem.

Islam factor: Bloody Londonistan, mate, and not like the good old Londonistan we replaced Persia with back in the day—one that fucks over white people. I KNOW!

Danger rating: Too crippled by inadequacy and impotence to do much damage today, but made up for it with a whole history of danger-bating.

SOUTH AFRICA

The situation: Thirty-two groups of men from 32 different countries are going to be descending on South Africa to play the game of football. There'll be delight, tears and fan-on-fan violence.

Islam factor: A number of teams will feature Muslims, yes.

Danger rating: There's a high risk—a high risk things will get dangerously exciting, that is!

AFGHANISTAN

The situation: Is that the Doors on the stereo? Because it's all feeling a little like Vietnam in here. We got a Democrat president determined to prove he's not a gay coward by sending thousands and thousands of American boys to the other side of the world, and a hardy native people fond of using their "local knowledge" (where the caves are; which goats are informants; who let the dogs out) to consistently fuck up those American boys. This time around, Britain's along for the ride. I mean, Vietnam looked so fun (rice, hilarious accents, napalm) that we didn't want to miss out on part two.

Islam factor: Through the roof.

Danger rating: If we don't stop the Taliban now, they will invade London.

ISRAEL & PALESTINE

The situation: It's like *Sliver*, with Israel obsessively watching Iran, unsure if it wants to kill it or embark on some kind of tumultuous, filth-ridden affair with it. Meanwhile, back at home, the peace process has stalled and each side has gone back to calling the other one a bunch of land-grabbing infidels. The Palestinians are fighting each other, but you know that's only going to lead to a new round of suicide bombings—many of them, no doubt, planned for your neighbourhood (if your neighbourhood is the Gaza Strip, that is).

Islam factor: Being fought against by a new kid on the terror block: Jew factor.

Danger rating: 2010 is all about hip, new forms of danger. This danger seems like it's kind of been around for way too long. Get interesting, Israeli-Palestinian conflict! You're beginning to sound like a St Vincent album.

UNITED STATES

The situation: America is gonna take a blue and white striped boot and stick it right in your ass, and they're gonna blow up the moon and eat it as a starter before they move on to the main course: the Middle East. Dick Cheney's constant goading has deranged President Obama. He's wandering around the corridors of the West Wing mumbling, "I am a man, goddamn it, a real man," while drawing up plans to invade France and re-name it Poland. If there's a banner that ain't star-spangled, you can be sure Uncle Sam will find it and get painting.

Islam factor: Their elimination is the final piece in the puzzle.

Danger rating: If we don't stick solidly to our suck-up-to-America strategy we could be in an unquantifiable amount of danger.

DEMOCRATIC REPUBLIC OF CONGO

The situation: When you've got uranium, high-end weapons and all sorts of narcotics being smuggled out of a country to places like Iran, Yemen and North Korea, then you know you've also got a side order of fear. The DRC is like the Wild West, Hollywood or Silicon Valley in the early days: anyone can show up, do whatever the fuck they want, and try and make it as a big player. This is the sort of country where everyone you meet you kind of suspect has killed someone.

Islam factor: It's in the mix, but it's not really top of the agenda.

Danger rating: Did you ever have nightmares about a place far away in which there were no rules and fear stalked you like a stalker? Well, this is like that nightmare, except without the sweet relief of waking up to find that the only thing you have to deal with is the urine-soaked sheets you're sleeping in.

RUSSIA & THE CAUCASUS

The situation: Russians don't like people from the Caucasus. I was once, for some reason, at a meeting of a Russian society. There was a strong Chechen presence there, and the Russians didn't like it. One guy, Yevgeny, told them to "fuck off back to the mountains". Tensions rose. In the end, the two sides agreed to settle it by putting their "champions" in a

ring and letting them sort it out with their fists. The Russian guy confidently stepped forward, only to be faced by an Islamic mountain troll who crushed him with one hand. The Caucasus may have won that night, but the real-life situation is kind of the other way round.

Islam factor: Praise Allah for the trolls you provide.

Danger rating: Is anyone ever not afraid of Russians? They're distressingly good at chess…

YEMEN

The situation: The terror country *du jour*, Yemen has suddenly put itself right in the middle of the fear map. And why not? It has it all: Muslim extremists, Al Qaeda cells, links to Somali pirates, a history as a British colony, and a prime location at the hub of the world's most alarming body of water, the Gulf of Aden. The media are bored with Somalia, the celebrities don't go to Sudan anymore, and there are no longer any people left in Iraq, so step forward Yemen and take your place at the top of the fear table. You are an Arab Poseidon hopped up on terrorism, piracy and weapons-grade narcotics.

Islam factor: The new Afghanistan.

Danger rating: I'd tell you to cry and run home to your mummy, but she's been beheaded by a bunch of Yemenis.

COLOMBIA

The situation: Everyone seems to have forgotten about Colombia, but it brings with it the kind of Latin American dread you just can't rely on from anyone else. We're talking about an old-school, coked-up fight for the right to produce and sell massive quantities of racket. We're talking about sweaty, paranoid dudes with moustaches shooting their cousins because they think they're CIA informants.

Islam factor: Allah has no place here.

Danger rating: If wearing a white suit and getting a nice tan is danger, then yeah, it's pretty dangerous.

AL QAEDA
FROM DAY ONE

SIMON REEVE KNOWS HIS SHIT | AS TOLD TO EDDY MORETTI
ILLUSTRATION BY PADDY JONES

Published November 2005

I don't think of myself as a journalist. I never went to university, I never went to college. I was 18, came from this very crappy part of London, Acton, and had been on the dole when I got a job in the post room of the *Sunday Times*. One night I started talking to this guy who was this sort of legendary old reporter who worked on all the investigations, and he got me working on a couple of projects with him.

Initially I was just photocopying things and then I was making phone calls, and then I was going out and doing a bit of research. So it was sort of the classic old way of doing things. By the time I was 19 or 20 I was running around doing surveillance on all these incredibly dangerous people. It was just an adventure. And then I started specialising, I suppose, in studying terrorism. And then the 1993 World Trade Center bombing happened, and I began researching and studying it within hours of it happening. It became clear, after looking at it for weeks and then months, that there was a much bigger story behind it than people thought. If you looked at the conventional news on it, they were saying it was just a bunch of crazies, but what they were ignoring or not seeing was that they were just the tip of the iceberg. And that iceberg is what we now call Al Qaeda. I realised there was a book that could be written about it, so I left the *Sunday Times*, and started researching and writing *The New Jackals,* which was published in 1998.

When it came out, nobody was interested. We couldn't find a publisher for it in the United States. It was a very small university press—Northeastern University Press—that eventually published it. And the amount of money they gave me for the rights was the price of a ham sandwich. Most of the money came from a British publisher. But even then it was just ridiculous. Nobody would take it seriously. And yet, when you looked at the issue and you looked at the guys who were supporting bin Laden, it was quite clear that they were capable of doing things that nobody believed possible. The whole conclusion of my book was that we were entering a new age of apocalyptic terrorism and these guys, Al Qaeda, were going to launch apocalyptic-style attacks. So I can't say I predicted exactly the attack on the World Trade Center, but certainly it was fairly simple to predict that they were going to launch attacks on that scale, if not larger.

I'm not 100 percent critical of how the American administration has dealt with the aftermath of 9/11. But I am 80 to 90 percent critical because I think they've failed to put in place the long-term policies that are needed not only to protect Americans, but also to make the world a safer place. The war in Iraq is the biggest engine for creating or for encouraging global terrorism that we or Al Qaeda have ever seen. It's Al Qaeda's greatest recruiting tool. We all know the figures. The effects of Iraq will last for many, many years. But the situation in Afghanistan as well is something that's being largely overlooked now. Al Qaeda in Iraq was hit with a very large fist. Al Qaeda and the Taliban. But neither was obliterated. They were just sort of splintered.

You can't destroy them; you can't destroy an idea with military might. And that's really what Al Qaeda is. It's gone from being Osama bin Laden to Osama bin Laden-ism. It's a way of thinking. You can't defeat that by having 300,000 troops on the ground in Iraq.

I think the main issue is that the root causes are not being addressed. Now, that's not only some fairly ludicrous US foreign policies, but also the policies of other countries. Not so much poverty, though. Most terrorists tend to be middle-class and well educated, but certainly the swamp in which they breed is largely fed by images of poverty, the idea that there's a lot of suffering around the world, and that the United States is largely responsible for it. Which isn't really true, of course, but it certainly doesn't help that the United States provides ongoing backing for corrupt regimes in the Middle East and Central Asia.

The US can't really win this situation because it is the only hyper-power. It is going to be the target of a lot of anger around the world. That's not only because people are angry about America's freedoms, as George Bush would have you believe, but it's also people are jealous, people feel inadequate compared to the US.

From my own experience, it's quite staggering how high the hatred people around the world feel for America is running. Higher than any point in modern history. It never reached this stage during the Vietnam War.

There are training camps in Afghanistan—ad hoc, temporary camps. There are places like this of varying scale all around the world. There are places in Africa where people are trained how to use weapons and explosives. There are places in Yemen, the deserts of Saudi Arabia, the cities and tribal regions of Pakistan—loads of them in Karachi. In Afghanistan as well, but probably less there than in countries like Chechnya, or other places where there aren't tens of thousands of troops on the ground with satellites. Camps or any new structures that spring up in Afghanistan have a habit of being overflown by predator drones and satellites. And you don't even need to go to a camp; you can download the instructions from the internet.

Iraq, much more than Afghanistan, is the main training ground now. Al Qaeda emerged from the battlefields of Afghanistan during the 1980s when there was a total war situation going on there, with everybody trying to kick out the Soviet Army. Iraq is now serving that purpose for the next generation of Al Qaeda recruits. I was in Saudi Arabia last year travelling around. The talk there is of the thousands of young men who have disappeared from the villages and the towns and gone north into Iraq to fight against American troops. Many of those Saudis and other nationalities will die in Iraq, but a lot of them will be battle-hardened. You only need a handful, but if you've got hundreds, then it's obviously more worrying. And if you've got thousands, you just can't catch all of them. The dictum for the intelligence agencies for the last ten years has been that we have to be lucky every single time. They only have to be lucky once. And that's really the cat-and-mouse game. When there're 10,000 mice, you can't catch them all. So yes, there is a serious risk of more attacks in London or America or Italy or Denmark

or Australia. It's a global terrorist organisation, the likes of which we've never seen before, and it poses a very unique threat.

But at the same time, if we look a bit more long-term, there are actually positive signs out there. The number of global wars is falling, the incidences of world conflict is going down. Almost every country is reducing its military spending, except the United States. In fact, war is now running at a much lower rate than it has in human history. There've been some interesting studies that say that a human being has a smaller chance of being killed now in armed conflict than at any other point in human history. We're all talking about how the world is going to hell in a hand basket, but unless you're a Kurd or member of the Burmese minority or something, things are looking up. Eighty countries have become democracies in the last 20 years. Things can be made better—it's not a case of "the world's fucked and there's nothing we can do about it".

The threat Al Qaeda presents is nothing compared to the risk of climate change or environmental collapse. When we talk about terrorism, we have to get it in perspective.

In many ways Al Qaeda can just rest up now. If they look at what happened with Katrina, they can develop a strand of thinking whereby they don't really need to worry about attacking the West, because the way we're fucking up the environment is going to kill us all anyway. The response to Katrina was just absolutely gob-smacking. I don't think Americans realise how this has been playing out around the world. It just destroys any notion of America as the benevolent super power.

Working through all this has sort of been my education in journalism. I've found more about seeking out information and knowledge than just attempting to report on it. I go out and work on projects that are interesting for me, not because they're interesting to everybody else or they're things that will be news worthy. I started investigating what we call Al Qaeda in the mid-90s when it wasn't really clear what they were or even what sort of threat they were. It was only as the years ticked by that it became clear how huge a threat they pose.

SADDAM SUCKS

BUT THAT'S MY PROBLEM | BY HALA QADAR KHAN

Published March 2003

Hello, everybody. I am a busty Iraqi girl who escaped to New York with her wealthy parents seven years ago. I thought I'd take a little time out of my incredibly boring school day to tell you about the man you call "the most evil dictator of all time" (you think you know, but you have no idea).

However, before I let you in on the secret life of this horrible monster, you have to promise not to throw the Iraqi people in there with him. Love Iraq. Hate Saddam. As with America, we have nothing in common with our leader. We despise him and are shocked daily by his actions. You know what it's like. You have the same thing with your king. Anyway, check it out...

L'ENFANT TERRIBLE

Saddam's life story reads like an Arabic version of *The Omen*. In March of 1936, a notorious slut named Subha Al-Tikriti realised she was pregnant. She was what we call "desert trash", and knew she was totally incapable of raising a child. She decided to give herself an abortion, but come on, this is 1937 here and her mudbrick house wasn't exactly overflowing with coat hangers. After nine months of belting herself in the stomach almost daily, this unfortunate tramp gave birth to Saddam Hussein Al-Tikriti. She showed her disdain for the incident by combining the words "great misfortune" (sad-mah) and "confrontation" (isti-dam) to make the word "Saddam" (a name nobody had ever heard before). Back then you would incorporate your village into your name, too, but Saddam comes from Al-Awja, which translates as "crooked town". That means his actual name is "The crooked troublemaker, son of Hussein". As soon as Saddam got into power, he abolished the village rule, leaving him with simply "The troublemaker, son of Hussein" (more on that later). The name is still painful for him today, because Hussein got the fuck out of there hours after Great Misfortune Collision was born.

As a single mother, Subha prostituted herself to make ends meet and soon settled in with a total asshole named Hassan (The Liar). Hassan's kids were much older than Saddam and ruled over him with an iron fist (that's called foreshadowing).

These were very shitty times for our beloved leader. His first job involved risking his life all day by stealing livestock only to come home at night to a five-person mudbrick house filled with two chickens, a sheep, and a donkey. In the crowded hut Saddam would get his head kicked in by everyone but his mother (which is maybe why he worships her so much and still uses "mother" as the ultimate adjective: "mother of all wars", etc. He recently built a shrine for her in Al-Awja, honouring her with the title "Mother of All Militants").

Remote areas like Awja are the lowest of the low. A highly underdeveloped infrastructure and stifling poverty led to heinous crime and the hillbilly "Bedouin" mentality of "you fucked my sister! I'll kill your mother!" Diseases like tapeworm and malaria were common, and most of the kids from these areas were, put simply, bad eggs. "They spent most of their time outside in narrow, dung-filled alleys," says Said K Aburish, who's written a few books on the area. "They formed gangs, stole from farmers and each other, and conducted feuds and clan wars

which often lasted for years. These children were tough, courageous, and vicious at a very early age."

SCHOOL DAZE

Normally a kid like Saddam would have died in a gang fight, never to be heard from again, but his mother did the future Iraqi people a huge disservice by sending him to live with his uncle Khairallah when he was nine years old. Khairallah was a schoolteacher and member of a rebel movement, and he forced Saddam to brave the laughter (being fatherless, poor, and illiterate was not exactly a recipe for popularity) and go to school.

Being known as "the big, barefoot bastard" made Saddam study hard and act even harder, until, at age 13, Saddam blew his cousin's head off. Despite having no friends, Saddam did quite well at school because he has an incredible memory, which was apparent a few years ago when Saddam had all his old school bullies executed. It was 27 years after the fact, but he got every single one.

TEENAGE REBELLION

During his teenage years, Saddam became obsessed with revolutionary politics and Stalinist ideology. Failing the entrance exam for the Baghdad Military Academy (a way out of the lower classes for bright young Iraqis) only added to Saddam's sense of inadequacy. Kind of like when Hitler didn't get into art school. Feeling dejected, he began taking part in antigovernment demonstrations and eventually joined the Ba'ath Party. He studied Egypt's Nasser and had dreams of a fully Arab Iraq, independent of the British powers that had dissected and infected the Middle East with political instability for so long. In 1959, he was involved in the attempted assassination of Iraqi leader Abdul Karim Qassem. Being the self-proclaimed superstar hero that he is, Saddam produced a film, *The Long Days*, which recounts this event in all its supposed glory. He is depicted as having been severely wounded by the incident, courageously stitching up his bullet wounds with his own bloody hands, à la Rambo. Truth is, he played a rather minor role in what was really a very clumsy operation. In any event, Saddam then fled to Egypt, where he and his Ba'athist buddies devised what would be a successful coup thanks to the CIA. Qassem was finally overthrown in 1963, and Saddam climbed the political ladder ruthlessly throughout the late 60s, destroying anyone who crossed him as if he was back in Crooked Town. He finally appointed himself "The Mother of All Leaders" in 1979.

FAMILY IS FOREVER

At the lowest point of his life, there was only one person who didn't pound the shit out of him: his mother. Blood. That taught Saddam a lesson: the family reigns supreme (no matter how unqualified they are to reign). Remember Uncle Khairallah? He's the minister of defence. When Saddam's two sons, Qusay and Uday, were old enough to work they became Saddam's dreaded security apparatus. Nobody has to worry about how conspicuous it is that everyone has the same last name, because last names were the first thing Saddam abolished (I told you there'd be more on that—there it is).

Hiring only family has its drawbacks. When Saddam appointed his son-in-law Hussein Kamil the head of the Atomic Energy Administration, he neglected to note that the guy barely had high-school physics. Kamil went nuts trying to keep up and tried to quit, so Saddam killed him.

THE BOY TODAY

Saddam's life of late still revolves around the manic paranoia he developed while getting pounded in the womb. Phone taps are a given, and many Iraqis have been executed for using his name in vain during casual conversation. His lookalikes regularly undergo plastic surgery to get at those not-so-Saddamish features and are giving more and more of his public addresses. Having built more than 21 over- and underground palaces, he never sleeps in the same bed for more than two nights at a time. His food tasters are easily replaceable. Many speculate that Saddam

himself was the mastermind behind the 1996 assassination attempt on his eldest son, Uday (even more of a reckless thug/rapist/crook, but that's a whole other article), because Uday was getting way too crazy and becoming an embarrassment to the Hussein family. Saddam shot him in the lower back, paralysing the boy for life.

His motto is: "Maintain power by any means necessary," even if it means the elimination of half the population of Iraq. As he puts it, "If there is a person, there is a problem. If there is no person, there is no problem".

MADNESS TAKES ITS TOLL

As Saddam gets older, he gets more and more perverted and insane. Unfortunately, absolute power and paranoia are not the best things to mix with an overwhelming libido. If he likes your wife, she instantly becomes his property. His second wife, Samara, was actually courted after Saddam personally asked her first husband to step aside. Saddam duly gave him a raise after the wedding.

And if you happen to be a member of his circle, be it the army or the elite of Iraqi society, you'd better be wearing deodorant, as "His Excellency" deems body odour to be so offensive that it is worth murder. For example, there was a time when Saddam's subordinates were allowed to greet him with the standard two kisses on the cheeks, but he's grown so wary of bacteria that he demands to be greeted with two tender pecks on either sides of his chest, close to the armpits. His emphasis on cleanliness is an extension of his serious fixation on security.

Saddam has an addictive personality, and alcohol was his drug of choice. But when the trials of being a tyrant were taking their toll, he realised he had to curb his appetite for Jack Daniel's with sedatives. Naturally, the situation only worsened. According to a former palace doctor, Saddam needed to be regularly tended for withdrawal symptoms that led the Iraqi dictator to raging fits. On one occasion, the doctor was called in and duly put Saddam to sleep only to find a pretty young girl drenched in blood in the bathroom next door.

THE MAN AND HIS EGO

As my aunt reproachfully puts it, "Saddam only loves himself." Saddam's cool and calculating rule has developed into quite a case of rabid egomania. His propaganda machine is so extensive it's impossible to avoid his face on a day-to-day basis in Iraq. His pictures are dispersed all over the country, from office posters to gigantic murals, and I grew up looking at his face on the first page of every schoolbook I owned. He even has a statue of his likeness erected in a different neighbourhood every year for his birthday (now a national holiday). They say that there are 22 million pictures of Saddam in Iraq—one for every Iraqi citizen. He still makes a point to appear on Iraqi television five times a day to remind the Iraqi people of his ominous presence. He has even jokingly advised the nation—with his trademark creepily hearty chuckle—to stick a picture of him on their TV screens if they break. By the way, these monologues have to be heard to be believed. His favourite subject is personal hygiene. Things like, "Remember to never wear the same clothes twice before washing and to shower at least once a day" and "Always brush one's teeth frequently, and if a toothbrush is not available, use one's finger". Just before I left, the regime had published a compilation, The Sayings of His Excellency Our Leader, that Iraqi high-school students are required to memorise as the new bible for all future Ba'athists. The first piece of advice in the book sums up the madman perfectly: "Do not respect he whom you suspect is doubtful of your intentions towards him." Word to the mother of all philosophers.

Another example of the Iraqi dictator's campaign of self-aggrandisement is his architecture fetish. During the 80s, he commissioned the Celebration Arch, a grotesque edifice consisting of two sword-bearing arms (modelled after his very own, of course) towering over a main street in Baghdad. At the base of the two structures are large collections of military headgear that once belonged to captured Iranian soldiers. Saddam even had the nerve to "restore" the Tower of Babel, one of the most precious archaelogical sites of earlier civilisations. Every brick that was laid in the construction of this magnificent building was inscribed with King Nebuchadnezzar's name, but at renovation time, Saddam had his people go in there and inscribe his name on every hundredth brick instead. Saddam's latest project is of unprecedented magnitude: while the Iraqi people are suffering tremendous poverty, plans are underway to build the biggest mosque in the world, with minarets taller than the Eiffel Tower. To complement the mosque, an artificial island will be built in the contours of—are you ready for this?—his fucking thumbprint! Not only is Saddam a leader among Arab leaders, he intends to be the Muslim that gets the closest as humanly possible to God.

DON'T BOMB US

It's strange to think that if I said the past two thousand words in my hometown, I would have been tortured and executed within a day. In America I just pound it out on my keyboard like it ain't no thing. Weird.

This probably isn't the best time to be letting you all in on what a psycho Saddam is. It's our problem. For the record, I am as petrified of American intervention as I am of Saddam. Like Subha, we never wanted him to be born, either. Saddam took Iraq out of its glorious days and dragged it into its darkest era. UN sanctions were implemented after the Gulf War "to destabilise the regime," but after ten years they've destabilised everything BUT the regime. Iraq once boasted the highest literacy rate in the Arab world, but today we are in the lower brackets of international living standards. Iraq has been bombed back to the Stone Age, and at least two generations have been wasted. I don't know how to get rid of him. America put him there in the first place, but ironically I don't think America should be the one to get him out. No offence, but every time you try to clean up this mess, you just make it worse. Tell you what, promise that you'll remove economic sanctions if he steps down, and we'll take care of the rest. This is an Iraqi affair.

WATERBOARDING'S FOR PANTYWAISTS

BY JULIANE LIEBERT AND FELIX NICKLAS | PHOTOS BY CHRISTOPH VOY

Published August 2009

When I first met Felix I had no idea that only three months later I'd end up torturing him with a 100,000-volt electro-shocker. Actually, I'd never planned on torturing anyone before at all. To me it was something that strangers did to other strangers in strange lands, one of those things that's constantly talked about but becomes more and more abstract with each new version of the Milgram experiment and each sensational new Guantanamo discovery. At some point this problem found its niche between the ozone hole and the extinction of species. It became normal. But all that talking about it never made it quite clear what it feels like; it just happens to some poor sod on TV. Plain old torture is nothing new, though, so instead of doing a little bit of waterboarding at some house party, Felix and I decided to try out some historical torture methods ourselves.

We talked to an expert to learn about the details (and risks involved) and then set out on a journey into the ugly depths of the human psyche that we had been told about—but could have lived without ever getting to know for real, now that we're looking back at it. Disclaimer: the following scenes might look pretty tempting, but please don't try to reenact them. The experiments were actually dangerous and took place under medical supervision. DON'T DO IT! JUST DON'T!

BOX

Torture pretty much works like playing poker. You either have to start on the lowest level or just bank everything on one card. It's up to you whether you find being locked up in the tiniest of spaces without being able to move your arms and legs because they're tied to your body MORE or LESS terrible. Forced postures belong to torture methods that are commonly used all over the place. This one here is

referred to as the "sardine can". The constricted position causes unbearable pain and joint inflammation. Apparently some tortured Falun Gong followers were locked up in metal boxes in the torrid heat for up to 80 hours. That's why I thought Felix was being a bit of a wuss when he started going mental inside the box and hitting against the walls and crying before we'd even really started.

Felix: In the beginning I thought this was going to be cool and totally relaxed and doable because the first couple of minutes felt like a trip back in utero. Then I realised I was crouched in this perpetuum of agony while breathing my body temperature up to new heights and straining my brain with calculations as to how long it would take until I'd suffocate. Then the pain set in and spiced up things a little. It started out with infernal cramps in my legs and every attempt to slightly change my position just resulted in even more pain. I never thought before that my toes could

make me scream with pain. Then I lost my sense of time and with that, the control over my body. My limbs started twitching and hitting against the walls of the box. So basically I was beating myself up.

HANGING UPSIDE DOWN

According to our expert, the true nature of torture comes out with the breaks between each set, when you know you've been extradited but don't know what they'll do to you next. Felix, however, knew everything he was in for. I explained the whole process to him thoroughly: the "grilled chicken" method of hanging someone upside down to make all the blood run into the torturee's head so it swells and causes shortness of breath, dizziness, and indescribable, migraine-ish attacks of pain. Some torturers also like to set up a little electro stove underneath the person dangling off the ceiling. In short, if no one chooses to take you down, you'll eventually crap out. It proved fairly difficult to tie Felix up, but I have to say, the time he spent hanging there was the first stretch of time since I met him where he managed not to bum a cigarette off anyone for more than an hour.

Felix: After the box I thought this "hanging upside down" would be a fucking spa treatment for my still-aching and convulsing body. But it turned out

it was pretty much the same thing, just shittier, if that makes any sense. The cramps returned and all the blood from my legs flowed into my skull, which made my eyeballs feel as if they were hard-boiled. I seriously believed they'd pop out of the sockets. Even minutes after I was taken down I still couldn't see properly. The world looked as if it had been run through a giant brownish batik-dyeing machine.

CHINESE WATERDROP TORTURE

It might not be appropriate to ask for sympathy in my position, but torturing really sucks. No wonder they blamed the water drop torture on the Chinese (the truth is the Italians came up with it). The procedure is classic. The head of the the torturee is fixed so he can't move it the slightest bit and then water keeps dropping on his forehead. Felix wasn't much help, lying in the corner feeling sorry himself after the hanging part, so I had to construct this on my own. The mean thing about this is not the water, it's waiting for the next drop. And the next. That's what drives you crazy. In the beginning I didn't see much of that though. Felix looked all peaches and cream in the face.

Felix: Ever kissed a girl in the rain and thought this moment is perfect and then she kicked you in the balls? After all this shit I thought this must be the

honeymoon of torture methods. In the beginning I relaxed and watched the drops that were about to drop on my forehead. Then I started getting really impatient. Very, very impatient. Strangely impatient. About as impatient as you get waiting in front of the train card machine and you hear your train's doors just closing and you really have to pee and you realise you have lost your wallet and this was the last train that could have possibly brought you home to your family for Christmas just before you piss yourself. I was pretty close to that actually.

NOISE TORTURE

Noise is one of the oldest torture methods, invented around 300 BC. That means that a whopping 2,300 years before the invention of techno, they already used to drum blasphemers to death. So the Guantánamo prisoners weren't off too badly after all: they were only tied to a chair, naked, in the cold, without food but with Metallica instead. However, I didn't want to put Felix through Metallica, so I just looked for the worst crap I could possibly lay my hands on. I taped a set of headphones to his head and put iTunes on repeat. A couple of minutes were enough to drive me crazy and I could only hear what the headphones gave off to its surroundings. Felix was squirming in his chair. But somehow I couldn't get rid of the feeling that he somehow enjoyed this.

Felix: The thumping gabber became a bit meditative after a while and slowly boomed me into the moron's nirvana. Blind and deaf from exhaustion, I almost fell asleep a couple of times. The isolation part was a bit annoying, but actually I could have endured this for hours. I began asking myself if there was some way I could release myself from this because the ties were chafing my skin. Maybe I was also having thoughts about breaking my torturer's neck. Almost dislocating my thumb in the attempt to break my shackles was probably the worst part about this whole thing though. If you consider that a weekend at Mayday is the best thing that some people will ever experience in their lives, two hours of noise torture are a pretty fair deal.

ELECTRO SHOCKS

The expert advised us to stay clear from Felix's head with the taser because that could cause epileptic attacks. That's why I decided to go for his leg. In Germany any idiot can walk into a store or go on the internet to buy a 700,000-volt taser without even showing his ID. So that's how we reached the climax of our little experiment. I put the taser against his leg and shocked him. He shuddered and screamed. I kept going until he was lying on the floor and didn't move any more.

Felix: The pain wasn't the problem, even though I must say that I ended up squirming on the floor after just the second shock. The pain goes away. What stays though is the echo in your nerves. I think everybody who had an experience with electro shocks before knows what I'm talking about here. But that's not really the point. This part of the torture was where I truly looked into the core evil of all this crap: man and his degenerated soul in action. A couple of 100,000 volts melt away any constraints—and suddenly you find your colleague turning into the asshole who'd shoot you in the back in some rundown prison.

When torture was banned in Europe in 1820 that didn't happen due to its inhumanity but its impracticable character. In times where torture is gaining more and more acceptance behind the scenes there's a little Kang Kek Iew in all of us. I know that I was a privileged victim assuming something like this exists. Compared to the poor guys who're suffering in random cellar holes around the world, I could have aborted this shit any minute and could have stormed out the door after screaming "fuck off" into my colleague's face. That's why I can't say that I was tortured for real. The pain isn't what it's all about; it's just a side effect of the concept. You learn to put up with it and get used to it while your body is drugging up itself with its own chemicals. The human body can put up with a lot of crap, that's for sure. However, losing your personal freedom, the option to say "No!", being delivered to complete unprotection—*that* is truly hell on earth. I'm sure for Juliane this was merely another job, but I still cringe when she starts talking to me.

ATHENS

INSIDE U OF A(NARCHY)
WORDS AND PHOTOS BY FREDDIE F AND STATHIS MAMALAKIS

Published December 2008

Why's everybody so up in arms over the riots in Greece? These are the same kids who went fucking bonkers when the Vandals played a USO show over there. Do you really think they're going to sit on their hands after a cop shoots a 15-year-old without just cause? Anyhow, while every major media outlet has been sputtering commentary from their ergonomic desk chairs about the situation, we went right to the source and got in touch with some Greeks to see what was really going on. A day and a half later they sent over a bunch of amazing photos. They also sent us some interviews with the protesters.

Most of what they gave us took place at the National Technical University of Athens, all shot the night after the riot police attacked them with smoke bombs, stun bombs, and tear gas. They ran in through the gates of the university compound as the riot squads were closing in and beating them down.

Historically, the university's been a place for revolutionary-minded individuals to organise and mix Molotov cocktails in peace. In 1973 it was the site of the Athens Polytechnic uprising, a giant, fiery fuck you to the dickwad junta in power at the time. University campuses are supposed to be neutral ground under Greek law—a sort of asylum that is technically off-limits to police and government officials. Being that this whole thing erupted because cops in Greece don't give a shit about "rules", we're wondering how long before they drive a tank through the gates of the

school just like they did in '73. Not very long from the looks of things (although there are reports that things are cooling off).

In case you haven't been following this as closely as you should have been, allow us to make it crystal clear that it isn't just anarchists who're firebombing buildings and setting cars ablaze. A lot of these rabble-rousers are just fed-up students. They're kids who are pissed about having no future in a country where the government is a joke. They wholeheartedly believe that the system is beyond busted and there is no way to fix it. Obviously they aren't letting the press slither around the place, so you're not going to find stuff like this anywhere else. As far as we know, this is the first time anyone has published photographs from inside the walls of the university during this week's riots.

71

Mike, a 15-year-old anarchist, with petrol, his weapon of choice, which is thrown on the cops and then lit.

Top: Breaking the university marbles for ammunition. Left: An extinguisher to put out the fires caused when the protesters get hit by plastic bullets and fall with their bombs, which end up burning the shit out of them. Right: At one point the guys got stuck in the university. It was impossible to leave—at one entrance riot police were going crazy and at the other some skinheads were stabbing everyone.

Top: An impromptu lesson in making bombs at the Polytechnic University. Left: Anarchists with a flag from Alpha Bank, one of the banks they destroyed. Right: A scorched car.

This is Leo with his gun. Photo by the author.

HOW TO BUY A GUN

FROM THE MILANO MAFIA | BY FRANCESCO VECCHIOLINI, AS TOLD TO TIM SMALL

Published November 2005

MILAN, OCTOBER 14, 1:45 PM

I'm sitting in a bar on the outskirts of town. The décor is squalid. Over at the fruit machines an old guy with a moustache has already stuck around 100 euros in the machine. Now he's shouting about his "full" not showing. Leo is late. Leo is 27, and now he's convinced himself he wants to be an actor. Of course he's never been to school, but he's bright, capable, and I think he might have the talent for it—even though he hides behind the mask of the "soldier".

"Of course, man, ten years of squares are better than any school," he says, proud. The "square", or "piazza", in Italy, is like "The Block" for LA's gangs: the theatre of all illegal activities. Today, the Perspicace, the Flachi and the Morabito, the three leading families of the 'Ndrangheta (Calabrian mafia), the Sicilians (or Cosa Nostra) and the Camorra (Neapolitan mafia) have taken a step back and are happy to control all action from above, leaving the details to immigrants. The square remains the ultimate measure of criminal power. The strength of one crew, or that of a single hot-headed "maranza", is judged on the reputation of the square they control, the territory they possess, and how dangerous it is for members of other crews; squares such as Corvetto, Odazio, Barona, Giambellino, Bruzzano.

Since the 70s, Milan has been a crossroads of international drug trafficking, where you can easily find everything you desire, be it Colombian coke, Moroccan hash, Spanish opium, Turkish heroin, Dutch skunk, or London's finest ketamine.

Milan is Italy's crime capital, when you consider the level of the individual drug peddler coupled to that of the billion euros of money laundering. I have decided to explore these criminal squares, to immerse myself in their world by pretending to be a maranza looking for a gun. I ask Leo for help, as Leo has been through all of this before. He used to be loosely affiliated to one of the families, started running jobs for them when he was only 14. He was a good-looking kid, so no-one ever suspected him

By 16 he never left his house without a gun. Drug-smuggling quickly became his thing, selling mainly pills and coke. But in 2002 one of his oldest mates, a kid he was running with, was shot dead during a robbery. Leo quit, got out of the family, but he never ratted anyone out, so he's still around to move a dozen grams here and there.

He likes my idea, he thinks it's fun—"like a movie"—so here he is, my chaperone, showing me around these two days as a criminal in the underbelly of Milan.

It's already 2 PM when he shows up wearing more perfume than a Japanese male whore. He doesn't apologise for his lateness. He just nods hello and stares at me, sizing me up, taking in my new outfit. I'm wearing exactly what he asked, from head to toe: cap, tracksuit, sneakers, gold chain outside my sweatshirt. The tracksuit is important: in many Italian prisons it may be worn instead of the regulation striped uniform, which has transformed it into a symbol of respect. It means you just got out, and jail is always a plus on the Mafioso's CV.

"Minchia Frà, stylish… where you coming from, Opera (a Camorra square) or San Vittore (Milan's largest prison)?"

He means it as a compliment, one of those constant jokes that these kids never seem to tire of. Nevertheless, I feel like touching wood. After a quick coffee and Sambuca we start moving for our first meet, at the end of Via Ripamonti. Beppe is also here, another guy from his crew, his driver for today, and Leo's brother-in-law. They tell me about the night before; they did too much coke, and ended up getting in a fight—the usual bullshit: women, money owed.

"It's the coke," adds Leo, "it makes you too fucking horny and too fucking mouthy, it's not a good combination. That's why I still have this with me," he continues, patting the gun under his t-shirt. I ask how it all ended, concerned, when Beppe cuts in. "Nothing happened," he says. "We beat one of theirs, they beat one of ours, then we made peace and ended up at my house. We smoked freebase till morning, playing Playstation."

4 PM

We still need the gun, but it's too early. There's a change of plan: we're going to Beppe's place, to prepare the cuts he's going to sell tonight. In his basement, Beppe takes a coffee can, full of beans. But something is strange. They don't smell like coffee. In fact, they're pure cocaine, pressed. Beppe cleans about ten beans with vinegar, then he crushes them and mixes them with mannite, the cutting agent, resulting in about 40 baggies ready to be sold. The whole procedure must have taken him about half an hour. While he's at it, I give him my bean back, as I wasn't gonna do it anyway. He asks me if I don't like it, I mumble something about panic and insomnia, and as soon as I do, I realise I've just lost a lot of respect. He must think I'm a depressed maranza. Luckily Leo comes to my rescue, vouching for me, even though "I quit doing it".

I ask Beppe about his background. He tells me, plainfaced, that for a while he was almost "in" one of the families, but it ended up going the other way. I ask him how. "Four years ago, I used to deal big time. Always in Piazza Caneva, pot and coke. Once, at the Number club in Brescia, a guy from Corvetto introduces me to Tony, his cousin from Calabria who robs jewellery stores. A total cokehead. To cut a long story short, we become best buddies, as well as accomplices. It was wild: parties every single night, orgies, Viagra and more coke than Tony Montana. We hit jewellery stores every week, between Piedmont and Liguria, a different hotel every night, we're fucking hot. I mean, he was already wanted, and now we literally can't spend more than two nights in the same place. Until one fine day that Venezuelan whore disappears with 200 grams of uncut blow."

The next hour is spent in the piazza, selling Beppe's stuff, a little courtyard beneath his house, a hangout for kids on their scooters. In that hour, the 40 baggies are sold at the price of 70 euros per bag. You do the maths, because if I were to attempt that I'd probably be here for the next two months.

Before we leave, Beppe, much more relaxed now, insists on showing me his 50,000-euro Mini-S motor car. "You like it? Give me 4,000 euros and I can get an identical one for you, regular, no problems with the paperwork."

"Pretty clean, huh? Too bad they put serial numbers on fucking screws now, so you can't run this operation on Mercs or Audis. Pity," adds Leo.

We head to the Hotel Diana for drinks. Leo introduces me to Pino, an alcoholic Pugliese who has been dealing with the families for years. Upon finding out that I support FC Inter, he gets pissed off at me, but then is moved to tears when I give him a saint-card of Padre Pio, which was given to me years ago in Puglia.

11 PM

We still haven't had dinner, and we head out to the Central Station. We get into a private club where we meet Karim, a 30-year-old Serbian who, as well as running a small prostitution operation, also deals in firearms. This time nobody's late: the gun dealer, the owner of the club, Pino, and his brother. The owner lets us in, and closes the heavy doors behind us. From behind a fridge, weapons start popping out rapidly, effortlessly, and then they are laid out on a table: a Beretta, a Colt Python, and a .357 Magnum.

Their serial numbers have all been scratched off. They cost 170, 300, and 800 euros respectively. I buy the cheapest, the Beretta, the police ordnance gun. "A good weapon," says Leo, trying to calm me down, as he studies it, caresses it. Maybe. But I'm feeling seriously uneasy: the realisation that this gun has already taken a life dawns on me and brings about a wave of nausea. I don't really feel like a Goodfella right now. More like a fraud. I'm suddenly panicking that they'll discover I'm not who I say I am. I mean, I'm not a cop, but journalists aren't exactly welcome within the fold either.

The more I want to leave and the more they want me to stay, hang out, drink some more wine, eat some more aubergines in olive oil, do one more line. All in about four squared metres. It's ridiculous and sad: I feel nauseous and panicked, claustophobic. I manage to lay off the coke (Leo told them I have a heart condition) but the rest I can't possibly refuse: the bottles of wine, grappa, vodka, Sambuca, and all the time food, tomatoes, aubergines. I couldn't tell them I've been on the wagon for about ten years. So, at around 3 AM, we leave the club's basement, and I'm drunk out of my head, and I have a gun. I don't know where the fuck to put it. Sometimes my curiosity pisses me off.

Leo starts telling me about Karim's organised orgies, and about his best friend's death, shot in the face after having spoken too much. All I can think about is how to get rid of this gun, which, it now dawns on me, is clearly hot. What the fuck am I doing? I feel like throwing up. Before I know what to do with the gun, and as Leo movingly tells me about his friend's mistakes, I pass out, and I remember the good thing about booze: it makes you sleep. I had forgotten about that these past ten years (I used to be an alcoholic).

LET'S GO PAKISTAN!

KALASHNIKOV CULTURE FROM NORTH TO SOUTH
WORDS AND PHOTOS BY SUROOSH ALVI

Published March 2004

From the American perspective, Pakistan isn't far from joining the so-called axis of evil. After September 11, this generally spineless nation conveniently became a buddy in the fight against terrorism. But make no mistake—if its current government should fall, impoverished and overpopulated Pakistan will flip-flop to redheaded-stepchild status faster than you can say "Flight 77".

Islamic extremists are hungry to assassinate Pakistan's President Musharraf (aka Bush's lil' bitch), and in recent months they've come close more than once. Should they succeed, the United States' greatest jingoistic fear will be realised—crackpot fundamentalists will get their dirty brown paws on a nice little cache of nuclear weapons. You think this country has a bad rap now? Just wait.

I've been to Pakistan 13 times since the 1970s, and I've witnessed the steady deterioration of a country that was built on a bad idea in the first place. Religious ideals are not firm bedrock for nation building. Mix in a dash of illiteracy (the *New York Times* puts it at 44 percent), some classic poverty, and more barefaced corruption than if Boss Tweed and Henry Kissinger co-ruled the universe, and it's a wonder that all of Pakistan isn't already a smoking crater.

Yet despite all this—and call me a pussy if you must—there's something about this tepid cesspool of failed dreams that I can't help but love.

My journeys back to the city of Lahore (the cultural centre of Pakistan in the Punjab province), usually consist of typical Punjabi laziness: watching Indian MTV on the satellite dish, eating rich food three times a day, and checking out girls at the nightly weddings. (Our family is so big that every December, which is wedding season, we marry a few young female cousins and nieces off to nerdy, sexually repressed guys they've never met before. It's Pakistan's sole form of legal entertainment, and it's fucking boring.)

To make sure things were status quo in these especially "troubled" days, I decided to arrange a visit this past December. This time, however, it wouldn't be all nuptials and Paki pop. This time I wanted to get around a little more.

After a few preparatory phone calls and emails, I'd inadvertently created the perfect itinerary to discover the hidden treasures that Pakistan can offer the typical tourist. But one quick word of caution first: if you aren't brown (I am) and you don't have multiple armed militiamen escorting you everywhere (I did), you might want to keep your jaunt to the motherland on a strictly armchair basis.

Ready? Let's go!

MUST-SEE ATTRACTIONS
PESHAWAR
Capital of the Northwest Frontier Province
(NWFP)

Despite the bad reputation, there is a ton of fun stuff to do in this country, from normal urban sightseeing (we'll get to that) to the northern areas (K2 is in Pakistan) to really fun stuff like exploring a spot that the BBC recently dubbed "the most dangerous place in the world"—the semi-autonomous tribal areas that run along the border of Pakistan and Afghanistan. The gateway to the heavy shit is Peshawar, a place that's renowned as a centre of religious conservatism, and more recently has been depicted by Western media as the first Pakistani city to fall victim to heavy Taliban influence (but I call bullshit on that). The Peshawar I saw was pretty laid back—lots of people goofing around on the streets (seriously). And even though the Taliban leftovers have tried to ban billboards that depict women and music from weddings, the central government in Islamabad successfully shut them down. So despite the intraprovincial and transnational chaos, there is some form of central leadership that still regulates the country.

DARRA ADAMKHEL
(THE ARMS MARKET)
Frontier Agency, Northwest Frontier Province
(NWFP)

From Peshawar it's only about an hour drive southwest to my favourite arms market in the world. The town is restricted to outsiders, so you can't really get in unless you have some kind of hook-up.

Our driver stopped at a security point just outside the town centre, where I was introduced to some members of the Frontier Agency militia, six angry-dad-looking bastards with AKs and sidearms, who became my personal bodyguards. My little A-Team followed me through a tight warren of gun shops and factories, and I'm not talking the GM plant in Detroit here, Michael Moore. These are barren little brick rooms where components are laboured over all day long in conditions that make Nike sweatshops look like Santa's workshop.

Peshawar; Darra Ademkhel; Karachi.

Darra Adamkhel is the largest illegal arms market in the world. They handmake, sell, and export everything from 9mm handguns to M-16s, but they specialise in the Pakistani man's new best friend, the Kalashnikov (AK-47). A Pakistani-made AK runs about $50 (50 fucking bucks!), while the Russian and Iranian versions start at $300 and up. You do the math. Darra Adamkhel is to guns what Canal Street is to Louis Vuitton bags.

The vendors are ethnic Pashtuns, some of the toughest people in the world, fierce fighters who can survive in conditions that would make normal people cry like babies and then die (Pashtuns comprised the majority of the mujahideen soldiers, the badasses who kicked the Soviets out of Afghanistan using their bare hands in the late 80s). Using primitive machinery, they perfectly replicate military hardware from across the spectrum. When the guns in Afghanistan ran out after the American invasion, Pashtuns provided military sustenance for the Taliban resistance, and are also credited with the illustrious achievements of covertly supplying weapons to the IRA, the Middle East, the Muslims in Kashmir, and the warlords that run all of Afghanistan (save for Kabul).

KARACHI
(POP. 16 MILLION)
Sindh Province in Southern Pakistan,
on the Arabian Sea

This megalopolis is the most cosmopolitan and volatile city in Pakistan, and has long been its centre of finance. The people are fashion-conscious, the cars are worth more than entire towns in other parts of the nation, and the stratification of wealth is fucking major. The rich are filthy rich and the poor are living in their own filth (with an estimated five million squatters). Karachi also rivals Bogotá, Colombia, as the world's capital for kidnappings and killings.

Karachi's main attraction is the nouveau riche kids, who live in a decadent, morally bankrupt bubble—a lapsed-Muslim *Less Than Zero*. The young rich kids have split into two groups: the ones who choose to speak English, who rock Gucci, Armani, and Burberry; and the Urdu-speaking, more conservative Muslim youth (boring!). The former are out of control, necking down E and sniffing cocaine like drugs were just invented. They're torn between the old-world values of the East and the nascent Pakistani pop culture and full-on liberalism of the West.

THE KHYBER PASS
NWFP

It's the most historic pass in the history of the history of the world, okay? If you don't know something about the Khyber Pass, you didn't go to school. It's 33 miles long, it starts on the outskirts of Peshawar and connects the northwestern frontier of Pakistan with Afghanistan. It goes way the fuck back, as in the Aryans came through here in 1500 BC.

In 326 BC, Alexander the Great and his army bludgeoned their way through. Persian and Greek armies came through also, and a bunch of other dudes like the Scythians, White Huns, Seljuks, Tartars, Mongols, Sassanians, Turks, Mughals, and Durranis all had their battles and meetings and shit up in here. In 1842, 16,000 British and Indian troops

The Khyber Pass; Red-light district in Lahore.

were killed by Afghani soldiers (Pashtuns, duh) in the Khyber Pass. How about that?

In recent years, the pass has been a pipeline for human misery: refugees constantly flowing back and forth, along with arms, heroin, and gold.

I drove the length of the pass with serious fucking security. At the edge of the Khyber region, we met up with two pickups full of soldiers that acted as an escort sandwich, one in front of my jeep and the other behind, and they freeeaaakkked out when I started taking pictures. They were speaking Pashto, not Urdu, but the message was clear: "Put the fucking camera away before you get shot." These guys were part of the Khyber Rifles, a militia organisation that's protected the pass from conquering armies for centuries.

Right now, the Khyber Pass is a spot-on summation of the effort to rebuild Afghanistan since America's recent high-octane "hello". Stunning scenery, the beautiful Hindu Kush mountain range for as far as the eye can see, with small mountain roads zigazagging through the Khyber pass filled with pure desperation: Pakistani supply trucks—a non-stop convoy of refugees, troops, food, rubber tubes, and rice, slowly making their way to the border. It was fucking intense and it made me kind of sad.

RED-LIGHT DISTRICT
(HIRA MUNDI)
Old City, Lahore

After eating at Cooco's Den (see the Dining Out listings), take a stroll through Lahore's red-light district in the Old City. From dragon-chasing junkies,

to snooker halls filled with ten-year-olds at 2 AM, to open rooms with whores on display, it's a South Asian Amsterdam, and definitely not in the next Islamic theocracy. I recommend buying some paan (tobacco in a betel leaf with a thin slice of areca nut and lime paste—it's been a cultural mainstay here for centuries). Chew on it for a while (make sure you spit, not swallow), cop a real nice buzz, and take in the sights (that's what I did).

A high-ranking Pakistani politician describes his home as a country where "there are fires everywhere, but no one to put [them] out." Others call it a place where everyone is landlord but nobody owns any land. The Western media sees it as a time bomb that's set to blow. The reality is that Pakistan has deep issues that are insanely complex, nothing is what it seems, and it's a country that's stigmatised beyond belief. No one from the West has any interest in going there, and that really makes it worth visiting.

All in all, countries with a bad rap are a helluva lot more compelling to visit than places condoned by *Condé Nast Traveler*. I'm surrounded by Americans every day, and I have absolutely no desire to see Americans when I travel. Cancun? No thanks. It's a fucking frat party.

Who would you rather emulate: the cast of *The Real World* or Graham Greene? Next time you're planning a trip, don't be a wimp. Try something off the beaten path, some place that CNN or the *New York Times* says is a dangerous shithole. Remember—it isn't a real journey unless there's a good chance you'll get shot, catch dysentery, or disappear forever.

Rubina (left) and an unidentified friend. Photo by the author

DICKLESS WONDERS

BE CAREFUL, OR THE HIJRAS WILL HEX YOU
INTERVIEW BY SARAH HARRIS

Published February 2009

India's proud community of boys who would rather be girls has officially breached the half-million mark, and we wish we could hug every one of these crazy, lovable, mixed-up bastards. They're a ubiquitous breed known as *hijras*, or "impotent ones", with a thousand-plus-year tradition of bringing good luck.

However, in these cynical times in which we live, the concept of luck is about as easy to believe in as the concept of leprechauns, and so the *hijras* have just become endearingly empowered street hustlers.

Vice recently caught up with Rubina, a 35-year-old from Mysore (ha ha ha, a town called "my sore"—only in India, folks!), who kindly invited us back to her place to discuss her transformation. It cost 1,000 rupees (about £15) for her time, and it was money gladly paid.

Vice: Rubina is a lovely name.
Rubina: Before I was Rubina, I was a boy called Sadiq. But I wanted to be a woman for as long as I can remember. From birth, I had flowery actions like a girl. I loved to dance, sing, grow my hair, and wear a bra and ladies' underwear.

And when did you actually claim your place among the impotent ones?
I ran away to Mumbai to join the hijra family at 18. A guru performed a special ceremony for me—like a marriage, with new saris, bangles, and decorations. It was a happy day. At home, I felt like I was in a cage, but when I joined my new family I felt like I was in the open air for the first time.

And this guru also surgically removed your penis. Is that legal for him to do?
No, but our guru performs the operation secretly. Removing the male parts was very painful. We see it like the delivery of a baby, because we are reborn as women. Some people die from it, but we have to bear it. I was very scared, but when it was over I felt so happy. I love my new body, even though I am quite fat. How do you think I look?

Gorgeous! How did your parents react?
They were very angry. I told them I would move away permanently if they didn't accept me. Because I am an only child and I make very good money from being a hijra, my parents now accept me.

What differentiates a hijra from a run-of-the mill tranny?
We are more like God's gift. The problem is we are born the wrong gender. Hijras have thousands of years' history in India. And we have responsibilities. People pay us a lot of rupees to perform weddings and births because they think we are good luck. But most days, we make money by approaching shop-keepers or the general public and saying things like, "Hello, darling, sweetie, namaste my dear, give me some money." Then we touch them and say rude things until they are a little embarrassed and give us cash. In return, we take away the evil eye. If they don't give us trouble, we don't give them any.

Define "trouble".
If they refuse to pay us any money, we will pull our saris up and show ourselves to them. They usually give us money so we stop making a scene. Then again, some men believe it is good luck to see our nakedness, so they ask us politely and give us money and we do it. Sometimes they kiss us and touch our breasts too, but in an affectionate way.

Are some people afraid of hijras?
Yes, some fearful people shout vulgar things like, "Homosexual eunuch, you have no penis!" I usually say something bad back to them, like, "Go to hell! You are going to die in a road accident." And what I say will probably come true. Just last month, a woman came to my house and said, "My husband is so rich that we could buy ten bitches like you." I got angry and said, "Soon your husband will die." The next week he did. This is the power of the hijra.

Bobbing into view, the grey seawall's artificial angling of the island gives it the shape of a battleship— hence its Japanese name in popular mythology, "Gunkanjima"—Battleship Island.

BATTLESHIP ISLAND

JAPAN'S ROTTING METROPOLIS | WORDS AND PHOTOS BY ALEX HOBAN

Published April 2009

These days the only things that land on Hashima Island are the shits of passing seagulls. An hour or so's sail from the port of Nagasaki, the abandoned island silently crumbles. A former coal mining facility owned by Mitsubishi Motors, it was once the most densely populated place on earth, packing over 13,000 people into each square kilometre of its residential high-rises. It operated from 1887 until 1974, after which the coal industry fell into decline and the mines were shut for good. With their jobs gone and no other reason to stay in this mini urban nightmare, almost overnight the entire population fled back to the mainland, leaving most of their stuff behind to rot.

Getting closer, talks with the fisherman continued slowly—it was only as we were actually setting foot on the landing jetty that he finally agreed to give us a couple of hours to explore before returning to pick us up.

Today it is illegal to go anywhere near the place as it's beyond restoration and totally unsafe. The Japanese government aren't keen to draw unwanted attention to this testament to the hardship of the country's post-war industrial revolution either.

The punishment for being caught visiting Hashima Island is 30 days in prison followed by immediate deportation. But the other week, after getting up before sunrise and cutting a secret deal with a local fisherman, some friends and I landed on Hashima Island.

The port of Nagasaki is an international hub where you're more likely to find granny-laden cruise ships and large oil tankers filling the docks than buck-toothed fisherman willing to break the law for a few extra bob, so we took the early morning ferry to the still-inhabited Takashima, the closest island to Hashima. After asking around—and being politely turned away by every Japanese we mentioned it to—we finally found our man. The rules of Japanese politeness dictate you never say what you want directly, so even once we were aboard the boat we weren't sure we were actually going to set foot on Hashima—we'd only agreed for our fisherman to take us close enough to see it.

In some areas the entire façades of buildings had fallen to the ground, revealing grids of homes, each exposed with their 70s television sets smashed after the TV stands had eroded away. It was difficult to gauge exactly what it might have been like to live here, although with the complete lack of outdoor space and the prison-like seawall keeping you in, I can't imagine it to have been anything other than claustrophobic, uncomfortable, and a bit like living in an ant farm.

Personal artefacts lay littered everywhere— old shoes, bottles of shampoo, newspapers, and even posters left on teenagers' walls. These were the most vivid clues that people had once been here.

We explored the empty classrooms of the island's huge school. The rusted carcasses of desks and chairs lay in front of blackboards displaying the withered dusty marks of the last class to have taken place there 30 years before.

From the top-floor gymnasium we looked down into the main auditorium, whose roof had caved in long before. It was clearly structurally unsafe. We were walking over large slabs which had fallen previously from the ceilings above us.

On roughly the ninth floor of an apartment block, I stepped into one of the rooms to admire the sea view from the window. The traditional woven tatami floor beneath my feet, unused to human contact, gave way, sending a tremendous ripping sound through the building's shell. I fell...

...about one metre, but it was enough to freak us out and from here on we took more care where we trod.

At only 1.2 km squared, the island is tiny, but you never can quite grasp this when you're winding through its perspective-warping high-risers. To get

a better overall look we scaled the central watch-tower—precarious as its old access paths were now overgrown beyond usability.

It never crossed our minds that the fisherman wouldn't come back. We were more worried that we only had those two hours on the island, an arbitrary frame of time my friend picked in the moment of excitement when we got the green light for transport. There was enough stuff there to keep us busy for an entire day.

And then, two days after this was written, the government re-opened it.

LIBERIAN GIRLS AND BOYS

HAVE BETTER VINTAGE T-SHIRTS THAN YOU
WORDS AND PHOTOS BY ANDY CAPPER & MYLES ESTEY

Published November 2009

VBS recently visited Monrovia, Liberia, where we made a film with three warlords called General Bin Laden, General Rambo, and General Butt Naked.

During our week there we filmed in the slums, on top of burned-out banks that have become squats, in graveyards that ex-child soldiers use to sleep in at night and, ill-advisedly, at midnight in the gnarliest brothel in the worst slum in the city. We noticed how everybody there looked like they'd been getting their clothes from vintage stores on eBay.

"How weird," I said. "We're in a country where only one-fifth of people have electricity or running water and there's a kid with a vintage Exploited shirt that somebody in LA currently lists for £200 on eBay so a stylist can put an MTV emo-rock band in it for an awards ceremony."

Just as those words left my lips, our fixer there, a Canadian journalist called Myles Estey, interrupted me with a sigh, and explained where all these shirts are coming from. What you are about to read is that explanation in written-down form.

Supply and demand comes with completely different connotations in Liberia. Demand does not control the goods supplied; it's the other way around.

Clothing exemplifies this inverted chain. Liberia's struggling economy does not have enough buying power to dictate what comes into one of the most import-dependent countries in the world. Its war-destroyed infrastructure means there's very little domestic production of anything.

Some new clothes do make it into the country. But outside the cheap Chinese kitsch sold in the potholed and rubbish-strewn Waterside Market, most new clothing is far outside the affordability of the average Liberian; as many as 60 percent of the country are said to live on a dollar a day.

So demand creates a different supply chain where low cost is the trump. Donations from the US and the wholesale purchase of massive amounts of used clothes fill hundreds of sea cans with clothing no longer wanted by Americans. These end up all over Africa, but Monrovia—the capital city of a country built by freed slaves of the 19th century in the image of the United States—receives a high proportion of used American garb.

It's these packed sea cans that set the parameters

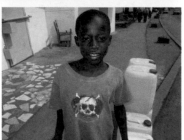

of style. Trends get set by what shows up in the shipping containers, not the other way around. For example, around Christmas last year, a multi-colour striped t-shirt made of cheap cloth could be found for about 80 cents anywhere in the country. It's near impossible to pass a day without seeing the "Be the Reds" shirt, produced by the millions to promote South Korea's football team as they hosted the 2002 World Cup. And sometime in the spring, a wave of cheap top hats showed up on the street, starting a trend for young men on the streets of the capital.

Yet these identifiable shipments are dwarfed by the mixed assortments of used digs that decorate pedestrians along the streets. The variation and contrasts can be truly spectacular. Boiled-peanut sellers in "Allman Brothers Live at the Fillmore" shirts. Ex-child soldiers with rippling muscles sporting white "Tickle me Elmo" shirts or black t-shirts adorned with a giant pink Barbie doll. Shockingly beautiful women in baggy shirts with a stupid logo aimed at lame American male middle-agers: "It's Not a Bald Patch... It's a Solar Panel for Love". Old women in yellow shirts bearing the classic DIY stencilling "Rock Out With Your Cock Out".

No trace of irony can be found. In fact, what the t-shirt actually says is generally ignored by the buyer in favour of size, colour, shirt quality, and personal perception of the design.

Rusty wheelbarrows stuffed with shirts serve as the shopping centres for these items. These sellers can be found pacing the city's streets, or they line the shirts in rows in busy areas, markets and roadsides, selling them for around two bucks each, often with a small crowd hovered around, finding the right mix of ingredients to bargain for a purchase. The US$2 price tag is a large investment for many Liberians.

Shirts live hard lives here. Most people have small wardrobes and so the shirts are worn repeatedly under the sweat, sun and humidity of equatorial Africa. Liberian kids are the last stop on this international hand-me-down chain. They wear shirts outgrown by older siblings, cousins and neighbours, often until ripped and dirty beyond recognition.

Even so, no one bitches that their shirt is not the newest, not the coolest, not the right colour, and certainly that it's not the right brand name—although these were most likely the reasons the shirts were given up in the first place. In Liberia, few kids have any clue of the disparity of privilege between themselves and those who tossed the shirt into a donation bin a million miles away.

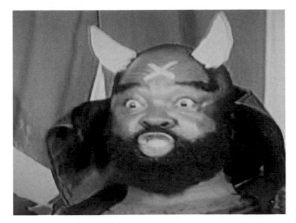

This is the devil saying: "I am Lucifer! I will take over the world!"

This is one of his slaves, gravely agreeing that what his master says is true.

NOLLYWOOD OMEN

NIGERIAN CHRISTIANS MAKE THE BEST DRUG-PARTY FILM EVER | BY ANDY CAPPER

Published September 2009

"Nollywood is the answer to CNN," says a star of *Nollywood Babylon*, a Canadian documentary about the Nigerian film industry—a veritable movie factory that churns out 25,000 films a year at a budget of less than $10,000 each. I was so intrigued by the idea of cheaply made Nigerian films that on a recent trip to Monrovia, Liberia, I picked up a bunch of Nollywood movies from a downtown DVD shack called Trans International Entertainment Business Center. It doubled as a barbecued-chicken-feet outlet.

I bought films called *Deadly Consequence, Emotional Problems,* and *Romantic Issues* and then watched them all with intense disappointment. They were little more than American soap operas set in dusty Nigerian villages. They had plots so unfollowable and audio so bad that they were impossible to watch for more than ten minutes each.

But then I started watching a film, or should I say a QUARTET of films, by Pastor Kenneth Okonkwo, who's regarded as one of Nollywood's most important producers. The film is called *666,* and it is

the most retarded-hilarious-fucked-film-to-watch-while-everybody-in-the-room-is-high-as-shit-at-4-AM thing I have seen since we covered that Turkish remake of *Star Wars* back in 2002.

The four episodes of *666* (each has its own DVD) follow the efforts of the devil to take over the world and how he enlists the people of Nigerian villages to do so. The devil is a large, bald Nigerian man with a beard. He has a team of female concubines who sit beside his throne in hell. He is constantly surrounded by flames and is always laughing

Here the devil sends a laser beam down to one of his slaves in an effort to destroy the world by using the laser beam to open up a grave for another devil, who is blue.

The slave gladly receives the laser beam.

Here, Pastor Okonkwo prays that the devil's laser beam does not awaken the other devil.

The devil's slave is hit by Christian lightning generated by Pastor Okonkwo's prayers.

maniacally about how much he's going to destroy the world. "I am Lucifer! I will take over the world!" he shouts while his evil bitches laugh.

In the first scene of *666,* the devil sends two assassins up to earth to kidnap a pregnant woman. They cut her belly open in a tunnel and steal the baby, whom they baptise in the service of Satan. Throughout the movie, Satan terrorises the people of Nigeria despite the efforts of Pastor Okonkwo (yes, he also stars in the film). Okonkwo often sends lightning bolts down to hell by the power of extreme prayer.

In part two of the quartet, the kidnapped child returns to earth and causes all manner of problems. He seduces a woman in her late 20s by flashing lasers out of his eyes; he goes on a bar crawl and possesses a woman who then kills a priest. Then, when a gang of Christians capture him and attempt to ritually stab him to death, he uses his powers to brand each of their foreheads with a lovely 666.

Weird shit happens every five minutes in these movies. The special effects (wobbly devil eyes and laser beams shooting down from heaven) are accompanied by *zow*! and *zap*! noises that sound like they're from a late-70s arcade game. It is the most fun ever, and while hardly an answer to CNN, it must be sought out by everybody reading this and made into a cult classic. I don't know how many of you will make it to Liberia or Nigeria to buy DVDs anytime soon, so you know what? I'll put them up on YouTube. Search "666, Nigeria, Vice". Deal? Deal.

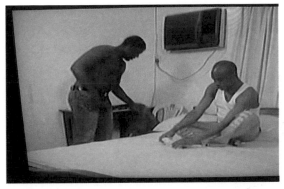

In this scene, two men have just had sex. This was put into the movie to show that the devil is at work in Nigeria even when he's not firing laser beams into graveyards.

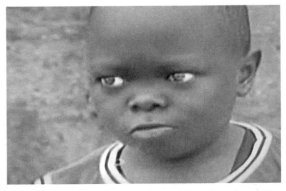

This is the Nigerian version of Damien from The Omen. *Here he is using his devil powers to tempt an older woman into bed.*

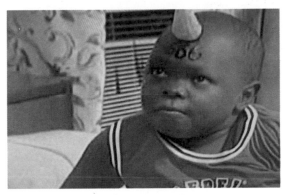

Here he is postcoitus.

This is one of the devil's concubines. She is about to threaten a Christian man with a drill to the head because he is refusing to accept the 666 stamp

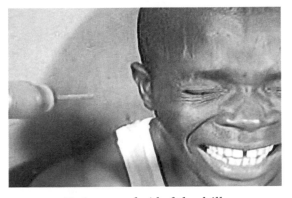

He is very afraid of the drill.

The film ends with another Christian man having his eyeball sucked out by a vacuum, whereupon this guy (who isn't actually Pastor Okonkwo) tells us to repent at once because the end times are upon us and you wouldn't like it if you had your eyeball sucked out by a vacuum. Fin!

Narcocinema actor Mario Almada and producer/actor/director Jorge Reynoso.
Photos by Abelardo Martín

NARCOTIC FILMS FOR ILLEGAL FANS

THE MEXICAN VIDEOHOME INDUSTRY MAKES MOVIES FOR THE MASSES
BY BERNARDO LOYOLA

Published September 2009

During the last few years, Mexican directors have received unprecedented international recognition. Movies like *Babel, Amores perros, Silent Light, Y tu mamá también* and *Pan's Labyrinth* have won awards at film festivals all over the world. Actors like Gael García Bernal and Diego Luna have drawn attention to a new generation of Mexican thespians. Hooray for them. But can we get some Mexican movies that aren't all arty and heavy and full of good acting and clever directing? Why isn't there a Mexican film scene that cranks out movies for the lady making tacos by the side of the road in Juárez instead of for the intellectual guy who teaches film studies in Mexico City? Aren't the poor and working classes of Mexico clamouring for films that they can relate to?

Well, I guess you aren't Mexican like I am. If you were you wouldn't have asked those dumb questions that I just put into your mouth because you'd know about the magic world of Mexican narcocinema. Come on, I'll tell you all about it.

For over 40 years, a hugely active B-movie industry has been producing super-low-budget films about drug dealers, bad cops, corrupt politicians, trucks, and prostitutes, catering mostly to the blue collar back home and the millions of Mexicans living in the US. In Mexico, this industry is called "videohome" because the movies go straight to video. If you go to a video-rental place in East LA, you'll find one copy of *Amores perros*, but it will be surrounded by hundreds of other movies like *Sinaloa, Land of Men; A Violent Man; The Dead Squad; Her Price Was Just a Few Dollars; Coca Inc.; I Got Screwed by the Gringos; Weapons, Robbery, and Death;* and *Robbery in Tijuana*.

This industry is frowned upon by embarrassed and ashamed middle- and upper-class Mexicans, and many people we tried to interview about it felt offended by the fact that we were even interested in narcocinema. A movie like *Chrysler 300* sold thousands and thousands of DVDs last year, but many people in the trendy neighbourhoods of Mexico City have never heard of it even though it was playing on every TV in the working-class areas. As Hugo Villa, a former official at the Mexican Institute of Cinematography, told us, "This is not a surprise when you realise that only 18 percent of the population in Mexico can afford to go to see movies in the theatres." The reality is that videohomes are a far truer reflection of the tastes of Mexico than the kind of stuff that makes Frenchmen pee champagne into their tux pants at Cannes.

These low-budget action flicks are often based on violent stories from local newspapers. They can be written, produced, and released mere weeks after the stories are published. They are also often based on myths and legends about the all-mighty drug cartels from the northwest region of Mexico and stories about Mexicans crossing the border. Also, hilariously, tons of narcocinema movies revolve around cars or trucks. In any store that carries videohomes, you can easily find movies like *The Black Hummer, The White Ram, The Red Durango*, and two of the most famous classics of the genre, *The Gray Truck* and *The Band of the Red Car*.

In the mainstream Mexican film industry, it is rare to find a movie that eventually gets a sequel. There's no *Y tu mamá también Part 2*. But in the videohome industry, any successful movie will become a franchise, so you have *Dos plebes 5, An Expensive Gift 4, Chrysler 300 Part 3*, and so on. Most sequels are revenge stories based on the original movies.

A few decades ago, these movies used to be westerns or straight action movies, but over the last two decades, the focus has shifted to drug trafficking. Mexico is the number two producer of both marijuana and poppies in the Americas, the majority of meth that seeps into the States is being made in Mexico, and the whole country is basically a superhighway for US-bound cocaine. Drug trafficking is a $100-billion-a-year business, and about 30 percent of that is estimated to go into paying off the government and the police.

Today, the narco wars going on in Mexico are out of control. Every day on the news you hear about shootings, executions, beheadings, and corruption. But it's not only the cartels that are at war with each other. The current government has tried to stop the cartels, effectively militarising entire areas of the country. This has sparked even more violence. So we have the cartels fighting the government, the government fighting the cartels, the cartels fighting each other, brutal killings every single day, and a group of dedicated workhorse filmmakers turning the whole thing into video faster than you can say *arriba*.

We recently met and spoke with two of the biggest narcocinema men in Mexico. Here's what they had to say.

NARCOCINEMA ACTOR MARIO ALMADA

If there's one person who represents this industry, it's Mario Almada. He's kind of like the John Wayne of Mexico—a total legend. He's 86 years old and he's still making movies. He actually holds the Guinness World Record for the living actor who's appeared in the most movies. We visited him at his house in Cuernavaca.

Vice: Have you made any movies lately?
Mario Almada: I just came back from Dallas. I was shooting a video there.

How many movies have you made?
I've starred as the lead in well over 300 films shot on 35 mm. That's just counting films shot on film. I'm not counting videohomes. I've probably acted in more than 1,000 of those.

Hence your winning the Guinness record.
That's what I've been told, but I've never seen it.

What's the difference between working in 35 mm and in videohomes?
It's very different. The big movies are shot over months and videos are made in six days. That's why I've managed to act in so many movies.

And do you usually play the good guy or the bad guy?
Usually I'm the hero: an avenger, a cop, a sergeant, a sheriff. I've played priests and pretty much everything else. Except for a gay guy. Not that. If I played that, it wouldn't even be believable. My characters always fight against violence and against the drug traffickers. Always. The only time I played the role of a drug trafficker was in *The Band of the Red Car*.

Who watches your movies?
Mostly the working-class people, but very often I run into women from the super-rich neighbourhood of Lomas de Chapultepec and they tell me, "Mr. Almada, I watched one of your movies on TV last night. They are great. Please keep making them." But the main audience is the working class in Mexico, the US, and South and Central America.

Is it true that a lot of these movies are shot in the US?
We've shot a lot of great movies in Brownsville, Texas. *The Band of the Red Car* was shot between Brownsville and Matamoros, Mexico.

And is that because the millions of Mexicans living in the US are really the market for your movies?
People there really like Mexican songs, but they also like the stories about the border, about illegal immigrants, and about drug trafficking. Movies like *The Death of the Jackal* and *The Revenge of the Jackal* were huge hits. We also shot those in Brownsville.

You just mentioned Mexican songs. There's a very close relationship between *narcocorridos* [drug ballads] and the videohome industry, right?
There are so many of these songs. There are lots of characters who have been very famous, like bandits and such, and eventually someone writes a corrido about them. And based on that corrido, a movie gets made. And they are always very successful, because they are based on a song that's already well known. For example, *The Band of the Red Car*. That started as a corrido that was made famous by Los Tigres del Norte, one of the biggest bands in Mexico. It tells the story of four friends who get killed. They were carrying 100 kilos of coke in the tyres of the car. The movie came out of that song. You can see it all in the movie. We take the tyres apart and all that.

You made other movies based on songs by Los Tigres del Norte, right?
Well, there was that one in 1978, but yes, we also made *The Golden Cage, The Gray Truck,* and *Three Times Wetback*. In *The Gray Truck* I play the father of a young guy who's a drug trafficker. I'm his father but I'm also a cop, and that's the main conflict in the movie.

Dos carteles *(2000), starring Mario Almada.*

I love the lyrics of that song. "It was a grey truck, with California plates/The truck was tuned out/ Pedro Marquez and his girlfriend had tons of dollars to buy drugs/Their destination was Acapulco, that was their plan/Enjoy their honeymoon and on their way back carry 100 kilos of the fine stuff/ Back in Sinaloa, Pedro tells Inez/'Someone is following us, you know what you have to do/Take out the machine gun and make them disappear.'" And in the end, they crash into a train and die. I love that movie too.

Yeah, it was a very beautiful movie. *The Golden Cage* was very good too. That's about a guy who wants to go back to the US, but his family doesn't want to go with him. In the end, he manages to cross the border and takes his family with him.

Now, I've heard that some of these movies are financed by…

By drug traffickers? Well, yes. It might be true. I've never looked into it. I have a lot of producer friends who wear gold chains and diamonds, but I don't try to find out if they are drug traffickers or not, because they're nice. They're good people.

Have you ever met any big drug dealers? Any capos?

I met Rafael Caro Quintero in the 80s in Guadalajara. He invited us to his table at a restaurant and I had drinks with him. He was a very charming man, a very generous man who did a lot for his people. He built schools. We made *Operation: Marijuana* about the beginnings of Caro Quintero, when he had those plantations everywhere. He got into something illegal and he ended up in jail, but he was a good man.

99

What do you think of mainstream Mexican films being made today?

There are a lot of good movies being made today, but they are not for the majority of the people. They are made for an elite. There need to be films that everybody can watch, not like *Y tu mamá también*. That's pornography! Filmmakers come out of school today with weird ideas. People don't like those complicated themes that they make their movies about.

Will you continue making movies?

I will, long as my body allows me, but it might not be for too long. I'm 86. That's too many years! I've seen so many things in my life!

NARCOCINEMA PRODUCER/ACTOR/ DIRECTOR JORGE REYNOSO

We really wanted to talk to film entrepreneur, director, producer, and actor Jorge Reynoso. As opposed to Mario Almada, Jorge usually plays the most badass of bad guys. He was hard to pin down. He cancelled on us a couple of times, and when we finally met him in Mexico City while he was supervising the editing of his latest movie, he explained to us that he had been busy, travelling in Asia on someone's yacht, visiting factories in China to start the production of his very own hot sauce: *Rico, Picante y Sabroso, el Sabor de Jorge Reynoso* [Good, Spicy and Delicious, the Flavor of Jorge Reynoso], which he plans to sell at Walmarts in the US next to the DVDs of his movies.

Vice: What's the difference between making films and making videohomes?

Jorge Reynoso: It comes down to distribution. Theatrical films are shot in HD or 35 mm and then they are projected in theatres. Videohomes are shot in 16 mm, HD, or DVCAM and they go straight to video and are distributed in supermarkets or video stores.

So how much money and how much time does it actually take to make these movies?

The costs are between $40,000 and $50,000 for a well-made movie. We ask someone to write the script, which is done in three or four days. There are some great Mexican writers. So in a week and a half, I have the preproduction of the movie ready. After that, we have two weeks to shoot it. So in five weeks, the movie is already on the market. I've made as many as 26 movies in a year.

That's incredible. What do you think of the Mexican film industry? What's the difference between the mainstream Mexican films that are known internationally and the kind of movies you make?

I think there are some great movies being made today, but I also think that they are made for people who can afford to watch them. They are not really films for the majority of the people, because the working class doesn't have access to them. First, there are no movie theatres in the small towns and rural areas, and second, I think that the themes they talk about are a bit off from where they should be, in terms of culture and values. I think those movies are too risqué. I think they've gone too far, but they win awards and compete at the major film festivals. The kinds of movies we make are very different.

How so?

This style of action movie that we make today, based on news stories, about the mafia, was started by me, and I made them popular by working with the record labels and by including popular corridos in them. People actually know me as "The Lord of the Guns", because I've killed lots of people... in my movies. Most of the movies I've made are about the mafia. These movies are very well received by the Mexicans living in the US, because they can relate to the characters in them, who are very respected, and loved by people that live in small towns, and also by the musical groups that sing corridos.

So you are saying that Mexicans celebrate their drug dealers?

What happens is that drug traffickers in Mexico come from the countryside. They are people who make their way out of poverty. Once they succeed, they do good things for their hometowns. They build schools and hospitals, they create jobs, and, obviously, people

La Hummer negra *(2005), starring Jorge Reynoso.*

love them. There's even a patron saint of the drug traffickers. His name is Jesús Malverde and his shrine is in Culiacán, Sinaloa. People go there and they leave candles and they sing songs for him. It's a fascinating culture, and it's the reality of Mexico.

Have you ever met any big drug dealers while making your movies?
I've had the opportunity to meet many of them. In fact, we've made some important movies with these people where they've worked with us. They've been with us, but obviously I was never a snitch and that's why I'm still alive. I've never betrayed the trust of any of them, who always gave us and continue to give us their friendship. The first movie that I made about the mafia was called *The Mafia Trembles*, a movie made about Rafael Caro Quintero, who was a very important drug trafficker in Mexico. We made

La Mafia 1, La Mafia 2 and *La Mafia 3*. They were highly successful.

Yeah, in the 80s he was one of the biggest drug dealers in the world. I remember that when they captured him in Costa Rica, he actually offered to pay off the foreign debt of the country if they let him go, and he said the same when he was extradited to Mexico.
Yeah, but I think he's still in jail today.

Do the police ever come and ask you where you get the information to write your movies?
It has happened in the past. The State Department would call me to ask me if I knew where such and such person was hiding. I would answer them, "You should know where he is. You are the police, I'm just an actor."

101

Did you start out making mafia movies, or were there other genres for you first?

In the beginning we started making movies about the illegal immigrants. More than making movies, we were making an homage to those people who make it to the "other side" despite all the difficulties. We feel very proud of them. Then we started making movies about the mafia. Although it was somewhat risky because the Mexican mafia is the second- or third-most powerful in the world, I continued making them, often based on narcocorridos. The record labels would approach us and give us songs, and we would make movies about the songs that were playing on the radio. We still do that today. People used to tell me that I looked like a mafioso and that I should play that kind of character, so that's what I do, and I play those characters with a lot of pride and dignity.

It's interesting that a lot of these movies are Mexican productions but are shot in the US. Why shoot there instead of Mexico?

We get a lot of support from the Mexicans who live there. People know us and they get very excited when they see us there. When you shoot in the places where they live, like Houston, Dallas, California, or Chicago, the people get very involved. Also, the mayors of many American towns are of Mexican origin, and they help us a lot.

Where do you sell the majority of your movies?

Our main market is the Mexicans living in the United States. Piracy was hitting us really hard, but we realised that if we sold lots of DVDs of our movies at supermarkets at very accessible prices we could make a profit. Walmart has more than 2,000 stores in the US. If we sell five copies at each store, we are talking about 10,000 copies, and they can be sold in just a few days. At Walmart they place our DVDs next to Mexican food products. For example, you can find a movie starring Jorge Reynoso next to some delicious enchiladas. We put four or five movies on a single DVD. We also sell our movies to TV stations in California, Texas, and Illinois. You give the people movies they want, with songs, with a

beautiful actress, a handsome guy, and a killer, and they will buy them.

You've mentioned narcocorridos. It's very interesting how this music has changed over the years.

Corridos were songs originally from the Mexican Revolution, from the beginning of the last century. They would make songs for the fighters and heroes like Pancho Villa and Emiliano Zapata or the women fighting with them on the front lines. In recent times, this kind of song is made for and about important characters of the Mexican cartels—dignifying them, and making them into larger-than-life heroes. People in the Mexican mafia love this kind of music.

A lot of these kind of movies are based on popular narcocorridos, but I know that in the past three years, there have been over 25 violent killings of musicians, like Valentín Elizalde and Sergio Gómez, attributed to the drug cartels, supposedly for singing in the wrong territory or about the wrong people. Do you ever get in trouble for making a movie based on the "wrong" song?

The song gives you the synopsis for the movie and, based on that, we make the adaptation. But of course, you have to ask for permission. You need to have good relations with these people so you don't get in trouble. Because if you make changes to the story that they don't like, then you will have some problems. God bless, we've always done things the way they should be done.

There are a lot of recurring stars in your movies, but it seems that non-actors play a lot of the characters too.

The scripts are written in such a way that everybody can participate. Like the strippers, who are always great with us. They are awesome girls. The security guards, the cops, the drunk guys, the hitmen, and all the people who are in that kind of environment always work with us. What you see is what you get. The prostitute is a prostitute, the cop is a cop, and the drug dealer is a drug dealer.

GARAGELAND

INNER-CITY LONDON TAKES THE MEDITERRANEAN
BY ANDY CAPPER | PHOTO BY WILL ROBSON-SCOTT

Published March 2004

British people who work in the media will tell you things like "The UK underground is dead", but that's because they get all their articles and ideas by googling their lives away on friendster.com and gayclub.org.

Anybody who actually lives outside the ridiculous world of fashion-culture magazines or the totally-out-of-touch mainstream radio and TV will tell you there's a million different underground scenes going on all over England all at once.

Just look at the young, black, violent MCs of east London's grime/sublow/eski garage scene (known to most as simply the underground garage scene circa right now). They've created an underground so alive and thriving that it's a mystery why the entire world isn't taking lessons on how to be like them.

Even though Dizzee Rascal made it quite big recently and the *Guardian* newspaper just wrote a story about grime, Dizzee and our boy Mike Skinner are like trillionaire violinist pop stars compared to the hundreds of underground MCs who make the garage music of today. In fact, most of these MCs have never heard of the Streets and see Dizzee as a successful rapper who used to do garage.

Made by some of the poorest kids in inner-city London, the new music consists of rhymes and beats so bristly and violent and fucking brutal and totally unplayable by any radio station ever that the first time you hear it you go, "Errrrwoaah phheeeeewwwwwwooooooohhhh," like when you've had too many Es and you're trapped in a scary place between ultimate joy and lust and total fear for your life.

Slew Dem's Tempa T at home in Stratford, northeast London.

Some of it's like Napalm Death (first album) crossed with dark fucking rock-slinging east London grimness and The Specials, and it makes Luther Vandross-sampling American hip-hop like Kanye West stand in the music-for-parents corner like it should. MC/producers like Wiley—who used to be Dizzee Rascal's right-hand man in the Roll Deep entourage—make simple, two-note, minor-chord beats out of Playstation 2s, and then press up white labels and sell them out of the boot of their cars at raves. There's no chains or ice, just kids in black Barbour jackets and Evisu jeans who climb to the top of 38-storey tower blocks to place a radio transmitter out of the way of the cops and the DTI (Department of Trade and Industry).

If you live in London, there are so many illegal pirate radio stations that it's almost impossible to get the main radio stations on your dial. The stations are hidden away in council-estate kitchens and factory tearooms and underneath railway stations. They're where MCs and producers make their names by spitting lines like "It ain't over 'til the fat lady sings/And I'll slap the fat lady/And if she gets up, BLAM! BLAM!/I'll shoot her back down again" (that's a Ruff Sqwad lyric).

The MCs and producers all have to pay to play on the stations, and they get nothing back from it apart from love and respect from their fellow kids, so it's clear that nothing really matters to them besides their scene.

Now the story here is that these kids work harder than most of their parents, and they need a good holiday now and again. Britain is cold and rainy 363 days of the year, and the working-class tradition of cheap package holidays to the Mediterranean makes life worth living for a lot of us, so that's how you get places like Ibiza, where the faggy, white, ecstasy-riddled house scene still thrives.

But while Spain gets didgeridoo-playing, technical-sandal-wearing E casualties chewing their faces off and dancing in the sea to Judge Jules, the violent-digital-cacophony scene of grime goes to the Cypriot resort of Ayia Napa. Because the police there are so strict on drug use and the garage scene used to be ruled by rollneck-sporting DJs like Artful Dodger and

Dreem Team, Napa was once quite a happy, trouble-free, completely boring place to go.

Mainly, it was a lot of fat middle-class white girls out for black cock and tons of embarrassing red-wine-and-shagpile-carpet people in fake Moschino jeans.

This year, though, the grime crews are going to descend on Napa in all their spitting glory. All drunk on Alizé and high as kites on skunk with zero females anywhere to take their bloodlust out on, they're going to tear Napa ten new holes and then piss all over its bleeding sores and laugh like hyenas.

"Grime is just bare noise, bruv," explains ex-N.A.S.T.Y Crew MC D Double E. "It means 'dark'. Just spitting bare anger. I reckon Napa is grimy. They always hold grime back, put it with some R&B, but when grime comes on pure it always gets the crowd shock."

The whole island is a powder keg waiting to go off. Most of the grime kids are going to be living in cheap, self-catering, package-holiday accommodations, where the food tastes worse than the supermarket shit in the east London ghetto. They're also going to be deprived of sleep thanks to the constant, unforgiving sound of 10,000-miles-an-hour music battering their brains all day and night for four weeks straight.

MC D Double continues: "The food in Ayia tastes fucked up. The clubs are all tight. The police are a bit crazy out there. I was on my moped and the police was following me, shouting bare ["bare" means "a lot"] shit at me. They tried to get me to the police station, but I got away. There's going to be random trouble everywhere next time we go."

"Grime brings out the anger in MCs," said N.A.S.T.Y Crew MC Ghetto when *Vice* spoke to him and rhyming partner Kano recently.

"In Napa, everyone is drunk," deadpanned Kano. "Everyone's having a good time, travelling round in cars or on their mopeds. There's always trouble. One of my friend's friends got stabbed and they had to extend their tickets. This year there'll be N.A.S.T.Y Crew, East Connection, Roll Deep. I would like to see Eskimo [Wiley's rave] out there. A lot of kids in England can't get to Eski in London, but in Napa you'll have people from Manchester, Cardiff, Leeds, Luton, everywhere. It's mad, 'cos they can't get our records or hear us on radio, but they all come down to Napa."

Shit. We feel a little bad writing all this stuff down, because we don't want to be harbingers of doom or see the grime kids—some of whom have written stuff for us and played our parties and helped us out—stabbed or shot or fucked up in any way at all, but everybody we spoke to about this year's Napa seemed to say the same thing.

Like UK garage bible *RWD* and their writer Rosa Ahmed said: "Grime music creates a tension in the clubs because you can't really dance to it."

She told us over the phone: "Grime creates a different kind of mood than the garage music that Ayia Napa is used to. It makes you want to punch somebody in the face, or else just sit in a corner and smoke weed and get paranoid. The old Ayia Napa crew was the Artful Dodger brigade, where all they sang about was girls and stuff, but grimy lyrics is all about violence and keeping it raw and angry. The kids are 21 and 22, and it's always tense at those raves."

We then proposed to Rosa that if all the rival gangs on mopeds are racing down to the beach and staying out all night dancing and getting tense, Ayia Napa '04 will basically be the black sequel to *Quadrophenia*, only twice as intense and potentially culturally relevant to Britain—ie, it could signal the start of a new musical movement as invigorating to bored working-class Brits as ska, punk, or two-tone was.

"What's *Quadroplegia*?" she replied. "I've never heard of it."

GARAGE

Named after Manhattan's Paradise Garage, this fast-paced form of dance music has changed drastically since its inception. Most recently it's gone from bourgeois turtleneck funk to catchy urban underground dance (The Streets) to minimalist rap (Dizzee Rascal) to pure digital cacophony (what it is today). Though definitions seem to change daily, and it is often called things like eski-beat, sublow, and grime (the genre's latest hero Wiley, just recorded a track called "Wot Do U Call It?"), the garage music of today is just a few sparse beats laid out on a Sony PlayStation with a barrage of lightning-fast MCs screaming out the kind of thing you'd hear on incredibly violent ragga. Most of the tracks are too loud and raw to be released, so they can only exist live. That is to say, the beats are made in some poor kid's bedroom, then played on an illegal radio station where an MC can rap over them live. If you're at home, you can hit "record" on your tape player and, bang, you have the song—nobody else does. Despite most of these tracks never being released, most kids at raves (any organised garage night) know all the lyrics. About 70 percent of young people in London listen to underground garage even though it has virtually no commercial appeal.

PIRATE RADIO

Most kids get their music from illegal radio stations. It is the only way to hear today's underground garage. A bunch of young kids (usually white) take over a small residential apartment in the ghettos of east London. They build a soundproof room and set up 90 percent of the station—the turntables, microphones, link box, and antennae. The antennae then sends a microwave signal to the transmitter, which is usually miles away on the top of a tower block (see the cover of *Original Pirate Material*). The transmitter is far away for two reasons: 1) it can be placed on the highest building in London and can therefore broadcast much farther than the flat they took over, and 2) when the DTI finds the signal, it can only confiscate the transmitter (worth about £400) and will still have no idea where the actual radio station is. The biggest expense a pirate radio owner has, by far, is replacing confiscated transmitters. The DTI contends that pirate radio stations inadvertently scramble emergency services signals and people are dying because of it. We think that's malarkey and they're just trying to justify their government-funded jobs.

AYIA NAPA

A small village in Cyprus that the underground garage scene has randomly chosen as their summer home. Where the house scene has Ibiza, these kids have Ayia Napa. You have all the pirate radio owners and DJs, all the MCs, all the fans (not just from inner-city London but from all over Britain), all the crews, and all the criminals. These are the poorest and most dangerous kids in London, all drunk and high and ready to rumble. Dizzee Rascal was stabbed here, and plenty more people will inevitably go down this summer.

THE UK GARAGE BEEFS

DIZZEE RASCAL VS VICE

Vice wrote about Dizzee back in April 2003 for the West Is the Best Issue. We took photos of Dizzee boxing, punching holes in walls, and finally, holding his knife. Dizzee's manager asked us not to use the picture of the knife, but we used it anyway because we're not a PR agency. When he saw the article, his manager hit the fucking roof and threatened to rip our UK editor "limb from limb". Dizzee got stabbed about nine months later, and his manager sees that as proof that he was right and that *Vice* endangered Dizzee's life by not following his instructions. When anything about this story is mentioned, his manager turns beet-red with rage and runs out of the room. Most recently, he was in the offices of a large American record label talking about it and he almost punched a hole through the wall. Meanwhile, Dizzee is shrugging his shoulders in the background and telling us, "It was the realest article anybody wrote about me."

DIZZEE RASCAL VS SO SOLID CREW

As we just mentioned, Dizzee Rascal was stabbed numerous times in broad daylight by somebody who was allegedly upset that he allegedly pinched the bum of the first lady of So Solid, Lisa Maffia, in a club the night before. While Dizzee doesn't really roll with that much of a crew now—he split from Roll Deep on signing to XL—there's still bad feeling over the incident.

SO SOLID CREW VS EVERYBODY IN GRIME

Because they inadvertently invented grime by introducing gangsta elements to a previously "red wine and roses"–obsessed scene, So Solid feel pissed off that none of the grime kids take them seriously. The 29-strong Brixton crew also owns a villa in Napa and its members have various beefs on a weekly basis with everybody. When grime invades Napa this year, So Solid is going to be ready and waiting for it to go off. So Solid (mostly in their mid-20s upwards) and the young scamps that make up crews like Ruff Sqwad and East Connection are going to make them look old and redundant and nothing's meaner than an old dog who can't get it up any more.

MARCUS NASTY VS D DOUBLE AND JAMMER

N.A.S.T.Y Crew founding member Marcus Nasty was in jail for a while, so a dreadlocked producer called Jammer took over the beats/management of Forest Gate's premier crew. When Marcus got out of prison, he sacked Jammer and dissed him in the garage press. D Double, N.A.S.T.Y's most popular MC next to Kano, also left in loyalty to Jammer, and MC Monkey left too. When this happened, Marcus Nasty went apeshit and even slapped D Double on stage at a rave in east London in January. D Double and Jammer are now working together with Monkey, while N.A.S.T.Y is now Marcus Nasty, Sharky, Kano, Hyper, and Ghetto. Both sides of the split are going to be in Napa this year. Look out.

WILEY VS EVERYBODY

Everybody's saying that Wiley's Eskimo rave will be at Club Ice this year, and if this happens, there's going to be beefs every night. Not so much violent beefs, rather, every new MC who wants to make his name usually does it by dissing Wiley—considered the Dr Dre of grime—and then having a face-off with him on the mic. This is how Durrty Doogz made his name. Recently, Wiley broke his hand single-handedly taking on the security at one of his own Eskimo Dance raves because they wouldn't let one of his boys in.

Right now, Wiley=God.

Wigan Pier donk night. Middle left: Blackout Crew's DJ Cover with adoring fans.

The Blackout Crew. From left to right: MCs Dowie, Zak K, Viper, Cover, Rapid and DJs Siddy B and Jonezy at Harmony Youth Centre.

PUT A DONK ON IT

**ON THE ROAD WITH BRITAIN'S NEWEST INSANE MUSICAL TREND | BY JAIMIE HODGSON
PHOTOS BY SCOTT KERSHAW, ANDY CAPPER AND STU BENTLEY**

Published February 2009

Those looking to shatter their last, lingering hopes for the future of Britain should visit Burnley. What used to be a prosperous cotton-mill town is now decimated by the terminal decline of industry, with entire square miles of housing steel-boarded-up, repossessed and marked for demolition by the local council. Unemployment is all-consuming, violence is a popular pastime—as is the rampant theft of expensive copper pipes from condemned houses to sell as scrap to pay for heroin and crack. It's practically a ghost town these days, but instead of headless cavaliers with chains clanging around their wrists and ankles, there are gaggles of toothless, skeletal smackheads waddling around in skid-mark-stained tracksuit bottoms. Actually, scratch that—it's more zombie town than ghost town.

Burnley is also one of the focal points of the planet's most terrifying and hilarious forms of dance music: donk. It's pretty much the only thing kids live for there. But drive 40 minutes down the motorway, away from the cluster of northwest donk satellites (Bolton, Wigan, Burnley, Blackpool), and barely anyone's heard of the genre.

There's a bit of debate about donk's origins, but generally people attribute early-90s Dutch producers like Ultrabeat for pioneering the sound. It's a rave-based dance music created around no-budget 150 bpm bouncy beats, intrusive fog-horned synth stabs, cartoon-y samples, and unsettlingly saccharine highs. It's basically happy hardcore on a crippling steroid comedown. The word "donk" comes from the relentless, maddening "donk" sound that's overlaid on the beats. The fact that a whole subculture stems from a noise that originated from an old-school keyboard sound-effect that emulates an empty drainpipe being hit by a paddle tells you pretty much all you need to know. The genre has also been called "scouse house", which refers to its early proliferation in Liverpool, and "bounce", which many locals still use today. Donk has come to represent the sound's recent influx of MC culture. Inspired by Eminem-copying white-boy rabbiting and early-90s rave MCing, the real donk stars these days are its hype men, whose rhyming has become the focus for most young fans. To some, this sounds like a *Daily Mail* caricature of an ASBO northerner assaulting a crystal-meth-smoking oompah band.

People outside the northwest are finally starting to hear donk through its very own boy band, Blackout Crew. The Bolton outfit are the only donk MCs to have recorded actual proper songs with verses and choruses. Blackburn dance label All Around the World spied the group through homemade YouTube videos and quickly cashed in by commissioning a series of proper-budget promo videos and releases.

They became our entry into the world of donk after a bunch of their videos were sent in a circular email to *Vice* staff and friends a few months ago. One track really stood out. It was called "Put a Donk On It". It's based around the concept that any type of music can be improved by the simple addition of a "donk". Go

on YouTube now if you haven't seen it.

In broad accents, Blackout rap about everyday stuff like tits, fighting, weed, shagging, knife crime, cars, ecstasy and their favourite brands of chocolate bar. It's not your typical boy-band fare, but even so, their fan base is almost exclusively teenage girls and boys. Recently, VBS.TV spent a week travelling round the northwest with the band, soaking up every last drop of donk culture.

Blackout Crew was formed at a community centre in Bolton called Harmony. It's similar to many youth clubs: lots of shiny veneer, bright yellow lights, table-tennis tables, and a tuck shop selling Panda Pops and Space Raiders crisps. But Harmony just happens to have rehearsal rooms and recording studios down the corridor, and every Tuesday and Thursday the place is transformed into a cross between *Shameless* and *8 Mile*. Swarms of kids in matching flammable ensembles with Nike logos shaved into their heads cram into any available space. Donk blares at deafening levels as the kids try to look mean, and occasionally launch into their own version of a "battle rap". Maybe it's because I'm a southern poof, but I could only understand every third line or so. Blackout were basically a dream-team of the best MCs who attended Harmony's open-mic nights, put together by Tony and Charlie, who run the centre. They consist of MCs Cover, Viper, Zak K, Dowie, and Rapid, alongside DJs Jonezy and Siddy B.

After police shut down Harmony's open mic night that we were attending, owing to aspiring rappers chuffing hash in the car park, we escorted Blackout (who had made a kind of special homecoming goodwill appearance for our benefit) to a gig at an under-18s club just out of the centre of town. There they were met by about a thousand sweaty, red-faced pubescents, all of whom were hyperventilating with excitement. As Blackout opened with "Put a Donk On It", the venue erupted into surreal pandemonium. The hordes grabbed at them, screaming every syllable like it was donk scripture. After the show, anxious teens scrambled to get close to them and begged members to sign autographs, with one over-excited 12-year-old, who called himself MC Scott, reporting breathlessly that his favourite rappers are "Eminem

Top row: Scenic Burnley. Middle row: Wigan Pier Clientele. Below: Blackout Crew fans.

and MC Dowie".

All the members of Blackout Crew either live at home with their parents or in council houses. This is what gives them such strong local appeal. The tangibility of having their heroes scuff their heels round the same shopping centres seems to have given many kids a refreshing perspective on the concept of celebrity. "I'd love to be a famous MC when I grow up," said Scott. "At the weekends, mind. I want a proper job too, like selling cars."

The day after watching Blackout Crew get mobbed like the intro sequence to *A Hard Day's Night*, we travelled to nearby Wigan, donk's Mecca. Wigan houses one record shop, Power Records, that exclusively sells one genre: donk. Outside, kids played bootleg donk remixes on their mobile phones with tracks such as the Red Hot Chili Peppers' "Other Side", Katy Perry's "I Kissed a Girl", and Chris Isaak's

"Wicked Game" getting bouncy makeovers. We were able to evade a pair of gummy thugs from Salford who appeared to have just smoked all of Moss Side's yearly crack production and caught up with Power Records co-owner, Pam, a girl who'd moved down from Scotland to be closer to the throbbing heart of donk. She explained how they'd tried selling other kinds of music in the shop, stuff you would think may crossover like hardcore or hard house, but to no avail.

"Och, if it doesn't have a donk on it, Wiganers just don't want to know," she said. Asking for a description of your archetypal donk fan, she explained: "The guys are meatheads. They're all pumped up on steroids, no tops, shaved chests and shaved heads. They wear white trainers and shorts in the winter."

And how about the girls?

"The girls won't be wearing much," she said. "Either fluorescent bikinis and face paint, or just their underwear. Usually they will wear furry boots and have scraped-back gelled hair."

Later that night we witnessed a crowd of nearly 3,000 of these self-professed "donkeys" welcome Blackout Crew onstage at Wigan Pier nightclub, which, it's worth pointing out, is the only real club in Wigan, and which these days only plays donk.

Hedonistic weekend escapist culture in Wigan is nothing new. In the 1960s, Wigan Casino became the iconic home to the massive northern soul dances. But when rave culture arrived at the end of the 80s, things changed. As rave evolved, places with African and Caribbean immigrant communities like London and Bristol took to the rolling breakbeats of jungle. Places such as Wigan embraced techno and the deranged euphoria of happy hardcore, and later donk, as their own. Clinging to the bag of pills for dear life and refusing to give up on the weekender dream of 48 hours of chemical heaven, these white working-class areas allowed apocalyptic scenes like those at Wigan Pier to ferment and the careers of people such as Burnley's MC Grimzie—arguably donk's most respected MC—to flourish.

"I worked out that the best response I got from crowds was when I say the sickest shit I could think of," Grimzie explained to us during our Burnley excursion. MC Grimzie's best-known rap is called "Sexy Nun". It consists of a rhyme chronicling his seduction, rape, and eventual mutilation and murder of a lady of the cloth. He also likes to dip his wick in the political sphere, expressing his views on issues such as the occupation of Iraq and immigration in verses like this one, from "Asylum Seeker": "I am no racist, I'm just sick of this shit/A couple of years illegal, then next they're raping your kids." Who says politics has no place in music, eh?

Standing at Wigan Pier on our last evening of our northwest pilgrimage, it became apparent that listening to donk for seven hours straight was a bit like being sodomised by a Black & Decker drill in every orifice. But at the same time, the night wasn't an entirely demoralising experience. The level of frenzied euphoria and commitment on display eclipsed anything we'd ever seen. From the second the doors opened, shaven-headed, topless, gurning young men ran onto the dancefloor to pump their limbs with intimidating ferocity, totally losing their shit. There was no queue for the bar because people were far too preoccupied with pumping their fists and popping endless amounts of pills. The crowd was a mixture of skimpily dressed, emaciated rave bunnies and some of the most gruesome thugs you'd ever come across—blokes whose faces had been permanently disfigured by a lifetime of being pummelled by fists every weekend, who've probably washed down massive doses of steroids with gallons of Stella for breakfast every morning since they were 11 years old. You could smell the testosterone and adrenaline oozing from their pores. We spoke to one massive bloke from Liverpool who told us that he'd just got out of prison and his main aim of the night was: "Beak (cocaine), bladdered (drunk) and then I'm gonna go and fill someone's bum in."

After a week in the northwest immersed in donk culture, it was impossible to deny that it's the bottom-feeder of the already bottomed-out dance-music food chain. It's parochial, drug-centred, racist, sexist and violent, and that's what makes it so, well, special. For all its flaws, donk perfectly mirrors the generation of kids and the society that created it: totally and hopelessly fucked, in every sense of the word.

112

First, fly to Glasgow and then drive four hours through mountains and wilderness to the Ardnamurchan Estate in the West Highlands. It's the most westerly point of the British Isles.

HOOTS MON!
IT'S HAGGIS TIME!

THE TECHNOLOGY BEHIND SCOTLAND'S NATIONAL DISH
WORDS AND PHOTOS BY ANDY CAPPER

Published April 2009

Meet up with a gamekeeper who will take you on a deer stalk in the wilds of the mountains. Ours was called Niall Rowntree and he ran the estate with the help of his "gilly", Grant.

Take one German-manufactured Blaser rifle. It's a high-end gun favoured by hunters and sportsmen all around the world. Your basic rig costs around £1,200. The rounds are held in the belly of the gun. The reason hunters prefer Blaser rifles is for the strength of the tube and the clean, easy operating system.

Then use some binoculars. Zeiss also makes the lenses for everyone's favourite point-and-shoot camera, the Yashica T4. Look through these to find a herd of deer to stalk and kill. At this point, it's worth telling yourself something like what our guide told us just before we pulled the trigger: "Nothing neutralises mountain grass and destroys natural habitats more than deer. You're doing something positive for biodiversity by shooting this deer. Remember this is just a population-control exercise."

Take two .308 Winchester soft-point cartridges and insert them into the Blaser by pulling the bolt action backward.

Use an Austrian-made Swarovski scope—it's the same firm that makes the crystals your grandma loves. The scope will cost you about £700.

Och aye, Jimmeh! Is there anything more satisfying in life than a wee dram and a haggis after a hard day's kilt-wearing and Sassenach-hating? And is any haggis more dreamy to eat than a venison haggis made from the innards of a fine West Highlands deer that yee shot yerself? The answer is: "Och no, Jimmeh! There cannae be a tastier puddin' anywhere on this fine earth!"

We recently travelled to the West Highlands to film something called *Deer Diary* for VBS.TV and this is what I learned about the technology that goes into the making of Scotland's national dish. Here's a recipe so you can make one at home for yer wee bairns!

Shoot the deer with your gun. It will die from the shock of the impact, rather than any damage to the vital organs. Our guide told us that "it's like being hit by an anvil at 100 miles an hour". Now you're halfway to creating your haggis. To test if your beautiful Bambi is dead, touch her on the eyes while fighting back the urge to cry out, "Oh God! What have I done??!!"

Next, you "bleed" the deer by cutting through the windpipe with a knife. Then pull out the oesophagus and tie it in a knot to prevent any of the stomach contents from leaking into the meat that you will cut up later to make a tasty meal.

Carefully remove the stomach. Don't panic if the intestines are still squirming around or if the stomach cavity is giving off a very earthy, steamy scent. Are you still hungry for that haggis? Good. Let's continue.

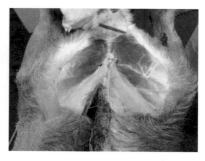

Tie a rope around the deer's neck and drag it two miles down a hillside. Here, Grant demonstrates this. "I hate doing this part of the job," he told us before he set off on his merry way, the deer's bones breaking down each hobble and bobble of the hill, its mouth agape and tongue dragging across the grass.

It's slaughterhouse time! Here you have to put on latex gloves, then cover them with chainmail gloves to prevent your fingers from being cut by pieces of deer bone or your butchery knife.

Ready to get involved? It's worth remembering here what Niall told us: "Everything in life has lines and seams." So use your knife gently but firmly to cut down the animal's middle and it will come apart like magic, revealing two delicious cuts of venison. Weight watchers take note, it's got less fat than chicken.

Uh-oh. Sometimes female deer are pregnant when you shoot them and this can make the butchery process a little traumatic for the person who shot the deer. Glad it wasn't me, guys!

Mmmm, starving yet? What you're looking at here is the main ingredients of your venison haggis. It's the heart, lungs, and liver of the deer, and you need to extract that before you get down to business in the kitchen.

It's fucking heavy, so make sure you chop it up into component parts before cooking it all up. This is the heart.

Now the boring bit. Acquire a sheep's stomach from your gamekeeper. Chop up the liver, lungs, and heart and mix them with suet, onions, oats, salt, pepper and whiskey. Stir it all up in a bowl, put it in the sheep's stomach, sew it up, and cook it in the oven for about an hour. It should end up looking as gorgeous as this.

Hey, presto! One delicious-looking haggis that's great for kids!

Serve with mashed potatoes, mashed turnip, and mashed parsnips and drink with two bottles of wine and a bottle of whiskey while tons of wasted Scottish men with kilts recite poems from Robbie Burns's back catalogue. All together now: "Fair is your honest happy face/Great chieftain of the pudding race/Above them all you take your place/Stomach, tripe, or guts/Well are you worthy of a grace/As long as my arm!"

VBS, OR THE REVOLUTION WILL BE TELEVISED (JUST NOT ON TELEVISION)

VBS is our film and documentary division, which was set up in February 2007 under the guidance of Spike Jonze.

Spike Jonze and Shane Smith shooting in Yemen, 2010.

VICE BROADCASTING SYSTEMS

HOW WE LEARNED TO START MAKING MOVIES | BY ANDY CAPPER

VBS stands for Vice Broadcasting Systems, which is the big important-sounding name for Vice's internet TV and film division.

We started in February 2007 on the advice of the director Spike Jonze, who went onto become VBS's creative director, while at the same time keeping himself busy with lesser-known things like being the creator of *Jackass* and making films such as *Where The Wild Things Are*. The first thing we made was the *Vice Guide to Travel* DVD, which includes short films of Vice CEO Shane Smith hunting radioactive wild boar and Vice co-founder Suroosh Alvi visiting the gun markets of Pakistan. The more we got the hang of making films, the more we loved it and, predictably, became addicted to going to make films in as many exciting places as possible. We travelled all over the world, met tons of incredible people, and filmed it all. Over the next few pages you'll read about some of it.

To begin this section, here is a conversation between myself and my boss Shane, who started the whole thing. We did this a few days before we sent the book off to be printed. He'd just stepped off a plane from Libya where he'd been placed under house arrest for a week and the only thing they'd let him eat or drink was milk and dates. Dictatorships are terrible for the bowels.

Andy Capper: Hello Shane. I understand you may feel a bit weird after the week you've just had, but I would like to ask you about the history of VBS for this book we're doing.
Shane Smith: Okay, well it all started when Spike Jonze called us up one day and said, "Hey! Do you guys film your articles?" He said it like it was a *fait accompli*, because he's a film guy and films everything, but we were magazine guys who didn't film anything. And so we did what we always do and we lied and said, "Yes." And then we had to work out how to do it.

And how did that go?
Well, at first we didn't know how to shoot films but we decided to try anyway. We knew that some of our magazine stories could look good in films but when you're a magazine guy you're used to doing the story after it's happened and not while it's happening. And even when you're shooting the story while it's happening, sometimes things don't happen visually, so that was a problem. Another problem was that we didn't know how to edit the films. In fact, Eddy Moretti handed in his resignation to me after me and [Vice Media Group EU CEO] Andrew Creighton watched the first lot of films he'd put together for the *Vice Guide to Travel* DVD. We were on the train and watched it and Andrew was like, "This stuff isn't very good." Meanwhile, Eddy's back at the office working with editors who were saying stuff like,

"Is this gonna lead to a full-time gig 'cos I gotta let Starbucks know."

I think I remember that guy.
And so the first thing we delivered was a C-minus, and we knew it wasn't great but we were astounded by the response it received. We showed it at a film festival in Tribeca and it got a standing ovation. I knew then that we could keep learning and making stuff that we weren't 100 percent happy with yet but still have an audience. And so we got some better editors and Eddy didn't resign and now he's creative director of the entire company.

Was there a grand design behind the idea?
No, never. Truth be told, we were thinking we'd only make things for DVD and TV and then we met a guy called Jeff Yapp from MTV, who's a visionary genius, and he said that TV on the internet is the future and so we started putting the films we made onto VBS. TV and now we're always thinking of ways of where to take it next. Regarding "grand designs", I think anybody who says, "Okay team, we're going to do it like this and it's going to be A, B, C and D, etc, etc"—anybody who does that is trying to be a fortune teller and is working with nothing but absolute horseshit."

Some of the people behind VBS will now talk you through the highlights of the films we've made so far.

Left: Suroosh Alvi fires a $50 AK into the hills of Pakistan. Eddy Moretti (centre) and Suroosh Alvi (right) arrive in Baghdad, 2006.

THE GUN MARKETS OF PAKISTAN

This was one of the first pieces we shot and which made it on to the *Vice Guide To Travel* DVD, and still it's one of our most popular pieces. This has Suroosh and Eddy travelling to nearby where Bin Laden is meant to be hiding out and firing AK-47s into the air, which they bought down the road.

Suroosh Alvi, Vice co-founder: The Pakistan shoot was so much fun. It was one of the first things we did and little did we know that we were making a piece that would go on to get watched millions of times for years afterwards, as well as winning prizes. I guess geopolitics worked in our favour with this one. Incidentally, the market where we shot our footage has become the homebase for the Tehrik-i-Taliban, which is the main Taliban militant umbrella group in Pakistan.

HEAVY METAL IN BAGHDAD

Following a *Vice* magazine article that uncovered a heavy metal band from Baghdad called Acrassicauda, we decided to fly into Iraq during the heaviest part of the conflict to meet the guys in the band. This would develop into a VBS series, then an award-winning documentary, a book, countless paragraphs like this one written about it and, coming soon, an album.

Suroosh Alvi: This story defined the early days of VBS. We literally snuck into Iraq to get this story and it went on to become a feature-length doc, a book, and, thanks to a massive humanitarian effort on the part of *Vice* and the UNHCR, we got the subjects of the film resettled to America, then signed them to our record label. It was very important for us.

Eddy Moretti, VBS creative director: This was the first piece we ever ran on VBS. It was us going to the heart of the shit storm. It was 2006, which was not good. It was the opposite of good. But Iraq was the biggest story in the world and every journalist was covering it, so it was impossible not to have an opinion on it. It was the most violent time to go. At first the whole thing was just meant to be a really great 15-minute piece and then [VBS producer/editor] Bernardo Layola looked at the footage and told us we could make it bigger. In October of that year, some of the guys in the band got out of Iraq and became refugees in Damascus. And that's when we thought: "Well, there's our third act. Let's go."

We made Vice Kills Jamaica *shirts for our visit there but ironically it was Jamaica that almost killed us. Photo by Rob Semmer*

Santiago Stelley and Bernardo Loyola make the pages of Alarma! *magazine.*

VICE KILLS JAMAICA

The Jamaican trip saw 11 staff members fly off to Kingston after somebody told us we could get intimate access to (the then relatively un-famous) Christopher "Dudus" Coke and his Shower Posse. What transpired was less than ideal but still noteworthy.

Rob Semmer, VBS producer: We got to Jamaica, 11 of us, and the girl who said she could fix it for us to meet Dudus and the Shower Posse asked for five times more money than was agreed upon or we were fucked, no story. So we were fucked, with no story. We hustled something up eventually and ended up finding a guy who took us to a big event where all the Shower Posse were hanging out at, but that got really, really heavy and we had to leave. The next day the girl in London called us in Jamaica and said, "What the fuck were you doing at that thing last night?" There were 2,000 people there and it was pitch black, so how she knew we were there I do not know. We got back to New York and had a phone call at the office from a member of the Shower Posse telling us we couldn't use the footage of the event.

That's why there's no episode two in the film.

ALARMA!

Shot in the sketchiest parts of Mexico City at night, this doc follows the staff of Mexican true crime magazine/newspaper *Alarma!* as they chase ambulances from drug murder scene to drug murder scene.

Bernardo Loyola, VBS producer/editor: We screened the movie at the Mexico City Film Festival in February 2009. We invited the editor of *Alarma!* and the photographers and they were pretty excited. They took the photos at the premiere, then we had a party where the Mystery Jets DJed and the photographer's wife sold sandwiches. So random. It was a sketchy shoot because I went to places in Mexico City I would never go and I had never seen a murdered body before. But the driving was the scariest part because we were driving like crazy, chasing ambulances, not stopping at ANY traffic lights, in a shitty VW Beetle with no seat belts while the guy was on two mobile phones and two walkie-talkies!

Eddy Moretti in front of the Alberta oil refinery.
Photo by Meredith Danluck

The captain of the boat that took us out to garbage
island shot this, printed it out and signed it for
Thomas Morton, who said: "In six years of working
for Vice, *I have had no greater plaudit."*

TOXIC: ALBERTA

The Toxic series was developed by Eddy Moretti and the idea behind it was to make an environmental show that would have a camera crew drive right into the most polluted areas on earth and do a report while trying not to choke to death on garbage and thick, foul, black air. The Alberta episodes reported on the huge hole in the middle of Canada that pukes out oil into the air so voraciously that it creates its own artificial atmosphere, complete with fake snow made out of oil particles. We went to one of the oil plants there and met the people who lived in it and around it and who ate the three-eyed fish that swam in the rivers.

Eddy Moretti: It was an ambition of mine to do some environmental stories because I guess I'm what you call an irrational eco-nut. It should be the easiest, simplest thing for us to rally around but nobody really does. It's not just about fossil fuels or global warming. It's much bigger than that and it's a more immediate, general thing than that. Look around you, there's garbage everywhere. The world is filthy. I made *Toxic: Alberta* with a girl called Meredith who I knew from the old days of *Vice* and who had the contacts to make the *Toxic: West Virginia* piece and then went on to sail the oceans to make *Garbage Island*, which was about how in the middle of the Pacific ocean there is a huge island made completely out of things that humans have thrown away.

TOXIC: GARBAGE ISLAND

Thomas Morton, VBS presenter: Shooting *Garbage Island* was like being on a family car trip that lasts three weeks. And there are no stops for hotels or pinball, and you have severe carsickness the whole time, and the sights you see along the way are mostly things that other humans have thrown out and which greatly diminish your hope for the continuance of the species. We were dead centre in the Pacific Ocean. The story was depressing as hell because there's basically no solution to the problem, and the duration and tight quarters of the trip made us all ready to kill each other by about hour two. We went swimming and the second you put your head under with goggles on, you could see these tiny flecks of confetti. And when Jake, the camera guy, came up from our swim he was covered in so many tiny chunks of plastic it looked like he had body glitter on. The whole trip changed me. I wouldn't have described myself as a "sceptic" or anything when it comes to environmental stuff, but I have long been of the mind that every generation of people thinks they live at the most crucial point of history and is generally being a little dramatic about its own importance. Seeing this mess at the farthest remove from direct human contact on Earth made me realise we've actually hit a point with technology and development where we actually can and may be fucking both the planet and the DNA of our species.

Ivar Berglin tries on Gaahl's spikes as they cook pasta together during the shoot for True Norwegian Black Metal. *Photo by Peter Beste*

Jared Swilley from the Black Lips visits holy ground on the Palestine vs Israel tour. Photos by Rob Semmer

TRUE NORWEGIAN BLACK METAL

This is based around a ten-day trip to the wilds of Norway to stay at the solitary home of Gorgoroth singer Gaahl. The photographer Peter Beste knew Gaahl from his work in the black metal scene, which was documented in the Vice publication *True Norwegian Black Metal*. Peter arranged for us to go and visit "the most feared man in Norway" not long after he'd been released from prison for torturing a man for six hours while collecting his blood in a cup, to drink (Gaahl, not Peter).

Rob Semmer: What I remember most about this trip was the fact that the only form of entertainment Gaahl had in his house was music by either Judas Priest or David Bowie. He also had a TV and DVD player he had to pull out of a closet, but the only DVD he had was *Blackadder*. We ended up watching a whole season of *Blackadder* with Gaahl while drinking fine wines.

PALESTINE VS ISRAEL

An ill-advised holiday to one of the angriest, most divided places in the world had a surreal twist as we also had the Atlanta garage rock band Black Lips in tow with us. In between playing shows with them in Palestine, Suroosh and Rob got into a lot of trouble with some Israeli police.

Suroosh Alvi: I didn't enjoy Israel. The place is weird and depressing. My producer Rob got shot in the stomach with a rubber bullet by an Israeli soldier. We spent our days in Palestine and evenings in Israel partying with the Black Lips, who were on tour there. The dichotomy of the days and experience did my head in and I was left with the feeling that things are only ever going to get worse here and there's no end in sight, ever.

Rob Semmer: People were so freaked out by Suroosh in Israel. They were waiting for him to get off the plane and they questioned him for like three hours. Then we were strip-searched when we went home. And then we were at a demonstration and I got shot for real. There was tear gas and police, but it's not like the police suddenly say, "Time out! We are now switching to rubber bullets." All I saw was tear gas and then felt the bullet. And that thing came out of an M16. All I could think was, "I've just been shot, and I'm in the West Bank with Suroosh and all we have is a rental car and we are totally fucked." Eventually it was OK, but I had a softball-size black bruise on my stomach by the time I left. Just after I'd been shot, the Israeli police kept shooting and I saw a 12-year-old get hit like eight times at once. Knocked him off his feet and cold. In the video you see people carrying him away.

John Cardiel. Photo by Patrick O'Dell

Keex, star of the London episode of
Shot by Kern Europe.

EPICLY LATER'D: JOHN CARDIEL

Veteran skater/photographer Pat O'Dell came up with the format for this regular skate show and it quickly turned out to be one of the most popular things on VBS. What made *Epicly Later'd* different from a lot of mainstream skate documentaries was that the series didn't profile skateboarding's richest sportsmen but rather the skaters' favourite skaters. And that's probably why the one about John Cardiel was watched by so many people.

Eddy Moretti: The whole thing was O'Dell's idea. It was just going to be another special edition of *Epicly* and I had no idea who the fuck John Cardiel was. I liked the show a lot but it's not my world so I didn't have a relationship with it. Making the Cardiel film changed everything. It was a totally eye-opening and amazing story. I've never really understood the whole culture of skateboarding, but the story of this guy's life I found it to encapsulate everything that is the culture of skateboarding and how it relates to aesthetics, youth, athletics, and a whole complex world view, which I thought was previously very simple. This film made me respect it a lot more.

SHOT BY KERN

The idea behind this show came from *Vice*'s main NY editor, Jesse Pearson, who you read about at the start of this book and without whom a lot of the stories you're reading in here would never have come to pass. *Shot by Kern* follows the legendary New York art/sex photographer Richard Kern around the world as he photographs young women as they disrobe in front of him. Jesse then interviews the girls about the intimacies of their lives. For reasons we can't comprehend, it's one of the most popular shows we have.

Jesse Pearson, series producer, *Vice* editor: I'd already been shooting with Kern for the magazine for a few years, and we'd become friends. Not every issue's theme would allow me to run his usual sort of photo, so we developed the show together as a way for me to be able to go on his shoots. Pretty simple. I love all of the girls we've done. It's hard to pick a favourite.

Left: Joshua Milton Blahyi, aka ex-General Butt Naked, a former cannibal who used to eat a baby's heart every day, contemplates lunch. Photo by Andy Capper. Right: Joshua Milton Blahyi, Andy Capper and Shane Smith get ready to go to church in Liberia. Photo by Myles Estey

THE VICE GUIDE TO NORTH KOREA

In which we travel to North Korea under false pretences and secretly film the whole thing despite the fact that if we were caught doing so we would be in jail for the rest of our lives while having nasty things poked into us every so often.

Shane Smith: North Korea—I hated it but it made me who I am today because when people reference me they reference that documentary. It was a crazy trip. We snuck in there pretending to not be who we actually are and got the whole official guided tour while armed guards stood by us at all times. My favourite part would have to be at the karaoke bar where I sang Sex Pistols. That was what really made the film. I was singing "God Save the Queen" in a strict authoritarian dictatorship while everybody looked on horrified but unable to bring themselves to do anything about it. It was western subculture colliding head-on with the North Korean secret police at a karaoke bar and, to this day, whenever I hear that song, I can feel disapproving eyes glaring at me, coupled with a feeling of "Am I going to be in jail soon?". Still, it gives me the giggly shudders.

THE VICE GUIDE TO LIBERIA

When ex-Liberian president Charles Taylor went on trial for war crimes, we decided to go to Liberia to find out what some other, lesser-known warlords were up to now that the UN was keeping peace there. We arranged meetings with General Rambo, General Bin Laden, and the star of our film, General Butt Naked, an ex-cannibal, nudist warlord who claimed responsibility for 20,000 deaths. It was as scary as it was inspirational.

Shane Smith: My three favourite VBS films are *...North Korea* because of what I just said, *Heavy Metal In Baghdad* because it put us on the map, and *...Liberia*. It was a happy accident that General Butt Naked turned out to be such a charming guy, and despite the chaos we encountered it all fell together.

Andy Capper, VBS producer: My favourite moment in Liberia was walking through the swamp with Joshua over some hills and towards his compound, where he rehabilitates ex-child soldiers. Joshua waved at them and they started singing West African gospel music. I get chills remembering it.

Shane Smith meets Mohammad Ali Zam, Imam and supporter of progressive Iranian film-making.

Hamilton Morris is stung by poisonous frog drugs. Photo by Santiago Stelley

THE VICE GUIDE TO IRANIAN CINEMA

Conceived by Shane and Eddy, the Vice Guide to Film has taken us all over the world. The series covered amazing, unseen cinema, a lot of which turned out to be funded by gangsters and dictators. The Iran leg of the series turned out to be one of the most bizarre episodes in the history of VBS.

Shane Smith: Places like Iran are totally surreal. It's impossible to get around without being shepherded by handlers. They won't let you talk to people or go out in public and usually they treat you like shit and you're afraid for your life. There was a Canadian journalist that was raped and brutally beaten to death in 2003, and one of our British correspondents, Ben Anderson, was kidnapped and tortured when he went there.

It was a scary place to be but we managed to get invited to a film festival in Iran and they gave permission to film. Along the way we met the doyens. We went to their version of the Academy Awards and the organisers asked me to impersonate the Canadian director Guy Maddin because he couldn't make it. So I agreed and I got on stage, I did a speech and ending up getting a hug from the mayor of Tehran.

HAMILTON'S PHARMACOPEIA: THE SAPO DIARIES

Conceived by our drugs correspondent Hamilton Morris and VBS head of content Santiago Stelley, this show follows Hamilton travelling around the globe in search of different ways to get as high as he can on as many different strange things as he can lay his hands on.

Hamilton Morris, VBS correspondent: *The Sapo Diaries* was interesting but not fun to film. I was criticised by a lot of people for having whined too much—but the pain of being out there was unimaginable and there was almost nothing to do but complain.

I was being stung and having my blood sucked by thousands of different insects at all times. It was fun as well, but long books could be written about the heights of itchiness I experienced. Your mind ceases to think about anything past the transcendent, agonising, pulsating itchiness. When it came to being poisoned by the frog, well that was an interesting, novel experience, but the high was more discombobulating than pleasurable. When I got back from the Amazon I was horrified to find that you could order the venom quite easily online.

Leo Leigh shoots the alleyway scene in Swansea Love Story. *Photo by Andy Capper*

B Company waits for dusk, on the shoot for Afghanistan in the UK. *Photo by Stuart Griffiths*

SWANSEA LOVE STORY

Swansea Love Story is part of the Rule Britannia series created by Andy Capper, which is based on a loose theme of "The Decline of British Civilisation". This documentary follows the lives of a gang of young people caught up in a heroin epidemic and was the first feature-length film that the UK office had ever made. It was co-directed by Andy Capper and Leo Leigh, whose dad is the British film director Mike Leigh. The *Guardian* called it the "must-see British film of the year".

Andy Capper: At times, making this doc felt sketchier than being in Liberia. I'd never been mugged with an axe in a crack den before and I'm hoping it's something I never have to do again. Despite that, the majority of the people we followed around in this film were lovely and I still keep in touch with a couple of them. When people ask me if we exaggerated the problem in Swansea I always tell them to look at the caption of the scene at the beginning of the film when Amy and Cornelius are shooting up in an alleyway off the high street while people walk by on their way to work, barely batting an eyelid: it's 9:15 AM.

Leo Leigh: It was nuts that they were so relaxed about shooting up in such a public space, and looking back now it's crazy that people were just walking past as if it was no big deal. At the time I was concentrating on shooting the moment in the right way,

so I wasn't really thinking about it. Despite all her many problems, Amy is a kind girl who only really wanted a good future for her and Cornelius.

AFGHANISTAN IN THE UK

Here we were living alongside B Company of the 2nd Parachute Regiment at a training facility in Thetford. The army has built a huge fake-Afghanistan village in the countryside and so we went there with two cameras and tried to keep up with them.

Andy Capper: Before we went I had no idea that I would be expected to take part in four 36-hour back-to-back training missions, being woken at 3 AM by mortars, sleeping in freezing cold swamps and marching for up to 30 miles a day. After day two of no sleep, I gave into the routine of it all and almost didn't want to go back to my sissy job, save for the fact I hadn't changed my clothes for a week.

Jason Mojica, co-producer: Show up anywhere with a camera and the most charismatic people in the group will manage to insert themselves into your story. With the Paras, though, the people I wanted to talk to most were the people who didn't want to talk to us—at least not on camera: young soldiers who were nervous about deploying to Afghanistan for the first time and others who couldn't wait to go back. It's strange to meet someone for the first time and wonder if they're going to be alive next year.

(DON'T) TRY THIS AT HOME

Back in 2005 we put out the Immersionism Issue of the magazine. It featured stories on living with refugees, terrorists, junkies, child prostitutes and the mafia, among others. After that we never really looked back and rather than interviewing people about things, or running stories about things, we decided to try the things out for ourselves—from reviewing whatever the latest awful legal drug out there is by doing it for three days straight, to actually massaging our own prostates, all so you guys out there didn't have to. Every now and then this approach to journalism goes horribly wrong, like the time staff writer Thomas Morton was nearly flamethrowered out of a Bogotá sewer. But on the whole, it makes a story seem a whole heap more real than if it was being reported by a guy with a bad tie behind a desk made out of cardboard 5,000 miles away from where the story is actually happening.

BLACKS VS WHITES

WHO CAN DRINK MORE? | WORDS AND PHOTOS BY VITO FUN

Published May 2005

How come black people never get totally shit-faced? White people are always getting so wasted they can barely stand but, outside of bums, you almost never see black dudes slurring their words. Is it because they drink really expensive shit like Courvoisier and Hennessy and to get slur-drunk on that is about £300? Or does it have deeper cultural meanings? Do blacks feel vulnerable in this white world and think they can't afford to let themselves be too self-indulgent? Maybe it's as simple as blacks in America are of a particularly fit stock and can break down toxins better than whites. What is it?

"I don't fucking know," says Probe, an MC from the Brooklyn-based hip-hop group Nuclear Family. "I have noticed that though. I know it's not the Courvoisier thing because I drink the same shit white people do. Beer and shots and all that." Instead of sitting around like a bunch of faggot academics, we decided to settle this like men. We got a black guy and a white guy and made them drink till they puked. We decided to use Probe as the black guy because he drinks the same drinks whites do and his friends say they are a pube away from "having an intervention on him". We chose screenwriter Dave TheBest (yes, that's what he calls himself) as the white guy because he is about the same age and weight as Probe and he used to be in a frat. Dave is 27 years old, 5'11", and weighs in at 164 pounds. Probe is 26 years old, 6'2", and weighs 169 pounds.

Here are the highlights:

11:15 We arrive at Bar Reis in Brooklyn. Everyone is amped. The white people are secretly rooting for the white guy and the black guy is really happy to get free booze all night. We order some quesadillas from upstairs because you're supposed to have food in your stomach. The owner has laid out some shot ideas.

11:23 First shot—Seagram's gin

11:25 First sip of beer

11:31 Spanish lady finds out what we are doing and becomes indignant. She wants to know why this competition is only for blacks and whites. We can't believe she's serious. She is. She insists we have a new competition with her husband next Friday. We tell her to fuck off.

11:42 Dave suggests they shoot the next shot, Probe wants to finish his last bite of food. The racial and ethnic tension is palpable.

11:50 Water is introduced to the experiment. The bartender genuinely cares about these guys and doesn't want anyone to die.

11:55 Sixth shot—Bacardi Superior rum

12:14 Eighth shot—Cosmopolitan

12:16 Bartender blends Malibu rum smoothie

12:23 Progress check. I ask them to rate their drunkenness on a scale of 1 to 10. 1 represents schoolgirl tipsy and 10 represents blackout drunk. Both parties give themselves a 3.

12:24 Tenth shot—Jagermeister

12:30 Bar patrons are getting curious. Coming over. This feels like when someone is winning at craps.

12:53 "This is an honour" is overheard.

12:54 Fourteenth shot—Sex on the Beach. A first for each contender.

12:55 Progress check. Dave claims to be an 8 out of 10. Probe says he is only a 7.

1:07 Sixteenth shot—Black Magic. Dave goes to pee, Probe decides to do a shot without him in order to get the advantage. We try to tell him that's not an effective way to cheat. Dave comes back and we "snitch" on Probe and make Dave do a shot.

1:26 Twentieth shot—French Martini

1:33 Racial harmony is achieved. Due to the name of the competition the subject of race keeps coming up. "Everybody is equal in their eyes" is overheard. No idea who "their" is. Could be the patrons.

1:37 Pseudo-sobriety test is set up. They take turns walking a strip of toilet paper on the floor. They both do really badly. Cops are right to do that test.

1:40 Twenty-second shot—Barracuda

1:49 I ask the bartender for two racial shots. He pours a shot of red wine and a shot of Hennessy.

1:50 Twenty-third shot—Hennessy. Dave groans, "That was bad news." He looks like shit.

1:53 Dave suggests a draw because he is a pussy.

2:19 Twenty-eighth shot—Crème de menthe

2:20 Pot break

2:32 Bartender shuts down bar. "This is unholy," he says.

2:37 Outside bar, Probe laughs at Dave's sandals.

2:37–3:02 Walking half a mile to the next bar.

3:02 New bar, Patio Lounge

3:02 Twenty-ninth shot—Soju (Korean liquor). There is a dog at this bar and they both are fascinated by it.

3:09 PBR can downed.

3:19 Dave wants to quit.

3:23 Thirty-first shot—Soju

3:23–3:30 Dave not doing too well, he seems to have ants in his pants. Probe is doing surprisingly well. He's confident and rapping a lot.

3:30 Bartender offers both another beer, Probe drinks it, but Dave can't get it down. The crowd starts going, "Oooooh" in an anticipatory "Here we go, boys!" kind of way. Like a crescendo. The yelling seems to turn Dave's stomach even more.

3:31 Dave pushes through the crowd and pukes the entire white race onto the street. He has let down 80 percent of the American population. Dave blew it after 31 shots and Probe had at least 40.

Probe stays at the bar, rapping to the bartender and doing pretty OK. She takes him home but he barfs all over her house and starts screaming gibberish like a fucking maniac. She tries to give him water but he thinks it's booze and begs her to leave him alone. "I don't want that," he says and falls asleep.

Blacks can drink more than whites.

ASS INVADERS

THE VICE GUIDE TO MILKING YOUR PROSTATE | BY JAMES KNIGHT
PHOTOS BY BEN RAYNER

Published August 2008

Hey, guess what? If you are a British man you are more likely to have cancer in your prostate than any other part of you. It's also more likely to kill you than any other form of cancer. Oh, and there is also the extra bonus of a 35 percent higher chance of your prostate going sour than your girlfriend getting breast cancer. Bummer.

But in fact, if you are literally a bummer, you are more likely than a straight guy to avoid dying from prostate cancer. Want to know why? Then listen up...

Over the last five years, prostate milking has exploded in popularity within the queer and BDSM scenes. Draining the little fella involves getting something stimulating stuck up your bum and jiggling the walnut-sized prostate sack until it gets so excited it makes you involuntarily secrete a dollop of seminal fluid. PS: Why can't I stop laughing every time I reread that last sentence?

As fun as shooting your wad without even fiddling with your dick might sound, getting over the whole fingering your asshole bit has kept milking mainly confined to ye gayes—espccially the fisting fetishists among them. But with increasing medical evidence showing that relieving the prostate of fluid buildups (coupled with regular checkups) can help prevent the big C word, maybe we all need to start shoving things up our asses and frantically rubbing.

I, for one, would rather not have ass cancer. So I learned how to milk my prostate, and I did so while my friend Ben took photos.

It's important to make sure that your passage is as empty as possible, so be sure to take a nice big dump before you get to milking. Amyl poppers, in addition to making you feel like a 14-year-old girl, relax your sphincter muscles. Why do you think they sell them in every store on Old Compton Street? (That's where all the bummers hang out.)

Fingernails can tear your rectal wall, so wear surgical gloves throughout the process. This also helps to make you feel a bit like Patrick Bateman in *American Psycho*—particularly if you are doing the whole thing in your brand-new apartment while your flatmates are at work. Sorry, Jess and Lynsey.

If the poppers don't give you the necessary Dutch courage then maybe resort to something a little stronger. Anything powdery and above class C should help. That bag you left in your top drawer for emergencies? Perfect.

Procrastinating is only natural. You are about to stick a massive piece of plastic up your arse. Go on. Have a cigarette.

This is the point where you have to keep telling yourself "it'sallgoingtobefine" really fast over and over in your head.

Once you've lubed up, it's time to slip it in. Initially it will feel a little like a plastic slug is trying to burrow into your anus. After a while though, your sphincter muscles relax and with a little prayer and a lot of lube things really get moving...

No matter how many objects you've slid up there before, this bit is going to feel weird. Remember that the prostate is hidden pretty far up your tunnel. Try and relax, fight the urge to poop, and search for that magic walnut!

Maybe, to relax, try thinking of something completely different. Like what your mum would say if she could see you now writhing around on some cardboard boxes trying to ward off cancer by buggering yourself with a big red dildo while your buddy takes photos.

Once you get past the initial fear, it actually starts to feel kind of OK. Does that mean I'm gay? Because after 15 minutes I was almost into it. Pain and pleasure are pretty much partners in crime so don't go doing anything too fast or too sudden. It can get pretty excruciating real quick. Remember that a lot of people out there do this for fun but an equal number of people end up causing themselves internal damage.

It felt like I was a split second away from crapping all over the floor. And despite going pretty deep I am also not entirely sure whether I was hitting the prostate—but I was definitely feeling weirdly horny.

Then I went to the toilet and this popped out. Pretty milky. While it was hardly the biggest barrel of laughs I've had, the whole experience was not totally awful. Regular practitioners claim that a prostate orgasm is 400 percent more intense than a regular orgasm and can last for up to five minutes. Beat that, Sting.

Once you are all done, take a shower. You have just been sticking stuff in your ass, so it's not like you can go straight to the bar and avoid eye contact with everyone you have ever known while stinking of shit and cum, is it?

I DESTROYED BANKSY'S RAT

BY LILY EVANS | ILLUSTRATION BY PADDY JONES

Published November 2009

A long time ago I lived in an old London warehouse with a guy called Steve, who was a questionable character and a cocktail of mental illnesses. Steve and I were both penniless; I worked full-time for a respectable fashion label but got awful pay for incredible PR, sales and marketing skills, whereas Steve was a bum and deserved to be broke. On the outside of our building, near our front door, was some graffiti: a Banksy rat. The most famous of Banksy's work, the one in all the coffee table books, the one that drew in hipster tourists every day to photograph it. I liked the rat. It made me smile a little each morning as I left the house.

One night Steve's drug dealer came over. He was also some kind of art collector. While snorting blow or some kind of flour mixed with bleach or whatever it is that dirty coke dealers give you now, he started telling Steve and I about how much the small graffiti rat on the side of our building was worth. Then he told us that if we get it off the wall all in one piece he can sell it for us for "about £50,000". And now I'm thinking, fuck, I could live off that money for a long time. I could be one of those people who gets their hand blown off when the printer in the office explodes and gets a lump sum of compensation money, except I don't even have to have a fucked-up hand: I just have to sell out and be a bad person. At the time that sounded just fine.

The dealer left and Steve and I discussed our moral dilemma. "Well, I mean, I'm sure Banksy himself would be fine with it because it would be like we were preserving it in a way, selling it to an art dealer and all." I looked at him and we both knew I was lying.

We decided that we needed a truly expert builder to survey the situation and see if it would be feasible to even attempt to remove the rat all in one perfect piece. I left Steve to find this builder on the account that I was too busy and important, seeing as I was the one with the job. I came home that evening and there was a Polish guy in our apartment. He had one of those creepy faces that did not belie his age: he could have been 20 or 50, for all I knew. He looked like he was drunk and bad-smelling but I didn't go close enough to find out because I have a strong sense of smell and it probably would have upset me.

As the guy walked past me and down the stairs, the only tool I could see was a red plastic bucket, and that worried me a little. I asked Steve what was going on and he told me that the guy had successfully been given detailed instructions of what he was to do. "So he speaks English?" I asked. Come on, I had to check. Steve assured me that yes he did in a annoyedly self-satisfied voice. He was on the computer trying to look all work-like, proud that he had, in his eyes, found "The Builder" for the job. He said he was researching Banksy but I knew he was on MySpace.

I sat down to eat and heard something that made me run outside. It was horrifying. Clearly not the sound of a piece of art being carefully removed from a wall. I went outside and the alcoholic builder was there chipping the rat off the wall in tiny bits into the red bucket. All that was left was his rat head. The rest of the famous landmark was in splinters of stone and paint in the bucket. I shouted at him to stop and he made some noises that confirmed to me that he couldn't speak English. I wanted to cry but I didn't, I just told him to stick some paper over the rest of the rat's head and fuck off. I took the red bucket inside, cradling it as if the shards of graffiti rat were ashes of the deceased. And, in a way, they were.

I couldn't breathe. I thought I was about to have an epileptic fit (I really do have epilepsy). I can't re-member what happened next but after a while Steve came upstairs with the rat's head all in one piece, which made me mad as hell because it proved that it should have been such a simple process to remove the graffiti in one piece.

We didn't say anything to each other. I sat the red bucket of guilt and grief in the corner of the sitting room, took lots of Valium, and went to sleep.

The next day I go to work and found a crazy amount of hate mail in my inbox from people that had witnessed the catastrophe. Stuff like:

"I live opposite you and saw your housemate pour-ing the remains of the Banksy rat from your wall into a bucket last night. What the fuck is wrong with you you dumb bitch, that was an urban landmark." Apparently all of my details were online due to my being the main contact for the fashion label I work for.

I replied to the first couple, trying to explain that it was simply an accident, but then as more come flooding in, I give up. Damn the Fashion Council with their helpful list of contacts. That night I came home to discover Steve had plastered up and painted over the hole in the wall, which made some of my bad feelings disappear.

Days passed and the red bucket was still in the corner, haunting us like the body we murdered but didn't bury. I'm very good at ignoring it because I have a true talent for repressing bad memories and experiences. More days pass. Steve eventually got a big tray and a bag of sand and a plan to slowly try to piece the rat back together, as if he were a special archeologist mapping together a dinosaur's bone from fossil fragments and I were his assistant. But we weren't: we were just a failed bum and failed fashionista who had done a bad thing.

I spent the whole weekend sitting at the sandbox trying and trying to find just two pieces that would match. But every time I put my hand in the stupid red bucket, the pieces seemed to become smaller and flakier. I knew that soon it would just be a pile of dust, my hopes and dreams of living my sweet life of luxury over.

GAYS OR GIRLS?

SLOBBING THE KNOB FOR SCIENCE | BY ANDY CAPPER
PHOTOS BY JAMES STAFFORD

Published February 2005

Men have simple sexual needs. They want to cum. That's about it. They might sometimes cum in ways that they think are inventive, like on your face or your tits, but it all comes down to the same end: a squirt of some white ropey stuff followed by a brief Xanax-y stupor. After about 20,000 orgasms, most men start to wonder, "Is that all there is to this cumming thing?" They get bored with orgasms.

Men in Britain are suffering uninspired blowjobs from girlfriends on a daily basis. Is it any wonder a growing number of guys are thinking that maybe the best way to wrestle themselves out of their carnal torpor would be to try a blowjob from a bona fide homosexual? After all, every gay man they've ever met has told them a queer blowjob is so much more exciting and enjoyable than a boring woman blowjob. "Nobody knows how to make a penis happy like a person who owns a penis of their own!" (That's what gay guys say to get straight penises in their mouths.)

But remember this: most "bi-curious" men aren't thinking about how delicious it might feel to have another man's dick buried in their ass. They're just thinking about how the inside of a dude's mouth is technically the same as a woman's, especially if you're drunk. Especially especially if you're drunk, ugly, and lonely. Bisexuality, quite simply, doubles your chances. It's the refuge of the pathetically horny.

New statistics from Italy say that, weekly, one gay man sucks more dicks than 12.7 women. Can you say, "Man alive!"? Who's receiving all these BJs from gay men? Not just other gay men—there aren't enough of those around for 13 (I rounded up) times more head sessions than girls perform a week.

Especially in Italy—those sluts suck dick as casually as our women choke down Apple Martinis. There is only one answer: straight guys are getting their joints coughed by benders with reckless abandon.

The only question left to ask is, "Who's better at it?" Do we have to go gay to get the best head? To find out, we got a gay man and a straight man to get blowjobs from a gay man and a straight woman. We blindfolded both of our suckees and built a glory hole. Then we sat back and basked in the heady milieu of the most erotic and revealing experiment ever conducted in the name of sensual truth.

THE RULES

The safeguards were made to prevent giving the suckees a clue to the sucker's gender.

Our female sucker was given orders not to make any erotic moaning noises and to keep her expen-

SUCKEE ONE
Rick is a 24-year-old Londoner with an eight-and-a-half-inch cock. He works as a gay male escort.

"The greatest blowjob I ever had was from a client a few weeks ago," he told us nervously.

"It lasted for about 15 minutes, and it was mind blowing. I've not taken part in anything involving a so-called 'glory hole' before, but I'm looking forward to it immensely."

SUCKEE TWO
Sam is a 20-year-old model from London. He's straight. This will be the first time ever that another man will touch Sam's thing.

SUCKER ONE
Avalon is a 26-year-old who's worked in the adult film industry since she moved to London from Malaysia in her teens.

She prepared to give head by sucking on a menthol lozenge, which she always brings to blowjob shoots because they numb the throat and the menthol tickles the recipient's glans, thus enhancing his pleasure. (Oooh-kaye.)

SUCKER TWO
Daniel is a poet from France who was extremely confident that he'd win the challenge. He even invoked the old "men know what other men want" chestnut. We pointed out that with that reasoning, there would be no war, politics, or conflict, and no babies born ever again, but Daniel maintained his sangfroid.

sively painted and lengthy fingernails away from the shafts. Ewww.

Our male sucker had his face freshly shaved and was not allowed to whimper things like, "Ooh, your cock is divine" in his manly French baritone. Again: ewww.

ROUND ONE

First up was Rick in his stained, grey shell-suit trousers. As soon as he popped through the hole, Daniel moved in for the kill, lapping away excitedly at Rick's trunk as if the reputation of every gay man in the world depended on it.

After ten floppy minutes of Daniel's best efforts, Rick's dick was still quite shy of the promised eight-and-a-half inches.

Just before he pulled out, he told us, "To be completely truthful, it's not the best I've ever had. But it wasn't the worst either."

It was obvious to all present that these were just words of kindness and encouragement for poor Daniel, who seemed genuinely confused by his inability to stir the snake.

Time to move on to mouth two.

After struggling to get the condom on his flaccid member, we encouraged Rick to just put it through the hole au naturel. Avalon sprung into action with a condom ready to roll on with her mouth. She made his dick disappear and within a minute, it was growing in her mouth at an alarming rate. Her effortless glide- and-lick technique impressed all present, most importantly Rick, who, in between murmuring and closing his eyes, told the judges: "Can I just say something? I think this is the male. This one's a lot better than the first one."

A minute later, he filled his condom with jets of hot gay spunk and Avalon leaped to her feet and punched the air like a lottery winner.

Result: Womankind 1, Gay Men 0.

ROUND TWO

Sam prepped by jerking off behind the glory booth to a copy of *Maxim*. "It can take me up to an hour to

cum sometimes, but I can always get my dick hard in a matter of minutes," he told us.

Daniel sunk to his knees while blindfolded Sam shuffled his wobbling sword into the glory hole. Our disheartened gay friend got to work immediately, this time using teeth, spit, face rubbing and the "licking down the side" technique that he learned in the "nightclub toilets of Brighton".

It soon became apparent that this rough lick-and-tickle technique wasn't doing the business, as Sam started to become droopy. He looked around the room as if desperately seeking a way out.

"I think I'll give No. 2 a go, please," he pleaded. "This one is very rough."

Fearing that the contest was already over, we decided to tip the scales and add a handicap—we told Avalon to give Sam the worst blowjob she could. She dallied around with his cock like an Iraqi prisoner of war forced to suck his best friend off for the pleasure of American troops. Still, though, Sam's member responded immediately. This was turning into a bloodbath.

Drunk on her success and given the nod to go in for the kill, Avalon sunk to her knees and showed off the smooth yet firm deep-throat technique that wowed Rick so much. Within a couple of minutes, Sam's features had relaxed and he gazed into the ceiling while telling us, "This one is a lot more sensual. Umm, uh, that's important, when you're, uh, doing a thing like this."

Just to be 100 percent sure, we gave Daniel a last chance to uphold his reputation. Sam still wasn't feeling his efforts.

"No," he sighed. "I like the vigour of this, but I definitely prefer the other." With that, Avalon took over and brought the young man to an intense, shuddering climax.

Result: Womankind 2, Gay Men 0.

So that's that—girls suck better cock than gays. It's a good thing, too, because if men had continued to waste their precious seed inside other men, the human race could have ended up extinct within, say, 2,000 years.

CAPTAIN BRING DOWN SAYS...

PARTIES AREN'T SO GREAT | BY DANIEL KITSON | PHOTO BY SANNA CHARLES

Published June 2004

In fact, parties* are terrible things. Horrific piles of nonsense full of lost souls wandering around looking desperately for someone drunk or lonely enough to throw their decorum to the wind and engage in something heart-crippling in a toilet or nearby bedroom. This is parties. Parties are darkness, noise, sticky floors, tears, hatred, jealousy and regret drizzled all over a seething heap of vapidity. This is what parties are and they are not for me.

My first party was an occasion of optimism at Jonathan Lodge's house. I had my dad's long coat and aftershave and my mum's confidence, coupled with my own castrating insecurities. After an hour of watching girls I liked at school getting a bit weird and stupid and generally unpleasant after having some of a bottle of cider, I placed my lemonade back on the floor and left. I'm pretty certain that I walked home in tears. Maybe I took the death of innocence as a personal bereavement. Maybe there was something implicitly hostile about that level of planned, preordained fun, that "pencilled in" debauchery. Whatever it was, I had a fairly violent reaction to it. And so I steered pretty clear of it until about three years later.

By that time I had a friend. A party companion. He was called Sam. He liked to get drunk, particularly when at parties attended by the various objects of his massive unrequited affection. He was great. I don't remember any of the parties I went to with him. I remember walking him home to my mum and dad's house. Holding him up for a two-mile stretch of main road as he staggered again and again towards the middle of the road, pointing out that it was actually the ideal place to piss. I tried to convince him that actually the toilet was the best place for that sort of business.

Since then I have used various tactics at parties. I have sat on the stairs and let the party come to me. I have ensconced myself in the music, naming myself as the DJ and choosing various songs. Basically I always needed a role beyond socialising. Because I couldn't do that. I knew the people at the party I wanted to be talking to. And they were normally one girl. Who was generally busy.

I avoid parties now. I would far rather be in a quieter room. With fewer people (all of whom I like), more food and less desperation.

* The "parties" I refer to are the teenage parties of yore. Borne out by some in adulthood only with fewer children and more money lavished on them. I have been to lovely parties. But they are not parties of the "Paaaaaarrty" school. They are tiny little parties. Birthday parties with four other people I very much care about. Food. Charlie's Angels. Ice cream. Midnight food. They are dinner parties with 14 courses and little talking. They are parties I left early with the girl I arrived with. These are the parties I care about. And they are not the parties the majority of you would like. But you are wrong. They are brilliant.

A NIGHTMARE ON ME STREET

SIX HYPNAGOGIC HALLUCINATIONS AND ONE GUY WHO PEED ON HIS GRAN
ILLUSTRATIONS BY J. PENRY

Published October 2007

Hypnagogia: it's the phenomenon of experiencing very real and quite often terrifying dream-like sensations while falling asleep or waking up. The horrible thing about this is that it goes hand in hand with sleep paralysis, meaning you are trapped and unable to move while having the worst time of your life. Also horrible is that you think you're awake while the scary stuff is happening to you. In fact, Wes Craven based the whole idea of *A Nightmare on Elm Street* on it.

Sufferers of hypnagogia, or "the wide-awake nightmare", often complain of having dark figures standing over them, of visitations by aliens, or of feeling somebody pushing down on their chest while they lie paralysed, unable to wake up until they finally force out a terrified scream that sounds like "Wuh wuh WUH WUH WAAAAAAGHHOOOOOFFF!!!"

We spoke to seven regular hypnagogia sufferers and this is what they told us. We're praying that this condition is not contagious, the way nightmares sometimes are, because if it is, we—not to mention our roommates and loved ones—are all now totally fucked.

PORTAL TO THE DEAD

About five years ago I was drinking heavily and doing about two grams of cocaine a night. My substance-abuse problems really took off at about the same time my aunt and my grandmother passed away in front of my eyes in close proximity.

Early one morning I got home from partying all night, drinking whiskey, and doing cocaine. I'd passed out in all my clothes on my bed (again) and was woken at 8 AM by the light coming through the crack in the curtains in my room. I remember not being able to move and hearing a voice outside my bedroom door asking me if I wanted a cup of tea. To my horror, it was my dead grandmother's voice, and at that moment of realisation, my nose was filled with the smell of her house, a mixture of Mr Sheen polish and boiled cabbage. Things got worse when my door handle started going up and down and Grandma started barging into the door, making it rattle against the frame. I was totally paralysed. It was like the end scene of *Suspiria*, when Suzy Bannion's dead best friend walks through the door in the head witch's bedroom. It was like a portal of the dead was opening into my room and it was really fucking scary. I remember breathing about three breaths a second and feeling extremely cold. Then, to top it all off, an invisible hand started to scrawl the word "PIG" in blood on my bedroom wall.

This set me off and I let out a bloodcurdling scream. I woke trembling and covered in sweat. I hope the neighbours didn't hear it. After that I resolved to put the blow aside for at least three days.

ANDY CAPPER

NOSEBLEEDING INDIAN

I've always been fascinated by the topic of sleep paralysis. The last time it happened I was awake in my bed but totally unable to move. I saw a guy with his face painted. He looked kind of like a Native American with a headdress. I was paralysed in my bed and he was standing over me. The more I looked at him, the more the red paint on his face appeared to be turning into blood. It was pretty scary.

When I finally forced myself to wake up I saw that my nose was bleeding.

KEVIN FIELDS

CANCER FUNERAL

Two years ago this girl from my hometown died of cancer. I wasn't around for the funeral, but apparently it was incredibly disturbing—her mother broke down as the girl's coffin was lowered into the grave, her father was literally tearing his clothes in grief, and her two older brothers were in hysterics.

Hearing about it, I began to feel incredibly guilty about not going to the funeral, not calling the girl in her final days, not having done anything to help the family. For days I would replay what I imagined the funeral to be like, until one afternoon I guess I became emotionally and physically exhausted. It was around 4 PM, and suddenly, replaying the funeral once again, I had to lie down. I began to think of the funeral again, but for some reason it was much, much more real, and the scene that played out was somehow above me, as if I were in the bottom of the grave. Above, I could see my mother going berserk as she looked down at me and I could hear the distinct wail of my father as he broke down in grief.

"This is fucking ridiculous, I'm not dead, that girl is," I thought, but my incredulity at the situation quickly turned to panic, since I couldn't remove myself from the grave. I kept on trying to get their attention, but they were too busy freaking out to notice me. I tried to alert them for what seemed like hours but it was totally useless, and finally I began to cry out of frustration. When I felt a tear on my cheek I suddenly snapped out of it and was back in my room.

CINDY McCULLOUGH

I TRIED TO EAT MY GIRLFRIEND

I suffer from sleep terrors. It's a more physical version of nightmares where you act out what you are dreaming. Apparently it's caused by anxiety. There have been cases of people committing stabbings and murders in their sleep. It gets pretty extreme.

Personally I have always suffered from horrible nightmares. When I was little I used to wake up in odd places around the house, shaking, with my heart beating out of my chest. Once I pulled a stack of shelves off my wall in my sleep. I woke up with a TV and a stereo system on top of me. Another time I woke up screaming next to my open window. I've gotten wiser, though. Now before I go to sleep I make sure all windows are locked and there are no scissors or sharp objects around.

The worst experience I ever had happened about a year ago. I was asleep next to my girlfriend and I was dreaming that something was attacking me. When I woke up I had her hand in my mouth and blood all over my face. I had bitten her in my sleep and taken a huge chunk out of her hand. It was so horrible. It's weird, but in my dream I thought I was saving her.

DORAN EDWARDS

I PEED ON MY GRAN'S HEAD

I went back to my hometown and stayed at my grandmother's house for a couple of days. One night I went to a local bar with some old friends and got really drunk. Somehow I staggered back to my gran's house and went to bed.

149

In the morning, all bleary-eyed, I got up and started eating breakfast. As I was doing this I noticed my grandma dragging her wet mattress out to the balcony to dry. She was silently fuming and refused to talk to me. Finally, after an hour of me asking her what was wrong, she started crying and asked me, "Are you proud of yourself?"

I had no idea what she was talking about. She proceeded to tell me that I had gotten up in the middle of the night, stumbled into her bedroom, unzipped, and started pissing on her bed while she was sleeping in it. With my pee raining down on her, she shouted at me to stop, but I screamed back at her, telling her to fuck off, and then toddled off to bed.

DARREN COUPON

PSYCHOPATHIC ROOMMATE

In my freshman year of college I shared a room with a small, muscled Indian kid named Jay. The day we moved in he hung a massive framed poster of a football player's backside covered in mud, with the words: "Winners Never Quit, Quitters Never Win: NEVER QUIT."

We were both weirded out by each other, but whereas his discomfort with me was based primarily on my cleanliness and taste in music, I was genuinely convinced that he was going to kill me. It was totally arbitrary and stupid, but as the weeks progressed I started attending an "everyday self-defence course" and sleeping with a knife underneath my pillow.

The height of my paranoia was nicely realised one morning when I woke up to find myself paralysed. I was lying flat on my back staring up at the ceiling and could move nothing but my neck side to side. My roommate was standing over me with this sick little smile on his face, and immediately I was engulfed by a white, urgent terror. He floated closer and closer to me at a painstakingly slow pace. All I wanted to do was get to the knife under my pillow, but as much as I strained I couldn't even lift a finger. I tried to scream for help but the only sound that came out was a low gurgle, and he just kept on moving closer.

Finally our faces were so close that I couldn't focus on his eyes anymore, but with a sudden burst of adrenaline I snapped out of my paralysis, and that was when I woke up to find myself covered in sweat, holding a knife, and screaming my roommate's name.

After that, my taste in Wagner became less of an issue and my "undiagnosed but undeniably psychotic behavior," as he called it in his formal complaint to the housing board, came to the fore. He moved out one week later.

JAMES TARMY

SONIC HEART ATTACK

The last episode of sleep paralysis I had was one of the scariest moments in my life. I remember I had gone to bed really late and was woken up by a high-pitched screaming noise followed by a pain in my chest. All I could hear was an unbearable sharp screaming sound like the one when you've stood too close to the amps without earplugs at a concert. I was paralysed and surrounded by darkness except for this kind of bright energy field that sucked all the force out of me. I felt weaker and weaker, and I tried to scream but no sound came out. I couldn't move. I was terrified, and the more frightened I got, the weaker I felt and the less I could move.

Since I'd been through it before I knew that freaking out would only make things worse, so I tried to calm down. I was completely conscious and I didn't allow it to scare me, I stayed calm. With a huge effort I managed to crawl out of my bed. There was a resistance forcing me back and I tried to scream, but there was still nothing. I tried to get to the door handle, but I couldn't reach it. I gathered my last strength and went for it again. I opened the door and the whole thing just stopped.

I awoke in my bed. My head felt heavy, my arm was asleep, and I was gasping for air. The following day I was still weak with a strange sensation in my chest. I think that the scariest thing about sleep paralysis is that you have NO idea what's happening to you, you have no point of reference for what you're going through. It's like a supernatural experience.

MARY MURPHY

A GIANT CHINESE FINGER TRAP MADE OF RAINBOWS TRIED TO SUCK ME INTO THE SKY

MY MANY TRIPS INTO THE WORLD OF CHEMICAL PSYCHEDELICS
BY D. H. TICKLISH | ILLUSTRATIONS BY TARA SINN

Published February 2008

I have spent the last year of my life on an exhausting psychedelic journey. I managed to get my hands on some of the most potent and rare hallucinogenic drugs ever made, drugs that are mainly illegal. The ones that are not illegal are only approved for analytic studies on things like MP range, mass spectrometry, and receptor binding affinity. If you have no idea what I'm talking about it might be better to stick with mushrooms.

But if you know a naughty chemist, you might be able to get your hands on a few of these compounds. How did I get them? For simplicity's sake, let's just say that I pretend to be a doctor. It isn't easy and I don't want to risk arrest or competition by divulging anything about my methods.

These drugs are as rare as they come. They are super potent and not recreational by most people's definition. People have died from taking these drugs for reasons nobody yet understands because there is no research being done on their toxicity. It is quite possible that I could wake up ten years from now with irreversible brain damage, or I could screw up a dose by a few milligrams and end up dead—and from what I gather, tripping to death is not a lot of fun.

It might seem odd that I would spend so much time experimenting with substances that have no guarantee of being safe or enjoyable, but to me that's the entire point of psychedelic exploration—to dive into the unknown. Why drink alcohol every night when you can drink gamma-Butyrolactone? Why snort coke when you can eat N-ethylcathinone? The psychedelic revolution has come cloaked in drug names that are difficult to pronounce, and it's time to wake up and smell the 4-fluoroamphetamine.

A quick note on dosage: these are the doses I take. Don't take the same as me and then get mad when you die. All of these drugs are dose sensitive, so 1 milligram can be the difference between a good time and a permanent psychotic break.

Also, they almost always come as powdered white crystals, usually with the characteristic taste of one chemical precursor called iodole, which is abundant in human shit. It is wise to keep track of which white crystals are which, to avoid a potentially lethal trip cocktail. In other words, if you are going anywhere near this stuff please be really, really careful.

DPT
DOSE: ORAL 140 MG, NASAL 100 MG
MY PROPOSED STREET NAME: CHRIST
There is a cult/church on the Lower East Side of New York called the Temple of the True Inner Light that has been taking this drug as the Eucharist for the last 30 years. Apparently it's tough to join because they already have enough people willing to participate in Holy Communions where they smoke Christ's psychedelic flesh out of a communal pipe instead of eating a flavorless wafer. Understandable.

The first time I snorted DPT it terrified me so much I felt like I had just railed a line of haunted houses. Eyeballs were peeping out of everything around me and when I looked up I saw a giant Chinese finger trap made of rainbows try to suck me into the sky. Also, snorting it was so painful it made me cry. I would rather snort a handful of sand.

2C-T-21
DOSE: ORAL 12 MG
MY PROPOSED STREET NAME: HEAT STROKE

This drug had a brief stint about five years ago as a legal ecstasy alternative, but it was taken off the market when a quadriplegic from Florida tried to lick an unknown amount out of a vial he bought online, gave himself a massive overdose, and literally fried his brains. That paralysed man was the infamous party pooper of this entire drug scene, and it was his overdose that got many of these unknown drugs scheduled by the DEA.

I tried 2C-T-21 about a week ago. While walking around my neighbourhood, I got so hot that I had to take off my shirt. My body was actually steaming. I decided to go swimming in the East River but instead threw my house keys into the water just to see what it looked like when they splashed.

4-ACO-DMT
DOSE: ORAL 24 MG
MY PROPOSED STREET NAME: THE GREATEST DRUG IN THE WORLD (SOME PEOPLE CALL IT AURORA BUT THAT'LL NEVER CATCH ON.)

Some wayward chemists figured out a way to twist around the structure of psychedelic mushrooms to fit them into a legal loophole so they could be sold from grey-market laboratories. Thus, 4-AcO-DMT was born. The second it touches your gut it gets converted into the active ingredient of mushrooms. But one big difference is if you eat too many mushrooms you vomit, which prevents many overdoses. With 4-AcO-DMT it's easy to accidentally swallow what would be equivalent to a bin bag of shrooms. My friend took too much in the middle of Times Square, went nuts, and ended up strapped down in a hospital. As soon as he got out he attacked his mum for lying to him about Santa Claus as a child.

DOC
DOSE: ORAL 3 MG
MY PROPOSED STREET NAME: DOC FEELGOOD

Since a scale that is accurate down to the microgram would cost more than all of these drugs combined, I measure DOC in a liquid solution. I dissolve 10 milligrams of DOC in 10 millilitres of vodka and then use a syringe to measure doses. 1ml = 1mg. Easy!

DOC is a psychedelic amphetamine that is al-

most unrivalled in potency. A lot of the acid that people think has angel dust in it is actually adulterated with DOC. The big difference between DOC and acid is that DOC lasts about 24 hours, and since it's an amphetamine, you're looking at 24 sweaty hours. This is the kind of drug you really want to have some Valium around for. Any food I put in my mouth tasted like polyester. By the end of the trip I ate a potted plant and the dirt it was growing in.

5-MEO-DMT
DOSE: SMOKED 5 MG, NASAL 15 MG
MY PROPOSED STREET NAME: CRYSTAL DEATH

This one actually occurs in nature. A rare variety of desert toad squirts it on predators in order to render them defenceless in a psychedelicised stupor. The dose is about the size of one grain of salt and when smoked it sends the user into a death trance. It is not uncommon for people high on this stuff to pee their pants.

"Psychedelic" does not quite describe the 5-MeO-DMT experience. If there was a chemical way to shoot yourself in the face and survive, this is it. Once I gave it to a drunk guy who didn't believe there was such a thing as psychedelic toad venom. Within moments his eyes rolled back in his head and he fell to the floor motionless. When he regained consciousness (after vomiting on me while passed out), he said he had touched God.

2C-T-7
DOSE: ORAL 22 MG
MY PROPOSED STREET NAME: 7-UP

Another psychedelic phenethylamine that is totally synthetic and never gained any significant level of popularity in the United States. Around 2001 a couple of suburban teens overdosed on it and the DEA immediately put it in the same legal schedule as heroin. Last time I took 2C-T-7, the moment I began to hallucinate I decided to get on the $15 Fung Wah bus to Boston. I closed myself in the bathroom and pretended I was time-travelling in a septic tank, and when we arrived at our destination the driver had to pry open the bathroom door.

AMT
DOSE: ORAL 40 MG
MY PROPOSED STREET NAME: JAW CLENCH VOMIT POWDER

This drug was born in Russia 50 years ago. Pharmaceutical companies marketed it as an antidepressant called Indopan. I think the problem was that it worked too well and it didn't take long before people realised it was capable of sending them into an insane vibrating notionscape if they simply took twice the dosage.

During my first trip on AMT, I was supposed to stop briefly at a party before going to a friend's house. I foolishly took the pill beforehand and ended up staying at the party the entire night exchanging pleasantries with strangers while watching them melt into the carpet. I was actually having the time of my life until I had to pee and realised that it was a psychological impossibility.

2C-E
DOSE: ORAL 17 MG
MY PROPOSED STREET NAME: C-ESSPOOL

This one is somewhat related to mescaline but about 20 times stronger. It made me so violently nauseous that I vomited out of my nose. Later that night I collapsed on a bench and watched the trees lining the roads slowly grow genitalia—splintery leafed penises and big sappy vaginas. I sat watching this in awe with two friends while taking an occasional whippit, but after a while a passing woman suddenly started beating the shit out of her boyfriend ten feet in front of me. It was more of a downer than a thousand Chris Farley overdoses. When the cops showed up I was climbing one of the vagina trees to get a better view.

DIPT
DOSE: ORAL 70 MG
MY PROPOSED STREET NAME: DIPTHONG

Whenever people ask me what DIPT is like, I have trouble explaining it. It is vaguely related to mushrooms, but at the same time not really. It's totally synthetic—a lab-made psychedelic anomaly that only affects the regions of your brain dedicated to auditory perception. DIPT gives you ultra-sensitive canine hearing and drops the pitch of all sounds down a couple of octaves. Sound waves that fall below the human range of hearing are called infrasound and are associated with earthquakes, exploding volcanoes, and screaming whales. On DIPT, I was listening to a steady infrasonic thrum being generated by a parking meter. Everything sounds like you're underwater, in a broken transistor radio, talking to a bullfrog. I could hear people having conversations inside their apartments as I walked down the street. I also learned to translate the language birds speak. I still have the notebook I was carrying, which has about 40 pages of phonetically transcribed bird chirps that read like this: "percheap twererp cherwerp".

DIPT is like a fun version of being schizophrenic, but I stopped taking it after a high-dose trip where I had an epiphany and figured out that fire-engine and ambulance sirens are a city-wide conspiracy to give people headaches. Also (and in retrospect I should never have done this), riding a crowded A-train through Bed-Stuy while on this drug was comparable to listening to a thousand howler monkeys being burned alive—through a stethoscope.

DMT
DOSE: SMOKED 50 MG
MY PROPOSED STREET NAME: DEMETRI

This one is a classic but still a lot of people have never tried it. You can inject it, snort it, smoke it, or eat it—and have a totally different experience each time. Once I smoked 50 mg after taking a special type of antidepressant that makes it impossible for your body to break down the drug. I began having a vicious argument with my left hand, speaking from both sides—my hand's point of view and my face's. I said, "I'm sorry. I will never do drugs again," and my hand replied, "It's too late!" I thought I was every crazy person that had ever lived in the past, present, and future simultaneously. A lot of people report having sexual encounters with aliens while on this drug but I think before experimenting with DMT, those people experimented with being molested.

Photos courtesy of the author

I WAS UDAY HUSSEIN

A STAND-IN SPEAKS | BY LATIF YAHIA

Published March 2007

The hand that rocks the oil pumps controls the world. Between 1979 and 2003, that hand was Saddam Hussein's. He would also use it to sign death warrants on dissenters, to murder his own countrymen, to plot disastrous wars with neighbouring countries, and to be the puppet master of his entire population. In September 1987, Saddam—or more accurately, his son, Uday—picked up my strings. Uday wanted a double, and I was unlucky enough to resemble him.

This was not my first encounter with Uday. Because of my father's wealth I was sent to the best school in Iraq, and a young, spoiled, arrogant Uday became my classmate. We all hated him even then. He would cruise the streets in his cars and, with the assistance of his bodyguards, would pick up girls whether they wanted to go with him or not—and most did not. At least one girl who refused to be taken by him was kidnapped and thrown to his starving dogs. In class he would act like his father, showing no enthusiasm for lessons and acting threateningly toward anyone who crossed him. A teacher who reprimanded him for bringing his girlfriend into class disappeared and was never seen again. My classmates used to tease me and call me Uday because even at that age I resembled him. I used to imitate him for laughs.

When my second encounter with Uday came about, I was a captain on the front in Iraq's pointless war with Iran. My unit's command received a dispatch saying that I should be sent to the presidential palace. I was taken there and informed that I was to become Uday Hussein's fiday, or body double. This would involve attending functions, making appearances, and assuming his persona when rumours of assassination were circulating. Saddam had several fidays already, and Uday obviously longed for one just like his daddy. I was to be his first. My initial refusal was met with a long spell of solitary confinement and mental torture in a cramped cell without so much as a toilet to maintain my dignity. Eventually, this treatment, and vile threats against my family, forced me to agree to Uday's demands.

Throughout a lengthy period I was trained to act like him and to speak like him. I was also, through cosmetic surgery, made to look even more like him. Indeed, having my front teeth filed down and being given a set of caps that mimicked Uday's gave me a lisp just like his. I was, during my "training", desensitised to the ugly barbarity of the regime by being forced to watch endless, excruciating videos of real torture, mutilation, and murder perpetrated by them on dozens of men, women, and children of Iraq, usually prisoners or prisoners' family members. These films also served as a warning as to what I could

expect were I to decide to challenge the regime at any time in the future.

My first public appearance as Uday was at a football match in Baghdad's People's Stadium. My job was to wave at the crowd from a dignitaries box and present medals to the players at the end. When Uday saw the appearance on television he was impressed. He congratulated my trainers and accepted me as a member of his circle, albeit on the outer reaches. He could not allow anyone to become too close to him, particularly anyone from outside the Tikriti clan from which the majority of the regime was drawn. Indeed, I had been the first fiday to be plucked from the outside world.

From then on my days were spent living in his palaces, effectively a prisoner, as I was not allowed to do anything without permission. But it was a prison of opulence and luxury, with access to the finest food and drink the world had to offer. Swimming pools and other such charmed diversions made the time a little more bearable.

But the captivity grew stultifying. Most of the time I would not be making appearances; I would be bored out of my mind, intellectually and socially unchallenged. I had graduated with a degree in law and had dreamed of following in my father's footsteps and becoming a businessman. This had never been part of my master plan. I was living a brainless, useless existence with no independence or exercise of free will. But worse was to come. I got sucked closer to Uday and he started to treat me as one of his bodyguards, taking me out with him as protection against assassination at the hands of any of his multitude of enemies. This is when I witnessed the depravity of Uday firsthand. I saw him rape, murder, bully, and destroy anyone who dared to question his will. This could be anyone from friends of his father to innocent passersby. On one occasion a honeymooning couple, the wife of which Uday took a liking to, was split apart forever when she threw herself to her death from a balcony after being raped by Uday.

I was saved by the beginning of the invasion of the US-led forces, which seemed to give the regime other things to think about. Uday came to visit me

one day. He had me shaved from head to toe and dumped on the doorstep of my parents' home. My mother discovered me but did not recognise the bald, skeletal figure at her feet until I spoke to tell her who I was.

I eventually managed to flee to Austria, but Uday was not finished with me. Two of Uday's men arrived at my family's home and told my father that Uday wanted to see him in his office. They said the meeting would not take too long and that they would pick him up and bring him back. The meeting took place in the headquarters of the Iraqi Olympic Committee, the organization led by Uday more as something for him to do than through any interest he might have had in sports. At 4 AM my father was dropped off at home. The family was still awake, terrified that he had been kidnapped, tortured, or murdered. He said he did not feel well, and just sat there in the lounge, obviously in some distress. In time he started to feel dizzy. Everyone assumed he was tired, as the past few hours would have been a serious drain on his physical resources. But his skin was changing colour, at first unnoticeably but eventually unmistakably, to a sickly shade of yellow. He eventually keeled over and took his last breath.

A few hours after my father was dropped off, Uday's bodyguards arrived at the house and imposed a no-funeral rule. They told my family simply to put his body in a grave and unceremoniously bury him. They must have known he would be dead by then, which confirmed to anyone in any doubt that he had been deliberately poisoned. Their rationale was that he was killed because he was the father of Latif Yahia, in their view one of the country's greatest criminals, one of its traitors, who was working alongside the CIA to overthrow Saddam.

I continue to blame myself for the death of my father. And I cannot see the day when I will forgive myself. I could have stayed in Iraq and faced the music. Perhaps I would have been the one to accept the orange juice, to have my bones broken, my soul forced through the mangle. Perhaps then my father would have been the one blaming himself—for sending me to the same school as Uday, for being wealthy. Who knows? It is pointless thinking about it. All I knew was that he was the biggest thing in my life—my father, my friend, my teacher, my confidante, a line of continuity in a place where arbitrary acts of violence and mayhem kept its inhabitants in fear and obedience. And now he is gone.

PHOTOJOURNALISM

Soon after we started the magazine we realised that we could commission enthusiastic young photographers who had no qualms about going to terrifying places and (quite literally) risking life and limb to take photos and bring them back to us. Since then, we stopped dealing with agencies and agents and have established a network of hard-working professional photographers whose amazing array of work includes stories on embedding with troops in Afghanistan, pet fashion parties, and looking at life inside a hospice for alcoholics.

CASTLES MADE OF TECHNOSAND

INSIDE DUBAI'S TERRORDOME
WORDS AND PHOTOS BY ADAM PATTERSON

Published April 2009

Dubai is a city where oil-rich Emiratis are willing to pay £10 million just to drive around with a license plate bearing the number "1". (Yes, that really happened.) It's a place filled with vast, multibillion-pound palaces of unholy decadence, a kingdom of greed and consumption where hotels provide westerners with 24-carat-gold facials and food prepared by Prince Charles's ex–personal chef is

This was taken at around 4:30 AM. These workers must walk to work from their labour camps, which are often miles outside the city. Others are shuttled on prison-style buses with faces peering through barred windows. They are part of an approximated one million migrant labour force mainly from India, Pakistan, Bangladesh and the Philippines. They look here much like they are within Emirate society: the ghosts of the great highway, the men building the dreams of Dubai.

In the rush to modernise, the Emirate of Dubai has ploughed any evidence of its past into the sand. There is no culture here, no way of doing things. Tourists are herded through the predictable turns like the gold souk, a rebuilt fabrication catering to the western craving of how things might have been.

served in garish dining rooms 70 feet below sea level. Even the thousands of tropical fish on display eat better than you do, feasting on nearly 500 pounds of restaurant-quality seafood buddies each day.

The contrast between the lifestyles of the tourists and those who build Dubai— the construction workers, not the faceless financiers—could not be more stark. Often they are paid £70 a month for working sweatshop hours in 120-degree heat. Employers usually confiscate their passports in exchange for jobs, as if a license to travel does a destitute worker much good. Unofficial figures say that around 1,000 of these illegally imported slaves from India and Pakistan suffered labour-related deaths last year.

As the global economy limps toward bankruptcy and the tourist trade that the city relies on dwindles, the pounds that once poured in are drying up, and layoffs have begun.

While £483 billion in building projects move ahead as planned, another £406 billion worth have been put on hold due to the economic slowdown. What will happen to Dubai's huge monoliths of futurist architecture gone wild when there is no one to stay in them? Will they stand there and rust until they crumble? In 2008, the *Wall Street Journal* placed Dubai's debt relative to gross domestic product at 42 percent. Neighbouring Abu Dhabi's debt relative to GDP is just 2.9 percent.

In 2007, reports claimed that Dubai retail and commercial space covered 1.3 million square feet. 15-25 percent of the world's cranes are in Dubai.

The push for western construction butts up against the pitfalls of religious tradition. Often workers collapse and fall to their deaths by dehydration.

Rest during a lunch break. During the month of Ramadan, when nothing may pass the mouth during daylight, deaths related to dehydration are common.

Many workers aspire to be taxi drivers. As a taxi driver they earn as little as construction workers—about 500 dirhams a month (£80)—and will work 13-hour shifts, with only one holiday every two years to see their family.

Hygiene is basic, but the hand wash offers a chance for respite. Most earn ten times what they would at home in India or Bangladesh. Sometimes this is not enough. In 2006, 87 migrant workers took their lives, many of whom would be sending the life insurance to their families.

In March 2006, workers rioted on the site of the Burj Dubai, causing around £650,000 of damage. Their protests led to a 20 percent increase in salary, but failure to deliver led to further riots in October 2007 with 4,000 workers being imprisoned and deported without pay.

The oldest tower in Dubai hails from the 1970s. Its original facade was a completely different incarnation to the one we see today. English financiers first saw potential in the region as a tax-free zone and, with Arabic backing, exploited it. Dubai law states that companies have to be headed by at least one Dubai national, and that ten percent of a company's staff must be nationals. If a national is fired, the company will be fined by the government.

Together, Arabic families and British professionals turned a desert into a metropolis, forging a relationship in the process. It is estimated that within two years there will be more British residents than nationals in Dubai. Judging by the streets full of mini skirt-wearing, beer-swilling English who don't even try to tone down their national tongues, let alone learn Arabic words, and malls of snogging couples, this statistic is quite believable and a world away from the workforces building their playgrounds.

UAE labour laws, particularly in the "free zones", are constructed to benefit the employer and undermine any rights the labour force have. Migrant exploitation is almost literally government sanctioned.

The day finally ends at sunset, usually around 7:30 PM. The workers walk along worn paths, tossing dust into the air and leaving a line of gritty, ghostly silhouettes moving into the distance.

This was taken in Sonapur ("land of gold" in Hindi), Dubai's largest labour camp, which embassies estimate houses upwards of 50,000 workers. Despite the number of labourers being in excess of millions, there are currently only 400 government building inspectors. And that is more than double the 2007 figure.

This is Ikram on the left with his friends in a rare moment of relaxation. As the economy begins to fail they have been given a ticket home. They are not sure when they travel, but they are expected to feel lucky for this small mercy. Over the next few days they will be taken to the airport and shipped back to the mountains of Pakistan.

These men can't wait to see their families again, but many are worried about debt and visits from the collectors. They are prodigal sons returning from Dubai, but without the bounty. Workers have one month to leave following the termination of employment. Whether they've worked two months or 20 years, no one can retire. It is not an option.

Life in Sonapur is squalid. Open rubbish bins and sewage are everywhere, leading to high levels of disease among workers with little to no access to medical care.

These are the huge pumps that pour the sewage out of the camps. They look like huge octopus tentacles snaking through the refuse-strewn streets.

Imran was a goat herder from northern Pakistan. His family came together and pooled the cash for his flight to Dubai, where he was promised a decent wage and solid work. On arrival he was informed that this wage would be halved and two months later Imran was told that he must leave Dubai within three days. There is no work. He now has no job.

This is a workers' camp I visited on the edge of nowhere. It wasn't even a village. In fact, all signs prior to arrival indicated that we should immediately turn around, or risk being lost, forgotten and never found. We had left Dubai only an hour before, but this was like being in another world. Around 30 Indian workers were living here, mere months after being miscounted and left to survive on dates that had fallen from trees. They are looking healthier now, thanks to the woman who had taken me to see them. She was a company director that found them nearing starvation only months before and decided to blow the whistle.

Sewage left in acrid open pools. You could smell this from within the camp and as you approached, miles before the camp was even in sight.

A security guard for a small-scale development.

Here a Filipino domestic worker I met called Jenny enjoys some respite in the Global Village, one of the few leisure areas domestic servants are allowed to enter in Dubai.

The government has ruled that families must live in villas or flats, but female staff like Miss Suzi cannot afford the 150,000 dirhams cost. She lives with 24 others in a three-bedroom villa. She told me: "My dream is to go back to the Philippines and not come back to Dubai. There is no future here with the freeze. They have stopped hiring and people are losing their jobs."

167

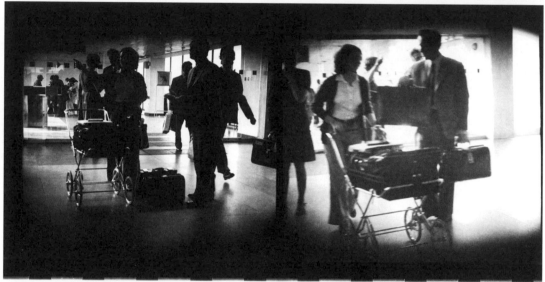

STATE-SPONSORED VOYEURISM

**PHOTOGRAPHY FROM THE CZECHOSLOVAKIAN SECURITY SERVICES ARCHIVE
BY PAVEL CEJKA**

Published July 2009

We will probably never know the proper names of some of our favourite photographers of the last century. You see, these people were not working for the sake of artistic glory. Instead, they served a totalitarian state apparatus that was not at all unlike the cheerful government in George Orwell's *Nineteen Eighty-Four*. And so what follows, dear comrades, are surveillance photographs taken by the Communist secret police in Czechoslovakia in the 1970s and 80s.

They were spying full-time on average citizens, hoping to catch them in a situation that could lead to a swift arrest and a lengthy incarceration in some dank, hidden cell. With their cameras secreted in a suitcase or under a coat, the agents had no idea what was being captured while they were taking these pictures. Their negatives, in which one finds brilliant snatches of street life from a time that few outsiders were able to see, are full of unexpected gems. Total art from a bunch of Communist lackeys and thugs. Who would have thunk it?

These photographs and more are collected in the book *Prague Through the Lens of the Secret Police*, which was released earlier this year by the Institute for the Study of Totalitarian Regimes, Prague, www.ustrcr.cz.

BORDERLINE BIGOTS

MEXICO TELLS IMMIGRANTS: "NO WAY, JOSÉ"
WORDS AND PHOTOS BY LUIS AGUILAR

Published June 2009

Each year hundreds of thousands of optimistic South and Central Americans travel north to see whether things might be less crappy for them in the United States. The problem is they have to cross Mexico to get there. And Mexico is riddled with inhospitable local authorities and migrants who are as eager as they are possessive of the American passage. Both groups treat Southern transients the same way US authorities treat illegal Mexican aliens: like human refuse.

I wanted to witness and document just how bad things are for South and Central Americans, so I caught up with a group of Guatemalan *chapines* and Honduran *catrachos* in Chiapas, near Mexico's southern border, as they made their way up to the States. It's a prime spot to observe. In broad daylight you can witness legions prancing over the increasingly defined line that divides one country from another.

I soon saw that immigrants have two options northward: riding a bus or hopping a train. Either way, Mexicans with machine guns and shitty attitudes await them.

If you are an illegal immigrant riding a bus, known as a tijuanero, across the border, you'll need to be ready to talk your way through numerous police checkpoints. Rides cost about £50 and take travellers from the south of Mexico to the primary crossing hubs of the northern frontier. The idea is to blend with the Mexican crowd to ensure safe passage.

In broad daylight and yards away from the border-inspection point, dozens of people cross the Suchiate River, which divides Mexico from Guatemala. That is a baby in that teen's lap. Good times.

One morning I met a group of immigrants scoping out potential trains to jump. After hours of looking for a place hidden from the view of the border patrol, we found a shaded spot and relaxed for a bit. The travellers talked about what it was like to live in Honduras and the daredevil act of entering and exiting Mexican trains. Suddenly, we heard a whistle. Everybody went silent and prepared for a sprint to the rails.

Travellers grabbed their backpacks and tied five-litre water containers to their trousers. The mood was tense. Everyone remained hidden until the conductor's car passed, and then, a few moments later, they started to run and jump aboard—women and children first.

Some didn't make it onto the train, but those who did smiled in relief as they waved goodbye. Their trip, however, was far from over. These are cargo trains, so passengers must climb to the rooftops or tie themselves to the stairs so they don't fall overboard while sleeping. They also have to be mindful of the metal, which can get so hot that you can fry an egg on it or so cold that it causes hypothermia.

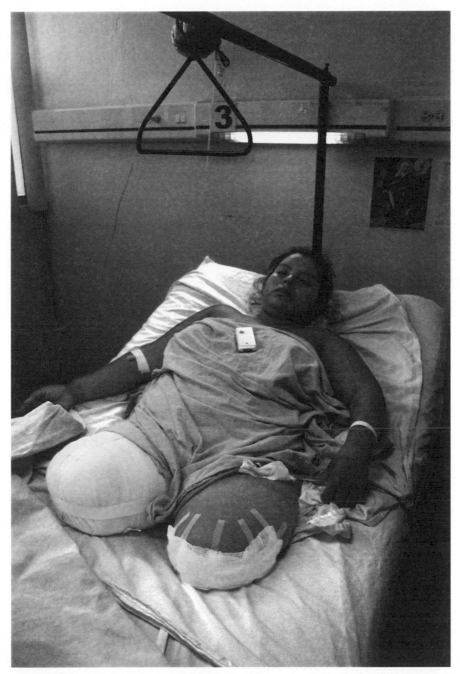

Later I met Ester, a Honduran immigrant who lost her legs while trying to catch a train. I asked her what had happened: "All my dreams are lost now. Sometimes I just can't take it anymore and wish I were dead because of everything that has happened to me. Everything went downhill when I lost $300—the only money I had. I went from train to train for 15 days, and when I got to Tierra Blanca I phoned my mum and told her I'd call when I got further. Two days later, I phoned her again: 'Mum, I lost my legs. I fell from the train. I know I'm still alive and I can hear you and my son, but it's tough being here.'"

PUSS IN BOOTS (AND HATS AND CAPES AND WIGS AND LITTLE RUFFLED COLLARS)

CAT PRIN CLOTHES ARE DICTATED BY THE COSMOS
INTERVIEW AND PHOTOS BY TOMOKAZU KOSUGA | TRANSLATED BY LENA OISHI

Published April 2008

You've probably seen Cat Prin: The Tailor of a Cat. It's a Japanese webstore that sells the most ridiculously adorable cat outfits with names like "Frog Transformation Set", "Young Lady Blouse", and "Shawl of a Rabbit". The site has tons of photos of two little Scottish Folds wearing all these funny getups and staring right at you with dazed expressions. It's one of those wacky websites that gets emailed around a lot, often with a subject heading like "omg, sooooo cute!" In fact, Amy Kellner, who does *The Cute Show* for VBS, says she gets it forwarded to her at least once a day, which is even more than she gets links to catsthatlooklikehitler.com.

For a while, everyone we know was using photos of the Cat Prin cats in their dazzling ensembles as their MySpace photo icons. It was everywhere, but because the site is in Japanese, it was still so mysterious. Is it a real store? And if so, who is the lunatic making this stuff? The few bits of English text on the site don't explain much. It says things like: "You need to dress a cat. And you will say to a cat together with a family, 'It has changed just for a moment.' You will pass pleasant one time." And: "I am the feeling which became a daughter." Hmm. That's awesome and poetic and stuff, but we still don't get it. Luckily, our pals over at *Vice* Japan were able to contact and interview the one and only cat tailor, Takako Iwase, and answer all of our pressing questions about her delightful cat-fashion creations.

Vice: Tell us how you first began the world's best clothing store for cats.
Takako Iwase: In August 2000, a booming voice suddenly rang out over my head that said, "Do something this year!" I panicked and didn't know what to do. I could hear the voice while I walked down the street. "Do something this year!" I kept looking around to see who was telling me to do this but no one around me seemed to notice it, and that's when it finally clicked that I was the only one who could hear it. But it was so loud, and right above my head! I don't know how to explain it, but I realised that this must be a revelation of God! I accepted it as that. So although I was a little freaked out, I began the online store called Cat Prin on December 10 of the same year. I was relieved that I made the deadline that God gave me.

I'll bet! Were there any particular events that led up to you hearing the voice of God commanding you to make cat clothes?
No, it was so sudden. I was actually suffering from a serious illness for about eight years around that time, and I was getting anxious about whether there was any work that I could do at home since working outside was no longer possible. Then one day I saw a story on TV about a 16-year-old girl from rural Japan who started her own business.

Apparently she started out by selling t-shirts online that she bought wholesale, and when those sold out, she borrowed some money from her dad and opened her own little shop in the village. She would ride the night bus to Tokyo over the weekend to stock up on clothes, and people would snatch them up as soon as she sold them in the store. She's only 16, but she's now the boss of her own company. When I saw her, something inside of me crumbled away, and I realised what a wonderful country Japan is. I mean, it's a country where if someone is selling something, and someone else wants to buy it, then it's accepted as a legitimate business. I was surfing the net with my computer, which was the only thing I purchased with my retirement money, and I realised that this was what I had to do. Also, my mother is a great seamstress and had made a little cape for my cat Prin, who was lying right in front of me. A computer, clothes for cats, and Japan, a country where anyone can do business! Cat Prin is all these things combined. And it coincided exactly with when I heard that voice telling me to "do something".

That is one inspirational story. Did you think there would be a big market for cat fashion?
Well, I'm sure that people have been making clothes for cats privately, but I didn't come across anybody who was publicly announcing that they were "cat tailors" back then. It wasn't exactly a taboo, but I think that generally you were frowned upon, like, "Clothes for cats? Ridiculous!" But after I started the shop I realised that there was actually a big demand for these things, and customers would come up to me and say, "I had been wanting to dress my kitty up for so long, I used to dress them up in dog clothes before you came along," like they were waiting for something like this forever. Even before I began the business, for some reason I got it into my head that there must be at least five people in Japan who would love my clothes. I don't know why. Anyway, I decided to do my best, even if it was just for those five people. And if other people didn't like it, I would quit, because it would mean that I was out of sync with the rhythms of the universe.

But as it turns out, you and the universe were very much as one.

Yes, to my surprise I didn't hear any complaints, just happy customers saying, "I was waiting for a shop like this!" Maybe it's because similar shops already existed for dogs. Apparently dog-clothing stores had a hard time at first. But now that society has been through that, I feel that we're living in a time of choices, whether it's "I don't want my cat to wear anything" or "I want to dress up my cat". Initially, I had only planned on making simple items like necklaces and shirt collars rather than entire outfits, but it gradually evolved from there. I always consider my products fashionable. They're not dress-up costumes to transform your cat into something else. It's more about aesthetics.

So once you had the idea, was it tough getting it off the ground?

Yes, I made a lot of mistakes at the beginning. You can't ask for advice because nobody has done it before. At first, some pet stores offered to sell a few of my products, but even then they said, "You should make dog costumes instead, that's where the money is." After that, I decided not to listen to anybody else's opinion except fortune-tellers and people with mystical powers, and they all told me the same two things, which reassured me immensely. What do you think they said? The first thing was "You will succeed" and the second thing was "You will have to live with your sickness for the rest of your life." They all said that these were absolute truths.

That's a whole lot of truth. Do you make all of the clothing by hand?

Generally yes, although sometimes I ask ladies in the neighbourhood to help out. If I need to bulk-produce a certain product then I ask a factory, but even then it's still two ladies sewing everything by hand. Dogs are fairly big so you can sew everything with a machine in one go, but only a tiny amount of cloth is used for cat's clothes so they always have to be hand-sewn. I didn't even know how to sew at first, so I didn't know that you don't have to make every single stitch look perfect, especially if it's a part that isn't visible. I was often told to take it easy with the

stitching. I'm not so concerned with whether they sell, seeing as the whole thing started because I wanted to make my cat Prin look cute.

Prin is the white Scottish Fold who models some of the costumes, right?

Yes. Back then I wanted to own a completely white Scottish Fold, which was pretty rare at the time. Then one day I was flipping through a magazine and I saw the words "White angels are born". Before I knew it, I was calling them up, and I went to the breeder's house to see the kittens. Health-wise I was in a terrible state and I can't believe I actually went, but I did and found out that there were seven kittens altogether. They were all tangled up and playing with each other. I stared at them for about two hours but I still couldn't see any of their faces properly, plus I was sick, and I didn't know what to do. But at the very end, this one kitten with a bright red nose came up to me, so I decided to get that one and eventually named her Prin. Looking back, I think that she actually chose me, like we were meant to be. She turns nine in March. She's a very strange cat. When I was sick, she never woke me up to ask for breakfast, and when I did wake up, I would find a toy mouse next to my pillow. She showed a lot of concern for me and would only play in my eyesight when I was lying in bed. Even now, she never wakes me, no matter how hungry she is.

She's so cute and seems so mellow. My cat would never let me put all those hats and cloaks on her.

Yes, I only recommend my designs for cats who are OK with wearing collars at the very least. If they can't even wear those, then there's no way they can wear my clothes. Same with slightly untamed cats. When you see Prin wearing them you think, "Oh, maybe my cat can wear these too," but actually it's not that simple. For example, if it's a helmet-shaped headpiece, most cats don't like their ears folded over. That's why I separate my products into three types: advanced level, mid-level, and beginners. The beginner products are mostly items that you place around the neck. I use Velcro for most of the clothes so that they're easy to fasten. I recommend these for cats who can wear collars. Mid-level products are clothes that have long bits hanging from the neck. Cats seem to really hate this. A lot of cats can't wear the sailor-style school uniform because of the hanging gold bit in the front. Hats and capes are the advanced products. We also have a "natural" level for cats who can't wear anything, which basically means, "You don't have to wear anything, just browse through the site and enjoy the photos!"

Funny. Who are your customers?

A lot of them are regulars. There are a few very passionate customers who always buy my new costumes. I have about 1,500 customers right now.

Have you had any strange requests?

Yes, mostly from men. Usually it's something like, "I want to dress my cat up as a bunny rabbit, and I also want rabbit ears myself. Can you make matching ones for us?" to which I say, "Sorry, I don't make human costumes." Numerous men have asked me to make matching costumes with their cats, but no women yet. It's very interesting.

Do you have any pointers on how to convince a cat to wear clothes?

Always think about the cat's personality beforehand, and don't force the costumes upon them. Try to do it when they're in a good mood, and say encouraging words to them. Cats love to be complimented. You can't be half-assed about it either. You've got to be like, "OH MY GOD, you are so CUTE, you're the best cat EVER!!" and they will actually feel it and feel better about wearing the clothes. Compliment your cat, and they will definitely get better at wearing clothes.

Which is your favourite cat outfit?

I love them all. They're like my children. But I guess I especially find the Versailles series interesting. I was awestruck when I found the material for the blond wig used in that series. I went to buy a tiara at a wholesaler that had a huge selection of pins and other things to put in your hair, and that's when I found these wigs. The hats look so much better with the hair! Prin looks fantastic with blond hair, by the way. I'm surprised how far I've come with the intricacy of the costumes myself.

You've even made an official Hello Kitty costume for cats.

Yes, the first Hello Kitty headpiece ever. My costumes are usually only two-sided but this one is fully three-dimensional. It was interesting to see how you can three-dimensionalise flat objects, and it was around this time that I came to love the whole craftwork thing. It took six months and 22 prototypes until we got it right. I was near tears. Sanrio had to check every single name tag and they would pick out the ones that weren't good enough. The embroidered

Hello Kitty mark also had to be checked one by one, and they'd say, "The nose isn't right, the eyes aren't right," and so on. There were so many problems I was about to give up! But the Hello Kitty symbol embroidered on this costume is wearing a blouse, and this is a Cat Prin and Sanrio original mark that can't be found anywhere else, so it's quite valuable. In terms of the shape, it was really difficult trying to express the roundness of Hello Kitty on a cat's head, which is actually oval shaped.

What's your ultimate dream outfit?

I'm interested in old England at the moment, like the clothes that the British ladies and gentlemen wore 200 or 300 years ago. Vests, ties, and hats like what Peter Rabbit wears, long flowing skirts, that kind of thing. I've made about 150 costumes so far. I always thought that one day I wouldn't be able to design any new costumes anymore because I'm not really a designer type, but the inspiration just keeps coming. There's never a time when I don't have a new costume idea in my head. I think that the more I make them, the more inspiration will keep flowing. That, and encountering new material.

Tell us about your plans for the future.

To tell you the truth, I don't believe that I was born just for Cat Prin. I think that I am still in the process of reaching my true destiny. My ultimate dream is actually to become a fantasy writer. I'm a terrible writer, but I feel like I can write about things that are out of this world. It's a long time ago now, but about two years ago a title for a book popped into my head: Christina's Children. It's a three-part series, and I already have a pretty good idea of the whole story. It seems like I won't be working on it for another year or two, though, since I'm so busy with other things. But it will be interesting if I can make this happen, and maybe even have a Hollywood movie based on it. But if it doesn't happen, that's OK too. More realistically, it would be nice to have a Japanese TV series based on this book. I often talk with my friends about which actors I want playing which characters. I think that's when I feel happiest.

Carl Wareham, 20, received a five-year order banning him from entering the Dorset village of Lytchett Matravers. He is also banned from the local pubs and off-licences. He told me that although he was a serial offender when he was young, he received his ASBO after being the subject of only two minor charges over a period of several years.

Adam Rooney, 20, told me he had only ever had two minor charges against him before he and his twin brother, Liam, were given ASBOs. Liam is now in prison for breaching his ASBO and Adam's picture is on the back of buses on three local bus routes. Adam now finds it impossible to get a job. I arranged another meeting with Adam after I took this picture, but when I arrived I found out he was in custody again.

ASBOS

WORDS AND PHOTOS BY ALEX STURROCK

Published August 2007

Last year I travelled up and down Britain for six months to meet and take photographs of people with Anti-Social Behaviour Orders. In case you didn't know, an ASBO is something invented by the Labour government to give out to people who are seen as a menace to the community they live in. I decided to do this because at the time there was so much coverage on things like "chavs" and "ASBOs" in the tabloid press that I wanted to find out what life was really like for the people who'd been labelled "anti-social" by the government. Originally, only a limited number of ASBOs were meant to be handed out and then only under very special circumstances. Once they started making front page headlines, however, the government started chucking them out like they were lottery tickets. When I began the project, over 9,853 people had ASBOs. At one point the rate of increase was so dramatic that if it had continued most of the country would have their own personal ASBO by the end of the decade. I wonder what mine would have been for?

Bobby, 13, left, and Craig, 11, right, pictured with their mum and sister. After both boys received ASBOs, Craig made the front page of the local paper and leaflets were distributed with his name and face on. Craig now finds himself on the receiving end of threats and abuse from adults in the street.

Billy is from Dagenham in Essex. He has an ASBO for hoarding rubbish and livestock in his house. When the council cleaned his house they removed over 20 tons of rubbish in 700 bin bags.

MERSEY INFANTICIDE

INSIDE THE VIOLENT LIVES OF LIVERPOOL'S 11-YEAR-OLDS
INTERVIEW BY ANDY CAPPER | PHOTOS BY STUART GRIFFITHS

Published September 2008

In the northeast of Scouserland, aka Croxteth, Liverpool, there lies a delightful old stately home. About 500 acres of it were made into a country park in 1972 and all through the year, families take day trips there to frolic in the fields, eat ice cream, and have a go on the swings. It's bloody lovely, it is.

But sadly for the holidaymakers, the area directly surrounding the park is run by a multitude of sub-machine-gun-firing gangs, the average age of which is around 15 years old. These kids were all busy getting on with their day-to-day trade of shooting each other and supplying the city's junkies with regular supplies of crack and heroin, all well underneath the public radar, until one of them mistakenly shot an 11-year-old named Rhys Jones in the back of the head during a gang fight just over a year ago.

Soon after, British true-crime author and undercover reporter par excellence Graham Johnson travelled up to Croxteth with photographer Stuart Griffiths to get in good with the children who run these gangs. This is what they came back with.

Vice: Tell us about some of the teenage gang members you met.
Graham Johnson: There's one kid from the Huyton area. He was in a gang called the Moss Edz. He was 14. Let's call him John. We talked in his mum's back kitchen while he was doing the dishes and he told me he'd been involved in over 30 firearms incidents, including shooting at rival gang members, being shot at, and "spraying up" houses with rapid-fire machine guns. He told me how he would avoid getting caught through forensic evidences by burning his "Lowies"—the gang's all-black uniform of Lowe Alpine mountain gear with all-black Reebok classic trainers and black trapper's hats. Oh, and they wear ski masks too.

I like it. It's a strong look.
They also wash their hands in gasoline to get rid of gunpowder traces. He told me all this while eating a dinner made up of Haribo sweets, packs of crisps, a chocolate bar, and a bottle of Lucozade.

Sounds delicious—but not very nutritious. Did you meet any of his friends?
Yeah. The leader of John's gang was a kid called Lee and he was also 14. I met him with a kid called Kevin who received a gunshot wound in his leg when he was 12. They told me that Kevin's 17-year-old brother Alfie had just got shot in the arse, then took

a taxi to hospital. I met Alfie later that day and when I asked him what it was like to be shot he said he "wasn't arsed" and that it was normal to be shot.

Why was he shot?
He insulted a local drug dealer's mum.

And what happened after he got out of the hospital?
They shot a rifle at said local drug dealer's mum's house. In response, the drug dealer walked down the street where Alfie, Kevin, and Lee lived and he just shot a semiautomatic into the air and into houses and down the alleyways where the kids sell drugs.

Um, so then the cops came and shot this guy down in the street, right?
Nope. They told me nobody could be bothered to call the police so they left it alone. The drug dealer was connected to a rival gang called the Dovey Edz, from the neighbouring Dovecot area, and stuff like this happens all the time. Maybe ten years ago or so it would have been settled with a fistfight or a knife but now the little kids all have access to powerful firearms. You can see it's true for yourself by going on YouTube. They make videos of themselves carrying guns and driving stolen cars through council estates and set them to rap music. Often the films have messages to rival gangs in them to the effect of "We are going to come and kill you using all of our guns."

What sort of firearms do they have?
There was one kid I heard about, nicknamed Fuji, who shot himself in his own foot while he was threatening another gang member. When the police eventually raided his house they found an SA-80 army-issue assault rifle—the same used by British soldiers in Afghanistan—underneath his bed next to a load of Xbox games. This gun fires 110 rounds a minute. The police said the weapon had been used to spray up a house in an unrelated incident.

So is it all shooting houses and accidental foot wounds?
No. Not at all. As you know, there's a big trial com-

ing up concerning the death of the 11-year-old boy who was shot by, they say, a 14-year-old, as he was coming back from football practice. And I met a lady called Donna Smith whose son, Liam "Smigger" Smith, was a member of a gang called Noggadogz and had his head blown off with a shotgun by the gates of a prison because he'd had cross words with a rival gang member on a visit to one of his mates. His mother described to me how she'd never seen blood pour out of anyone like that. "It was like running a tap," she said.

Poor lady. Are you still in touch with her?
No. Sadly, she died shortly afterward of natural causes. That was the only interview she gave.

So we've got the Moss Edz, the Dovey Edz, and now the Noggadogz. What kind of environments do they live in?

Well, the Noggadogz live in places like the Boot Estate, which used to be the largest council estate in Europe.

I bet it's nice there, yeah?
Hmm. It actually looks like a cross between a war-torn Bosnian village and the set of *Escape From New York*. It's the perfect environment for gangs to operate in. There are plenty of nooks and crannies to stash weapons and drugs. They need the weapons because there's currently a war going on between them and their main rivals, the Croxteth Crew. They say that this war is what could have lead to innocent Rhys Jones to getting shot.

Who's the older guy standing in front of the BMW [above]?
That's Stephen French. He's known as "The Devil" in Liverpool.

How come?

He used to kidnap and torture young drug dealers in the Norris Green area of Liverpool and take the money they'd make from selling heroin and crack. He said he needed to feed his family and help pay his friend's electricity bills.

Ha ha ha.

Yeah, he's been likened to a black Robin Hood in Liverpool by his allies. He was totally feared by the drug dealers though because nobody knew who this mysterious kidnapper guy was. I wrote a book about his life and when I went up north with Stuart Griffiths to photograph these teenage gangs we bumped into each other and I asked him what he thought about it all.

What did he say?

Well, he blames himself partially for the rise of firearm use by children in the city because when he started operation, some ten to 15 years ago, he created this climate of fear in the younger, small-time dealers who'd previously only really had rival gang stabbings or short custodial sentences to worry about. When they found out they were directly at risk from a guy called "The Devil" who was kidnapping and torturing them and stealing their money they all started to arm themselves for protection.

Makes sense.

Yeah. Anyway, now he's given up crime and is involved in something called the Andrew John Centre where kids from deprived areas like the one we're talking about can learn things like wallpapering, motor mechanics, and woodwork. These days "The Devil" is a social campaigner.

Yeah, I still wouldn't fuck with him though. What does he think about all these gang members now?

He said that he's terrified of them.

Amy and Cornelius taking their mattress to an old garage they believe to be vacant, which would provide good shelter for the night ahead.

Amy sleeping on the street while Cornelius searches for money for more cider.

This is Amy. At 14, her mother got her hooked on heroin and turned her to the brothels to make money for the family.

A POSTCARD FROM WALES

DEAR MUM AND DAD, I'M LIVING IN A HEROIN EPIDEMIC
WORDS AND PHOTOS BY ADAM PATTERSON

Published November 2009

The small South Wales city of Swansea is in the grip of a heroin epidemic. How do I know? Well, I've been living with a group of young Welsh heroin addicts, on and off, for the last three months. The needle exchange where they flock to every day to change their works recently reported that in the last four years there has been a 178 percent increase in the number of registered heroin users in the city.

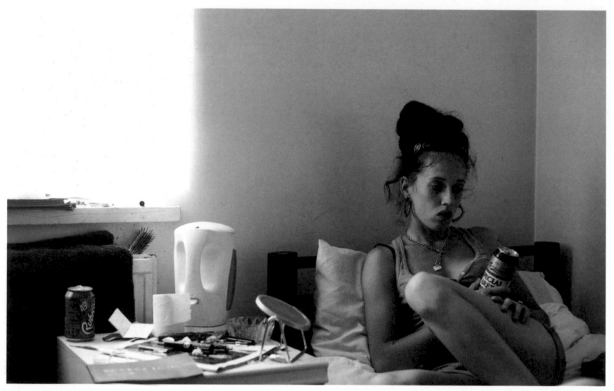

This is Becky in her flat. Weeks later she would be evicted after being accused of selling drugs by another resident.

Why has this happened? From what I discovered, the supply is driving the demand. Swansea was once a thriving port with a lot of heavy industry, but the Thatcher years and outsourcing to foreign labour has meant that unemployment is high and chances for working-class young people to obtain work is low. It is, however, possible to make upwards of £1,500 a DAY as a medium-level heroin dealer.

The people I met in my time here told me that heroin has become easier to acquire than cannabis in Swansea, leading to a rise in long-term addiction and the associated spiral of decline.

The result? Lots more heroin dealers selling cheap, cut heroin to an increasingly younger market. If that wasn't enough, another report recently revealed that in Wales, in 13 years, the number of people contracting hepatitis C through needles is up 1,612 percent.

What else did I find out? Well, lots of other things

that statistics can't record. In an hour you can know more about someone than three months of mindless commuter talk in London. Life is different here.

On a Sunday morning a local man called John Frith, who works for the Swansea Drugs Project (SANDS), walks me around the city. John has seen more than most and has the courage to use this to help out those addicted to heroin. He is well respected here and I am quickly introduced to a number of different faces and opinions that will shape my next four days.

I fall quickly into the lives of people who move very fast. There is Becky, talking aloud to herself with no control of the roaming voices she says are tormenting her thoughts, her fingers badly bent from diabetes. And there is Max, deep vein thrombosis rotting his legs, ridden with hepatitis C, 42 and facing a bleak future. After years on the streets, this couple

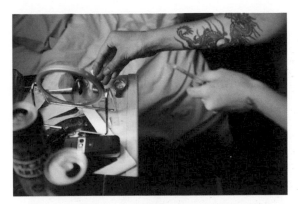

Here's Becky preparing a clean rig for using heroin.

Becky and Neil, her partner, preparing the heroin for use.

Becky and Neil after taking heroin. Becky has recently been housed at a project for people on heroin. At 21, she had been on and off the streets for more than seven years.

Becky showing her tattoos shortly after taking a hit.

Becky fixes her phone while her boyfriend Max works on his computer. Though Becky is only 29, the couple have been together for 14 years. The first eight of these were spent on the streets, but now they share a council flat and enjoy the space and the security.

After years of prolonged drug use, Becky has developed severe headaches and paranoia.

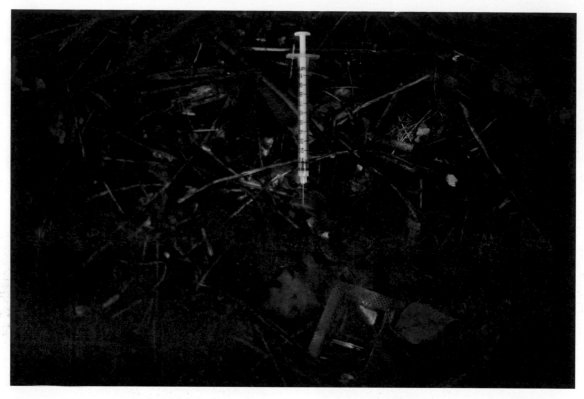

Discarded needles are often found in parks and alleys. Many users condemn this lazy practice because disposal kits are available at the Swansea Drugs Project. However, with limited funding, the facility is closed on evenings and weekends.

hold down a council house together on the edge of the city.

Walking by the water, I see Simon fishing for mullet, his dog Charlie feeding on scraps from the adjacent pub. He scratches his thick beard and recalls youthful trips to Ireland by boat, surviving only with "eyes on the back of my head". The boats don't go to Cork anymore.

Walking up Wind Street, I stop with a girl called Joanne, who is very nervous. The man who assaulted her has been released from prison and is expected back in the city soon. Her story bears a saddening resemblance to many others I spoke with. "I started drinking after my father [committed suicide], but when my mother went [when I was 15], then it got worse and worse," the story usually goes.

Becky and Neil have been together a short time.

They lie back on Becky's bed and talk of stealing fish-tanks to flog for drug money. Becky is not long out of prison, having been caught attempting to sell drugs to an undercover policeman. As they prepare to shoot up, the routine flows well—all the elements are clean, having been obtained from SANDS—and soon they float away. In most cases, heroin addiction often seems to start young, and more often with the involvement of a family member who has the wrong set of ideas.

I meet some people only once and then they are gone, often in no real direction but with a sense of urgency. Lee and Leanne are hunting for bond money, for example. They need a £200 deposit for a six-month lease. At night they are sofa-surfing with friends—part of the "hidden homeless" the statistics never account for.

This homeless person wakes early each morning with the sun. He prefers sleeping at the beach to the town because he can be alone. Here, he is drying his dew-sodden mattress.

John had told me about a young couple who could be too chaotic for me to follow and engage with. Neither Amy nor Cornelius had a phone and so it took a chance encounter and introduction at a breakfast run for the homcless to start the talk. Amy was just out of hospital after impaling herself on a fence; Cornelius helped her through. They have been together almost four years. Over the next few days I would spend a lot of time with them, mostly at night when they would drink big bottles of White Storm cider. They describe trying to come off heroin as being "like the flu, but a thousand times worse". Living on the streets, their life is like a twisted game of musical chairs. For example, sleeping in the gap behind the solicitors' wall is no longer an option because they had just been chased from there. Later that day, Cor-

nelius finds an old mattress, and the new plan is to squat a vacant garage they spotted earlier. They talk openly about wanting the life most of us know. Amy would like to study psychology. "You can see people working and doing things with their lives, and I don't—that's what depresses me the most," she says.

These two are not used to a support system of any kind. A family member of Amy's turned her to heroin and prostitution when she was 14. The last night I saw them, they'd had a row. They'd downed three litres of White Storm in under 40 minutes. Amy, who is only 18, lost a child last year. She and Cornelius are both on methadone and each drinks three three-litre bottles of cider a day. Without the drink, they have morning shakes and wild sweats, distorted logic and a desperate struggle.

This was in The Meadows housing estate. A couple of weeks earlier, Nathan Williams, 17, was shot in the estate's shopping centre. It happened in broad daylight and witnesses say it was after an argument over a pushbike. Here one of his friends pays tribute by wearing her specially made "R.I.P Nathan" hoodie.

IN MEMORIAM

WORDS AND PHOTOS BY ALEX STURROCK

Published November 2006

For our Poverty Issue, we spent a week sleeping on people's floors in one of Nottingham's most rundown areas, Radford. Because of the lack of decent employment opportunities in Nottingham, crime has gone through the roof and it's estimated that crimes like burglary are FIVE times the national average. High-profile gun crime cases, where teenagers have been shot in broad daylight, have also added to the city's woes. At the time we went, house prices were down by 14 percent (the worst in the country). The hospital had a deficit of £20 million and forecast job losses of 1,300. Poverty doesn't just exist in far-flung places that celebrities visit to generate press for themselves. Sometimes it's just down the road.

This is the shrine family and friends made for Nathan at the spot where he was killed.

A detail from Nathan's shrine.

We met this girl in Radford the day before we went to The Meadows. She had a simliar tracksuit print to the girl who was a friend of Nathan, but this one was dedicated to her deceased niece.

ANDY JULIEN

SHREDDED BY WAR

BRITISH SOLDIERS ARE COMING HOME IN PIECES
WORDS AND PHOTOS BY STUART GRIFFITHS

Published October 2007

Andy Julien was 18 years old and had been serving in Iraq for two months with the Queen's Royal Lancers when his Challenger tank came under fire south of Basra. Andy and Lance Corporal Daniel Twiddy had been asleep on top of the tank when they were attacked. An eyewitness later told a Ministry of Defence board of inquiry that after "the boom of a heavy weapon and a bright flash of light" the tank became "an exploding ball of fire". Andy and Daniel were thrown to the ground, engulfed in flames. Two of their fellow soldiers were killed inside the tank on impact.

Now here's the really hilarious part: Andy's tank had come under fire from allied troops. This incident was caused by what was described in the inquiry as a "catalogue of errors". The laws of combat immunity protect the identities of those responsible for the attack, so nobody will be charged. In fact, Andy has heard rumours that since the incident, crew members of the tank that fired on him have been promoted.

After mistakenly informing his parents of his death, the Ministry of Defence flew Andy back to Broomfield Hospital in Essex. His mother and father did not initially recognise the swollen, bloody heap of flesh that they were told was their son. After 20 operations and six months in a wheelchair, Andy was medically discharged from the army without even the offer of a desk job.

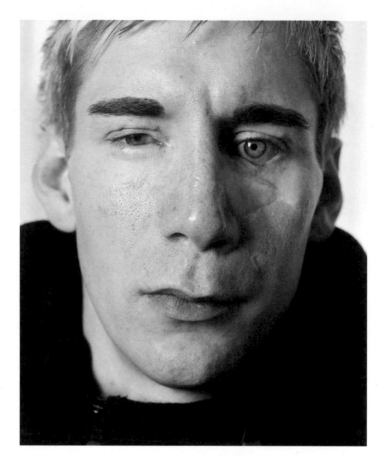

DANIEL TWIDDY

Five days into the war in Iraq in March 2003, Daniel Twiddy was blown off the top of a Challenger tank outside Basra by a round of friendly fire. It was a 120-millimetre high-explosive squash-head shell from another British tank. He remembers bursting into flames as a second round impacted on the turret of the vehicle, killing two of his colleagues. He also remembers being on his hands and knees, on fire, screaming during what he thought would be the last seconds of his life.

He awoke a month later in Broomfield Hospital, Chelmsford. His skin was burned over 80 percent of his body and there was a large hole in his face. He considers himself very lucky.

Daniel told *Vice*, "I've been a gunner myself and when you hit hard targets like tanks, it's unbelievable. 120-millimetre high-explosive squash-heads are designed to destroy bunkers. They fired two. That's how lucky I was.

"When I joined the British Army I respected the Ministry of Defence. I thought that it was their duty to support you through thick and thin. But when you're at the parade they have for graduation from training and they say, 'Not only is your son part of our family, you're all part of our family now,' it's bollocks—total shit. As soon as something like what happened to me occurs, they toss you aside like a number. They're not bothered about you. Physically, I can heal up. What hurts the most is that I've been left behind. I'll always remember what they've done to me. Friendly fire is something that should never have happened, so they should be looking after me. But they won't admit it. That's what makes me the most angry."

DAVID MCGOUGH

David McGough was one of the first British soldiers to arrive in Iraq. He was a lance corporal in the Royal Army Medical Corps at the age of 21.

David told us, "We medics did exactly what the other soldiers did—patrols and stuff. The difference with us is we saw the after-effects of war as well. We saw the casualties. We had to deal with the carnage and death and destruction." David would spend 17 hours a day dressing bodies that had been blown apart by shrapnel and ordnance, sewing the living dead back together, and watching others die. One incident in particular haunts him to this day. "There was a little girl about eight or nine. Her family had died. We were trying to do a nice thing by giving her water and bits of chocolate. One day we spotted a militia hanging her in an alleyway and we had to make the decision whether to go in and save her—which would have led to a riot and many more deaths—or just allow one person to die." In the end, she was hanged.

"When the militia left, we took her down and buried her. Most 21-year-olds are out getting drunk, but I've got that little girl on my conscience and I will until I die."

David was medically discharged after six months, with a diagnosis of post-traumatic stress disorder a year later. Once back home, his weight plummeted, he couldn't sleep, and he broke up with his girlfriend. He claims that his former colleagues were told not to speak to him. "I wouldn't go out of the house. There was no contact and everything was failing around me and I felt like shit. The nightmares would make me go into the bathroom, lock the door, and cry for hours."

David has since attempted suicide twice—once with a knife and once with a gun that misfired.

MARK DRYDEN

During his second tour of Iraq, in 2005, Mark Dryden was on a routine patrol. It was a Sunday. Fridays in Iraq are fairly quiet because everyone goes to mosques. Sunday, for Iraqis, is a fairly normal working day. But on this particular Sunday, it struck Mark that there was no one on the street.

Mark told us, "It was like the Iraqi people knew what was going to happen. The road we drove up is usually one of the busiest ones in Basra but there were no kids, no cars, nothing. Suddenly there were two explosions. The first one was in the engine block, and the second came through my door. It all happened in seconds, but everything slowed down from the point of the second explosion going off. I knew I was badly injured. I was sent back to the medical recovery station in a hotel nearby, where they can stabilise you and get you ready for the helicopter evacuation to the main hospital.

"I don't think that the British public have slagged the army off—they've slagged off the government for sending us. Now it's like, why are we still out there? Why are we still getting killed and injured? I'd already done fighting in Iraq in 2003. I've been to Bosnia, Kosovo, and done two tours of Ireland, but I was more scared to go back to Iraq in 2005 than I ever was in my life. I even changed my life insurance and made sure my will was bang up-to-date before I went out there. When I look back to Northern Ireland in the 1970s, Iraq seems very similar. I think we will be there for another ten or 15 years at least."

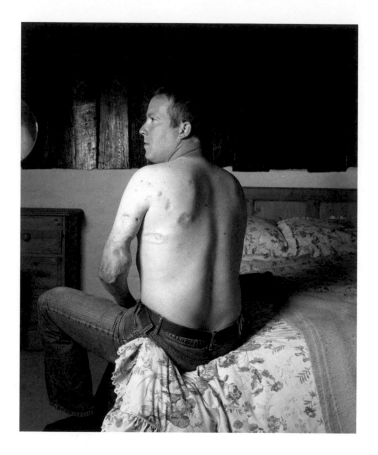

DAVE HART

Dave Hart had been with the Territorial Army for years when the call came through that there would be opportunities to serve in Afghanistan. He had already done a tour in South Armagh and really enjoyed it. It reaffirmed why he had joined in the first place. He readily signed up for Afghanistan.

Dave recalls, "The patrol that day was nothing out of the ordinary. There were four vehicles in line and I was in the first one, which was a stripped-down Land Rover. A suicide bomber had tried to get into Bagram US airbase, which was a few miles from us, but came to a vehicle checkpoint and decided to turn around. We had a couple of UN compounds down the road from us and he probably wanted to hit one of those, but he happened upon us instead. We were probably too much of a target to miss. I've been told that I was blown out of the vehicle. I don't remember it. The driver was killed instantly. My mate Dave was

in the passenger seat and lost his eye. I was on the ground, on fire. A couple of UN workers came over and doused me. My platoon sergeant flagged down a vehicle at gunpoint and threw us all in the back and got us to the multinational camp in seven minutes. I had already lost eight pints of blood. A couple more minutes and it would have been the end.

"The next time I came round was in Germany. That diamorphine is pretty good stuff. I was off my tits for a while before I fell into a coma for about two and a half weeks. I was there for two months and was then flown back to the UK and taken to Selly Oak in Birmingham. It was a real comedown—really piss-poor to be honest. I went from intensive care in Germany with six nurses to Selly Oak, where you're dumped in bed for three days, seen by a consultant, then cheers—off you go. And then I got MRSA, a lovely virus you can pick up in hospitals in the UK."

ANDY BARLOW

Growing up in Bolton, Andy Barlow always fancied the military. As soon as he was done at school he joined up. He was 16. He completed relatively safe tours in Afghanistan and Iraq but then, on his second tour of Afghanistan, the shit hit the fan. Andy and his fellow soldiers walked right into a minefield.

Andy told us: "One of our guys' right legs had been blown off halfway down a mountain trail. The lads went down to give medical support and someone got on the radio asking for a chopper. Our corporal, whose name was Pearson, walked backward and set a mine off that took his leg as well. I began to tourniquet him when two other soldiers joined me—my friend Mark Wright and a medic I didn't know. We waited for about an hour for a chopper to come and pull us out. When it finally came in to land, another mine was set off by a rock. That mine hit Mark badly. I was knocked back six feet with shrapnel injuries to my arm, and the medic had also been hit. I took a step toward Mark, and then another mine blew my foot clean off.

"Mark passed away in the Chinook. He was next to me on the helicopter floor in a body bag. I knew that I was going to get my leg amputated—the fact that we had been waiting so long meant that gangrene had set in. I flew back to the UK, straight into Birmingham Airport, where they took me to Selly Oak Hospital. At the time Selly Oak were not prepared for as many casualties as it was getting. One of my main problems there was being on the same ward as civilians. Civvies are the last people you want to see after something like what happened to me."

I WENT UNDERCOVER IN THE WORLD OF SYRIAN WHOREHOUSES

WORDS BY VICE STAFF | PHOTOS BY FALKO SIEWERT

Published November 2007

While I was in Damascus last summer, my friends from the Serbian Embassy took me to a brothel. It looked like a regular nightclub. It was well lit, music blared, and people hung out. I would not have thought: This is a place to buy sex. I got to talking with a group of Iraqi girls. I told them I was a "colleague from East Germany" on vacation. They were slathered with makeup and topped by massive, overstyled hair. They explained their situation to me: they fuck for 20 or 30 dollars. They are forbidden from leaving their shady hotels during the day—they aren't allowed out until they are picked up for work at 8 PM. Then they go to the club and, until dawn, alternate between sitting around and having sex with Syrian strangers. This is what their day is like, every day.

As we were talking, the club's manager entered the room and clapped his hands. This was the signal for all the girls to get onto the dance floor. I followed them. It felt like the right thing to do. The girls didn't really know how to do pole dances, so I hopped on to give it a shot. It was my first time on one, but I had been drinking and they kept on cheering, so I really let loose. Afterward, the manager approached me and asked me whether I would work at his club. He said he could see I had fun doing what I was doing and he liked that, and his clients liked that.

I wanted to see what I was worth in Damascus, so I agreed to meet his boss the next day. He wore a suit and had an air-conditioned, windowless office in a building on the other side of town. After offering me tea, he told me my strengths and weaknesses. He said that I was a bit old, but I wasn't too insulted, because many prostitutes in Syria are 12 to 14 years old. He suggested that I would be suitable for "rich and demanding Saudis with elevated desires". It was sort of awful, but I was flattered that he said I was "not for a Syrian who is only looking for an extra-marital fuck". The boss said he would offer me at an hourly rate of $400. The club manager asked, somewhat heatedly, for a 15 percent commission.

I never went back to this club, nor did I answer the phone when the boss rang, but I had the hook in me. It had been a dumb and callous adventure, but it had stirred something up. I wanted to visit more brothels.

On the following Friday evening, I went—this time with an Arab friend—to the discotheque in the basement of the Hotel Meridien. After my friend had met a few of the girls there, he confirmed that they were all Iraqi refugees. Some had been prostitutes under Saddam's regime, and some were there following the very dark, violent, inconceivable cataclysms that the war had brought into their lives. All of them were drunk to the point of staggering up and down the carpeted stairs under the weak, cheap disco lights.

I had a relentless train of Saudi men in dresses grabbing my ass. Much of the clientele in Syrian brothels is from Saudi Arabia. All of them were drunk and I was turning out to be the main attraction. My friend explained to one of them that he had booked me for the night, and then he asked the man and his friends if there were any other places we could go. They told us that there was a whole red-light district in the suburbs now and said we should just get into a taxi and ask to be driven to a northern suburb called Sednaya. We got out of there and hopped in a cab.

We drove through the dark streets of Damascus, passing by Palestinian refugee camps. We were under the impression of having left the city altogether, when a sudden boom of bright, multicoloured lights appeared on the horizon. It looked like Las Vegas. On each side of the road there were countless signs pointing the way to the "touristic clubs and restaurants", which seemed to be the official term for "whorehouses full of underage refugees". There must have been well over a hundred clubs there on this one strip of road. It was unreal. We started at one end of the street and worked our way down from club to club.

In each club we found a circular stage on which very young girls—children, really—circled throughout the night. Only a very few of them could walk in their heels. We asked some of the girls where they came from, and most of them proudly answered, "Iraq". Some of them were Palestinian refugees from Lebanon. To set themselves apart from the Iraqi girls, they wrote "Lebanon" in Arabic on their upper arms. Even among underage refugee prostitutes, the social hierarchies of their parents and grandparents live on.

The girls wear tight, padded push-up bras, tight polyester dresses, and thick, dramatic make-up. They are chaperoned by their mothers, who gather in the dark corners of the club and scope the crowd for clients. When a mother sees a patron she likes, she shines a laser pointer on her daughter, who then goes to the man her mother has picked. Phone numbers are traded, assignations made. In these clubs, where ten- and 12-year-old girls are whored out, open prostitution is not allowed. Later that night, the clients and the mothers speak on the phone to arrange a rendezvous.

In one club, a fast Arab dance came up and a girl with terrible wounds—burns and cuts on her arms—asked me to turn her round and round. I twirled her for a long time, and when I stopped, 15 or 20 girls had gathered like butterflies to a candle. They were all begging to be twirled. They wanted to be turned like mad until they could not handle it anymore. So I did it for them, until I noticed the red flickering of a laser pointer on my shirt. A mother had noticed a guest giving me the eye, and wanted to help me with my business.

In Wadeye, over half of the town's population is under 20 years old. Couple this with the fact that there wasn't a high school in town until a few years ago (even now, the attendance record for both primary and high school is under a third) and you have a lot of bored kids roaming the streets with fuck-all to do besides fuck about. The community's solution? Hire a "kid wrangler" who drives around town in a flatbed truck with a cage mounted on it, rounding up errant kids. When that didn't accomplish anything, they built a swimming pool and instituted a "No School, No Pool" policy. Things looked up for a while, but then the school began to burst at its seams. Teachers were breaking down and the classrooms were too small to cope with the influx of students who wanted to be able to swim. The new solution? Encourage less kids to come to school. Welcome to Wadeye.

ABORIGINAL HEADBANGING

**THE MOST METAL TOWN IN THE WHOLE WIDE WORLD IS WADEYE
WORDS AND PHOTOS BY JONATHAN WEST**

Published August 2008

We had been told that there had not been any gang violence for a few months in Wadeye but it didn't stop us from feeling somewhat apprehensive when we were invited to a party that every rival gang in the town was also heading to. Instead of fighting or huddling in their respective corners glaring at each other, each gang brought with them their favourite album from their respective band and handed it to the DJ upon entering. So when, for example, "Run to the Hills" kicked in, the entire Maiden gang rushed to the front lawn to play air guitar and mosh in front of the other gangs to prove their allegiance to their mob and band.

At the beginning of 2008, the Australian national news reported on a small, isolated Aboriginal community deep in the Northern Territory, aka the middle of nowhere, aka Satan's Asshole, aka East Bumblefuck.

Violent riots had erupted between two of the town's largest gangs and for a moment it looked like the Australian army (because there really is such a thing) was going to have to be brought in to settle the fighting. But what really blew us away was that the town, which is named Wadeye (pronounced "Wad-air"), was split up into gangs named after heavy metal bands. There were the Judas Priest Boys, the Evil Warriors, and the Slayer Mob. We immediately dropped everything else we were working on and embarked north from Melbourne to Wadeye to see it for ourselves. Nothing could have prepared us for what we found.

This guy was incredible. His name is Sebastian and although he is a member of the Judas Priest gang he claimed he didn't like heavy metal but preferred country music and rock and roll. When it was his turn to rock the dance floor all the gangs cleared the front lawn and he came out of nowhere and absolutely killed it. When his song was up he disappeared back into his house without saying anything to anyone, then shut the door.

These photos were taken inside the family house of two brothers from the Slayer gang. You can see how the walls are covered in graffiti. Aside from that there was absolutely nothing else in the rooms. No tables, chairs, couches, or even beds.

For a town so obsessed with music, it was strange that these five CDs were the extent of the music available in the only store. And like everything for sale in Wadeye, they were really expensive—almost twice what you'd pay in a bigger city. When we asked, most of the people told us they get their music from Darwin, a six-hour drive northwest of Wadeye.

The kids in Wadeye are amazingly friendly and confident. And they all fucking love metal.

INTERROGATIONS

In the last decade, almost every publication in the world has turned its attention to the tawdry world of celebrity, so much so that it is now possible to buy magazines that feature interviews with Jordan's old breast implants. There is also a blog written by Paris Hilton's tampons. We hate this facile world and hope that you do too. However, sometimes there comes a time when a famous person turns out to be really amazing. And so in this section we've interviewed some of our favourite ones, and included a couple of our favourite non-famous-people interviews as well. WARNING: contains no interviews with girl-band members, in-the-closet gay boy-band members, or prostitutes that had sex with a footballer once.

WERNER HERZOG

INTERVIEW BY ROCCO CASTORO | ILLUSTRATION BY TED PEARCE

Published September 2009

Interviewing Werner Herzog is a guilt-ridden experience. That's not to say he makes the questioner feel stupid or inferior, but there's still a lingering notion that he could be drafting a screenplay or producing a film in the time it takes to ask him about doing those things. He's written, produced, or directed (more often than not it's all three) more than 50 movies. And it's well known that he'd rather talk about what he's doing than what he's done.

Following that line of reasoning, this is not an interview that attempts to analyse Herzog's work. That's been done to death. If you want to know more about the specifics of his movies, watch them. And if you still want to sift through more anecdotes and thoughts on "ecstatic truth" and Klaus Kinski, pick up a copy of *Herzog on Herzog*.

At this point, we want to know more about how the man is capable of doing what he does at such a speed and sustained level of quality. In the past year he has completed two big-screen features with marquee actors for miniscule amounts of money (compared with the sums other directors and producers squander on what usually turns out to be inexcusable garbage). *Bad Lieutenant: Port of Call New Orleans* stars Nicolas Cage in a liberal reimagining of Abel Ferrara's 1992 scumbag cop saga, while *My Son, My Son, What Have Ye Done* is loosely based on a true story about a son who stabs his mother with an antique saber and features Willem Dafoe and Chloë Sevigny.

Somehow Herzog has figured out a way to beat Hollywood at its own game. If the soulless opportunists who make up the putrid core of the show business industry had real hearts and brains, they would just copy what he's doing instead of spending $200 million on movies based on action figures. But that doesn't look like it's going to happen anytime soon, so the best we can do is to ask him about the logistics of the film industry and how the hell he acquired such a voracious work ethic. Hopefully someone out there in la-la land is listening.

Vice: You've lived in Los Angeles for a while now, and your assertion that it has more substance than any city in the United States is one that puzzles lots of people. I think many assume that you've always had an antagonistic relationship with Hollywood.

Werner Herzog: I am never speaking of Hollywood; I speak of Los Angeles. But I have never been antagonistic with Hollywood either. For example, I am a great fan of Fred Astaire. Hollywood is a specific culture of cinema and has created very, very fine films. I'm just not part of the purely mercantile industrial production of cinema. It doesn't affect me. You see, I have never been at parties, I've never been to red-carpet events, I do not see the films. I see maybe two films a year, three films a year. Hollywood doesn't really have any relevance for me.

Even though you're not part of the system, would you say that living in Los Angeles makes it easier to deal with the business aspects of filmmaking?
It's not making anything easier. Filmmaking has always had its complications, but I'm not in the culture of complaint. Los Angeles is just a very exciting city. There's great excitement, there's vibrant culture, and there are a lot of things going on here that I wouldn't relate to filmmaking, but yet they trigger films. For example, I was fascinated by the *Galileo* space probe, which at the end of an incredible odyssey was sent on a suicide mission into the atmosphere of Jupiter, where it burned into superheated plasma and was gone. Only 30 minutes from where I live there is a mission-control centre in Pasadena, and because of this fascination with *Galileo* I found out that there was a completely unknown NASA archive in downtown Pasadena in a warehouse. I discovered footage of astronauts who filmed on 16-mm celluloid back in 1989, and it is such fantastic footage. In a way it was the backbone of a science-fiction film I made called *The Wild Blue Yonder*. So you see, the excitements are everywhere, and they don't have to be connected with Hollywood or production companies.

You've run your own production company since your late teens. How are your practices different from Hollywood's? Are actors and other people in the film industry taken aback by the way you run the show?

I'm always wearing the hat of a businessman—always. For example, I recently completed a film called *Bad Lieutenant*. I gave the guarantee that I would, as usual, stay on budget and hopefully under budget. In my entire life I've never gone over budget. Five times I've been under budget. Every single day I struggled to contain the amount of people that were being tossed at certain problems. I said, "No, it's not a question of having four or five more people edit. It's a question of intelligence. Let's not hire these people, let's forget about it." So what happened is that I delivered the film two days ahead of schedule and $2.6 million under budget. Now the main producer, Avi Lerner, wants to marry me [*laughs*]. These are people who have done nothing but very, very commercial films, including the last *Rambo*. I'm totally at ease with these people, because I think like a producer as well. For example, I waived my right to have a trailer, a camping trailer on the set... What do you call it? What's the expression for it in the industry?

I would just call it a trailer.

Whatever. I'm not even familiar with the terminology. But anyway, I waived my right to have a trailer, I waived my right to have a personal assistant, I waived my right to have a shopper, and I waived my right to have a chair with my name on it, which saved the production 65 bucks! But I hate those chairs anyway. I loathe them. I've never had a chair like that. They asked me, "But where are you going to sit?" I said, "I'm going to sit on a metal box or film magazines or anything that's around." Most of the time I would be standing anyway. And this isn't just a personal quirk of mine—it set an example for the whole production. Some of the actors—some of them very big stars—seeing that, would not arrive with an entourage of 12 but with an entourage of two.

I want to ask you about some of your earliest days in America. You received a scholarship to study at a place of your choosing in the US. You chose Pittsburgh but quickly abandoned the scholarship. Then you were taken in by a rural family called the Franklins. I get the feeling that this period was pivotal in the way that you use American imagery in your films.

Very much of what you see in my film *Stroszek* is a distant echo of that time. I saw the best of America then. Of course, once I had abandoned my scholarship, I lost all the money. I lost my guest family, and I lost my free passage back. I had to live on my own and was taken in by a wonderful family. That's what the spirit of America can be at its best. I'm forever grateful to the Franklins, but they represent more than just great hospitality. There's also a frontier spirit still in them, and that's something I really like about America. I also have some ambivalent feelings about America, but that's OK.

Shortly after your time in Pittsburgh, you went to New York and then Mexico because you were facing deportation from the US. That was one of the first steps in what was to become a long-standing association with Latin America in your work.

My Bavarian spirit somehow seems close to Latin America, in particular to Amazonian Latin America. I think there's an affinity to this exuberance of fantasy and fever dreams and imagination.

South America is where you've taken some of your greatest chances, and you've always commented on how important it is to take "calculated risks" as a filmmaker. But how do you personally calculate such perilous risks?

I always test things out on myself first. I'm good at assessing risks. However, I have to admit that one or two or three times I took risks that were just blind lottery. For example, in *La Soufrière* I filmed on top of a volcano that was about to explode. Nobody knew if it would happen in the next two minutes or the next two hours or the next two days. That film was *about* the expectation. Still, you shouldn't do things like that too often.

La Soufrière **is a good example of one of your many**

films where athleticism, or at least enduring very harsh and inhospitable conditions, was essential to the making of it. Are you worried about aging to the point where taking these types of risks and putting your body through these intense experiences are no longer possible?

No, I don't really care about that. The connection between athleticism and cinema is in part, of course, metaphoric. It's about the understanding of movement in space. That's why I admire NBA players so much—how they move and how they understand space is just phenomenal. Besides, it is a statistical fact that a good amount of filmmakers have been quite athletic people. You don't see that among painters or among musicians. I have never met a composer who was an athlete.

Another activity you recommend for aspiring filmmakers and other creative types is walking. Is that a hard thing to do in a place like California that's overrun with freeways?

Here you have to have a car, otherwise you can't function. But I'm not speaking of walking, per se. It's something else—travelling on foot—that I am talking about. Normally it means longer distances. It does not mean ambling around, it doesn't mean hiking, and it doesn't mean backpacking. What I mean is *really* travelling on foot. I can only say one simple dictum: The world reveals itself to those who travel on foot.

You've also said that cooking is a similar undertaking. What do you like to make for supper?

Oxtail, Spanish style. It's a complicated one. I would say once a week I cook a decent meal. Many filmmakers are also very good cooks, including Les Blank, Francis Ford Coppola, and others whom I know.

You're known for using the same cinematographers, cameramen, and other crewmembers throughout different phases in your career. How do you know when you want to work with someone new?

That's a difficult question, but I think it's like casting. You have to have it in you to see who will work right away, like, that's the right actor for this film, or this is the right cinematographer for that film. If you don't have it, you shouldn't be a movie director. It's a prerequisite of understanding your craft. I've done the last 12 or 14 or whatever films with Peter Zeitlinger, an Austrian cinematographer. However, I must say, doing films here in America like *Bad Lieutenant* and *My Son, My Son, What Have Ye Done* immediately limits the possibilities because you have to use union people in some areas, and many of the people with whom I end up working are not whom I would work with if I were shooting somewhere like Peru or Europe. There are not union men in those places. But it doesn't really matter. I always connect well with real professional people.

Do you think things like YouTube and other digital distribution systems will help break apart the bureaucracy of filmmaking?

Well, the whole thing is still in its infancy, and crude and uncouth. When it comes to YouTube, you get the lowest common denominator out there, but in certain segments of it you may find very high-calibre things in the future.

These types of immediate distribution methods are also increasing the usage of digital editing and cameras. The latter is something you've always been wary of, but didn't you just finish shooting *My Son, My Son, What Have Ye Done* on video?

Yes, I did, but that was for financial reasons. You can't make a film for around $2 million if you start shooting on 35-mm celluloid. I like to edit digitally because I work much, much faster. With digital editing you can work just as fast as you are thinking. But it has been a trap for some filmmakers who cannot decide quickly enough, and then they create 22 parallel versions and can't decide which one to take. I plow through material very, very quickly. For example, *Grizzly Man* was edited in nine days. I also wrote the entire commentary, recorded it, and did a primitive mix—all in nine days.

In *Grizzly Man*, like most of your documentary films, you provide the narration.

I grew into this somehow. In the old days I had the feeling that, yes, I should do it, because I wouldn't know of anyone who would be as credible as my own voice.

It does seem like the best person to narrate a documentary would be its maker.
It's a question of credibility, and I don't care how bad my German accent is. I make myself understood anyway.

Is the audience something that you actively think about when making your films?
I must confess that my audience has always been a big mystery to me. I do not know exactly who they are, or how they change, or how have I survived so many years with shifting audiences. The strange thing is that today I get more mail from young people—15, 16, 17 years old—than from people who are over 30.

That doesn't surprise me. I think younger people might even appreciate you more than your own generation does.
I really do not know. However, I never make films for myself. I never circle around my own navel. I've always made films for audiences, even though I do not know who they are.

You've said that people should not intellectualise film, but what about your writing? Is that a different matter?
Literature does not need to be analytic, but you're asking me this at the moment where the last thing that I published was *Conquest of the Useless*, which is based on the diaries that I kept when I made my film *Fitzcarraldo*. I think my writing will outlive my films. I will be starting my film school very soon, and I will make a point about a sense of literature for young people who want to step into filmmaking. One of the prerequisites will be that those who apply have to read this, this, and this.

It's amazing that you're starting a film school. Can you give me a sampling of what will be on your syllabus?
For example, Virgil's *Georgics*. They don't have to

read it in Latin, but there are some good translations around.

I just watched your debut film, *Herakles*, for the first time the other day. You've said that it was your one great "blunder".
Making that film was my way of going to film school. As a film it's not that important, but what is significant about it is that, at that time, I was wondering, "How can I connect materials that have absolutely nothing to do with each other and combine them into a coherent sort of story line?" Combining the unthinkable is how you create film sometimes. It was a wonderful experience.

Outside of filming some operas, you haven't made a short in quite some time. You also haven't produced anything for television in almost ten years. Today, there are more channels and more ways of watching TV than ever, but that hasn't seemed to increase the overall quality of programming. Do you still feel it's a valid outlet?
I hardly watch any television, but I hardly watch any films either. And sometimes you don't need to have big meaningful things on television. If you watch WrestleMania, it does not have a big, deep, plowing concept behind it; however, it is interesting to watch because you have to understand what is going on in the collective audience. As a poet, you must not avert your eyes. You have to understand in what sort of world you are living.

If I didn't know your views on the subject, I'd assume you're being ironic. You've said that you have a sort of communication defect in that you are unable to understand irony.
You have to make a clear distinction between humour and irony. And most of my films have a lot of humour in them, including even *Grizzly Man* and *Encounters at the End of the World*. And now just you wait for the real hilarious one—*Bad Lieutenant*.

I can't wait. There's been quite a bit of controversy around that film and no one's even seen it yet. Abel Ferrara, the director of the original

Bad Lieutenant, was outraged that you were doing what he considered to be a remake. But you steadfastly deny that it's a remake and claim to have never even seen the original.

I don't need to see the film that was made sometime in the 90s. Mine has a completely different story and a completely different setup. Basically what happened is that one of the people who had produced the first *Bad Lieutenant* held rights to the title, and they were hoping to establish some sort of a franchise. I don't mind, I can live with the title, but I always felt it had to be something else. I tried to call it *Port of Call New Orleans*, but I couldn't prevail. So now it's *Bad Lieutenant* and then it has the subtitle of *Port of Call New Orleans*.

And if I'm not mistaken, you did not write this one, which is sort of an anomaly when compared to your other films.

Yes, it is a screenplay by Billy Finkelstein. However, I changed a lot in it. I changed the entire beginning and the entire ending. I have made a lot of modifications. I threw a lot of sequences out and replaced them with sequences that I wrote myself. But I won't have any credit in the screenplay because the Writers Guild doesn't allow that.

What drew you to this movie?

Well, there were a couple of things that were immediately intriguing. Nicolas Cage and I all of a sudden realised that we had always somehow eluded each other, and that was very strange. Secondly, the prospect to make some sort of a film noir was intriguing, because film noir is always a consequence of deep depressions and the insecurity of the times. Classic film noir is a bastard child of the Great Depression, in a way.

And why do you say that your *Bad Lieutenant* is so funny?

Just wait and see.

The other film you've just completed, *My Son, My Son, What Have Ye Done*, is based on a nugget of truth about a man who stabbed his mother after

becoming obsessed with Sophocles' *Orestes*.

It's loosely based on a real murder case. A friend of mine who has worked with me a lot, who is actually a professor of classics at Boston University, wrote the screenplay together with me. It fell dormant for a while, and then I had a conversation with David Lynch and I mentioned, "We should make films—real fine feature films—but not for more than $2 million, and we'll still use the best actors and a great story. It's possible," I said, "and that should be the answer to the financial crisis." And he said, "Do you have something in mind?" I said, "Yes." And he said, "Well, I'd love to be on board as an executive producer." I started to work on it a few days later. Otherwise Lynch doesn't have anything to do with the substance of the film or the style of the film. He only read the screenplay, and he hasn't seen the finished film yet.

There were some rumblings about you making a film based on *The Piano Tuner*, the historical novel by Daniel Mason. Are you working on that right now?

No. That's a project that kind of fell dormant. Focus Features wanted to do it with me, and how shall I say... there was once an attempt to do a purely Hollywood version, but it never got off the ground. They asked me to do something that was closer to the book, so I wrote a screenplay where I changed a lot of the novel, and then they didn't find it Hollywood enough [*laughs*]. It was kind of contradictory. They didn't really know how to handle it, and I said, "Let's wait. Things have to fall in place easily, otherwise we'll constantly be struggling about this phrase or that phrase and this twist of the story and that twist of the story—it wouldn't be healthy like that."

What are you actively working on now?

I have five or six things, each a film project, pushing me. I may do more writing. I'm going to India fairly soon just to listen to a story of someone for eight days. But I don't know what's going to happen with that. And as I said, I'm starting my film school, which will basically be weekend seminars in various locations. But I will be my own film school. I'm not going to be affiliated with anything else.

TERRY GILLIAM

INTERVIEW BY NICK GAZIN | PHOTO BY ALEX STURRROCK

Published September, 2009

Terry Gilliam got his start being the most beloved guy in his high school and then he went on to do every job that anyone has ever fantasised about and to collaborate with everyone that anyone has ever wanted to meet or be. He worked for Harvey Kurtzman on Harvey's longest-running post-*Mad* attempt at magazining. He was in Monty Python and did all those animations and distinctive visuals. Then he went on to make really big, great, depressing movies like *Time Bandits, Brazil, 12 Monkeys, The Fisher King,* and *Fear and Loathing in Las Vegas.* Also George Harrison, aka the best Beatle, was his number one fan. Gilliam is a genius. I think that so many things have come easily to him that he has to make the most difficult-to-film movies possible just to keep from getting bored.

The person who was originally supposed to conduct this interview died or something while working on a story in Detroit, and I was called up at the last minute to fill in. I didn't have time to do research although I'd spent much of my formative years obsessing over Terry Gilliam. That obsession waned once I started obsessing over how to *be* Terry Gilliam. So this interview contains some of the stock content that you get when you talk to someone as famous as him, but I also wanted to know about how, for him, depression and hope relate to making creative work. I don't know if I did a good job or not. I didn't see his last couple of films. I hope he didn't hang up the phone and say to himself, "What a jackass."

Vice: I'd like to start with something that's near and dear to me. I love *Mad* magazine and I love Harvey Kurtzman, so I'd like to ask you about growing up reading *Mad* and your eventual work with Harvey.
Terry Gilliam: Well, *Mad* was THE magazine when I was a teenager so far as I'm concerned. It was so smart and so funny and so... troublesome.

It was fantastic—the bomb in the mailbox on the letters page.
Yeah, all that stuff was freeing. It was like, "Wow!" You couldn't wait for the next issue. And the art was brilliant. Jack Davis, Wally Wood, Willie Elder... It wasn't just destructive anarchy. It was really intelligent. They were brilliant at satirising whatever was going on in the world, whether it was other comic strips, television, or movies. It was a fantastic, funny mirror held up to the world. So I became a huge fan of it and started learning how to cartoon like those guys. Wally Wood's women were so sexy that I felt that it was possibly a form of pornography, and I used to hide the magazine from my parents because I felt guilty.

That's how you know it's great art. I remember seeing the first six issues. My dad had them. I forget when the first issue came out. '52? '51? But it's still edgy today. The sex and anger are all on the surface.
There was nothing else like it at the time, so there was nothing to compete with it. Every cartoonist I know from my generation was totally affected and influenced by it. Harvey became kind of a god for all of us.

You got to work for Harvey at *Help!* magazine along with Robert Crumb and some other greats.
It was after Harvey walked out of *Mad* and his other magazines, *Humbug* and *Trump*, came and went. *Help!* was the one that seem to develop a life of its own. I was in college at the time, and some friends and I took over the school's art and literary journal and turned it into a humour magazine. *Help!* was in many ways the model. Our magazine was called *Fang*.

You went to Occidental College in Los Angeles, right?
Yes. We started doing parodies of things like *West Side Story*. I sent a copy of our magazine to Harvey and he wrote back a nice letter and that was the end of it for me—I just had to go to New York and meet this guy. I wanted to be part of that world. I wrote him back saying that I was thinking of coming to New York after I graduated and he wrote back again saying, "Forget about it, there's nothing for you here, we're self-sufficient." And I said, "No, no, I'm coming."

Nice.
It was really funny, that summer I had been reading a book called *Act One*. It's the autobiography of Moss Hart. He was an incredibly successful playwright. His story was of a callow youth going to New York to meet his hero and ending up being his partner in writing—and that's what happened to me. I met with Harvey at the Algonquin Hotel, which at that point was famous for the round table where Robert Benchley and Dorothy Parker and all these brilliant wits hung out in the 40s. I went up and knocked on the door of his suite, and it wasn't Harvey in there, but Willie Elder and Al Jaffee and Arnold Roth. All of these cartoonists were busy working on the first issue of *Little Annie Fanny*.

Oh my God.
It was like walking onto Mount Olympus and there were the gods. Eventually Harvey turned up, and this is where luck enters the whole picture. The guy who was the assistant editor was quitting and they were looking for someone else to work for next to nothing. I was the kid standing there, and that's how it happened.

What's it like to meet and then work with someone you idolise?
Well, for one thing they come off their godlike-status pedestals and become real people. Harvey was so meticulous in the way that he worked. He was a great teacher, but he also gave me incredible freedom. One of the things we used to do was take

photographs or engravings and then caption them. I would spend ages down in the New York Public Library going through old photos and books. I learned so much—about art, about history—just by having to do this work. The magazine's staff was basically four people: Jim Warren, the publisher who we never saw, Harvey, myself, and Harry Chester, who was the production guy. Harvey would be up in his attic in Mount Vernon working away and I'd be down in his office administering with Harry Chester and his pasteup guys. Because I was the assistant editor of the magazine, all of these other young cartoonists were turning up in New York and hanging out with me. Whether it was Gilbert Shelton from *Fabulous Furry Freak Brothers* or Bob Crumb, we were all roughly the same age. I guess they thought I was more successful since I was the assistant editor of *Help!*, but I was getting paid $2 less a week than I would have if I had been on the dole. [*laughs*]

Help! is also where you met John Cleese, which kind of started you moving through the creative industries like a shark. I envy that a lot, for an artist in one lifetime to work and move through so many different fields and become masterful in them.
What I really wanted to be was a film director. That was the goal, but I had no idea how you got there. I grew up in the San Fernando Valley, and it was there dangling just over the hills. From the summer camps I worked at, I knew all of these Hollywood kids—Danny Kaye's daughter, Hedy Lamarr's son, Burt Lancaster's daughters. I was a counsellor at the camp while I was working my way through college. Hollywood was so close, but I just couldn't see how you worked up through a system like that.

But you did start building connections to that world through Help!
Because of the fumettis—

We should just say, for those who don't know, that fumettis are comics that use photographs.
Right. And we needed actors for them. I would go down to theatres in the Village. We were only paying

$15 a day, but I kept meeting people through that. I met Cleese and Woody Allen that way.

Making fummetis must have taught you things that came in handy later, doing TV and then film.
I produced the fumettis by organising locations, costumes, and actors. I learned an awful lot. The thing about Harvey was that he always wanted to be a director, so the cartoons in *Mad* were very filmic. He used the frames like a camera.

What did you do after Help! folded?
I hitchhiked my way across Europe. When I was coming back from Turkey and I didn't have enough money to return to the States, I stopped in Paris. I went to see a friend who was editing a magazine there and asked for a job so I could get money to go home and he said, "OK, I want you to fill up two pages with as many jokes as you can about snowmen." And so I sat in this tiny little hotel room in Paris freezing my ass off drawing snowmen, and it got me enough money to get a plane ticket. When I got back I didn't have any place to stay but Harvey's attic. [*laughs*] It was grand, it was a great time.

Wow. And when you got back, was that when John Cleese asked you to do animations for Monty Python?
No. After living at Harvey's for a bit I moved to LA. Do you remember Joel Siegel, the film critic on *Good Morning America*? He was one of my best friends then, and he and I did a book called *The Cocktail People*. I think it made me 12 and a half dollars, but it did lead to Joel getting me a job at an advertising agency called Carson/Roberts. They invented two things: the smiley face and the phrase "Have a happy day". That's what the receptionists would say when you called. They inflicted that on the world. Joel and I worked there for a year, and when I'd had enough of it I wanted to move back to Europe since I had fallen in love with it. I was living with an English girl at the time, so the two of us came to London and I worked in magazines there for the better part of a year. Cleese was the one person I knew there, so I called him up one day. John, by then,

231

was very well known on television there. I asked him to introduce me to someone in television since I wanted to get out of magazines. I met a producer who was working on *Do Not Adjust Your Set*, where Mike Palin, Terry Jones, and Eric Idle were writing and performing. The producer was an amateur cartoonist. He liked my cartoons and he bought a couple of written sketches from me. So I was thrust upon the other three, much to the chagrin of Mike and Terry. Suddenly I was in that group, and when I did a cartoon for them, that was the beginning of the connection.

Was it an animated cartoon?
Yeah. Basically what happened was Eric and I became good friends and we started working on another show called *We Have Ways of Making You Laugh*. There were five or six of us who would sit around as the core group. I was the cartoonist. A guest would come on the show, I would finish off a caricature of them, and at the end the camera would mix to my drawing of the guest. One week I suggested doing an animated film. They gave me two weeks and £400 to make it. The only way to do that was to simply cut out the drawings and move them around.

So your famous stop-action collage style was a financial necessity at first.
No one had ever seen anything like that on television before, and overnight I became an animator. [*laughs*] That started a second season of *Do Not Adjust Your Set*. There were six of us then, and that became Python.

Talking about Monty Python is almost hard for me because it was such an omnipresent thing in my life at certain points.
Ah, another victim.

Every year there's a kid in every middle school doing the dead-parrot sketch. It just never goes away. Kids who don't fit in always discover Monty Python.
You know what's funny is that in the States they seem to start discovering it around 11 years old.

That seems like such a young audience for it. But they suddenly bump into Python and I think the absurdity of the whole thing gets them going.

That's when I got into it. I didn't like what was popular culture at the time and Python made sense to me.
That's what's interesting about Python—on one hand it's very intelligent and erudite stuff and on the other hand it's completely silly and juvenile. So it always appeals to smarter kids or more anarchic kids who have difficulty with authority. We were those people and we seem to pass on that attitude to new generations.

So yeah, I don't know what to ask because I know so much about Monty Python. [*laughs*] Maybe it's been talked about too much.
There's so much that's been written about it. When we are interviewed there's kind of a set thing we say. I don't recall the nightmares and the terrible times. I only remember the good bits. It was a very special time because the BBC was so laissez-faire. Once they said "yes" we could just get on with it.

I don't think that really happens anymore.
Well, you've got *The Simpsons* and *South Park*, and thank God for *Family Guy*, which is wonderful. Anyway, the BBC was an old and lazy organisation that just let things happen, but now it's become terribly bureaucratic. It's full of executives. It's almost like a Hollywood studio. There are so many people making a living managing and making decisions and passing the buck down. When we were there, the producer would be given the go-ahead, there would be the money, and you would just do it.

Since Monty Python has been covered as covered can be, let's move on. I rented your first feature film, *Jabberwocky*, from my public library expecting it to be Pythonesque, but I got something a lot different.
It was my escape from Python—or semi-escape, because you have Mike playing the lead character and Terry Jones in there too. People kept trying to sell it

as a Python film, which was a big mistake.

Movie-marketing people are fucking assholes. I live in New York and when you're walking down the subway platform, every movie poster just gives you less and less of an idea of what the movie is about. They're ugly and vague and bland.
You just get the two faces of the stars. What I used to love, I used to collect these old Polish movie posters. They were abstract and beautiful and they make your brain spin a bit.

So *Jabberwocky* had a big effect on me. It confused and upset me as a 13-year-old. It was funny and scary. The ending was not one that a teenager would have expected. And that made me think about you as a teenager. You were popular in high school. Weren't you the homecoming king?
I was very popular. I was a letterman, student-body president, homecoming king, and valedictorian. I was perfect as a human being. But none of it made any difference to me.

I wonder if being so popular back then helped you to be quick to make friends and connections in your career. I mean, being well adjusted couldn't hurt.
But I was always just creating my own little world. An outsider's view could have been like, "Boy, he must have been networking a lot." No. I've always been gregarious and I genuinely like people until they say no to my ideas and projects, and them I hate them and I want to kill. [*laughs*]

Still, you're so lucky to have not had to do a "real" job all your life.
The last proper job I had was on the assembly line at the Chevrolet plant in Sacramento Valley on the night shift when I was working my way through college. I just hated it. The repetitive nature of it, the stupid dumb mechanical nature of the eight hours I had to spend there every day. At the same time, I could look down the line and see that the other guys were quite happy putting their eight hours in. They got their pay and went home to their wives and families and that's

what they were happy to do. And then it also made me crazy working in an advertising agency; I felt like I was trapped in a bureaucracy. That kind of stuff is what led to *Brazil*, which was the catharsis against all of the jobs and situations I had found myself in and was angry about. The rest of the time I was just enjoying what I was doing, playing and cartooning. I could actually draw things and make these worlds. I think that was the difference. With a pen and a piece of paper I've got control of the world, in a sense. I think that's why a lot of writers get on. They may be solitary figures but they're not unhappy figures. Just give them a piece of paper and they start putting the words down. That's how you get through the mess that life is.

Would you say that you get bored easily?
I can get bored quite easily but then I get to doing something because I can't stand it. I occupy myself instead of going into a depression.

You just channel your positive energy?
Yeah, though it gets harder as you get older because it's easier to get bored. Things are less surprising. But, being visually excitable, I can sit and look at something and be amazed at, like, a wood carving over here or the shade on this lamp. Taking in the world around me and enjoying it on a visual level gets me through a lot of the boring moments of life.

Do you get depressed, though?
I get depressed a lot. I spend a lot of time being depressed. Rather than fighting it, I just go with it. I let the depression take me down to the bottom of the pit. When there's no lower to go, then suddenly you start crawling back up.

Sometimes a person who can confront depression and the grim aspects of life doesn't like other people. They don't want to talk to anyone, much less worry about selling an idea to a producer or an agent.
You're probably right. But I actually do like people. I'm not frightened by them and they surprise me. And also, talking to you now or talking to a group of

people, I'm slightly different from who I really am. I'm outside of myself, performing. Then I go back home and my wife gets to see the truth.

I can relate to that. And when you're by yourself and deprived of stimulus it's just you and your thoughts.

But actually that's one thing that I'm fighting for so much now. Because of Facebook and Twitter and all this crap, people don't have time to be alone and confront themselves and who they really are. It's the thing that really worries me the most about the modern world. People just seem to be extensions of a social order now. We have a house in Italy with no telephone or television. My son would be there, and he was used to playing his video games and blah, blah, blah, and he'd go there and get bored. My wife would say, "Well, we have to do something to keep him entertained," and I'd say, "No, let him get bored and you'll see what happens." After about two days of boredom and saying "There's fuck all to do here," he started inventing things. He was creating a really interesting world, because he was involved in creating it. He wasn't just having it created for him. I think so much of what we do is now done for us. It's digested, it's handed to you. I like video games but I also think they're dangerous because of how much time and energy they consume. It's not the same as reading a book.

You also read a book at your own pace, while TV and video games keep going even if you stop.

[*laughs*] Exactly. Then you're filled with this terrible feeling like [*sinister voice*], "They don't need you." Another thing is this: My son had the Tony Hawk video game and he was brilliant at it. Then he started skateboarding and he realised that it actually hurts. And this is what bothers me about so many of these video games. They've removed that element of pain. You just sit there and you watch your life force go down, but you're not experiencing pain. You're sat there flipping through the air, and then you try to go out and do it in the real world and: "Ouch!"

After *Jabberwocky*, you made *Time Bandits*, a

movie that I loved a lot as a child. It sits in my mind along with Jim Henson's *Labyrinth*. I wanted to watch it over and over again. It's also one of your most positive films even though it has a lot of scary elements. I mean, the main character's parents die in the end!

Part of it is the journey of a kid who has a lot of heroes. He goes through history meeting them, and he realises that they are not quite what he thought they were—not quite so heroic—and ultimately he earns the right to stand on his own two feet. His parents should be listening to him as opposed to ignoring him.

It's a common theme in comics, too, like in *Batman* and *Superman*. Kids secretly want to kill their parents and be free of the restrictions they put on them. Anyway, just thinking about *Time Bandits* now makes me happy. And George Harrison was involved in the film. He was my favourite Beatle. I don't want to get off topic here, but can I ask you what George was like?

He wasn't the quiet Beatle, which most people thought he was. He was very funny and outspoken. "Sardonic", I think, is the word. He was quite wicked and he was a great gardener. He spent the last 20 years of his life tending 37 acres of one of the greatest gardens in the world. He was spiritual but he could joke like the best, and he was the number-one Python fan.

Amazing.

George was a special guy. You don't meet many like him because his feet were so firmly on the ground even though his head and his heart were floating high.

***Time Bandits*, to me, has a happy ending. The main character ends up free of his parents and I can imagine his adventures continuing. I also liked that Sean Connery, who played King Agamemnon earlier in the film, turns out to be a fireman at the end.**

Connery wasn't supposed to be there at the end. He was supposed to die when they have the big battle with Evil—all of these archers were going to turn up and Evil gets turned into a pincushion. Connery was supposed to be leading that group, and then he was supposed to be crushed by a falling column. But we'd run out of time with him. We only had X number of days with Connery, so I had to kill the character Fidgit instead, which was a better idea anyway.

Even though it gutted me when I was a child.

So there was a point when I didn't quite have the ending of the film sorted out. I remember talking to Sean, and he had suggested that Agamemnon come back as the fireman. He was in tax exile, so he was just in London for a day on the way to his accountant when we grabbed him for literally an hour and got two shots of him, including the one in which he winks at the main character. It wasn't until a month or two later that I actually wrote the scenes around that. Films write themselves, ultimately.

Happy accidents. So *Time Bandits* ends with a hopeful note and *Brazil* ends with no hope—

That's where you're wrong. That was my altruistic ending! That was my happy ending! [*laughs*]

I guess I never saw that before. [*laughs*]

It goes back to what I was saying earlier about inventing my own world. That's what I did at the end of Brazil. Sam is inside his imagination, and he may be mad, but who gives a fuck? He's created a world that's satisfying to him. The outside world can't get at him and that, to me, is happiness. Now, today, in the modern world, this idea of somebody being alone, being separate from their peers, is frightening. But to me that's liberating.

Brazil does feel like a pretty scary and dark film, though.

There's a lot of badness out there, and *Brazil*, while I wouldn't say it was totally cynical, was getting that way. I just dumped my anger and all the bad things in the world on the screen to get them out of my life. But there must be far more altruism than not in the world. Otherwise we'd all be dead. I'm assuming that altruism is 51 percent of the world and the other 49 is shit. [*laughs*]

So we're more good than bad?

Yeah, we have to be. Otherwise wouldn't we all be gone?

It's nice to hear you say that.

Well, I think you have to believe that. When I left America I was so angry about what was going on in the late 60s that I wanted to start throwing bombs. I was just like, "There are a lot of shits out there and they all should die." So I actually left America because I thought I would probably make a better cartoonist than a bomb maker. I stayed with what I was good at.

You recently renounced your citizenship and now you can't come back for more than 30 days a year.

I punished myself for betraying my country. [*laughs*] No, I decided that I've been here in the UK for 42 years now. I thought, "Come on, stop pretending." But the real reason—the one that finally tipped the balance—was when I discovered that when I die, the American tax authorities would have assessed everything I own in the world and taxed me on capital gains for 40 percent or whatever it was. My wife would literally have had to sell the house in London to pay the death duties to America, a country I haven't lived in for 42 years. So I said, "Fuck this, time to say goodbye."

I've heard that there were serious production difficulties on *Brazil* and *Baron Munchausen*.

Filmmaking is really hard. I've had more books written and documentaries made about my difficulties than other people have, so everyone thinks I've had it worse. I haven't, though—I'm just more public and I like the idea of bursting the bubble about the joy of filmmaking. With *Brazil*, 12 weeks into the shoot I realised it was going to be a five-hour movie and we'd be millions and millions over budget. So I stopped shooting for two weeks and tore pages out of the script. I finished the film and then Universal decided it was unreleasable. Luckily I didn't have a Hollywood agent to calm me down, so I went to war and—surprise, surprise—the film was released. Nobody had ever done anything like what I did: take out a full-page ad in *Variety* with a little black frame surrounded by empty white with a letter in the middle saying, "Dear MCA President Sidney Sheinberg, when are you going to release my film *Brazil*? Signed, Terry Gilliam." That's just not done in that town. It created a lot of shit, but it was good fun. [*laughs*]

You get away with a lot of things that would get other people blacklisted.

That's because I don't have a career. Other people think in terms of a career, but the minute you start thinking like that you've already compromised yourself. I just do one thing at a time, and that one thing will be the most important or even the only thing in my life at that time. So fuck it. Until we get the movie out, the battle is on. [*laughs*]

***Brazil* is full of huge buildings that look like tombstones, much like the building at the beginning of *Monty Python's the Meaning of Life,* which are just imposing and horrible monsters.**

I think that comes from me living in New York for several years with no money. The place overwhelmed me, the scale of it, with humanity seeming very small in comparison—living and working in these great monolithic buildings with all these people trapped inside.

Let's talk about *The Adventures of Baron Munchausen*. I loved it but other people didn't.

I know. But *Munchausen* has come into its own over the years. And when it came out it got the best reviews that Columbia Studios had seen since *The Last Emperor*. But the company was in the process of selling itself to Sony and so they basically didn't release the film. They put it out in 52 cinemas and I think they went wide with 172 prints. That's all they ever made. It's very hard to judge how it would have done had it been distributed properly. It was sort of my *Magnificent Ambersons*, if you know Orson Welles's stuff. It was my comeuppance because I beat the system on *Brazil* and the system was going to beat me this time around. I really felt that.

It's another movie like *Time Bandits* that's so full of neat ideas. It's beautiful.

Kids loved that film because it was like a storybook. The kids would come out of the cinema dancing. And musicians loved it, artists loved it, theatre people loved it. I wanted to do a series of ads because I had all of these quotes from people like Pete Townsend from the Who. He said, "A fucking masterpiece." George Harrison and all of these guys wanted to rave about the film. There's a Blu-ray version of it that just came out this year, on the 20th anniversary of the film. So obviously over a longer period of time it's been appreciated. It's like a good wine—you have to lay it down for a few years.

A few years later *The Fisher King* came out. I saw it when I was 14 and I don't remember much about it.

You were the wrong age. Appreciating a film has a lot to do with the age at which you see it. *Fisher King* was a huge success among 20- to 30-year-olds. It was for people in love or people wanting to be in love with the possibility of being in love.

Who was in it?

It starred Jeff Bridges and Robin Williams. It was basically Jeff's movie, but Robin got nominated for a Golden Globe and won an Oscar for it. Mercedes Ruehl also got the Academy Award for her work in it. Richard LaGravenese wrote the script and I thought it was wonderful. I understood all of the characters in it. It was his first script and he had written it on spec. The studio had it and they kept trying to change it into a robbery caper. But it was about stealing the Holy Grail! It was absolutely bullshit what they were trying to do. Then they got me on board because I could get Robin and they wanted him.

And then there was *12 Monkeys*.

That was another great script. David Peoples wrote that. We moved it through the studio system by getting Bruce Willis and Brad Pitt on board. We were shooting during the moment when Brad became a superstar. We were working and no one was bothering us and then *Legends of the Fall* came out and we had to have security everywhere. It was just extraordinary to watch.

Everything looks so great in that movie. All the set design and the machines, that big tube you shove down Bruce Willis's throat. The animals moving around the abandoned city. It's just beautiful.
I have a hard time making things look ugly even when they are. [*laughs*] Even if it's some rotting corpse, I still find beauty in that. It's very hard for me to make something look truly ugly. *12 Monkeys* went smoothly. It was a nice chance to get Bruce and Brad to play opposite what they were usually cast as, and Madeleine Stowe was just wonderful. It was a simpler movie without a lot of special effects, but the animals running around Philadelphia were still a lot of fun.

And now you've got a movie coming out soon called *The Imaginarium of Doctor Parnassus*.
Wait, you missed *Tideland*. Have you seen *Tideland*?

No. I didn't see it. I'm sorry.
OK, well go see *Tideland* first just to punish yourself. It's one that divides people completely. Some of them get so angry with that movie. And when they get angry they don't shout and scream—they just pretend that it never happened. [laughs]

I also didn't bring up *Fear and Loathing* or *The Brothers Grimm*.
Those are classics in their own time and they will be discovered one day if we live long enough.

But hold on—how do you feel about *Tideland*?
I think it's great. Wonderful. I was doing something that I thought might spark a controversy or a dialogue or an argument—putting a young girl in what could be deemed jeopardy, into a very strange and disturbing experience. I thought it would get people screaming, but it didn't. I thought, "Oh my God, what has happened to society that they can't get angry about something that's worth arguing

about?" That was the disappointment with *Tideland* for me.

Do you want to tell me about your new movie at all?
Well I just went to Comic-Con and told 4,000 people how it's going to make their lives worth living.

"Go drop $10 if you want to live."
Yeah, that's it. Don't drop acid, drop dollars. And so many people have walked out of screenings of this movie saying things like, "I'm still tripping." By any measure this film shouldn't have been finished at all. This goes back to my argument about altruism and love in the world. Heath Ledger died in the middle of the shoot and so far as I was concerned, there was no way we could carry on without him. But I was surrounded by people who just would not let it go, who said that the film must go on, it must be finished for Heath's and for everybody's sake. So I called up Johnny Depp and he said, "Whatever you need, I'm there." Then we got Jude Law and Colin Farrell. They all came in and took over Heath's part. We ended up with three other actors to finish the part that Heath began. I think that says a lot about love and goodness.

And about being able to see past failure and keep going and improvising.
Yes. I was in my giving-up state when my daughter, who was a producer on the film and my cinematographer, just said, "No, you don't get out of it that easily. Go back to work." And that's the good thing about my films: They always have a magic quality. And that saved the day.

I'd just like to thank you for inspiring me as a teenager, and thanks for inspiring me right now. It was good talking about hope and art.
I think they go together. That's what the creative thing is about. Keep reinventing the world, keep making it worth living in—if only for yourself and nobody else.

We're all in it together.
I know. [*laughs*] I love that.

DAVID SIMON

INTERVIEW BY JESSE PEARSON | ILLUSTRATION BY TED PEARCE

Published December 2009

David Simon is responsible for one of the greatest feats of storytelling of the past century, and that's the entire five-season run of the television series *The Wire*. If that sounds like hyperbole to you, then you haven't watched the show yet. It is the most intricate web of character, motivation, insight, action, repercussion, and emotion that's ever been on TV, and it rivals the grand novels of the late 19th century, when novels actually, regularly, had scope. More hyperbole, but there you go. I and most of its fans are to *The Wire* as a Christian is to Christ or a junkie is to dope. It's basically A FUCKING GOD. Too much hyperbole there, maybe. But you're getting the point, right?

Before *The Wire*, David Simon was a reporter at the *Baltimore Sun*. During his time there, he wrote two meticulously researched and richly human books about his city. *Homicide: A Year on the Killing Streets* (1991) was the result of a year spent with the murder police of a town where murder seems to be a major mode of employment. *The Corner: A Year in the Life of an Inner-City Neighborhood* (1997, with writing partner Ed Burns) was the result of a year spent among the families, addicts, and dealers of one of Baltimore's more infamous drug corners. *Homicide* resulted in the long-running cop show *Homicide: Life on the Street*, which was cool and everything, better than most cop shows, but also kind of just a cop show. *The Corner* resulted in an HBO miniseries that was pretty much a direct antecedent to what *The Wire* would end up tackling.

After *The Wire*, Simon and Ed Burns, who is a for-mer Baltimore cop and schoolteacher, adapted Evan Wright's book *Generation Kill* into an HBO miniseries. It stands as the most effective document yet produced on the daily reality of the life of marines in the current Iraq war.

And now, today, as I type this, Simon is filming his new HBO series down in New Orleans. It's called *Tremé*, and it is said to take as its centre the lives of local musicians. But I have a feeling that would be like saying that *The Wire* took as its centre the Baltimore drug trade. Sure, it started there. But given Simon's obsessions with the American city and the decreasing institutional value of life in this great country of ours, we're pretty much guaranteed that *Tremé* will have the same reach and impact as *The Wire*. In other words, I wish I could be cryogenically frozen until the day this show debuts, because I can't fucking wait.

Simon recently spoke with *Vice* from the *Tremé* production offices in New Orleans. This is the longest interview we've ever run by a long shot, but come on. It's the guy who made *The Wire*. You're lucky the entire issue isn't about him.

Vice: I don't know if the people who set this interview up for us related this anecdote to you, but you and I actually had an interesting run-in last year. I was waiting to get into a Pogues show at Roseland in New York City and—
David Simon: The fucker who cut the line. Yeah.

Exactly.
The guy with Secretary of State's Disease.

That's the guy. I was right next to you, right ahead of you. I'd noticed it was you after I realised that multiple strangers were coming up to the guy behind me and saying things like "Thanks" and "I love your work." Then I looked behind me and saw a *Homicide: Life on the Street* Season 5 jacket and was like, "Fuck. That's David Simon." Next thing I knew some guy was cutting in front of us and you unleashed on him. You asked him if he thought he was the Queen of England.

Well, just don't cut the line. You know? I found that guy afterward.

Did you really?
Yeah, after we got our tickets I walked past him. We were both going to be on time for the concert. That was the thing. I said to him, "Was it worth it?" He just eye-fucked me.

He didn't seem to really understand.
Then later on we were both backstage after the show.

Oh, really? What was he, some kind of record-label guy or something?
I don't know who he was, but it was crowded back-stage, and I was back there to say hi to the people I know in the band. The last thing I wanted to do was to make it about me or him. So I wasn't going to pursue it. I was very scrupulous about not carrying it on with him then, but yeah, when I passed him before the show began, I was like, "You're in. I'm in. The people who were behind me are in. What the fuck?" I hate that shit. I'm a little embarrassed about how profane that moment got, but hey. Shit happens.

I loved it. I was like, man, he really fucking walks it like he talks it. I was happy.
I didn't fight the guy or anything. I wasn't going to swing first. That wouldn't have been right.

Well, I had your back.
And I also would have ended up getting thrown out of a concert that I had—

A good reason to be at. Right. So I've always been curious about the way a season of *The Wire* would be structured before shooting. Can you outline, even really roughly, the process of scriptwriting?
There would be a series of planning sessions. First, at the beginning of every season, we did a sort of retreat with the main writers, the guys who were going to be on staff the whole year. We'd discuss what we were trying to say, but we were really having a current-events/ideology/political argument. The

writers didn't all think the same. We weren't in lock-step on the issues of the day, whether it was the drug war or public education or the media. So we had to discuss the issue as an issue first. Never mind the characters, never mind plot.

A lot of the people who came to write for *The Wire* were not from a traditional TV-writing background.
If there's anything that distinguishes *The Wire* from a lot of the serialised drama you see, it was that the writers were not from television. None of us grew up thinking we wanted to get to Hollywood and write a TV show or a movie. Ed [Burns] was a cop, and then he was a schoolteacher. There were journalists on the writing staff. There were novelists. There were playwrights, too. Everyone began somewhere else.

That probably made all the difference.
Well, we weren't cynical about having been given ten, 12, 13 hours—whatever we had for any season from HBO. All of that was an incredible gift. *The Godfather* narrative, even including the third film, the weak one, is like... what? Nine hours?

Yeah, about nine hours.
And look how much story they were able to tell. We were getting more than that for each season. So goddamn it, you better have something to say. That sounds really simple, but it's actually a conversation that I don't think happens on a lot of serialised drama. Certainly not on American television. I think that a lot of people believe that our job as TV writers is to get the show up as a franchise and get as many viewers, as many eyeballs, as we can, and keep them. So if they like x, give them more of x. If they don't like y, don't do as much y.

Right. Between seasons of a lot of hit shows, adjustments will be made that are clearly based on network notes about what's perceived to be most popular with viewers.
We never had that dynamic in our heads. What we were asking was, "What should we spend 12 hours of television saying?" And that's a journalistic impulse. That was coming from the *Wire* writers who were journalists and, to an extent, the novelists who wrote for the show who write in a realistic framework, like researched fiction. People like Pelecanos, Price, and Lehane.

Those three guys seemed to have the perfect backgrounds to bring a lot of valuable stuff to *The Wire*.
It wasn't like we were putting Isaac Bashevis Singer on staff. I love his stuff, but we were looking for novelists who were doing researched fiction, and particularly in an urban environment. I'm also not mistaking *The Wire* for journalism. I have too much respect for journalism to make such a statement. But the impulse, the initial impulse behind doing the show? It was the same reason somebody sits down to write an editorial or an op-ed.

To make a statement or to sound an alarm.
Yeah: "Shit's going wrong. Here's where I think it's going wrong. Here's what I think might make it right." That impulse was the same in *The Wire* writing room as it would be at the editorial board of a good newspaper.

"Good" being the operative word there. I don't want to reduce *The Wire* to one big theme, but would you say that a major thrust of the series was the idea of institutions versus individuals?
Yeah, that permeated it. One of the things we were saying was that reform was becoming more and more problematic as moneyed interests—capitalism, which is sort of the ultimate Olympian god—become more entrenched in the postmodern world. Reform becomes more and more problematic because the status quo is arranged in such a way as to maximise profit and to exalt profit—particularly short-term profit—over long-term societal benefit and/or human beings.

Which is kind of the classic problem that comes up with capitalism and industry.
But I'm not a Marxist. I am often mistaken for a Marxist.

Oh, no, I wouldn't guess that about you. I think of

you as being, besides a writer, more of a critic and an observer.

It's one thing to recognise capitalism for the powerful economic tool it is and to acknowledge that, for better or for worse, we're stuck with it and, hey, thank God we have it. There's not a lot else that can produce mass wealth with the dexterity that capitalism can. But to mistake it for a social framework is an incredible intellectual corruption and it's one that the West has accepted as a given since 1980—since Reagan. Human beings—in this country in particular—are worth less and less. When capitalism triumphs unequivocally, labour is diminished. It's a zero-sum game. People paid a much higher tax rate when Eisenhower was president, a much higher tax rate for the benefit of society, and all of us had more of a sense that we were included. But this is not what you really want to talk about, I know.

Well, no, I do want to talk about this. It isn't technically about writing, but it's very relevant to your writing.

I guess what I'm saying is that the overall theme was: We've given ourselves over to the Olympian god that is capitalism and now we're reaping the whirlwind. This is the America that unencumbered capitalism has built. It's the America that we deserve because we let it happen. We don't deserve anything better. *The Wire* was trying to take the scales from people's eyes and say, "This is what you've built. Take a look at it." It's an accurate portrayal of the problems inherent in American cities.

Absolutely.

Are there other parts of those cities that are economically viable? Of course. You can climb higher up on the pyramid that is capitalism and find the upper-middle-class neighbourhoods and the private schools. You can find where the money went. But *The Wire* was dissent because of its choice to centre itself on the other America, the one that got left behind. That was the overall theme and that worked for all five seasons. So that's the institution versus the individual.

It seems that wrapping up these commentaries on

American society within fictions might be the only way to get a lot of people to engage with problems like poverty and drugs and the disappearance of industry. Have you seen the messages in *The Wire* resonate for viewers beyond the level of entertainment?

No. I think that some people got it and they may react differently the next time some shit-spitting politician shows up to say that with a little bit more of a business base and more cops and more lawyers we can win the war on drugs. There may be a little bit more dissent on some of the points we hit the hardest. But I don't believe that a television show or, for that matter, even the systemic efforts of journalism can change the dynamic. Not even very good journalism, of which there is less and less.

Why does reform seem so impossible?

We live in an oligarchy. The mother's milk of American politics is money, and the reason they can't reform financing, the reason that we can't have public funding of elections rather than private donations, the reason that K Street is K Street in Washington, is to make sure that no popular sentiment survives. You're witnessing it now with health care, with the marginalisation of any effort to rationally incorporate all Americans under a national banner that says, "We're in this together."

But then the critics of a system like that immediately cry socialism.

And of course it's socialism. These ignorant motherfuckers. What do they think group insurance is, other than socialism? Just the idea of buying group insurance! If socialism is a taint that you cannot abide by, then, goddamn it, you shouldn't be in any group insurance policy. You should just go out and pay the fucking doctors because when you get 100,000 people together as part of anything, from a union to the AARP, and you say, "Because we have this group actuarially, more of us are going to be healthier than not and therefore we'll be able to carry forward the idea of group insurance and everybody will have an affordable plan..." That's fuckin' socialism. That's nothing but socialism.

It is, literally.

So the whole idea of group insurance, which of course everyone believes in, like that fellow on YouTube, "Don't let the government take away my Medicare…" You look at that and you think there's only one thing that can make people this stupid, and that's money. When you pay people to change their votes on the basis of money, the wrong shit gets voted for. That's American democracy at this point. And you get to the Senate and you're looking at 100 votes, which don't represent anything in terms of popular representation. When 40 percent of the population controls 60 percent of the votes in the higher house of a bicameral legislature, it's an oligarchy.

I'm getting depressed.

Now you're listening to Joe Lieberman say that he will filibuster anything with a public option. Let me understand this: One guy from a small state in New England is going to decide on a singular basis what's good for the health care of 300 million people? That's our form of government, and I don't get it.

It's not good.

Well, it is what it is and it has been for years, and it's why we're able to marginalise larger and larger percentages of our population. Fuck 'em where they stand. Five percent, 10 percent, 15 percent. How many people are you going to keep out of the gated community? How many guards are you going hire?

The guards will be the only working-class people in the gated communities, I guess.

Right. You're going to hire people to guard your shit, but you're not going to give them health care.

Season 2 of *The Wire*, the story lines about the longshoremen's union, really hit me personally. Both of my grandfathers were steel-mill workers and—

Oh, really?

Yeah, and my uncles too, and there were always lots of layoffs and worrying about getting shifts. It was a constant refrain. This was outside Phil-adelphia, at the Fairless Works US Steel plant down there. It's completely shut down now and the neighbourhood where I was born has become a company town with no company, and the problems with addiction there seem worse than ever. And that's a postindustrial state, right? Watching season 2 made me wonder about how the drug trade relates to the postindustrial state.

My writing partner Ed Burns said it best: "When the economy shrugs, it throws more people onto the corners." It's simple as that. Addiction is a growth industry in America. Not just in black America, but all across the country. Look at methamphetamine. Ultimately, because the drug trade is in part an economic imperative, meaning it's the only factory still working in parts of America and therefore it is a viable employer where no other viable employer exists, it's going to have its own fundamental lure. But it actually goes beyond money in this sense. People are defined by what they do in this culture. I think it's the human condition. I don't think it's any different from any other time in history. You are what you do. You are your profession. You are your trade.

I agree.

When you no longer have a trade, then you ache for meaning in a way that strikes to the very core of your being. It's something that I think a lot of people don't understand about people in the drug trade or people in the throes of addiction, which is that the choice not only offers them money. From the point of view of people getting high, it offers them purpose.

It does. Addiction gives you a calling when you're desperate.

We pretend to educate the bottom 10 to 15 percent of American society to join the ranks of the existing economy, but it's all pretence. We're not really giving them a good enough education to make that leap into the service economy. We're really preparing them for the corner and ultimately for the prison complexes. And they may not be educated, but they're damn sure not stupid. They get it. So if they get it, what do you fucking expect? They understand that they're being built for the corners.

The role is all laid out for them.

Every dope fiend I ever met knew what he was supposed to do when he woke up in the morning in just the same way that anybody with any other profession ever does. He was supposed to get $10 in a world that didn't want to give him shit. He was supposed to get high and he needed $10 at the end of the day at a minimum.

It's a strong imperative.

And that guy had no existential crisis. Whereas a guy who accepts the economic cards that have been dealt to him by postindustrial America and just sits there on his porch and says, "Well, I'm not necessary…" In a way, that's far more brutal than addiction and death, but we don't get that. From our perch, from our middle-class or upper-middle-class perch, from the policymakers' perch, things like "Just Say No" sound relevant.

Yeah, that was a very effective campaign.

It draws on the morality that we can easily acquire and utilise—

And it also assumes that everyone has the same set of choices.

Right. Like, "What the fuck was I supposed to say yes to, motherfucker?"

The police department, schools, industry, the media—these are all institutions that were addressed on *The Wire*. I've always wondered if there were a couple more institutions that would have been dealt with if there had a season 6, like the finance industry or health care, maybe?

Immigration was a theme that I would have done. The problem was that there was actually a delay of almost two years between season 3 and season 4. It took HBO awhile to renew the show. They were on the fence about it. By the time they did and we got back together and got into their schedule, it had been two years. For us to then stop and to retool and to do the research on immigration…

Is there a large Latino population in Baltimore?

Just in the last decade. Baltimore had almost no Latino population when I was a reporter there, like minuscule. Then, suddenly, Central Americans began showing up in Southeast Baltimore. They've created an incredibly vibrant immigrant community.

It would have been fascinating to see how *The Wire* would have treated this.

All you've got to do is watch the national debate and realise that immigration is this incredibly potent source of friction and ideology, and maybe always has been in American life. So I would have loved to have done that, but none of us knew Spanish and none of us had done any research on it. It would have taken us a little time, as it always did. But we had researched the school system and we were ready to do that.

And that was the focus of season 4. See, this sort of comes back to my first question, which is how does a show like *The Wire* gradually weave its web together over the seasons? It's so intricate and yet all so clear, and all the pieces fit together. I wonder how the immigration thing could have fit in.

The problem was, if you think about how carefully it was created, coming up with the boys in season 4, you need the character of Marlo. You need the two-season arc of Marlo and the bodies in the vacant houses, and that was all planned out. And then we were going to have to go from there to the media. It was all of a piece. Seasons 4 and 5 are connected maybe more than any other two seasons of *The Wire*.

Yeah, and you can really see it in retrospect. I just went back and watched the entire series for the third or fourth time over the past few weeks.

One of the things that I have unbridled contempt for—well, not unbridled—I don't really give a shit, but when I read it I just laugh, is the amount of debate that happens over which is the best season and which is the worst season.

It's impossible to say because the entire run of the series is one big story. I don't think someone can

dislike season 2 but still really appreciate what comes after it. It's all essential and cumulative.
I know there are some artificial divisions in terms of when we end it for a season, and we'll end it at a certain point that gives it some resonance. I guess you can debate that. But it's like, to me, season 1 is the weakest. It created the crucible, the core values of what we were going to build beyond. It did everything it was supposed to do, but to me something happens in seasons 3, 4, and 5 and it's informed by everything you've seen in 36 or 48 or 60 episodes.

Definitely.
So the notion that it was in this pure state early on and then we spun deeper and deeper? No, no, no, it's the exact opposite. We were building toward the last 15 minutes of the show—and doing so for a long time.

It's great to go back and see things starting to dovetail. But yeah, I think the only really valid debate in terms of which season is better than which season is just which version of "Way Down in the Hole" is better. My vote goes to either the Blind Boys of Alabama or Steve Earle.
[*laughs*] To me it's like, you can say that we caught this aspect better than we caught that aspect or we executed this story line better than that story line. That's all legitimate. It's open to debate. I know the thing isn't perfect. All writing is just abandoned at some point to deadlines and budget and to whatever else limits it. But the problem was that once we thought of immigration, it couldn't be the last season. The media had to be the last season because the last critique had to be... Well, the critique is more than the media. It's more than critiquing a newspaper. It's critiquing us.

As consumers of the media, you mean.
Yes. Newspapers have less and less ambition and are demanding less and less of themselves as arbiters of what is actually important, of what our problems are and how we're addressing them. *The Wire* was trying to say, at the end, "Look, if anything in the first four seasons struck a nerve with you, don't think for a moment that anyone's going to address themselves

to it—least of all the watchdogs of society—because their teeth have been taken out." They've done it to themselves. We had to say that last because ultimately we were saying: "This is the America you built and if you think the first alarm is ever going to go off in any sense, guess again."

And if anybody in our culture were going to sound any sort of alarm, it would be nice if it were newspaper writers doing it.
Still, it was critiquing not only the newspaper but also the people reading the newspaper and by extension the people watching television. It was basically, to quote Pogo, "We have met the enemy and he is us."

Right. And after that was all wrapped up, you couldn't just go, "Oh, by the way, immigration, too!"
Yeah. "And by the way..." We also thought about health care and we thought about a few other things. And I mean, I could make an argument for a sixth season if immigration had been introduced between seasons 3 and 4.

It would need to have been starting to develop then.
Before the rise of Marlo. We could've held Marlo's rise, with the bodies in the vacants, held that off until subsequent seasons and then began it in the last two-season arc, but then we would have been off the air for three years and I would have had to go back to HBO when I'd just talked my way back into the last two seasons and go—

"I've got one more story I wanna tell."
Yeah. "I know that I said I'm out in five, but I meant six." So it wasn't going to happen for any number of reasons. Anyway, I've seen people say mistakenly that season 6 would've been immigration. No way. Season 4 would've been immigration if there had been six seasons.

Got it.
That's the only way it could've worked. And the only reason that we thought about other things and said

no was because, at a certain point, even if you're getting to address yourselves to some of the same dynamic—like the dynamic in health care, as we just discussed, it's the same as the dynamic with public education.

Right.

So even if you're making that point, and you're using a hospital setting to do it for another season of *The Wire*, say, you're basically making the same institutional points and the same points about the inability of the political and social and economic culture to reform—

Just relative to a different institution.

Yeah, you're just shifting it. And how many times are you going to make Kima and McNulty and Daniels and Bunk, how many times are they going to walk up the hill and then see the rock slip back? At a certain point the characterisations, the bricks and mortar, would start to show the wear. How many times is McNulty going to fuck an alligator in the sewer and then do an honest thing and then do a fucked-up thing the next minute?

[*Laughs.*]

At a certain point you have to honour that the characters have to have arcs. So just picking a continual litany of things to critique in society, I mean, listen, I'd love to tell a story about the issues of health care and public health, but maybe it's time to let the *Wire* universe go and do it with some other universe.

A big thing I wonder about in terms of writing *The Wire* is how you went about constructing composite characters from real-life influences, like Omar is a big one, of course, but—

Why don't I do Omar, because that's the one everybody always asks about. Here are some people that we used for the Omar story line—and they are real people and real names that would be known on the streets of Baltimore. Anthony Hollie, Ferdinand Harvin, and Cadillac and Low. I don't know their real names, but they were a team. And there's also Donnie Andrews. He was the big man who went to war

with Omar the last time. He got killed in the shootout in the apartment in the ambush. That's actually the real Donnie.

Oh man, the guy who was with Omar and Butchie and then he was Omar's backup against Marlo? Oh wow. No kidding.

Yeah, that's the guy.

The actor who plays the Deacon was also from the streets, right?

He was a major drug trafficker. Melvin Williams, little Melvin. He was famous going back to the 60s. He had maybe 30 years of selling heroin and coke in Baltimore. He was busted by Ed in '84 and got out in 2001. We all had lunch and then he came to work as an actor.

So out of all these people, did you pick and choose traits and stories from their realities for Omar? For instance, Omar carries a shotgun. He's gay. He's got all these really great characterisations.

Listen, when he jumps out the window during that shootout, that was something Donnie Andrews actually did. He jumped out of the sixth floor of the Murphy Homes when he was caught in an ambush and out of ammunition. Did he think about it? No, but he did it and he survived and he was able to limp away. It happened. He also jumped off the Poplar Grove rail bridge another time. It's legend. There are people who will tell you about it in West Baltimore other than Donnie. It's not just something he's making up. If you make that jump, you're dead. If I make that jump, I'm a puddle on the ground.

But he did it.

He needed to make the jump and he wasn't gonna die that time.

I love that Omar's jump was based on a real story, because that was one of the things in the series where people were like, "Ah, that would never happen. He'd be dead."

And we actually only had Omar jump from the fourth floor.

Whereas Donnie really jumped from the sixth.

The building we had only went up five and we said, "Eh, the fourth is fine. They're not gonna believe it anyway, but he did it." Some other things we just made up. None of those names I gave you I know to be homosexuals, but at one point I was mistaken in my own head. Somebody had told me when I was a reporter years ago that Cadillac and Low were a gay team—that they were a couple. I just thought that was true, and then at some point that's what got me to say, "This is an interesting character to have be gay because he can be openly gay because he's not beholden to anybody." It's impossible to be an openly gay male cop. It's OK to be a lesbian, but it's hard to be a gay male cop. And with all the homophobia it's hard to be openly gay in the organised drug trade.

Unless you're an outlaw even to the outlaws like Omar was.

Right. Omar's playing by his own fuckin' rules. So you look at that and you say this would be a good character for that and I thought I was referencing Cadillac and Low, but when I mentioned it to Ed four episodes into the show he said, "They weren't gay." So I just got that wrong. We also made up the Sunday truce. There are things we made up because they were fun. But we didn't make up how important church hats are to women in West Baltimore. There's actually a great picture book called *Crowns*.

Oh yeah? I'll check that out.

It's glorious—photos of women's Sunday hats in the black community. So you make some stuff up, you borrow from this guy, you borrow from that guy, and then you've got this guy Michael K. Williams playing the role, who just brings it and makes his own way into the characterisation. He brings his own toolbox. It's not like writing prose. Film is a synthesis, and television, since it's ongoing, is a synthesis between what the actor brings and what the director brings and what the writer brings and what the crew makes you capable of in a given day. It's very communal.

I've always wondered how much of a character's

ultimate arc was known to you and how early it was known. For instance, did Omar always have to die? Did Carcetti always have to become governor? Was it just built into their DNA as characters?

It was. It was built in. You have to know where you're going and one of the things that television in particular, more than film, certainly more than prose, suffers from is that there's so much money in the product that once you get an audience, once you achieve an audience, your job is to stay in that audience ad nauseam.

Meaning what?

Meaning if they love Omar, give them some more Omar. If they love Stringer, give them some more Stringer.

Yeah. It's not like they were going to kill Ross and Rachel on *Friends*.

Right. And they're never going to kill David Caruso on whatever show he's on, whichever one of the *CSI*s.

Or even Tony Soprano.

Well, you know.

That's debatable, I guess.

But ultimately, if something is all about character, then character has to be served at all costs. And you know, we loved our actors. We never killed an actor because he was pissing us off. The only reason we killed an actor was for story, and we'd go to them and say, "We love your work. We're going to work with you again sometime. I can't wait till that day comes, except maybe it won't because you'll be a frickin' movie star." But it was never about any contract issues. We never played that game with our actors and they knew it. That probably made it more terrifying for them—

That it had to be true to the story line.

I'll never forget J.D. Williams, who played Bodie, he saw himself starting to have these conversations with McNulty, and when I finally came to him and said, "This is your episode. You're goin' out." He said, "Oh, I knew it. I could see." I said, "OK."

Because he knows the character so well by then.
And he has to know the show at that point. So every time somebody rises up and tries to speak a little truth…

They die, basically.
And he was right. We were writing a Greek tragedy.

What did it feel like to kill characters like Omar and Bodie? Did you feel sentimental?
Every time. The first time was when we killed Wallace in the first season.

That was brutal, man.
The crew was fuckin' mad at us. The crew was like, "This is a bad scene, man." It was horrifying. We're hugging the actor—a great kid named Michael Jordan. He's got a good gig now. *Friday Night Lights*. I just put my arm around him and I said, "Look, people are going to remember this scene for a long time and they're going to know that this is a young man who can act. I can't write you a better scene than that." And he brought it. All three of the young actors in that room did.

Was it like that on the day Omar was killed, too?
Yeah, except by then we knew the show was going out. We knew it was our last season and so at that point if you're Michael K. you probably want a great death scene.

Right. And it was great.
But I guess where I was originally going is that nobody wants to write endings in television. They want to sustain the franchise. But if you don't write an ending for a story, you know what you are? You're a hack. You're not a storyteller. It may not be that you have the skills of a hack. You might be a hell of a writer, but you're taking a hack's road. You're on the road to hackdom and there's no stopping you because stories have a beginning, a middle, and an end.

It's impressive that HBO took the ride for this entire series.
We didn't know if we were going to get five seasons, and I certainly didn't go to HBO at the beginning and say, "We're going to build a whole city and there'll be this über-theme and it'll all build to this point where it's an indictment of—" They would have laughed me out of the room and said, "What the fuck was that guy talking about?"

Like, "Come on, now."
So the first thing I said was, "Through the course of a police investigation you're going to see the fraud of the drug war. You're going to see how the drug war is not worth it and how nothing works the way we think it does when you establish prohibition." And then it was after we came back to talk about season 2 that I had the honest conversation with Chris Albrecht and Carol Strauss from HBO about building a city. They said they could give me this and this and this.

Wow.
One of the reasons they renewed for seasons 4 and 5 was that I was able to go in to them with beat sheets for every episode, for the remaining… I think I had 22 episodes. But I didn't have specific episodes for season 4 or 5. I had storyboards for all of the characters, and I could tell them where everyone was going and what the theme not only of season 4 was, but of season 5—and how they were connected.

I was able to say to Chris Albrecht, "If you're in for a penny you're in for a pound. You're gonna have a hard time cancelling it after season 4 because all these bodies are going to be in these houses and they're going be discovered."

Yeah, can't leave that hanging.
So he was in for a penny, in for a pound. That was liberating in a way. And we knew where all the characters had to go no matter what. Clay Davis has to survive. No matter what, Carcetti has to thrive. He has to become governor. The city can go to hell, but he has to become governor.

That's another thing I was thinking about. People

like Clay Davis or Carcetti or Rawls or Levy, they all thrive. What unites them? I kind of know the answer to this, but I'd like to hear how you put it.
They sublimate any moral imperative to their own personal ambition. They wed themselves to the capitalist construct and they embrace the status quo at all costs. Some of them become that person by degrees, in the case of Carcetti, and some of them are that person from jump, like Levy or Clay Davis. Some people do it without a great deal of ambition or greed. Burrell, all he wanted to do was preserve his job. He wasn't looking to get promoted. He certainly didn't think he was going beyond commissioner in any way. He just wanted his institution not to be humiliated. He wanted to avoid all negative publicity. He's literally the guy in a Skinner box. He's a pigeon that doesn't want to be shot. So he lives life on those terms.

Even though that isn't as conniving as someone like Clay Davis, it's still pretty ignoble.
But all the characters who are serving the institutions, who are so self-preserving and self-aggrandising, they are rigorous about always making the wrong choice when it comes to a societal good, to a communal good. And you know what? I was a reporter for a lot of years. I actually believe that's how the city works or doesn't work. I wrote a book about what was wrong with the drug trade, the drug war. It was very carefully researched and it made clear that this was a fool's errand. I watched a councilman who was running for mayor go to the corner where I wrote the book, hold a copy of the book up in front of the TV cameras, and say that if he were elected mayor he would fight the drug war for real and he would win it. Well, he became mayor and he fought as a drug warrior and he clipped the stats and he made it sound like crime was going down when crime wasn't going down and now he's the governor of Maryland.

Jesus Christ.
And he didn't like *The Wire*. He didn't think *The Wire* was a good thing.

Not that surprising.
A lot of what *The Wire* was about sounds cynical to people. I think it's very cynical about institutions and their ability to reform. I don't deny that, but I don't think it's at all cynical about people.

On the contrary—it's very empathetic and human.
Which is why it's watchable. It embraces the idea of everybody's humanity at the same time that it says, "Oh yeah, we're fucked, but we're fucked together in our own way and we fucked ourselves."

I love the sense of humour that exists among cops. It's some of the best black, gallows humour there is. I think that's the stuff that really informs the humour of *The Wire*.
It's pretty good among anybody who deals with life and death on a daily basis or who sees the fraud and sin underlying the human condition. The guys I knew who worked in ERs in Baltimore, the nurses and ICU people, they were pretty funny in their own way. If you don't think a hospital's a funny place, get a book called *The House of God* by Samuel Shem. It was probably some of the source material for *St. Elsewhere* and some other shows. It was written back in the 70s. It's a book they give to every first-year resident in America.

I'll read that.
And if you think that it's not present in the military, read *Generation Kill*—

Of course. *Generation Kill* has real comedy in it.
I think that the closer you are to a flame and the more you see people getting burned, the funnier you get, if you're at all human. Or you put a gun in your mouth. Either you laugh or you cry.

This seems to play into what you mentioned earlier, that you were writing Greek tragedy, which certainly had comedic elements.
Yes. Before finishing the first season I'd reread most of Euripides, Sophocles, and Aeschylus, those three guys. I'd read some of it in college, but I hadn't read it systematically. That stuff is incredibly relevant today. As drama, the actual plays are a little bit stilted, but the message within the plays and the dramatic

impulses are profound for our time. We don't really realise it. I don't think we sense the power in there because we're really more in the Shakespearean construct of—

Yes, the individualism kind of thing.
The individual and the interior struggle for self. Macbeth and Hamlet and Lear and Othello. These are the great tragedies—the dramatic branch that leads to O'Neill and our modern theatre. But I saw a version of Aeschylus's *The Persians* done on the stage in Washington, and it made my jaw drop. They put it on during the height of the insurgency in Iraq—after that misadventure in Iraq had made itself apparent. If you read that play and if you saw this production of it, it was so dead-on. I don't know if you know the play.

I've never read it, but I know what it's about.
It's basically the people back in the Persian capital wondering what's happened to their army and, of course, bad things have happened to their army. And the young emperor who wants to be compared to his father—it's Darius the Great, I think—he wants to win the victory that was denied his father over the Greeks.

Sounds familiar.
Yeah. And of course they performed it in Republican ties and suits. It was a Washington audience. I was watching it and I was looking around, and some of these lines were landing, some of the dialogue was landing. I was looking around like, "Did everyone just catch that? Did they really just say that?" It was so ripe in its critique of Bush and Cheney and all those guys.

It seems to me that people want to be sort of special, unique snowflakes, and the Shakespearean thing addresses that more.
Right! Let's celebrate me and the wonder that is me. It's not about society. The Greeks, especially the Athenians, were consumed with questions about man and state. They gave Socrates hemlock because his ideas were antithetical to their notions of state.

Listen, that's totalitarianism in any sense, but for him, he was cynical about democracy and he was an iconoclast about the democratic principles. That went to the heart of Greek thinking. It was like, "Don't fuck with that." Now, the thing that has been exalted and the thing that American entertainment is consumed with is the individual being bigger than the institution. How many frickin' times are we gonna watch a story where somebody—

Rises up against the odds?
"You can't do that." "Yes, I can." "No, you can't." "I'll show you, see?" And in the end he's recognised as just a goodhearted rebel with right on his side, and eventually the town realises that dancing's not so bad. I can make up a million of 'em. That's the story we want to be told over and over again. And you know why? Because in our heart of hearts what we know about the 21st century is that every day we're going to be worth less and less, not more and more.

Worth less and less as people, you mean?
As human beings. Some of us are going to get more money and be worth more. There are some people who are destined for celebrity or wealth or power, but by and large, the average American, the average person in the world on planet Earth, is worth less and less. That's the triumph of capital, and that is the problem. You look at that, and you think that's what we've come to and that's where we're going and it's like, "Can you tell me another bedtime story about how people are special and every one of us matters? Can you tell me that shit?"

"Tell me again about that boxer who came out of the ghetto and became the champ."
"And what about that musician whose genius was never recognised? What about him? And, oh yeah, somebody else overcame addiction. That's great. Tell me that one again." Listen, I don't mind a victory if it's earned. But if all you do is victory, if that's your whole dramatic construct and that's 90 percent of American television—

It goes back to how you didn't want to put char-

acters like McNulty and Kima through the same framework again and again. But that's what this big tradition of storytelling is nowadays. It's just a tired retread. I found it kind of ironic that in season 5 there are a few really great scenes where you're mocking the editors of newspapers who are asking for a Dickensian vibe, and then a lot of critics and writers compared *The Wire* to Dickens.

It was fun goofing on the Dickens comparison because I understood what they meant by Dickensian when they said it. You get this sort of scope of society through the classes, the way Dickens would play with that in his novels. But that's true of Tolstoy's Moscow. That's true of Balzac's Paris. It's been done a lot in a lot of different places by a lot of writers. And I'm not the one doing the comparing. I'm just saying if you use those tropes you can go to a lot of places other than Dickens. The thing that made me laugh about it with Dickens was that Dickens is famous for being passionate about showing you the fault lines of industrial England and where money and power route themselves away from the poor. He would make the case for a much better social compact than existed in Victorian England, but then his verdict would always be, "But thank God a nice old uncle or this heroic lawyer is going to make things better." In the end, the guy would punk out.

Now that doesn't mean he wasn't a great writer and they're not great stories. They are. But *The Wire* was actually making a different argument than Dickens, and the comparison, while flattering, sort of fell badly on us.

Sure.

So there was a little bit of tongue-in-cheek satire on the show directed at people who were using Dickens to praise us. But the other thing is much more simple, which is the editor of the *Baltimore Sun* when I was covering the drug trade, when I was trying to explain what was happening in the city in terms that made economic sense to me... When I was coming back off of the reporting for *The Corner* and preparing to go back to the newspaper, this editor and I talked about writing columns about life on the streets

in West Baltimore. That, to me, would have been the narrative equivalent of telling some stories that you ultimately saw on *The Wire*, but using real people. The first one that I tried to tell, for a variety of reasons, some of them emotional and some of them due to the fact that we weren't getting along, he spiked. It was about a guy very much like the *Wire* character Bubbles who was harvesting metal—two guys harvesting metal, actually. This editor spiked the story without explanation.

Wow.

He came to me and said, "I want to do the stories that are about the Dickensian lives of children growing up in West Baltimore." What he was saying was, "If you give me a nice, cute eight-, nine-year-old kid who doesn't have a pencil, who doesn't have a schoolbook, who lives in poverty, who's big eyed and sweet and who I can make the reader fall in love with, I can win a fuckin' prize with that. Write me that shit."

"Don't hand me some struggling junkie."

"Don't give me a guy who's, like, trying to get high but maintain his dignity. Don't give me anything complicated." And he really used the word "Dickensian."

Fucker.

I still have the email he sent me. It happened over a period of about two months, but that was one of the moments where I knew I had to go. So I was really just quoting this editor, John Carroll. I came back trying to explain how utterly bereft economically West Baltimore was, how distanced it was from the world that we were pretending to be, how it was not even a part of our world anymore. All he wanted to do was reach back and grab some cute kids and run with them to win a prize. That's who he was.

It's the opposite of the impulse that we talked about for *The Wire* earlier, where you proceed from theme into character.

Exactly. First you do a bunch of reporting. You feel like you know the subject and then you ask, "What do we want to say that hasn't been said and that deserves to be said?" That was the first question we asked ourselves at the beginning of every season. That question never got asked at the *Baltimore Sun* when I was there. What got asked at the *Baltimore Sun* was, "How can we bite off a little morsel of outrage and run with it?"

And get a Pulitzer.

Yeah. "Let's do 50 stories on lead-paint poisoning between January and December. We're not going to do any more the next year because that's past the Pulitzer year. But we're going to show you how bad lead-paint poisoning is. In fact, we're going to show you that if it weren't for lead-paint poisoning, these kids would all be at fucking Ivy League schools. Never mind that their family lives have been decimated, that they're in a school system that's utterly dysfunctional, that the drug trade's the only industry where they live. Never mind all of that. If they'd just stop eating the fuckin' lead paint, they could all be at Princeton." You would look at that and you would say, "This is the highest ambition for journalism? This is what you got? What the fuck happened to us?"

It's the definition of pandering, basically.

It was pandering. It was prostitution of a kind. It was pornography, is what it was. The pornography of poverty. The stakes are too high for journalism to do that. I understand why politicians do it. I understand why police industries cook their stats. I understand why school administrators cook their test scores. I understand people in a bureaucracy doing that stuff because I expect so little of them at this point after years of being a reporter.

But the paper is supposed to be calling all the rest of them out.

Exactly. If the paper can't address itself to hard truths, then what the fuck? So that's where "Dickensian" came from. It was right out of John Carroll's mouth.

You worked with some great crime-fiction writ-

ers on *The Wire*. **You're also married to an excellent crime novelist named Laura Lippman. What do you think about the treatment of crime fiction by the literary establishment? I talked about this in an interview with Elmore Leonard earlier this year. I think that it's really ghettoised.**

It is ghettoised, but the funny part is that these writers wouldn't want to walk out of the ghetto if they could. Now, I'm sure they would all love to be recognised for the literary merits of what they do. I'm not saying that. They're not without professional pride. Richard Price, of course, began with literary cred and has not relinquished it. Dennis Lehane and George Pelecanos and Laura, they began as crime novelists. Price began as a young literary lion and has nonetheless taken the milieu of crime as part of his demimonde. But what's common to all of them is that they're looking for the fault lines in society. They're using crime to do it because that's where these things are readily apparent. It's where money and vanity and fraud and intellect and cultural dissonance all manage to show themselves in very blunt and fundamental ways. It's a great bunch of tools in your toolbox.

And it's true, crime fiction often addresses serious problems in American society with much more insight and attention than literature-literature does.

Yes, what's really notable about American crime fiction is how much more the best of it has managed to get to in terms of society and politics and economics—and how little the literary world has managed to address itself to those things. I was on this panel with this guy Walter Benn Michaels at the New York Public Library, and I didn't dig it because he was basically using *The Wire* as a cudgel to beat up on literary fiction. But I don't want to beat up on anybody. I don't want to generalize, because there are some good literary novels. There's also a lot of navel-gazing—and there's a lot of navel-gazing on the Upper West Side of Manhattan. I find that stuff unreadable and a waste of my time, but there's a lot of good stuff, too. And then there's a lot of really smart stuff and there's a lot of crap in crime writing.

Sure.

There's no reason to generalise. But the highest end of crime writing is doing everything right now that literary fiction claims for itself. That is true. And much of what passes for quality literary fiction is not accomplishing very much at all that I find to have merit. So that's my opinion. But having said that, this panelist took it to an extreme where he was literally saying, "Can we just write about economics and money and politics?" He was saying that literary fiction should be like *The Wire*, which is nice and flattering, but then he was saying, "Can we stop writing about slavery? Can we stop writing about the Holocaust?" He was basically saying that writing about cultural identity is bullshit. But it's like, I don't buy that either. I couldn't write effectively about people if these sort of core 20th-century experiences or 18th-century experiences that still influence us were not part of who we are.

Of course not.

I can't begin to write one black character—much less 30—and have them all be distinct and different and represent different things if I don't have some core understanding of where they came from. Not just them and their parents, but culturally—what they've acquired and what they expect of the world and what the world expects of them as blacks, as Catholics, as Jews, as whoever, as marines, as fuckin' South Texas Mexican marines serving in Iraq. So I'm standing on a lot of literature that has come before and that is contemporaneous with me. Thank God somebody wrote *Schindler's List*. Thank God somebody wrote *Beloved*.

And there are two different kinds of relevancy. There's current-events relevancy and then there's larger human-condition relevancy. Do you know what I mean?

Yeah. So what I'm saying is I agree with your high assessment of the high end of crime writing and I agree with your low assessment of the low end of literary fiction, but there's a lot of great literary fiction and there's a lot of shitty crime writing and I don't want *The Wire* used as a cudgel to beat up on any-body. Everybody should write the stories that matter to them and then we'll figure it out once everything exists.

I know that I'm not supposed to ask much about your new series, *Tremé*, here. But can I just ask if the framework in terms of institutions versus individuals is informing that series also?

Well, there's obviously a lot of that because New Orleans has been grossly affected by the aftermath of the storm and the behaviour or misbehaviour of institutions, but also in some ways this series is a little bit different in that it's a celebration of what we're capable of as Americans. *The Wire* tried to imply—and I felt it being from Baltimore, and I think Baltimoreans felt it, but I'm not sure how well it conveyed for the rest of the country—the value of the city as the essential American experience. We're an urban people. Eighty percent of us live in metro areas. I don't buy the whole Republican convention with its small-town values and "We represent the real Americans". I live in Baltimore. I'm concerned with big-city values and I live among real Americans. I could give a fuck about the other 20 percent of the country. I care about how we live together in cities. I think there were some people who watched *The Wire* and said to themselves, "You know, why don't they just all move away? That city's unredeemable." We never felt that. I'm vested in Baltimore and I love it, just as I now spend part of my year in New Orleans and I've always loved New Orleans.

And what's different in New Orleans?

Because New Orleans has created such unique cultural art in terms of music and dance, and it's a very idiosyncratic culture, it shows the value of what the American melting pot is capable of. It does it in a way that is visual and musical and demonstrable, and it does it in the fucking street every day. Somehow this city is trying to find a way to endure while the political essence of the country doesn't give a fuck. That, to me, is a fascinating dynamic.

Thanks to Tim Small and David Feinberg.

IAN HISLOP

INTERVIEW BY ANDY CAPPER | PHOTO BY ALEX STURROCK

Published October 2008

For those of you without taste or eyes, *Private Eye* is a fortnightly satirical news-print magazine that contains more actual news than all the other British news-papers made during the two weeks it takes to put their issue together. In fact, it is one of a very small number of news publications that remains worth a shit.

Not only is it consistently hilarious, informative and subversive, it wields a mighty punch. *Private Eye* has acted like a sharpened pin to the whoopee cushion of inces-sant lies and deceit that has become the common currency of modern British politics.

Its relentless and savage satire remains perhaps one of the truest checks on UK executive power. Without the magazine's fortnightly needling, the spin of Blair's authoritarian 90s rule may well have slickly skated into the imperious presidential model of government that smiling Tony always seemed to have such a massive hard-on for.

It is no coincidence that, as the longest-serving editor of the magazine, Ian Hislop is the most sued man in Britain and that the magazine keeps a "fighting fund" on hand to payroll the endless litigation they face.

We met him in his offices in Soho and drank tea with him while staring at all the amazing stuff on the walls and trying to concentrate on asking the questions. (He has a piano in there on which they play Mozart while they're coming up with jokes). He is my hero.

Vice: So what is the day-to-day of doing this job? I've always been fascinated by how *Private Eye* works. It's so consistent.

Ian Hislop: Nearly everybody works somewhere else. The journalists tend to have other jobs, and most of the writers do as well. The week before we go to press people turn up in batches really and the journalism tends to get done in there [the main office down the corridor] and the jokes tend to get done in here [his personal office]. The jokes are collaborative. There are usually three or four people doing it.

Who's in charge?

Essentially me.

Which other papers do your journalists work for? Do they write under different names?

A lot of them don't admit they write for us, which is fine.

Why do they write for you, though?

I think it's about the mischief really. And they can write stories they can't write in their own papers really because most of the national press have some other agenda depending who owns them or how friendly they are to the people you're trying to write about.

Who owns you guys now?

We used to be owned by the comedian Peter Cook (*Bedazzled, Derek & Clive*) but then he died and he left most of the shares to his sisters and to his wife.

So it's still completely independent.

The rest of the shares are owned by a sort of rag-bag of people that Peter borrowed money off in the 60s, so people like Jane Asher and Dirk Bogard, but he died so it's now his nephew. It's a pretty odd bunch.

When *Private Eye* was started, what do you think was its purpose? Was it set up to be a counter-culture magazine?

Well, no. It was started by a group of friends who went to college together. They thought they were funny, they made each other laugh and they thought: "This is better than working." I think that's what it was about. No one consciously starts a counter-culture because they're not aware of being counter-culture, it's just what they are. I think they were basically bolshy and quite rebellious people. Most of them didn't have fathers. They'd either died in the war or died early and the sons didn't get proper jobs and so they thought, "We can do this." The essential component was making each other laugh and then as it developed [founder] Richard Ingrams said, "We don't only want to make people laugh, we want to tell them things that they didn't know," so a sort of journalism culture attached itself, mostly because they had this brilliant man called Paul Foot. He was a very good journalist.

He was the guy who really brought the journalism into it?

Yeah, and sadly he's not with us any more.

Who's taking care of that now then?

I had to hire three people to replace Paul. One is a man called Richard Brooks, who is absolutely brilliant. He used to work for Customs and Excise and we lured him over to the dark side because most journalists are illiterate financially. He isn't, but his record on public finance is just fantastic. He's done some extraordinarily good stuff. I don't want to be that specific, but a lot of the best columns we run are by people outside the office. We run a health column that is entirely written by pissed-off doctors.

So your contributors are mainly people who have contacted you with dirt on people and you've kept them on as contacts.
Absolutely. There's the local council column that is written by local journalists who can't get stuff in their own papers so they send it to us. Council advertising is quite heavy and you know what you can't get in, but all that stuff comes from them. The TV column is also written by an insider.

Is he a secret insider?
Yes, and he would definitely be fired if they knew who it was.

Ha ha. Who is the person who writes from inside of the Houses of Parliament?
That's a couple of people. Most of whom we don't say who they are.

And so how many is your core team of contributors?
About 20.

And that's in the UK only. Have you ever thought of exporting *Private Eye* in to different countries?
No, we're not like you. We stay inside this country. It's what we do well. We know this place. We don't sell outside.

Your circulation has gone up recently hasn't it?
It's about 200,000, yeah.

What do you think drives people to keep buying your magazine? I thought British people were only meant to buy trashy crap about TV stars or interviews with footballers' girlfriends?
I think the intelligence of audiences in this country are always underestimated, especially with television and newspaper magazines. People say: "They'll only buy *Heat* or *Nuts*", but it's not true. If you provide something better people will go and get it. The worst

times for our circulation figures were the height of Blair's rule — when the economy was booming and everyone said he was marvellous and nobody wanted to read us.

Ha ha. Everybody was doing cocaine and listening to Oasis and going, "Waheeey!"
Yes. Ha ha.

What did the circulation go down to?
We were slipping down to sort of 180s, 190s. There was a sense of: "You guys you just complain all the time. You are a bunch of whiners." Over years of the magazine you can see those public perceptions change. They are periods of satisfaction.

How was it in the 80s, aka "the decade of excess"?
In the beginning of the 80s it was very good for us. Society was very polarised with Thatcher and the miners' strike. There was all that aggro around and that was good for us. Then the complacent 80s weren't very good for us. That's when I took over the mag actually.

So human suffering is great for circulation?
Ha, yes. It is on the whole. And so is dissatisfaction. When people start asking questions again they read us. When everything's fine, people don't really care.

I've met a lot of kids in the past few years. They were supposedly "underground" or "alternative" kids and they all want to vote Conservative in the next election which, before Blair, was anathema to a kid like that.
I think there are a lot of those kids about.

I remember saying things like, "But do you not remember what the Conservatives were like? I mean, they really weren't that great." And they came back to me saying things like: "We don't like Blair's stance on the war."
And that's enough for them.

Ha ha, yeah. They would have preferred the Con-

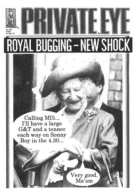

servatives' stance on the war, which would have been a lot more cool or something. What do you feel when you hear kids making statements like that?

Well, a) It's quite funny, and b) I think the current lot of Tories also don't remember what they were like before, so they don't know what they'll be like when they get in either. I think that is why people are prepared to give it a punt. Politics are very peculiar now, with the Conservative leader David Cameron saying "green taxes" and you're thinking, "Hang on, you're a Conservative, aren't you?" And then you have Labour leader Gordon Brown saying, "We'll build the power plant and we'll have some more nukes as well." It's no wonder the kids are very confused.

But they have more access to information than ever before now.

Yeah, they have a lot of information but there's less analysis. It's sort of a tsunami of information really

and no way to work out which bits of it matter.

From your insiders and knowledge of the workings of the Houses of Parliament, do you think the Conservatives will win the next election and, if so, what do you think they'll do?

I think the Tories will win the next one. I think they'll be exactly like Blair when he started. When you take over you don't do much, you sit there for a bit and see how the land lies. They've said things about keeping up the spending programmes. All the scare stories—about the Tories coming in and slashing the NHS and giving up on teachers—I don't think they'll do any of that.

Do you not?

No, those sort of Tories, on the whole, aren't there any more.

You don't think they would get rid of the National

Health Service?

No, I think they would be no more keen to privatise it than the current Labour lot are. I don't think they'll do that, particularly because Cameron's got a personal invested interest in having his child born in the NHS. That has done him pretty well.

What have you found out about that guy then?

About Cameron? Does anybody know anything more than: "What you see is what you get"? He's had one job working as a PR man for a television company, which is not the greatest CV you have ever seen, but then Brown's never had a job either. They've been full-time politicians all their life, that's what we get now. Politicians used to be people who had jobs first, then went to politics, but they don't now. They're all sort of the people you met at college who were very interested in politics very early. And you have to think: "Why?"

I always thought it's a weird thing to want to be a politician.

Being a politician is the thing that defines them. It's no more weird than wanting to be on TV or be in a band.

What about Boris Johnson?

Boris is the ultimate showman, but very effective. Very popular with your lot, I would guess.

What do you mean "our lot"?

Well, that younger readership. That seems to be where his base is.

I guess so, yeah. Are you pally with him?

It comes and goes. He's furious with me sometimes depending on what we've written about him. I've done three, four television shows with him, which were hysterical. I don't know how much he knew why they were funny but he is innately entertaining. There is something very appealing about him.

His mayoral acceptance speech was something else. I watched it a few times.

Well, the Beijing [his big speech about Britain host-ing the Olympics] thing was really funny too. There is part of you that thinks it's a mass-organised, synchronised display, and then you have this man who comes on who can't even do up the buttons on his suit.

Here's another thing I need your insider knowledge for. That must have been a prank at the Olympics when they flashed up the portrait of Myra Hindley during the "Come to England, it's lovely" video?

No, it's one of the Brit Art paintings.

Yeah, I know that, but surely it must have been a prank?

No, no, they were very serious about that. I promise you the cultural community think that a big portrait of Myra is absolutely terrific.

But when they flashed it up on the screen for a short time it just looks like the original mugshot of Myra.

It looks like someone that killed children, I agree. It certainly wasn't top of my list of what's to be proud of in Britain.

What is top of your list of what's to be proud of in Britain?

Obviously a tradition of questioning authority, that seems fairly high. Personal freedom. An ability to organise things. Lots of things that don't happen in Beijing. I do quite like this country and that's one of the reasons I'm very quick to jeopardise any deviation of the good things we have.

When was the last time you got sued? I guess it doesn't happen as much as it used to.

No, because people don't do it as much. We've got two as of last week.

That's how often?

This latest one is a copper.

How often do you get them? Every week?

We don't get them every week but they come in. A lot

of them disappear nowadays. A lot of people we get rid of, but on the whole, there's always something outstanding.

We're probably running 70 stories a week which people don't particularly like and at a certain point some of these people will sue. But it's nothing like the mad days of libel in the late 80s and early 90s.

Why do you think it changed?

Well, the law changed. The amount of damages came right down and the fees went up, so it costs a fortune now. It really costs a fortune now so people have become hesitant.

Have you had the same lawyers throughout the whole period?

Yes, and they're very, very rich.

Ha ha. So what stories are you working on right now that could get you sued?

The big stories we are working on are about Brown's reputation for economic competence. Our theory is the things people are known for are usually the things they can't do at all. I think he was useless at economics and most of the public finances are unravelling because of that.

How bad do you think it's going to get, "credit crunch" and recession-wise?

I'd like to think of myself as an optimist but when the Chancellor of the Exchequer says, "It's the worst thing for 60 years", you think, "Oh shit." I think it's going to get quite serious. Partly because we had a stupid obsession with the value of houses in this country and in the long-term I think that houses being worth less will be a good thing, but it will be very painful when you get there.

Is there any story you could pass on to us because you can't print it or you're scared of getting sued?

There's nothing I would give you, absolutely nothing, and I'm not going to tell you what we're going to print obviously because that would be pointless printing. People say to us, "You must know stuff that you don't print", and I say, "Well, if it's any good then I'd put it in." If I don't believe it I don't put it in because otherwise why would people buy you?

What were some of things that people have told you that were true that weren't put in there?

People are always telling you that politicians are gay, usually ones who aren't, and on the other hand people who knew John Major really well would come up to you and say it's very interesting that [Conservative MP] Peter Lilley was gay, which he wasn't. Him and his wife couldn't have children, and politicians are so unpleasant they spread the story that he was gay.

Anyway, the same time they were telling me this story, John Major was actually screwing Edwina Curry. No one knew it. On the whole I find the really good stories you find out afterwards because no one has told you.

You must have met Edwina Curry?

I have met Edwina Curry on a number of occasions, yes.

Have you ever imagined what it's like to screw her?

I'm just not going to comment on that.

How old are you now, if you don't mind me asking?

I'm 48.

Has anyone ever offered you another job, or offered to buy you out?

They have done, yeah.

Buy you out or offered you another job?

Both. I can't think of a better job, though. We are one of the few companies where the views of the shareholders aren't very important.

Do you think that's important?

There was a point when the widow was very unhappy with me and she said she might sell the magazine to Mohamed Al Fayed and I said that was fine, but I would torch the building. So she didn't.

YOU'RE NOT PUNK

AND I'M TELLING EVERYONE | BY PENNY RIMBAUD | PHOTO BY DAVID TITLOW

Published April 2005

I've got no allegiance whatsoever to punk as a form of music. Never really did. Punk as I knew it has a political purpose. What is classified as "punk" music these days is absolutely empty and gutless.

I genuinely believe that if it hadn't been for Crass and the movement which grew out of it, punk would now only be remembered as another old dame in the rock and roll pantomime; just the same old attitudes dressed up in a different costume. The Pistols certainly didn't do anything more radical than Elvis Presley, the only difference was that Elvis could handle his drugs better than they could.

Crass wanted to change the world, and in some respects we did, but nowhere to the degree that we set out to. We wanted to undermine the prime institutions of the State and everything that it represented. We went to great lengths to do that. The rock and roll swank of performing in a band was simply the platform we used.

What we did as activists was much more important to us than the music. We were always looking for some way of moving beyond being just a band. In our history we had dealings and run-ins with all sorts: Baader-Meinhof, the KGB, the CIA, the IRA, MI6, Margaret Thatcher. You name them, they all tried it on. When you compare that to bashing away on stage, you can see where we were at. I guess our interest in performance was secondary.

Punk in the hands of the showbiz world is an absolutely pointless farce. It means nothing. Fine, rock and roll can be fun, you can have a good night out, but what's that got to do with punk? All these reformed punk bands and major label acts who like to think of themselves as punk are okay if you want a laugh and a good old jump around, but it's nonsense to imagine that it's anything to do with what punk was really about. Punk was a way of life, not a pop fad.

If you're a band there's a degree to which you have to make a commitment to put forward a public image, and the only way you can do that is to keep up a personal front. In the end we found it impossible to keep up that front, which is one of the reasons we stopped—1984. Very Orwellian.

The lyrics, music and imagery of Crass were involved with global politics, but ultimately I think the effect we had on people was more on their personal politics. Punk used to be a massive cry against inequality and injustice, but then it became incorporated into the mainstream. I detest people who allow that incorporation to happen. It makes me angry. Time and time and time again you hear youth expressing its voice. Time and time and time again you see that voice destroyed by drugs, self-indulgence, stupidity and sell-outs. It's sad.

But for all that, you have to go on believing in possibilities, believing that people want something better in life, looking for something outside of ugliness, vulgarity, cruelty and exploitation; something that has a meaning, that's got connection. But every time there seems to be a possibility of that happening, it gets knocked down. It was like that with the Clash. Everyone was so excited because finally there was someone talking politics and saying things like "I'm so bored with the USA", and then the next month what are they doing? They're snorting coke and doing big gigs in the USA: big deal, guys.

People are so endlessly let down by their heroes, but I guess that's their fault. They shouldn't have heroes, but that's the society we live in: big heroes, little people. Sure, I acknowledge that there are people who might see us as heroes, but those are the people who completely missed our central message—"There is no authority but yourself". However, I know from the letters we continue to get from all over the world that many people were deeply and properly moved, not toward their pockets, but in their souls. That's because it wasn't a matter of us saying, "Come on, buy our latest fucking album." No, we were trying to let people know that their life was important, that it was the only one they'd ever have, and that they should try to live it their way, whatever that way was.

We offered information, and I do believe that a lot of that information was real and correct. When I say correct I mean actually presenting something of value which people could take hold of and say, "Yeah, maybe I could make something of my life." The thing we wanted to help people understand was a sense of autonomy and authenticity of the individual human soul. Just as soul is constantly de-

meaned in the media, so it is undermined by drugs, inside or outside, but in the end it's the only thing we've truly got. As personalities we're just a series of remarks picked up on our journey through life, and, sadly, this becomes what we think we are. But beneath all that we've got something we were born with, something we die with, something which exists beyond time, and that's our deepest inner soul. I guess I'm talking about a kind of immortality. To me the purpose of life is to connect with that inner soul, because by doing so we actually become part of life's continuum. If we exist as separate entities, as individual personalities, there's no reality to life and no continuity beyond it.

There's a connectedness between everybody and we all breathe, we all eat, we all sleep and we all have an inner soul which enables us to do that. It's all so obvious and natural. That's a starting point, and that's what we were actually (well, I was) attempting to promote through Crass. Yes, the lyrics of Crass were a lot to do with "the bomb" or "the State", but what I was saying was "look beneath all that, look beyond it, and where do you find yourself?" If you can do that, if you can find your soul, you connect with all humankind, with all of life.

We all exist in a day-to-day reality of lies and deceit, and nobody will ever make any sense of it. That's why we need to allow for tenderness, for silence, for contemplation. We need to find our own soul within all this mess. We've let ourselves become commodities, pawns in the marketplace. The only way we can get out of that is to realise that our personality, the very thing we think we are, is no more than a costume of ideas. We all like to think we're someone special, so we mouth the right words, dress up in the right gear, but it's all projection, all so fucking irrelevant.

But for all that, I believe people want to connect. Deep down they're tired of being no more than an idea of themselves. That's why people look for more, that's why they have sex, why they smoke dope, why they go on binges. They probably won't find the answer that way, but all the same, they want to connect. People want to know that they're alive, but let's face it, in a consumer society, that's no easy job.

LEMMY

INTERVIEW AND PHOTOS BY CHRIS SHONTING

Published November 2009

I thought about trying to make the intro to this interview sound like an impartial journalist wrote it. But fuck that. Lemmy is my hero and I'm not going to try and hide it because that'd be no fun. When I was meeting, photographing, and interviewing Lemmy backstage at a recent New York show, I felt like a young boy sidling up to the kitchen table with my grandfather when the houseful of relatives had finally gone silent and he decided that it was time for me to hear his stories. At first I was nervous because this was the big show, but within the first few words Lemmy had already disarmed me. Then he let it rip and told his tales. As a Motörhead fan, I can think of nothing greater.

Lemmy is by far one of the most down-to-earth people I've had the good fortune of coming across. He's a goddamn gentleman and not too shabby of a scholar either. Like his music, he is also quite savage. Some find him too brutal to handle. But offending those who are weak in constitution is just a byproduct of his total honesty. Lemmy has never changed in order to gain fanfare or subdue his critics. His entire existence speaks boundlessly about what it means to stick to your guns. There are no astronomical highs or abysmal lows in the story of Motörhead. There is simply the trajectory of a band plowing insolently through an endless blizzard of gigs, women, trends, naysayers, ass kissers, and industry swine. Lemmy is THE exemplary road dog for the ages.

Vice: What was it that made you say, "I'm going to be in a band"?
Lemmy: Women.

Women.
Hands down, women. Seeing them on TV flocking around rock singers. I came up in the 50s, you know, and that was kind of basic at the time. I got my first record in 1958. I was pretty young then, and I saw this English singer, Cliff Richard, who is still going but is very different now from what he was then. He was on TV, surrounded by chicks trying to pull his clothes off. I said, "That's for me. It doesn't even look like work." I found out later that it was, but it does have its advantages over working at the washing-machine factory.

Yeah, I would say so.
So that's what made me go for it. My mother played Hawaiian guitar, right, but there was really bad action on it, if you know what I mean. Nevertheless I put strings on it and took it to school during the week after exams, when you don't do anything.

When you're just sitting around.
Right. And I was immediately surrounded by chicks. It worked like a charm, and I couldn't even play the fucking thing.

How soon after that did you think, "Maybe I've got to learn"?
Oh, about two hours. I find it quite easy to play chords and, you know, that was all I ever did. I never wanted to be a lead guitarist. I didn't even realise there was such a thing as a bass player till later.

I understand.
So I was a good rhythm guitarist for a long time, but I was shit at lead. Really mediocre, man.

But you did try doing lead guitar?
Yeah. I played lead for two years in a band called the Rockin' Vicars. I just cheated, you know. I used to put on a lot of fuzz and move my fingers up and down really quick, and they thought it was a solo. I didn't want to tell them it wasn't.

Great bands usually implode after three albums or so, but you've kept Motörhead functioning for so long.
Coming up on 35 years now.

What are those other bands doing wrong?
They don't think the music is important enough to sink their personal differences for the sake of it. I always felt that no personal differences were big enough to break up the band. I mean, people have left the band, but I always carried on. I never considered doing anything else. This is what I'm supposed to do. This is what I'm supposed to be. I'm supposed to be in the fucking dressing room doing interviews. It's my life.

Yeah.
It's not a job anymore.

I want to ask you about Hawkwind, who you played bass for before you started Motörhead. How did you get it going with Hawkwind?
I went to see the band play live once before I joined them. Everybody was having this collective epileptic fit—the whole audience, 600 people. I thought, "Fuck it, I've got to join these guys."

What were the pros and cons of being in Hawkwind?

What I liked about it was that it was the first time I played bass, and I found out that I could be a good bass player. So I became a bass player and I *was* really good at it, you know? That was a great thing for me—kind of an eye-opener—and also there was a lot of freedom within that band to play bass. I did a lot of fill-ins and a lot of smart shit behind Dave, who played lead guitar. You know, I was showing off as usual.

For the chicks.
What's it for if you can't show off? It's rock 'n' roll, so you might as well.

What were the things that really bugged the shit out of you?
In Hawkwind? Their attitude. I mean, they never told me I was in the band.

Fuck. That was like five years.
Five years. They fired me, and I said, "You can't fire me, motherfuckers, you never told me I was in the band!"

Who ran that band?
Dave Brock, the lead guitarist. It's his band, lock, stock, and barrel.

I've always thought, from watching interviews, that he seemed like a pretty level-headed dude.
He was, but at the time we were very successful in Britain—number one and all that. And that gets to different people in different ways. They never really forgave me for being the singer on their only hit single. [*laughs*]

"Silver Machine". That song was kind of a ringer.
They tried everybody else singing it before me and none of them could do it. I got it in like two or three takes. That really pissed them off. Then *NME* printed my picture alone on the front page. "Hawkwind Goes to Number One" with my picture next to it.

Oh, that will make you some friends in the band.
Yeah. That really upset them. It was a funny bunch of people anyway. We were all cataclysmically stoned all the time. We were not even on a tour bus then, we were in the back of a van with two mattresses and blankets. That's how we used to travel at festival time.

Jesus.
And it was still a festival when we were going home in the fucking van. In fact, Dell's festival blanket wasn't washed for two years. The fucking thing could fucking stand up on its own if you leaned it against the wall.

One band you played in before Hawkwind that I actually still listen to a lot is Sam Gopal.
Oh yeah. You listen to that?

I have it on my iPod. I think someone emailed it to me because you can't get it.
You can now, apparently. It's been put out again by somebody.

What was the deal with that? I think it's some of the sickest music I've ever heard.
Well, I wrote all them songs in one night.

Fuck. You sang it too, right?
Yeah. That was in 1968. It was very rushed, obviously. But the speed was very good in those days. I sat up all night and wrote all the fucking songs. Eleven of them, I think.

When was the last time you listened to it?
Years ago.

It's great. You guys even had girls doing back-up vocals.
Yeah. Sue and Sunny were famous backing-group chicks at the time in London. They were on everybody's record. Like Dusty Springfield, they did all her records. They were really well known.

Oh, you know that song on there, "Season of the Witch"? I didn't write that one.

But the rest, in one night? Not too shabby.
Not too shabby.

What's your writing process like?

I get the title first and write around that. It's like a word exercise. You get on the theme and then you explore every possible avenue. So I'll get a title like "Overkill" and then figure out stuff to do after that.

I don't even know how many fucking songs you've written.

Plenty.

Who influenced you when you started out?

Everything I hear influences me. I can't tell you all my influences as a musician. I mean, all the early rock singers like Little Richard, Elvis, Buddy Holly, Chuck Berry, are important. All them guys. And all the Liverpool bands too. I was very lucky, man. I got to hear a lot of good shit. I saw the Beatles at the Cavern Club.

I remember reading about that in your book.

And Hendrix. I was working for him as a roadie just because I happened to be sleeping on his bassist Noel Redding's floor at the time, and they needed an extra guy. I got to watch that motherfucker twice a night for about six months.

So if you had to say what the greatest act you ever saw was…

Hendrix and the Beatles. No doubt. Those two… you will never see anything like them again, because they were at the peak of their game and they came in and fucking wiped everybody out. Even the Stones. The Stones were secondhand next to the Beatles. It was only when the Beatles were gone that they could start calling themselves the greatest rock 'n' roll band in the world, which they never were. They were always pretty ropey on stage. Without all that production they do now they would still be pretty ropy, because Keith is pretty ropey, isn't he?

Yeah.

He is a great rhythm guitarist, but he isn't a leader.

He is not the liveliest character I've seen.

He was livelier earlier on, but Brian Jones was the leader of the band for years. It was his band. He hired Jagger and Keith too, but they paced him out.

I wanted to ask you what your ideas are regarding success and failure. You are totally unchanged.

Why change if you're on a winner? [*laughs*]

Yeah. But when Motörhead dropped that first album it seems like the media were like, "What the fuck?"

We couldn't get released in America for about three years after we were a big hit in Britain. Then we were on fucking Legacy and Eclipse and then we got on Sony, which was actually worse. Then we got lucky. We got with… what was that label called? They got eaten by Sanctuary anyway.

Was it that German label?

No, we're on SPV, the German label, now. But they just filed for bankruptcy.

It's a common trend.

I know. Record companies are going under, and they don't even understand how it happened to them. They are so fucking stupid.

Can you give the industry a grade, like an F to an A+, in terms of the way people have handled Motörhead?

Oh, it's an F. It's the same with any other band that's a bit different. The industry has always been fucking surprised by the next breakout band. Like when the Liverpool bands went up—the Mersey Sound was a big craze right, and there was a small scene about Manchester, and then there was London with the Stones, and then it came over here with San Francisco, and then they did again with Seattle and Nirvana. After they have one hit with one band, they always run up to that city and sign everyone with a guitar around their neck. Half of them should have never even got a contract.

They were just kids with guitars who didn't know what the fuck they were doing.

THE WORLD ACCORDING TO VICE

They just happened to be from Seattle or from Liverpool. A lot of them industry people—even Brian Epstein, the Beatles' manager—didn't know what the fuck they were doing. He signed about four bands that never had a hit, and then they got cast by the wayside.

But if all the labels embraced you and knew what to do, would Motörhead be Motörhead?
Probably not.

Because you guys are like underdogs and legends all in one.
Yeah. We made sort of a career out of it. We had no choice, actually, because we weren't ever going to be the overdog. We're kind of too brutal to be universally popular. I never thought we were going to be that. Being up toward the top of the second echelon is fine with me. What it must have been like to be in the Beatles or the Stones, man. I cannot imagine. It must have been fucking torture. George Harrison said it was the worst time of his life and the best time of his life.

I'm sure there's a serious amount of 50/50 there.
Yeah, sure. Everything they did was under the microscope. One British daily paper had a Beatles page in it that was about whatever they did the day before. A mass-circulation paper—the *Daily Mirror*, it was—which was the biggest-selling paper in Britain at the time.

Do you think anyone could really stand that for a long time?
Stand being that big? No. You have to either give up or change. And the Beatles certainly did that.

I always liked how they were cast as goodie-goodies while the Stones were cast as Satanic tough guys.
The Beatles were from Liverpool. It's a hard town. The Stones weren't the hard men. They just dressed up. The Beatles were the hard men. Fucking Liverpool, man. The Stones are from the suburbs of London. Ringo was from the fucking Dingle, which is

the worst area, next to Glasgow, that I've ever seen in my life. What they did in both those places—they couldn't reform it, so they just knocked it down. They moved everybody out and razed it and built new housing projects. No way to make it civilised, you know what I mean? It was fucking lawless. The police wouldn't go in there.

Your song "Stone Deaf in the USA" is a tribute to partying in America.
Yeah.

And you moved to LA.
Yeah. But not when I wrote that song.

So the song isn't about that? That was just from touring?
Yeah. We did the Ozzy Osbourne tour—the first *Blizzard of Ozz* tour. Audiences were like this [*makes a disgusted face*].

Like, "What the fuck?"
All the way through the set. Most of them didn't understand anything about it, but a few did and that's our core fan base. Most of them were just there for the event of something, and they were appalled. But they were appalled by Ozzy too. Never mind us. What they did when Kiss joined the tour after we finished, I don't know.

Jesus Christ, Kiss took over from you guys opening for Ozzy? That's a schizophrenic tour.
Yeah. Kiss and Ozzy.

You are the most low-maintenance band, and then they needed their fucking makeup artist.
I know. Remember when they took the makeup off?

Yeah. That was awkward for everybody.
Very awkward. Because you found out, "Jesus, they're ugly."

They are not pretty men.
Except for Paul Stanley. He was still cute. But the other three?

It's like waking up next to a chick after you were blackout drunk and you're like, "Oh shit."
[*laughs*] Fucking hell, hiding in the bathroom till she leaves.

I like to play asleep.
It's like the fox-trap syndrome. You'd rather gnaw your arm off than wake her up.

We've all had that situation.
I remember one of our crew once, Paulie, there were these two chicks we took on all our German shows. We used to call them the "Monsters of Rock", right? One of them had one tooth. A terrible mess, but they were really big fans, you know? So this guy Paulie pulled one of them one night, and they were sharing a room with our sound guy, Dave Chamberlain. He woke and he could tell he was next to someone, but he had no idea who it was. Then he looks over at Dave, and Dave is in bed like this [*Lemmy makes more disgusted faces*]. And he went [*another disgusted face*]. And Dave went [*shakes his head*]. Then Paulie went to the bathroom and waited till she left.

That's a pretty relatable story for most people.
Most fans have been through that one.

Shit. I've dealt with that all over the Lower East Side. Really sounds like a good idea at first.
Yeah. Especially late night, drunk.

That's when all the fucking golden chicks start popping out.
That's when everybody becomes good looking, or at least manageable. But sometimes, it's like there's the last chicken in the shop and you don't seem to be able to help yourself. It's like having an out-of-body experience. You see yourself chatting up this dragon, and you know you're doing it but you still do it.

It's like the devil and the angel on the shoulder.
And the angel always loses.

The angel doesn't have a tolerance for alcohol.

And the devil is always shaped like a dick.

Pointing at her.
"Do it, do it." Like a fucking dog.

OK, this next one is kind of a cliché question.
I'll give you a cliché answer.

All right. Good. Line me up with a solid for this one. Where are the best women you've found from touring all over the world?
The best women are the ones who want to fuck you, and the worst are the ones who don't.

So that pretty much transcends all geographic boundaries.
It does, because there are only two kinds of women in the world—women who you want to fuck and succeed, and women who you don't want to. It's easy, really. It doesn't matter where they're from. I don't mind the accent. There's always sign language, even if you can't speak the same language.

There is. Especially in a barroom.
Yeah. Though it gets kind of confusing if you're really cataclysmically drunk. They often get the wrong idea. Many a guy has woken up married with tattoos on the chest.

I got a couple of friends like that. But listen, we have to also say that you've been very supportive of a lot of female musicians.
I like women in rock 'n' roll. I was brought up by two women—my mother and my grandmother. My father left when I was three months old. She didn't marry again till I was like ten or something, so I understand women a lot better than a lot of guys do from going out hunting with Dad. Mostly I like women more than guys. If you talk to guys, especially in America, it's always macho bullshit you talk about, like how much you hate politics and you're going to be in the militia and shoot something. There's a lot of that about, and it's a shame because this country is paradise. People here are shooting themselves in the foot and they don't even know it.

SPIKE JONZE

INTERVIEW BY SHANE SMITH | PHOTOS BY TERRY RICHARDSON

Published September 2009

In the five years since we've become friends with Spike Jonze, he has never not been working on his movie adaptation of Maurice Sendak's classic children's book *Where the Wild Things Are*. It's been a life-consuming, soul-questioning, long-day's-journey-into-night, half-decade quest for Spike to make this film according to his very specific vision for it, and it's been hugely inspiring to watch it grow and evolve. And now, like a beautiful little baby crowning the rim of the birth canal or a ripe, juicy tomato plumply twisting on the vine, *Where the Wild Things Are* is about to burst forth into the world. It's like no film we've seen before, and we can't wait to witness how the general moviegoing public reacts to it.

Vice founder Shane Smith went to London this summer to visit Spike as he completed effects work on *WTWTA* there. Shane was en route to Africa to film for VBS.TV, and he was reeling from the gargantuan doses of malaria medication he'd been taking. Before he met up with Spike, he attended a private viewing of *Where the Wild Things Are*. Then he rushed straight into Spike's arms and, overcome with emotion, sobbed awhile. And then the two of them sat in Shane's hotel room and talked all about Spike's new movie, life, and love.

Vice: I just saw your new film. It's called *Where the Wild Things Are*—
Spike Jonze: Yeah… [*laughs*]

I obviously read the book when I was a kid, and I remembered all of the characters, especially Max. But I couldn't remember a lot of the specifics. Like, does he use a boat in the book too?
He does. The basic elements are all taken from the book. But most important to me was to capture the spirit and tone of the book. At least what that was to me…

You read it when you were a kid too?
Oh yeah, definitely.

And it was one of your favourites?
For sure.

Was it in your brain for a long time that you wanted to make it into a film?

No, because it was one of those things that I loved but I wouldn't have wanted to touch. I didn't know what I could add to it that wouldn't ruin it. But I've gotten to know Maurice Sendak over the last 14 years and talked to him about it occasionally. He would ask me if I would want to do it and I would contemplate it and try to think of—

Hold on. So he asked you if you wanted to do it?
It was something he was developing into a movie for the last 20 years.

Do you know who else was ever going to do it?
I'm not sure who had gotten really close to it, but he talked to a lot of different people.

It must have felt amazing to be personally asked by him.
Oh yeah. I mean, I love him, and I love his books. And since I've loved them from when I was so young—*In the Night Kitchen* and *Where the Wild Things Are*

and *Pierre* and *The Nutshell Library*—those images are all so…

Ingrained in your head?
Right. When you love something from that age, you end up loving it really deeply because the images are there way down inside you. As you've grown, you've grown around them and they've just gotten deeper into you.

Sometimes I get mad when someone takes one of my favourite movies and then remakes it, or takes a great book and films it. There's a huge risk of misinterpreting the original thing. Were you worried about that? Like, "Wow, it's a huge responsibility to make the most beloved children's book of all time into a movie"?
Definitely. Not only did I not want to ruin it for other people, I didn't want to ruin it for myself. So, initially, I didn't want to do it because I didn't have an idea of *how* to do it.

And then one day it clicked?
Well, I think it was probably the third time Maurice talked to me about it. He sent me a script, a draft of a script—

So he had been writing it?
No, not Maurice himself. He had worked with different writers or directors over the years and tried different versions. I read this one draft and it wasn't bad. But I realised what it could be and I got really excited. It was a really simple idea—to take the feeling of the book and expand who Max is and who the Wild Things are. And my idea was the Wild Things are wild emotions. It was that simple, but it was enough for me to know I could explore that idea and still be true to the book. I think that as a kid, for me at least, wild emotions were probably the things that were the scariest.

Like freaking out but you didn't know why you were freaked out, getting hysterical.
Exactly. Maybe at the time I wouldn't have analysed it like this, but I think that wild emotions, both your own and those of the people around you, can be really confusing and disorienting as a kid.

And the most accepted interpretation of *Where the Wild Things Are* is that it's about emotions and control—or lack of control—over them as a kid.
Reading that script, suddenly I felt like with that idea, if you were going to be writing about our wild emotions, then it's sort of infinite in terms of where you can go with it. It just felt wide-open.

Did there end up being any of your own childhood in there? Is there a little bit of you in Max?
Yes, sure. I mean, even in things that I've made that I haven't written there is some of me. Even the movies I've done with Charlie [Kaufman]—I feel like I'm in those as well. But yeah, I am probably in this one to a higher degree.

You wrote this script with Dave Eggers. How long did it take you guys?
I probably worked on it on my own for around six months. That was just doing notes, free-associating, coming up with characters and ideas and themes and dialogues—really having no idea how it was going to come together. Then I went and started working with Dave and brought him all these notes and sort of dumped them on a table and we went from page 1 and just worked from there. I would say the first draft probably took four more months from that point. I moved to San Francisco and we worked every day.

Did you have a studio before or after the script?
First there was a studio, but it was a different studio than we ended up doing it with.

Why? Did the first studio hate the script when they read it?
I don't know if they loved it.

Well, I think you did a great job on the writing, but when I was watching the movie I was thinking to myself that this must have been a hard sell to a major studio for a tent-pole release. This is

obviously a big film, but it's also so intimate and artistic...

It's definitely not what they were picturing.

What did they want? *Shrek*?

I don't know, you should go interview them.

Did you feel any pressure when you were making it, or were you like, "Screw it, I'm going to do my own film and everybody can go to hell"?

Well, I wanted to be respectful of, you know, the people who were paying for it to be made. But at a certain point you've got to just make the movie you want to make. If you go off that track, you become lost and you're neither here nor there.

What about input from studio people?

You've got to be open to listening to see if it's a good idea, because a good idea can come from anywhere. But you've also got to not be swayed by other people's anxiety. In the end, I just tried to keep to my original intention.

Which was what?

To make a movie that felt true to being nine years old and trying to sort of navigate the world and your own emotions and the emotions of people around you.

I was thinking that this was a very brave film for you to have made because you made art even though it's financed by a conglomerate and there are so many millions of dollars involved and so many pressures against it. That's incredibly brave, and I'm proud of you.

Thanks. I'm excited that we got to make our movie and make it what it is, whatever it is. I don't even know what it is! It's just what we set out to make, and now because, you know, it's financed by Warner Bros., it's going to be released in a kind of big way. So that's exciting that there is this little thing that is going to be presented to the world in...

It's going to be huge. Are you nervous about that? You're not a public guy, and you made this thing for

five years and it's your little baby and everything, and now it's going to be in, like, *People* magazine. You're gonna be in *People*! Can you believe it?

Wait, Shane, I didn't get to finish my last answer!

Sorry. Go ahead.

It's my turn to talk!

And here's another thing! I have another thing! Just kidding, go ahead.

[*laughs*] This is my interview!

Go! Talk about your film!

No, I was just going to say that I think it's really hard to be a big company and still be about ideas, and I think it's amazing when I see a company that's about ideas over profit margins, or over deals. Or to trust that ideas can lead to profits.

It's pretty rare.

Businessmen, they make deals. That's such an abstract idea. I don't even know what that means. But they're out there making the deal, acquiring another company, deciding what percentage, what profits are they going to keep, which of their costs they can bill back to somebody in business with them...

All of that stuff is torturous.

Yeah. So I'm always impressed when companies are about ideas first, like Apple or Pixar. Those are two of my favourite companies because it's about an idea, it's about making something that means something. Branson too, everything Richard Branson does. To work on that scale, and—

So you like raves, then?

Does Branson rave?

No, but Virgin Atlantic Airlines, it's like, black lights and trip-hop.

I don't like the purple light.

You love the purple light!

No. That's the one thing about those Virgin airplanes.

It's the most unflattering, ugly, color-draining light. I have a feeling they're going to have to change that. Will you write them a letter?

If you insist. But can we talk a little about how you made the actual Wild Things for the film?
We started with the voice performances. We shot the whole movie with the voice actors on a soundstage, on video—

Before you had costumes?
As we were making the costumes. This was just to get the voice performances down. The whole movie is based on what those guys did on the soundstage. We shot it like a movie. They'd learn their scenes, block the scenes, and try takes exploring the dialogue. We videotaped the whole thing. We had seven cameras and seven actors. That became our reference footage for the making of the rest of the movie.

How do you do voice casting?
We listened to a lot of actors' voices from their previous roles as we looked at still images of the *Wild Things* characters. Once you start isolating somebody's voice, you know, you have to think very differently. It's such a different thing from what I'd normally need from an actor.

So I guess that's the first element of the Wild Things, the voices. What about the people inside the suits?
The suit performers. They are the second element. They would watch the tapes of the voice actors and take all those nuances of what those guys, like James Gandolfini and Forest Whitaker, had done.

Were the suits hot?
They were insanely hot. I mean, these guys were like soldiers. The movie was hard for everybody just because it was a long process, but for those guys it was a whole other level. They truly bled for it.

Wow.
They made the suits come alive, and that's not just a matter of keeping them moving. I think that sometimes there's a tendency in animation or puppetry where people are like, "Well, if it's alive it's always moving. So don't ever let it sit still." But a puppet is poorly designed if doesn't look alive when it's sitting still.

Yeah, I forget the name of the goat Wild Thing—
Oh, Alexander.

Right, Alexander. It was great how that character looks depressed even when he's just standing still.
Yeah. Those suits were built already with the look of the face and the way they would stand. But the suit performers found ways to enhance them. If they were just standing there relaxed, the suit would look dead. But if they got into the right position, the suit looked like a body with muscles and everything. So the idea was not to have them moving all the time, but to have them moving when there was an intention behind it. They would listen and hear the intention of what the voice actors did, then sort of adapt that to what the suit could do.

That's really pretty amazing.
And then the third element that makes the Wild Things is their faces.

Which came last out of all these things.
Right. A friend of mine was saying that it's almost like an experimental film because we didn't know how it was going to work until the very end. But maybe all visual-effects movies are like that.

The effects on the creatures' faces were really the touches that made them totally come alive.
It completes the character. It's not like a visual effect that is just going to make it look cool. These visual effects are going to complete the performances of the Wild Things.

It must have felt insane to finally see it all put together.
It's really exciting and it's also like, "Finally." Only in the last three months did we start seeing enough animation where it was like, "Ah, that's amazing." It really looks like they're thinking and they're alive.

You worked on this movie for something like five years.

I know. That's too long. Five years is too long to work on a movie. It's crazy.

Well you wrote it for two years, you were down in Australia shooting for a year, and then you did post work...

It's ridiculous. It seems like another lifetime when I started it. But we're getting close now. I feel like I've finished the movie in my head. We locked the picture last October and for the last eight months we've just been doing visual effects and music and sound.

Do you think that a movie is won or lost in the edit room?

The movie becomes what it is in the edit. Some people, like the Coen brothers, I think their movies are very close to their scripts. And I think that's amazing, but I've never done that before. My movies change a lot in the edit room.

Do you shoot knowing that? Is it like, "Oh, I'm going to do two wide shots so I can make a choice when I'm cutting the movie"?

Yeah. When we're shooting, we shoot in a very loose way. We cover it in a manner where you know it could go together this way or that way. Or, you know, we cover dialogue in different ways, to try stuff, to find stuff, to see what we can discover. If an idea comes up on set, we'll improvise. If something funny or interesting happens, or we discover something, or an actor has an idea, we incorporate that into it—as long as it gets you closer to the feeling you set out to capture. That is the catch... to be open to new ideas but to always keep your intention for that scene or the film in the forefront of your mind so you can know if an idea is getting you closer to that or further away.

What would you say you like doing better? TV, music videos, commercials, skate videos, or—loaded question—feature films?

I like them all in different ways. Even though it's a cliché answer, there's actually some truth to that. The thing about movies is that because of their length they can be so much. You can explore a lot more ideas and get deeper into characters. In that way they are the richest experiences because you can put so much of yourself into them.

Here's another important question. Do you want to go to the pub and get wasted?

[*laughs*] I've got to work in the morning. I'm animating all week. Animating hungover doesn't work that well. I've tried it.

Do you find that animating all week cuts into your partying? No, I'm just kidding. But do you feel like you are getting better at things just by making, making, making more things and working all the time?

I think my skills are getting better. I know how to talk to an actor in more of a helpful way or how to light a shot where, if I have a feeling of a shot in my head, I might know what lighting will give it that feeling more than I did before—what kind of light might give me the quality of light that I want. So, yes, technically I've gotten more knowledgeable. But I still feel like you only know what you're doing after you've done it.

You just jump in there.

I was always so excited to learn how to do things by putting myself into situations where I *had* to do them. I think that was something that I always liked doing. And this movie is no different.

You run a risk of not getting perfect results.

I think perfection is overrated. Me and my friend Eric, who edits my films, have talked about this a lot. I'm all for a shot that is sort of out of focus or flawed if it has the right feeling. For example, in *Adaptation,* Nicolas Cage plays two brothers and sometimes you can tell that Nicolas is one of the brothers and the other brother is a double that doesn't really look like him. There would be shots like that where I would want to hold on longer because Nicolas would be so good in a certain take, and Eric would be like, "No, we can't, this totally gives away the trick." But I'm always for, well, whatever. If it feels good, go for it.

And you also can get more confident as you make more and more things.

Even those videos that I did were all so homemade. It's not like we had a budget to do it any other way, but I kind of liked that it was, on a Beastie Boys video, just the three of them and me. I had probably like a 16-mm camera and the crew was whoever could fit in the van with all the props and wardrobe.

Is it strange to think of that progression from you, the Beastie Boys, and a Bolex 16 to these big Hollywood productions?

The amount of equipment and crew that was required for *Where the Wild Things Are* was much bigger than anything I've tried before just because, you know, the locations were far away and they needed a lot of art direction and design. We needed to get the Wild Things to do what we wanted and we needed big equipment to have, say, a Wild Thing walk up to a tree and rip it out of the ground. You can't just do that with a Bolex and a couple of people in a van.

Of course not. But what would be an example of the downside to having the sort of production where you can pull off something huge like that?

It makes it a real battle to stay spontaneous. Like if you are going to have a crane that's going to yank a tree from the ground, you've got to put that crane somewhere. So you've got to look at the location months before, and say, "OK, we are not going to look in that direction. All these other directions look good so we just won't look in that direction, and we can put the crane there." And then the day to shoot that scene comes and suddenly the light is different or the clouds are a certain way or the actors do something we hadn't imagined and it's like, "Fuck, we've *got* to look in that direction now." But you just can't move the crane, the crane is already rigged there with all its anchors and you're not going to waste half a day pulling it up and trying to figure out how to drive it through some trees to a different place.

That sounds incredibly stressful.

But I feel like I'm not going toward only making big

ideas. Only making things that require a huge crew and therefore a bigger budget would be really limiting. You would get stuck. The bigger it gets, the more isolated you get within that system.

OK, so let's review a few things.

OK.

***Where the Wild Things Are*. Directed by—**

Me.

Written by—

David Eggers and me.

Produced by—

Maurice Sendak. And his partner John Carls. And Tom Hanks and Gary Goetzman and my producing partner, Vince Landay.

You don't have a producer credit? Come on.

Why? I directed it, that's enough.

I guess. When does it come out?

October 16, 2009.

Are you excited?

[*laughs*] Yes. I'm excited that we're finishing it. And I'm excited about the movie we made.

When you launch a film like this, there must be crazy marketing plans.

You have to totally… you have to set the date, then you have to eat the movie, then you have to lick it, and then you have to grab it, and wrestle it—

Eat it and *then* lick it?

Then you have to kiss it softly and delicately massage it to bed. And then you tuck it in, and then you cuddle up with it, and then it doesn't want you to cuddle up with it anymore. And then you have to, like, give it its own space, and then you just check on it every now and then.

And then it's done.

Yes, and then it's done.

DAVID LYNCH

INTERVIEW BY JESSE PEARSON | ILLUSTRATION BY TED PEARCE

Published September 2009

I am a big-time David Lynch nut. I remember having to steal a copy of *Blue Velvet* and watch it at a friend's house because my parents thought it was too sketchy for me to see at 12. I watched each episode of *Twin Peaks* the night that it originally aired. I saw *Wild at Heart* and *Fire Walk With Me* on their opening days. For my money, this guy has made some of the most original, thrilling, deep, and beautiful cinema ever, ever, ever.

So just because you care, here are my favourite David Lynch things in descending order from the best on down to the simply very great:

- The episodes of *Twin Peaks* that he directed
- *Blue Velvet*
- *Inland Empire*
- *Mulholland Drive*
- *Wild at Heart* (this was at the top of the list when I was 15)
- *Fire Walk With Me*
- *The Elephant Man*
- *Eraserhead*
- *Dune*
- His early shorts
- *Catching the Big Fish*

I didn't like *Lost Highway*, but let's not bother getting into that.

Now here's the tricky part. David Lynch and I both practice this thing called Transcendental Meditation, which was invented by a guy named Maharishi Mahesh Yogi back in the 1950s. The Beatles did it; Howard Stern and Jerry Seinfeld do it too. Weird collection of people right there. I interviewed Lynch for *Vice* a few years ago, and we talked only about TM at that time. I figured that this time around we would talk about TM and more stuff, broader stuff, life and movie stuff. And we did, sort of. But you also have to realise that for Lynch, the tenets of TM are of the utmost importance. His whole life is inextricably linked to it. No matter what you ask him, he is likely to link it back to meditation. So, after we were done talking this time around and I listened to the tape, I thought, hmm, we really did talk about TM a lot here. Maybe it's weird to put all this TM talk into the magazine. Maybe it feels like a commercial for my and his brand of spirituality. Maybe I shouldn't do this.

But then I realised: I'm the editor of this magazine and the rest of you aren't. So fuck y'all if you don't want to hear about it. Here's me and Lynch talking about meditation, the unified field, total enlightenment, and cheese.

Vice: Hello, Mr. Lynch. I don't know if you remember, but I interviewed you a few years ago. We spoke mainly about Transcendental Meditation that time.
David Lynch: I'll be darned.

I'm a practitioner as well, since I was a little kid.
Fantastic, Jesse!

I want to touch on TM this time as well but also go

a little broader later on. I know that meditation is very important to you in terms of your creative process. I often find myself wanting to interrupt meditations to jot down ideas. Does this happen to you too?
Well, you know, the Beatles asked Maharishi the same question when they were with him in Rishikesh in '68. They'd get ideas in meditation too. He said, "Come out, write it down, and then go back to meditating."

Wow. I'll do that from now on.
See, the idea is very clear down there, and so it's really thrilling when it comes. But if you wait till after you finish to jot it down, chances are that you'll forget it.

That's happened to me a lot. Is it the same for you?
If I've really got a hot one, I come out and write it down, and then I go right back in.

Now that I think about it, if I'm interrupted I sometimes find it easier to go right back into a deep meditation as opposed to a shallower one.
I know what you mean, but a lot of times "shallow" and "deep" are sort of subjective things. If you saw yourself on an EEG machine, you might be surprised at how many times you were transcending during a meditation.

I guess it goes in peaks and valleys.
You dip in and dip out. Maybe you go in there and you didn't really get zapped, but you've still touched it many times, meaning the transcendent, which is the deepest level. You experience that many times in each meditation.

Just for different lengths of time.
Yeah.

That makes sense. It sounds familiar to me. I think I was around seven years old when I first started having experiences in meditation that felt transcendent to me.

[*laughs*] That's fantastic.

It was pretty funny. My grandparents and my friends thought I was in a cult.
Now, just for your readers, Transcendental Meditation is not a religion, not a cult, not a sect... It's a mental technique—an ancient form of meditation—that unlocks the human being's full potential. And the full potential of a human being is called enlightenment. It's really pretty foolish *not* to meditate.

Our readers might start to tune us out now if they aren't open to hearing about this stuff, but oh well. So yes, it's true for me too—not meditating is sort of a waste of one's own capabilities.
Yeah! You've got this potential, but you're not going to get it unless you experience transcendence—that deepest level. Pure consciousness. And every time you experience the transcendent, you infuse some of it and you grow in that consciousness. You grow in intelligence, creativity, happiness, love, energy, and peace.

All good stuff, basically.
And the side effect is that negativity starts to lift away. It's a win-win-win situation.

You don't have to tell me.
I know, but we have to tell your readers. [*laughs*] People get it at different times, and you've got to want it to do it. And hearing these things might make some people out there say, "Man, I gotta have that!" That happens—more and more these days.

If the reader comments on our website from the last time I talked to you about this stuff are any indication, we're going to get slammed. Anyway, based on what I've read about your working process, ideas might come to you and then not get used for years and years.
Sometimes, yeah.

What's your method for keeping track of ideas?
I write them on little pieces of paper and then I drop those in a box. So I have, like, an idea box. And then I sometimes go through there, and one idea is

suddenly like a little jewel. And so I'll start to think about it, and you know what they say: "Where the attention is, that becomes lively."

Right.
Focused attention has a magic quality. The idea does become lively, and it can make other ideas swim in, like little fish, and join it. And then a whole thing starts to emerge.

Is there also an element of the idea having a different context just because, say, five years—with all the changes that can happen in that amount of time—have gone by? Something that was mysterious to you when it popped into your head could be clear as day five years later.
Yeah! It's like all ideas have a time for being. And for some reason, at some specific time, you'll read an old idea and it just makes you crazy because you love it so much.

Do you ever go back and watch your old films?
Sometimes. My son Riley hadn't seen them before, so I saw them all with him recently. It's the same way with my older paintings—it's sometimes good to go back and look at your old stuff. It's just like the idea box. You might see something that you did way back when, and some part of that can feed into the work you're doing right now and jump-start it.

What do you call the place where ideas originate? The subconscious?
No. Everything—*everything*—originates in the unified field. It's an ocean of pure consciousness. It's the transcendent. And that's what quantum physics says now: Everything that is a thing has emerged from that field. New things are always emerging and bubbling up from it. So an idea will come, but you will not know the idea until it enters your conscious mind. Now, if you expand your consciousness you can catch ideas at deeper and deeper levels, and they'll have more information and more energy.

It's pretty intense.
Plus, as you understand things more, there's more

to understand!

That's true. It's almost kind of scary.
Everybody relies on ideas.

Your more recent work, specifically *Mulholland Drive* and *Inland Empire*, sort of has the rhythm of meditation to me. We drift, find focus, drift, and find focus. Is there anything to that, or am I reaching?
Well, I always say that those two films, like any other film, are based on ideas. I'm not trying to duplicate a meditation experience. I'm trying to translate ideas that came to me, to make them feel, in cinema, the way they did when they came to my mind. It's all based on the ideas that come.

Sure, without the idea there's nothing.
Exactly right.

Why do you think so many people have such a desire to know the meaning of your films?
I always say the same thing—we're like detectives. Films are another world, with new characters and new situations. When things are concrete in films, you don't have a problem understanding them. When they get abstract, then the understanding varies and people come up with different interpretations based on what's inside of themselves. When you look at life, we're always looking at stuff and wondering and thinking about this and that—trying to suss out what's going on, just like we're watching a film.

Just walking down any street could lead to a thousand different mysteries.
Ex-actly.

But even with all of that said, don't you get tired of people asking you what things in your work mean?
But I don't ever say what they mean. I say, "You know, for yourself, what it means. And that's valid."

Your films can be very scary. I know people who can't even watch the first Winkie's scene in *Mul-*

holland Drive. **What do you think an audience might get out of being so freaked out by a movie? I know that there is something valuable for me in it, but I can't put my finger on what it is.**

Well, I know that the images can be fearful, but those are just the ideas that came. Or they came *with* that fear. But there's nothing really scary there. It's just the way the scene goes, and the words that are said, and the way the expressions look, and the way the camera moves, and the way the sound is designed. It all conjures up a thing that makes people say "Whoa"—just like I said "Whoa" when I got the idea. And of course ideas can come up and conjure beautiful images too.

Of course.

Thank goodness for the ideas, because they tell you how to go. Intuition tells you how to go. Intuition is the number one tool for the artist.

Without that intuition, you can't make art.

You can't just read a book and become a painter or a filmmaker. There's some other abstract quality that has to be there too. And that's called intuition. Number one tool!

Going back to this fear thing for a second... You make it sound so simple, but a scary scene in one of your movies is way more than just the sum of its parts. Maybe you can tell me something that scares you.

I'm not any different from anybody else. The fear of death is the biggest fear. Everything else kind of falls away from that.

Are there specific ways that you're afraid you're going to die?

[*laughs*] It's like, you don't want to sit around and start thinking about that. But sometimes ideas come that involve death and fear—fear of the unknown— and not knowing where this path is leading.

Maybe part of the enjoyment in watching really scary stuff is that it's a safe way of experiencing that fear of death on a tiny scale.

See, that's the number one key. I always say, "Have the suffering on the screen. Not in your life." The artist doesn't have to suffer to show suffering. I could be a happy, happy camper shooting a death scene because it will have nothing to do with what's inside me. I'll just be translating ideas. And people can have a scary experience in the theatre, and then leave it and go into a world that's really a good world. Although a lot of times these days, people leave the theater and go into a world that's far worse than the horrific things they're seeing on the screen.

That's interesting, because a thing that gets said about you and your work a lot—especially since you've started talking so much in the press about meditation—is this question: "If this guy is so into the pursuit of bliss and enlightenment, why are his films so dark?" I think that's kind of a dumb way to look at it.

But it is a legitimate question.

I think what you say about putting suffering on the screen rather than in your life pretty much answers it. What would you say to my friend who is too much of a wimp to finish that Winkie's scene?

A film is like reading a book. You can read a book, and it can be a really frightening, horrendous story, and you can be really gripped by it. But you can stop reading at any moment and go get a cup of coffee and sit outside or whatever, you know? You choose to go into the world of that book.

Cinema can be much more immersive than a book, though.

But books are great too.

Oh sure, of course. Now, you might think this is goofy, but I've always wanted to ask you if you believe in the supernatural to any degree.

Well, this makes me think of my friend John Hagelin, who is one of the world's greatest quantum physicists. We know now that there are ten dimensions of space and one dimension of time. There are worlds upon worlds upon worlds, and there are all kinds of things going on. But a person can get lost in there—

for a long time. You want to go beyond all that and experience the transcendent. That's where all the power is that runs the whole universe and universes. Like Maharishi says, "Capture the fort first and then all the territories are yours."

That's a good analogy. You mentioned beauty a minute ago. What's a beautiful image you've seen in real life recently?

Pretty much everything! Here's another expression, and this one is Vedic: "The world is as you are." It's a secret. The world is as you are. If you want to see a better and better world, start expanding your consciousness. All of it's there inside every human being. The world starts looking brighter and more beautiful and people start looking more familiar and beautiful too. Everything starts getting really, really beautiful! An analogy is that if you're wearing filthy dark green glasses, then that's the world you see. But if you start cleaning those, and pumping in rose and gold, then *that* is the world you see.

I think that a lot of people fear that adjusting their attitude will take more sheer willpower than it actually does.

This is a natural process. It's not about trying. In TM, the word "trying" doesn't exist. It's effortless—easy. A ten-year-old child can do it.

I was just looking at your photo series of female nudes draped in smoke. That got me thinking about your female characters and how they are usually mysterious and dangerous, or at least the keepers of big secrets. Do you think that men are capable of really understanding women?

We're capable of understanding totality. But most of us don't understand women. [*laughs*] And they don't understand us. It's kind of an interesting thing. They are mysterious, and they are extremely beautiful. You could take photographs of women till the cows come home, and you'll always find something new.

It really never gets old.

It's just magic.

So you think that women don't understand men either?

Yeah. We don't understand one another, really, but you get more understanding when you start expanding your consciousness. Enlightenment is infinite understanding!

Maybe some people have a different idea of what "understanding" means. To me it's not about solving everything like a math problem. It's more about learning to coexist with whatever needs to be understood, and to sort of embody it, maybe.

It's knowingness.

Right. But it isn't about trying to reach the end of an equation.

Well, there's objective science and there's subjective science. And now the two are coming together. In other words, intellectual understanding alone will never get you there. It needs to be intellectual understanding coupled with the experience. The experience is what's missing in life.

There are rumours going around that you're done with narrative feature filmmaking.

No, no, no. [*laughs*] I'm done with *celluloid*. Even though it's so beautiful, it's going to be a digital world that I'll work in from now on.

Are you working on a feature now?

No, I'm going to do a documentary on Maharishi and then I don't know what I'll do after that.

We have an interview in this issue with Werner Herzog and he told us that you and he have talked about making good films for less money than the usual Hollywood budget. Do you feel like there's overspending and bloat in the film industry?

For sure. It still takes money to do things, but it doesn't take ridiculous money. I always say that film-making is about the size of the corral they put you in. If you're in a little corral and you've got like one million or half a million dollars, you're going to think of ways to do it for that much money. And that's really beautiful. In a 100-million-dollar corral, you're

THE WORLD ACCORDING TO VICE

not even going to think that much. You're just going to be able to throw money at stuff.

Do you shoot with your digital camera just for the hell of it, even when there's not a specific project going on?
No, I don't really like doing that. I guess if I had a Flip cam I might do more of that, but I like to have an idea and then try to realise that idea—not just go around willy-nilly.

Like the way that you worked on *Inland Empire*, where you shot a scene here and a scene there over the course of a couple of years.
I didn't say, "I want to do a film that's going to take a long time." That's just how it happened. You can go a long time without an idea, and then they start flooding in.

I'm going to shift gears a little bit here. I asked a friend of mine who knows you what I should ask you about, and he said to ask you about cheese. Was he messing with me?
Well, I like to eat cheese. And I sometimes like to think of cheese.

In what way?
How it came to be. The magic thing is that there's just, you know, a cow. And then there's the grass and the sunlight, and then here comes the cheese.

It's true.
It's kind of amazing.

Thinking about you and cheese reminded me of that extra on the *Inland Empire* DVD where you show us how you make quinoa. That made me wonder about what you like to eat for breakfast.
I don't eat breakfast. I like to have cappuccinos instead.

You drink a lot of caffeine.
Yes.

I've read that it's upward of 15 cups a day.

Sometimes, yeah. Maybe that's on average.

I'm sure you get asked this all the time, but do you think about the health implications of all the caffeine and all the smoking that you do?
You've got to just live your life. And these days—because of some people in San Francisco—everyone's really started going against smoking.

You can't smoke anywhere now.
Well, you still can in LA. It's so beautiful because there are outdoor restaurants here. So there are plenty of places you can smoke. But cars are everywhere, see? I think that anybody would say that they'd rather smoke a cigarette than stand behind a car's exhaust pipe for the amount of time it takes to smoke. Cars pollute way more than cigarettes do.

I guess that the anti-smoking activists are more concerned about getting cancer from second-hand smoke, which I think is kind of ridiculous when it's applied to public places.
If you were in a cabin all winter with a smoker and you were a non-smoker, I could see there being something to that. But nowadays if you light a cigarette 50 feet away from someone in a park, they freak out.

Smokers are becoming pariahs.
I know it's not healthy, but I've loved tobacco since I was very little.

How old were you when you started smoking?
I guess I was five or seven the first time I tried a cigarette.

Wow. So that's just like the behind-the-woodshed, sneaking-one-to-see-what's-it-like sort of smoking?
Right.

Are you the kind of guy who's going to just keep smoking as long as he can?
I don't know. I could just get a big urge to quit one day. But right now, I'm enjoying it and enjoying life.

THE (EX-) BIGGEST HEROIN DEALER IN THE WHOLE WIDE WORLD

INTERVIEW BY GRAHAM JOHNSON | PHOTO BY STUART GRIFFITHS

Published October 2008

By the time Suleyman Ergun was 21 years old, he was the world's most prolific and powerful seller of smack. Known throughout the junkie and police communities as the North London Turk, Ergun and his gang flooded Britain and Europe with heroin for five years.

For his pains, the former factory worker got mansions filled with cash and unlimited underworld cachet. At the height of his powers he was a multimillionaire and his favourite tipple was a bottle of champagne with eight grams of cocaine dumped into it. Today, he is almost penniless and lives with his mum. He's 39. What happened?

Vice: Tell me a fond memory of your drug-dealing days.

Suleyman Ergun: There's nothing like the feeling you get when you've got 100 kilos of heroin in the trunk of your car. Just to be near it, to smell it. Driving along at 120 mph in France somewhere and thinking: "I know what I've got in the car." Police stopping beside you. A gun under my seat. Wouldn't think twice about shooting them. Taking the risk. At the end of the day that's why I became a drug dealer. Not the money or the power, but the buzz.

Did you serve an underworld apprenticeship?

At 15 I was an errand boy working in the Turkish rag trade in north London. I was earning £70 a week. At 17, I started selling coke, E, and pot, and I was earning £1,000 a week. Then I muled a couple of kilos of coke direct from Colombia and sold it in the clubs, along with tablets. Someone tried to rob me in the toilets of the Camden Palace once—I shot him in the leg.

How does one go from selling coke in a bathroom in Camden to being the king of all heroin in Europe?

Me, my former brother-in-law Yilmaz Kaya, and an Istanbul babas [godfather] named the Vulcan founded the Turkish Connection—that's a network that smuggles heroin from Afghanistan across Turkey into Europe. Up until the early 90s, Turks had been bringing it in piecemeal. An immigrant would bring in ten keys, sell it, buy a shop in Green Lane and pack it in. We were the first to start bringing it in 100-kilo loads. Stack 'em high, sell 'em cheap....

It's that simple, eh?

No, that's only the supply. On the demand side, we bypassed all the usual gangsters and crime families in London. We fucked the Adams family off when they asked us to serve up to them. Instead, we sent it all to one distributor in Liverpool who sold the lot.

What was your role?

I was hands-on. The gear was driven from Istanbul to Paris in, say, a coach load of Turkish folk danc-ers. I coordinated the handover to the Scousers in France.

Then I'd drive up to Liverpool a few days later and come back with black bin bags full of cash—£140,000 one week, £100,000 the next, £68,000 the next, £150,000 the next, and so on. Then I'd count it, stack it, and box it in cereal packets and send it back to Turkey using a former Turkish army colonel disguised as a bone-china collector as a courier.

After a while, we rolled out the same system across Europe—Spain, Italy, Holland, and Germany. We dealt with the mafia, all of that. At one point we could afford to buy our own oil tanker.

Where did it all go wrong?

One of our workers was having an affair with a wom-an who was a police informant. He got nicked. Cus-toms put us under surveillance for a year, and then bingo. The whole thing got walloped in July '93.

What was the upshot?

Fourteen years, nine months. The gang got 123 years between them.

Did that teach you a lesson?

Did it fuck. I started dealing in prison within two days, trading heroin and coke for phone cards, food, tobacco. In September 1995 I used heroin for the first time, out of boredom and curiosity. It felt lovely and warm, like somebody putting an electric blanket over you. But the best thing about it, and this is why the jails are full of heroin, is that it makes time go by very quick. Twenty hours on heroin is like two hours normal. I got out ten years later and I didn't know I done the bird [prison time].

How did you get your heroin in jail?

Before I got nicked, I had five kilos of pure heroin straight from Turkey buried along with two Berettas, an Uzi, and four shotguns at St Pancras graveyard in north London. Every week I'd phone a girl up and use the word "brandy", which was code for brown—heroin—and she would go and get it. She dug up the stash and shaved off some, and then it was given to a second girl who had a boyfriend in my prison. It was wrapped in a condom and nylon sheeting, shaped up proper like a dildo. She stuck it up her cunt. On the visit, they'd snuggle up close, and her boyfriend would put his hand slyly down her knickers, get it, and then stick it up his arse. Back in my cell, he'd get 60 grams and I'd get 60 grams.

Didn't the prison wardens ever find out?

I had the DST—Dedicated Search Team—permanently on my case. They even used to take apart my batteries in the radio. But they never found gear in my cell because I used to hide it in my vegetable plot. I hollowed out an onion and put the gear inside and buried it. When the stalk wilted, I just taped a fresh one on. Take three grams out a day. Sell half a gram for my phone cards and that, and smoke the rest. Sometimes I would put it up my arse wrapped in tape so if the screws made me squat during a search, it wouldn't fall out.

Couldn't anyone smell you smoking it?

As long as you're not causing trouble, cutting people over deals, and fighting, then the screws turn a blind eye. They know you're on it because your pupils are like tiny pinholes and you start scratching and go red and raw. But the authorities let it go because if you stop the heroin it causes murders and they can't handle that. Withdrawal symptoms. Kicking doors. Drugs will never be stamped out in jail.

How many bent screws did you know?

About six all over. They approached me because I was rich. I never ate prison food. They brought me in Marks and Spencer salads. In one prison the screw brought me in four ounces of weed, half a carrier bag full of phone cards, half a bag of tobacco, a TV, a phone, and two bottles of brandy, every week, for £500 a week, plus the bill for the food. He'd wink and say: "Your box is under your bed." Then I'd pay another inmate to look after it. If you don't have money, you have nothing.

I suppose when you got out of prison in 2003 you gave up drugs?

No, it got much worse. I discovered crack cocaine. The world had changed so much. I couldn't cross the road—it was too fast. I used to see people talking to themselves on their hands-free and think they were off their heads.

What's crack like?

It's great. It blew my fucking head off. Over the next four years I blew half a million pounds on it. Sold my flat. My jewellery. Spent the few hundred grand I had stashed away.

What was the lowest point?

My mate robbed a rock off my table. I dragged him into the kitchen and chopped his little finger off with a knife on a chopping board. Then I flushed it down the toilet.

Some people would say that it was natural justice—that you were being punished for selling heroin by becoming a drug addict.

An eye for an eye. I'd created thousands and thousands of addicts. My past had caught up with me. I got depressed and then I took more crack and heroin to stop thinking.

How did you finally get off drugs?

I went for treatment in Turkey twice. A detox where they put you to sleep through withdrawal. It cost £20,000. My family paid. But when I got back onto the streets here in London, I kept slipping. Finally, I fell in love. It's as simple as that. I haven't touched a stone since.

Would you ever go back to being a heroin baron?

Not in a million fucking years. I've been offered a million pounds in cash to start up again. I could fly to Turkey now and get 100 keys and be away. £100,000 in cash by tomorrow. Mine. I get approached every week by someone or other, some of the country's biggest gangsters, to go into business. But I can't do it.

Why? Are you scared?

Fuck off. D'you want a smack?

ELMORE LEONARD IS THE MAN

A NICE LONG TALK WITH THE BEST CRIME NOVELIST EVER
INTERVIEW BY JESSE PEARSON | PHOTO BY RICHARD KERN

Published June 2009

We won't waste much time on an intro here because you should already know who this guy is. Let's just say this: Elmore Leonard, now going on 84 years old, is still cranking out perfectly detailed, thrilling, and hilarious stories of criminals at a pace that's hard to believe. He writes dialogue so well you'd think it's transcribed from real conversations, and he knows more about how to craft a living, breathing character out of thin air than God (or any other higher power—more on that later).

We recently sat with him in his hotel room in midtown New York City, where he was taking a short break from the tour to promote *Road Dogs*, his new novel. It brings together three previously existing Leonard characters—Jack Foley, Cundo Rey, and Dawn Navarro—in typically powder-keg fashion in Venice Beach, California. As with everything he's done, it's compulsively readable and 100 percent entertaining.

Vice: I just finished *Road Dogs* last night. I read it straight through. It took about ten hours.
Elmore Leonard: That's the way to do it, so that you can remember what's going on in it.

I really like the way you set up these situations that seem like they're going to be traditional thriller devices, but then you explode them almost immediately. Like when Jack Foley first arrives in California and meets Dawn Navarro, there's already been this tension set up of whether they'll have sex or not.
Right.

And in someone else's book, that would be stretched out for a long time. But you cut right to the chase and have them in bed together at their first meeting.

I remember my editor, while I was writing the book, said, "I don't think they should get that serious about each other within a couple of hours." I told him, "Don't worry, it will work OK."

It seemed very real the way you wrote it.
It works in this book because he's not going to wait until the third date or something to kiss her. He's just out of prison.

Yeah, he's not about to wait. And then there's the character of Danialle, when Jack and Dawn are supposed to be running this con on her. I expected that to be a long, suspenseful thread through the entire book but, bang, a few pages later you have her saying that she knew it was all a hoax and that she didn't mind.
That character is named Danialle Karmanos because

her husband paid $40,000 in an auction for me to use his wife's name. I've been doing that for I don't know how many books—fund-raising events where they'll have an auction at different schools: "Do you want to be in my next book?"

Oh, so Danialle Karmanos is named after a real person? That's funny.
Yeah! Karmanos is a cancer centre, a big, big cancer-research and treatment centre in Detroit. Her husband wanted to be in the book too, so he got into another auction and only had to pay $5,000 to win. But I gave him a lesser part.

Yeah, that character is a corpse!
He's dead. [*laughs*]

Do you let them know what their role in the book is going to be, or do they just find out when it's released?
I don't tell anybody anything.

I've heard about how you start with characters rather than with plot.
Yeah, well, characters in a situation. Like, Foley is going to get out of prison and so is Cundo Rey, who I used in my book *La Brava* in the early 80s. I liked Cundo Rey. He was in that older book, but it wasn't a real starring role. So I wanted to bring him back. I thought I could do a lot with him.

I figured he was dead at the end of *La Brava*.
I was afraid he was too. I remember looking it up in the book like, "God, I hope he's alive." He was shot in the chest three times. But he made it!

I guess so. Do you do character sketches or do you just drop them straight into situations?
Well, these three—Foley, Cundo, and Dawn—I knew. Clooney played Foley in *Out of Sight* and I was hoping that he would want to do it again, but he hasn't read it yet.

It seems to me like it's begging to be a movie.
It is. And so the three characters, I knew them.

I didn't have to worry about dreaming up anything for them outside of just plot. And I don't put a lot of time in on my plots. I like to make it up as I go along. No outline at all. You'll meet practically everybody who is going to be in the book in the first 100 pages. And then, for the second act, I have to do a little figuring about fitting in a subplot and what's going to happen next. In the third act, which I usually get to in my manuscript around page 300—my books are mostly 350 pages or so—I think of the ending.

Literally making it up as you go along. Is that a process you developed over the course of your career, or has it always been that way for you?
I've been doing it like that for 30 years.

Does it ever feel like a high-wire act, not knowing where you're going to go?
No. I don't worry about it. If it doesn't work, it doesn't work. But if I like the characters, I know it's going to be fine. I'll know that I'm going to have fun with them, and that's the main thing. The writing has to be fun or else forget it.

It must be fun for you, since you're always writing.
I'm writing a book right now. It's called *Djibouti*. It has to do with the Somalian pirates.

Wow.
A documentary filmmaker, a woman, 35, starts reading about them in the paper and decides she wants to do a film on them. She has made three films so far that have won awards. *Katrina*—she lives in New Orleans so she walked out the door and shot Katrina—and she did one on white supremacists called… I forgot what it was called.

So this character in your new book is based on this documentary filmmaker?
No, this is all my character.

She's a totally fictitious character? The way you're referring to her, I would have thought she was a real person.

I know. That's because they become real to me. By the end of the book, I wonder, "What are they doing now?"

That's great.
So she brings her assistant, who is a 72-year-old six-foot-six black guy who was a seafarer. He's been around the world 50 times. He's been through these waters, down through the Red Sea into the Gulf of Aden and the Indian Ocean, around the Horn of Africa—East Africa. That's where all the pirates are operating. In the book I even have the latest important move that they made on the American ship where they had the captain in that enclosed lifeboat and then the three snipers shot the three pirates—one shot each.

Yeah, that was incredible shooting.
They weren't that far away. The life raft was on a line to this destroyer. The snipers were in the back of the destroyer and I think they had their rifles somehow in a gyroscope so that they would stay level.

But three head shots from a huge boat bobbing in the sea to a small life raft in the dark... it's pretty impressive, gyroscope or not.
Three shots and that was it.

I kind of love those pirates.
Well, that's what she thinks too. She loves them. She has complete sympathy for them because their fishing grounds are being messed up with toxic waste. They also were getting a lot of competition from big companies from China and Japan that were sending fishermen there. So they turned to hijacking ships and asking for a lot of money. Ransom.

And your main character feels for them.
In the very first chapter, she lands in Djibouti. Her assistant is there. He's already leased a boat for them—a 30-foot trawler. That night, he's showing her around Djibouti, which is a real mess. They run into a pirate, who is in town to have some fun. He's got a Mercedes and he takes it for a ride. He's not just your everyday pirate. He's got some background

and a lot of money. Homes around Somalia. She's also met another guy on the plane from Paris. He goes around talking to pirates, trying to convince them that this won't end well.

Trying to talk them out of the path they've chosen.
Right. And he's Saudi... I think he's Saudi. He went to Oxford and he affects more of a British way. He's a cool guy. His name is Ari but everyone at school called him Harry. Idris is the name of the pirate leader. And then there are other people involved. There's a guy called Billy Wynn who's on a $2 million yacht with a girl that he likes a lot, but he's giving her a test. They go around the world and if she doesn't complain or get sick, he might marry her. He's fun. He's a little strange.

It's really interesting how you're talking about the book that you're writing now, but it sounds like you're just telling me about real people that you know. You're like, "I think he's a Saudi."
I've been into this book now all this year. *Road Dogs* I wrote at least a year ago.

Your pace is incredible.
I like to write books, so...

It's just what you do.
That's what I do. I don't take time off in between for any particular reason. I mean, if I do then maybe I'm just thinking of the next one.

A lot of writers will do something like three books in ten years—or even less.
Well, they go out to lunch and all that. They talk about it with their friends.

Instead of working. So one of my favourite scenes in *Road Dogs* is when Little Jimmy goes to confession. It's hilarious, with great comedic timing. And then at the end he says, "Anything I did to get God pissed off at me is forgiven," because he said ten Hail Marys and ten Our Fathers. You were raised Catholic. Does that reflect the way that you feel about it too?

Ten Our Fathers and ten Hail Marys was just—that was just rote. That's what you usually got! I mean, what could you do that would require a Rosary or something?

Sometimes you kind of want to go in there and see if you can get 20 or something.

[*laughs*] I don't know what it would take. I haven't been to confession in, God, how long… I haven't been to mass in probably 20 years. But I was in AA, you see. I'm still part of that because it worked. I haven't had a drink since '77.

And AA is quasi-religious.

Higher power. That's what keeps you straight. The higher power isn't defined necessarily as God, but because I was brought up Catholic, it's easy for me to do it that way.

Right.

And you go right directly to God in AA. You don't fool around with the saints.

Do you still attend meetings?

No, I haven't gone to a meeting in quite a while. The last time I went, the same guys were there and they were all telling the same stories. In my new book, a person who is in AA asks Dara—that's the documentary filmmaker—if she wants to do a documentary on AA. He tells her that there are these drunkologues where they stand up and tell these harrowing stories. Like the one where the guy all of a sudden realised he was going the wrong way on a turnpike—

I've heard that very story more than a couple of times in AA meetings.

[*laughs*] Sure, I'll bet you that every group has heard that one. But Dara says, "I don't think I'm good enough to just have someone telling a story rather than showing it." She can't show it. How are you going to shoot the guy going the wrong way?

Dramatic re-creation? Just kidding.

Yeah. Then it's not a documentary.

How do you feel about the cliché of all writers being drunks?

In the meetings that I've gone to, I've never met another writer. But that doesn't mean anything because in my area there are only one or two others that you've ever heard of. Maybe it's because you're alone, because you're by yourself writing and you need… I don't know what you need.

The solitude seems to get to some people.

It's like, I gave up smoking once for 30 days and I wrote 30 pages. And then I started smoking again, and in the next 30 days I wrote 100.

I don't meet many people your age who still smoke.

What have I got to lose? [*laughs*] And I know people who quit smoking and then their lives went to hell. They got sick and, you know…

Everybody has to have something. If it's going to be cigarettes, so be it. Are there any of your characters who you personally identify with more than others?

I usually identify with the main character. The way his mind works is the way mine does, and what's important and what isn't important to him is the same for me. But I like all my characters. I spend time with them and I get to know enough about them so that I don't have to describe them psychically in any detail unless there's something, a little something, that catches your eye.

That's one of your Ten Rules of Writing, correct? Don't overdescribe characters.

Yeah, right. Which I got from Steinbeck.

Right. I like your first rule: Never open with a description of the weather.

And leave out the parts that people tend to skip.

And if it sounds like writing—

Rewrite it. You know them.

I do. Can you tell me what's so interesting to you

about criminals?
There are all kinds of stories I can tell about a criminal. Has he done time and now he's out and he seems like a good guy? And there's that opportunity for him to go back into crime at any time. That's always up in the air. I like that. But really, I write crime because it's popular.

And you wrote Westerns when they were popular.
Very popular. There were probably 15 magazines you could sell to anytime you wanted. Pulp magazines paying two cents a word. Like *3:10 to Yuma*. Twice it's been a movie and I got $90 for the story—4,500 words.

Do you get anything from the movies?
First time I got $4,000. Second time I didn't get anything.

The ending of the remake was pretty different from your story. Does that make you unhappy?
Well, it's just dumb. In the new one, he shoots his own guys—

That was insane.
And then he gets on the train and whistles for his horse! I don't know what that means. I have no idea. Is the horse going to follow him all the way across Arizona?

Running alongside the train. Are there any new upcoming adaptations of your work?
My character Rayland Givens and his stories are being made into a pilot by Sony for the FX network.

Interesting.
That character wears a very particular kind of gentleman's Stetson hat. It's very small, and it's well worn. Now, he has been done once before. It was a movie for TV. And they got the wrong hat. I don't know why they got the wrong hat.

How hard can it be? Who is playing Givens this time around?
A guy named Olyphant. You know him?

Timothy Olyphant. He was on the HBO series *Deadwood*. He's really good. I hope they get the hat right this time.
I don't know why they can't just find an old hat.

You're probably tired of hearing about how great your dialogue is, but I'm just going to say it here once more because it really is the best.
I write dialogue because I don't want to have to describe things myself. I like point of view, and the points of view change. It's always how a character sees whatever is going on. The weather, even. In one of my books, a guy is having trouble and he walks out on the beach and he looks up at the sky and it's raining and he just yells out, "Fuck!" And that's my weather description, see?

It's perfect. "Fuck." Do you speak your dialogue out loud while you're writing it?
No. Nor do I laugh until years later, when I'm warming up by reading my old books. Before I start to write I'll open one of the books and just start reading so that I get into the rhythm of it again. I'm sitting there cold in front of my desk, and I'll read something and I'll laugh because I'm surprised by it. When I was working on a line, it was just a process of work. It wasn't something that just came out.

Do you have a particular place where you like to write?
I write in the living room.

Longhand?
Longhand at first. All the creating is longhand and then I type during the day as I go along. But I get to my desk later now than I used to. I get there at 10:30 or 11 o'clock and I used to always be there by 9. And before, when I was still working at an ad agency, I'd get up at 5.

That takes some serious dedication.
I had to start writing before I could put the water on for coffee.

Oh my God.

It took about three months to start getting up at 5 when the alarm went off.

For the first three months you'd just smack the snooze button.
Yeah, and roll over. But finally I started to get up. During the 50s, I wrote five books and 30 short stories in the dawn.

You've employed a researcher for a while now.
Greg Sutter. He's been working for me since at least '83.

Is Greg working on the Somalian-pirate book now?
Yes. We've got so much stuff. I've got stacks and stacks on my desk and on the floor. When we started in November there wasn't that much to really look for.

And it's become a huge story since then.
Huge! Now everybody wants to make a movie about it and there are a bunch of TV movies—my agent in Hollywood says—that they want to get into.

Is Greg also the person who's responsible for helping you to keep up with gang and criminal lingo?
That's him.

Do you stay in contact with any of the criminals who figure into your research?
I hear from them. They write to me and want to know if I've done time. I met a guy at Telluride who had done a few years in Colorado for selling marijuana. He said, "God, you've got it right down, the way these inmates talk." But where I usually get it from is an article where somebody will say a specific line.

And that line leads to something.
Right. But yeah, this guy in Colorado, he said, "In my trial, I maintained that the marijuana was for my own use." And I said, "Well, how much did you have?" and he said, "400 pounds."

Sure, personal use. Are you friends with any ex-cons?

No. Well, there is one guy. I'm not sure what he's in for, but he's done over 20 years and he's getting out soon. It was a federal offence. He's from Detroit. He had a plan once. Down by the naval armory on the Detroit River there was a submarine anchored forever. His idea was to steal it. But where are you going to go with a submarine, you know? [*laughs*]

That's a lot of scrap metal.
And then they moved the submarine. He thinks they found out about his plot.

You guys are pen pals?
He writes to me and sometimes I'll answer his letters. He's just kind of subversive.

Sub-versive. Ha.
Yeah. He's a socialist.

So stealing the submarine would have been a statement of some sort.
Yeah, right.

What do you think of the distinction in the publishing industry between genre writing and so-called literature?
I think most serious writing is boring. But one time I was on *Charlie Rose* with Martin Amis—

Amis has been a big champion of your work.
Yeah. And Amis was waiting. I was on first. Charlie said, "What are you doing here with Martin Amis?" I said, "Well, we're friends and he's interviewed me in front of 1,000 people. I should have been interviewing him, but I wouldn't know what to ask him." As a literary writer, he's using his voice all the way through because he has all the words and he knows how to put them together. But that doesn't appeal to me. I like the characters. I'm in the characters' heads all the time.

I agree with you that serious writing can be boring.
I guess that's kind of a dumb statement—

But I don't take it at face value. I know what you mean.

There's not much that I can read in my genre either. They're all the same. They have a favourite character, a lead character, who runs through all the books. I couldn't do that. I started to do it at one time. I was going to do a series based in Detroit Homicide. My publisher liked the idea. And so, in *City Primeval*, Lieutenant Raymond Cruz is in Squad 7. Then, in the next book, I do Raymond Cruz again. My agent said, "You've got to change this guy's name, because they bought one—but what if they don't like this one? Then we can't sell it to anybody else because they own Raymond Cruz." So I changed his name to Brian Heard in the second one. And that was it for the homicide cops.

It's such a commitment for a writer to do a series like that, like the Bourne books or all the Pelecanos books with recurring characters. It's like a relationship.

I was corresponding with John D. MacDonald and he was on his 28th Travis McGee book. He said, "I don't think I can do another one."

"I'm starting to hate this fucking guy."

As it turned out, he didn't have to. He went to one of the big hospitals in the north to have a bypass and he didn't come out.

He had a cosmic reprieve from Travis McGee. There's a funny part in *Road Dogs* where Lou tells Jack Foley, "The publishing business isn't about writing. It's about selling books."

Well… [*laughs*] it is. It took me nearly 30 years to get on the *Times* list. I was getting good reviews but then—which book was it—maybe *Unknown Man #89* was reviewed in the *Sunday Times* book review section and it was like the guy had just discovered me. But I'd been writing for 30 years.

That's ridiculous.

I have a lot of fans, there's no question about that, but I don't have a million fans, like James Patterson.

Who doesn't even write his own books…

He always has that help. He probably thinks up part of the plot, and yet his name is on there, and he gets all the credit and he gets all the money. If his first printing is a million, then he gets, what? Five million dollars? Something like that.

Let's be realistic, though. You have a lot of very dedicated fans. If it's the kind of writing that's meant for a certain reader, they can't just read one Elmore Leonard book and then stop.

Yeah.

You've said a lot of times that your first big inspiration was Hemingway.

For Whom the Bell Tolls. I used to open up that one up anywhere before I started to write. I looked at it as a Western in Spain in the mountains with horses and guns. But he did lack a sense of humour.

It's true. Hemingway is not known for his laughs.

And I was dying to say dry things. Then I found Richard Bissell—

The Pajama Game, right?

Exactly. *7 1/2 Cents* was his book that became *Pajama Game*. But the ones that he set on the Mississippi River, where he was a pilot, those are what taught me a lot. They weren't trying to be funny, but they were. They were about uneducated people on a towboat, and they just said funny things. Got into discussions about things that were ridiculous, almost. There's a line, might be in the opening of one of his books. It's in a hotel room early in the morning and the guy's looking out the window and the girl on the bed rolls over and looks at him and she says, "What in the world are you looking at?" And he says, "St. Louis, Missouri." I thought that was a great line!

It is.

I don't know why.

It's really good.

It's the "Missouri", I think, maybe, that makes it.

It's similar to the line that comes up a couple of times in *Out of Sight* from *Three Days of the Condor*—that kind of pithy bedroom talk.
Oh yeah. Uh-huh.

Detroit has been a big part of your life. You've lived there since you were young and you've set many of your books there. What is it like for you to witness its decline? There's so much unemployment there, and the car industry is dying.
When I was doing car ads, I was reading car magazines. It wasn't what I was interested in, but I read them because of my job. There were always complaints in these magazines that Detroit wasn't keeping up. They were still making these big boats, you know? And finally it caught up with them. I was writing Chevrolet ads, but I was driving a Fiat.

When was this?
In the 50s. It was 1961 when I left the agency. But then we bought a house and my profit sharing, which was like $11,500, was enough, I felt, to live on for at least six months and write a book—

But then you bought a house and there goes that.
Yeah. So I started doing a lot of freelance stuff. I wrote a bunch of history and geography movies for *Encyclopædia Britannica*.

Like educational films for schools?
Yeah.

I wonder if I saw any of those in elementary school. They were definitely still showing us film strips from the 60s when I was in school in the early 80s. Could you just crank those out?
First I would have to talk to an authority on the subject. That was always fun. I did things like the settlement of the Mississippi Valley, the French and Indian War…

Did any of that stuff ever lead to ideas for stories?
No. [*laughs*]

I just want to talk a little bit about other writ-
ers. You're the top of the crime genre. Who do you think is carrying on the tradition for a younger generation?
I like Pelecanos and I like Dennis Lehane. He wrote a blurb for *Road Dogs*. I was surprised—I didn't know he was that into it.

How could he not be?
A few years back I was the guest of honor at Bouchercon, which is a big assembly of mystery and crime writers. There were hundreds of writers there, but I only knew two of their names. I don't write or read mysteries.

Do you pay much attention to your reviews?
I read one recently where the woman who was writing said, "Well, he uses all of these F-words."

It's not you, it's your characters.
I don't, but they do! She thought that *Road Dogs* was the same old thing, like she always knew what was going to happen. Well, if she did, she knew more than I did. When I got to the part where [major character name] is shot—everybody is surprised by it…

I didn't see it coming in quite that way. But wait, do you want me to leave that detail out of the interview? Do you care if big plot points are spoiled for potential readers?
No. I don't know. It's more about how I tell it or how I write it. It's not the fact of it. I don't know how you might couch it without just saying he's shot. In the chest.

From a Walther with a silencer across a table at point-blank range?
[*laughs*] Yeah.

You got a really good review in the *New York Times* for this one.
Janet Maslin. That was a beauty. Great review.

You mentioned how Lehane blurbed your new book. That reminded me of how you blurbed some

of the books of Charles Willeford, one of the best and most underappreciated crime novelists. Do you have any memories of him?

He died shortly after I met him. In fact, the day I met him, which was down in the Florida Keys at some kind of a meeting, he had a portable dialysis machine, and he's drinking whiskey and smoking and having a time. But have you read *The Friends of Eddie Coyle* by George Higgins?

I haven't. Should I?

I think it's the best crime book ever written. It takes place in Boston. They're in and out of Massachusetts prisons. The main character is a guy who sells guns. He always has to come up with fresh guns for these guys who rob banks. And how they rob banks is they take the manager of the bank out of his house early in the morning. They break in and the guy comes down to breakfast and they're sitting there.

A good plan.

Higgins's dialogue was great. Very, very good. He wrote three books like that and then he got into monologues. His books would run for pages and pages of someone talking.

What did you think of that?

I didn't care for it.

Was Higgins an underappreciated writer too, like Willeford?

Yeah. Absolutely. And nowadays I don't think George Pelecanos has ever been on a list in the *Times*. I don't remember seeing him.

I would have thought he would have been by now.

He should be. Cormac McCarthy—of course he's on the list now—but he wasn't for a long time.

So do you like his writing?

Yeah, sure!

I do too, but it seems like in a lot of ways he's the opposite of what you write and talk about lik-

ing. His language is usually very dense and artful rather than terse and direct. Like in *Blood Meridian*, for example.

Blood Meridian is one I still haven't read and I don't know why.

You definitely should! I have a question here that I have to ask for my father-in-law. You're his favourite writer. He calls you "the man." He was in love with Karen Sisco and wants to know if she's ever coming back.

I don't know if she will. She's mentioned in *Road Dogs*. I was thinking of bringing her back at one point and I wrote the first chapter of a book where she has left the US Marshals service and was working for her dad, who is a private investigator. She's in a bar and she's waiting for her dad to meet her. She's in South Florida. And she starts talking to a guy and she just has this feeling that this guy is a wanted offender. Just something about him, you know? And she ends up shooting him.

Ha!

I sent it to my agent in Hollywood, who said, "Yeah it works, it's fine. But why don't you think of something else that you haven't done before, with none of your characters?" So I got into the piracy book.

I bet my father-in-law would like to strangle that agent. I noticed while we've been talking that you smoke Virginia Slims. That's what your character Dawn Navarro smoked too.

Yeah. And that's what the girl in *Mister Paradise* smoked. She was smoking Virginia Slims and then I started.

The women in your books are always great. A lot of your dialogue between men and women reminds me of stuff like Tracy and Hepburn.

There's that part in *Road Dogs* where Dawn is trying to get Jack to tell her something. She thinks she has him under hypnosis. He goes along with it. Then he turns his head and lets her know he hasn't been hypnotised and she says, "Well, aren't you a tricky motherfucker?"

ALAN MOORE

INTERVIEW BY JAMES KNIGHT | PHOTO BY JOSE VILLARRUBIA

Published December 2009

Alan Moore is the guy who just about anyone who has ever read a comic book agrees to be the best writer in the form's entire history. In the 80s, he was the person who almost singlehandedly made it OK for otherwise cowardly grown-ups to admit that they liked funny books.

A proud son of Northampton, who still lives near the area he grew up in, Moore cut his teeth in the early 1980s at *2000 AD*, the leading British comic factory of science fiction and fantasy. His Judge Dredd strips reimagined the character with hitherto unexplored complexities. His own creation, *Halo Jones*, was the first title in the medium not to portray a female character as a big-boobed superlady or a victim.

By the mid-80s, Moore had revolutionised American comics, first by jump-starting stagnant DC title *Swamp Thing*, turning it into a book of existential examination with ecological concerns, and then by creating *Watchmen*, which was the first comic to really turn the whole superhero trope on its ear, and which of course led to an abysmally terrible movie last year (which Moore, thankfully, disavows).

Several legal tussles over ownership and rights to his creations later, Moore started his own line, only half-jokingly entitled America's Best Comics. From 1991 to 1996, he produced *From Hell,* his own grim and beautiful take on the Jack the Ripper story. It, too, was made into a shitty movie that Moore disavows. *The League of Extraordinary Gentleman* series began in 1999 and has become a mammoth, sprawling beast of a book that happily mixes fictional and imagined history with versions of our own reality. Again: shitty movie, Moore disavows. In *V for Vendetta*, Moore gave us his take on totalitarianism. And yet again, itty-shay ovie-may, Oore-may isavows-day.

In recent years, Moore has produced a formally complex novel, *Voice of the Fire* (1996), and a long-form poem that deals with girls who like girls and guys who like guys called *The Mirror of Love* (2004). He also published *25,000 Years of Erotic Freedom* (2009), which examined pretty much what the title suggests, and *Lost Girls* (2006), which he created with Melinda Gebbie and which involves Wendy from *Peter Pan,* Alice from the *Alice in Wonderland* books, and Dorothy from *The Wizard of Oz* having lots of fairly explicit adventures. It's a real hoot.

Moore is currently working on *Dodgem Logic*, an underground magazine; his second novel, *Jerusalem*; and a guide to magic. You see, Moore is a practicing magician (not the top-hat-and-bunny-kind). We recently called him at his home in Northampton, and after he assured us that he had a cup of tea and "as many more cups on the way as it takes", it became apparent that Mr. Moore was willing to talk to us for quite a long time about his work and his ideas. And yes, it was pretty much magic.

Vice: *Dodgem Logic* is your new thing. Why don't you tell us about that to begin?

Alan Moore: *Dodgem Logic* is an aggressively random collision of all sorts of things, from absurdist pieces of fiction by Steve Aylett to new bits of work by Savage Pencil and Kevin O'Neill. Aesthetically and in terms of form it came from a fascination with the underground press, which is a culture that dates back to before the printed press itself, but which came to popular fruition in the 1960s and 1970s when it was a vital part of the counterculture.

What were the big underground-press entities in the UK back then?

The main papers here were the *International Times* and *Oz*, which started out as a satire magazine in Australia and then moved here, where it became a much more controversial and psychedelic affair. Those were intoxicating times and it was the underground press that acted as the glue that kept that whole element of society together and in touch with each other. Without those papers, you would have just had a few people who wore similar clothes, liked similar music, and took similar drugs. You would have had no coherent political or cultural discourse.

And *Dodgem Logic* is meant to be a continuation of that tradition?

We decided to make *Dodgem Logic* a very brightly coloured, 48-page magazine that is trying to reinvent the notion of underground publishing for the 21st century. We were constantly trying to leave it with some rough edges. We didn't want it to be slick because there can be something intimidating about slick. It can put up a barrier between the magazine and its audience. We've gone for a deliberately rough look.

It is fairly cut-and-paste in places, which makes it seem like a hybrid between an underground paper and a zine.

I take that as a compliment. Fanzines used to be such a vital part of the culture that I grew up in, from the poetry fanzines of the 1960s to the comic-book, science-fiction, and fantasy fanzines in the 1970s that produced so much of the talent that now dominates the comic and science-fiction genres. They were incredibly productive little publications and they contained such a lot of energy. Perhaps that came from how easy they were to produce. They were nowhere as easy as they would be to make these days, but now that all the technology is here to make something far more ambitious than we ever dreamed possible, the impetus has disappeared. Perhaps the degree of passion that was put into something like *Sniffin' Glue* or any of those zines associated with the punk movement does in fact exist now, but online. I don't know. I may sound old-fashioned, but I still believe that there will always be a difference between something that you look at on a screen and something that you can hold in your hand.

Physical things are better. They're more real.
There is more of a sense of an artefact that is part of a community and part of a culture.

A general dissatisfaction with government and the inexorable decline of civilisation, as well as a concern with the erosion of local community and culture, is a recurring theme in your work, from *Swamp Thing* to *Watchmen* and beyond. *Dodgem Logic* seems like a more direct means of addressing those issues, as opposed to the more oblique method of tackling them via comics.
To tell the truth, I am pretty much out of comics. I am pressing on with *The League of Extraordinary Gentlemen* and I am drawing some strips for *Dodgem Logic*, but I am detached from the comics industry. I no longer consider myself a part of it.

Could the things that you are tackling with *Dodgem Logic* be done in comics?
Yes, they could be addressed in comic form. However, while doing that might delight my comic-book audience, it wouldn't be addressing the wider world, which is where these issues need to be. I should point out that *Dodgem Logic* isn't a magazine specifically about Northampton. That just happens to be where I and some of the contributors are from. However, we look at it from the point of view that Northampton is in the exact centre of the country geographically, economically, and politically. It is a fairly good model representation of an everytown. The high streets are being boarded up, the people are being abused by the council, and there is rubbish everywhere.

What prompted you to address these issues so directly now? It's not like we lacked for social problems in the 80s.

A couple of years ago I was contacted by a group of ex-young offenders who had been working on music down in the Burrows area of Northampton. That is where I was born, where I grew up, and where most of my forthcoming novel is set. They had decided that they wanted to do a film about this deprived and neglected area. Since they knew that I came from there, they asked me if maybe I'd like to be interviewed for the film. They were actually working with the Central Museum in Northampton. I went down there, met them, and we got on very well. I wanted to stay in touch with them beyond the duration of that initial project, so I went down every week to the offices of a local community support organisation called CASPA that was doing brilliant work in the area. I met up with the boys and their wrangler, who was a wonderful young woman called Lucy, and I'd inevitably tell them about the local scene and the underground culture and arts clubs that were around when I was growing up that had done so much to shape me into the person that I am today. I would also tell them about how we'd produce magazines and fanzines and hold poetry readings and things like that. I'm sure it was very boring for them hearing all these stories, but the ideas seemed to stick. They decided to produce a magazine of their own, which I contributed to. Both myself and the boys wanted to talk about some of the genuine problems that afflicted that area and how it was a shame that we probably couldn't really address them in the magazine because it was council-funded. We discussed the possibility of doing an independent magazine and decided to give it a go. The issues seemed so important to the people of that area that we couldn't keep them from the local community. I wrote an article that was called "The Destructors". It was about an old incinerator that was in the Burrows area. It was where, in days gone by, the entire city would bring its rubbish and crap to be disposed of.

Right, which is a telling detail.
It gave a pretty clear message as to what the council thought of people who lived in that area, and while the incinerator was torn down in the 1930s, that message remains applicable to the area today. It is where

the council sends things that it doesn't want to have to deal with: immigrant groups, ex-convicts, and people who have been in care homes. All the problematic people are shoved down into this neighbourhood, often in accommodations that have been condemned by the fire services. Horrific things happen there every day.

And did the council end up blocking that piece?

Yes. We were told that we could not publish the article as it was critical of the council, so Lucy and I worked it out that she could drop down to three days a week at CASPA and spend the other two days working on an independent magazine with me. The council swiftly told her that if she was going to spend two days a week working on an independent magazine then she wouldn't have her job at the council on the other three days, at which point I decided that I'd had enough and I invited Lucy to work on *Dodgem Logic* full-time. The issues we are talking about are important, and the magazine offers a place where these things can be discussed. We're not bound by any constraint and we can say whatever we want. However, we don't just want to depress the hell out of people, so we have tried to get as much stuff in there as we can that is genuinely entertaining, as well as the social and political. These are strategies for getting people through difficult times—give them the information that they need, but also give them something to cheer them up.

It's a good cause.

I hadn't done much more than pass through that area for many years. Meeting the good people who lived there in this rotten situation actually made me decide that I wanted to do something focused on that area. The Burrows is in the top 2 percent of deprivation in the United Kingdom. There are areas like it all over the country, but they are swept under the carpet. I also feel an emotional attachment to the area, which I've always had, and I saw an opportunity to produce something beautiful and useful out of that environment while at the same time creating a model for other areas like it.

You have advocated anarchy both in your work and personally in the past. Would that be your answer to the social problems discussed in *Dodgem Logic*?

Well, in the second issue I will actually be writing an article introducing anarchy and explaining how it could practically be applied to our current situation. So, yes. One of the things that I will be looking at is the principle of the Athenian lottery and the concept of sortition. Sortition basically dictates that on any issue that needs to be settled on a national or administrative level, you appoint a jury by lottery. They can come from anywhere within the culture and they are appointed purely at random. The pros and cons of the case are then presented to the jury, which they then listen to, debate, and vote on. After the decision, they are no longer part of the jury. They melt back into society, and for the next issue another jury is appointed. That system seems to me like it might be approaching something like democracy, which is something that we do not have at the moment. The word "democracy" comes from "demos", the people, and "cratos", to rule—"the people rule". It doesn't say anything about the elected representatives of the people ruling, which is the system that we have at the moment. By moving to something closer to sortition, we would create a system safe from many of the abuses of our current model of government. It is quite difficult to buy people's favour if you don't know who the people you need to be buttering up are going to be. It would also be difficult for the temporary ruling body to act in their own interest, as it would make more sense for them to act in the interest of the society that they would be returning to.

This is interesting. It has elements of anarchy and democracy in it.

Yes, it would square the circle between the ideas of anarchy and government. My definition of anarchy is the Greek one: no leaders. It is difficult to think of an ordered society that conforms to that ideal, and yet with the Athenian lottery you wouldn't have leaders, you would have individual people making balanced decisions. It would take an enormous amount of constitutional change, but I like putting the idea out there so that it is a possibility and something to be discussed. Our current form of government clearly isn't working, and we can't just keep trying to make quick fixes on a model that is inherently flawed. It might be the time for a new model rather than putting continual patches on the radiator of the old Model T Ford that has come to the end of its natural lifetime.

Will you be tackling these themes through your fiction? I ask because *Dodgem Logic* deals with your local environment very directly, and your forthcoming novel is also set in the area, as was your first.

To a certain degree. Both methods complement each other. *Dodgem Logic* and *Jerusalem* essentially deal with the same neighbourhood and territory, albeit in wildly different ways. Reading an issue of *Dodgem Logic* will be a very different experience from reading a chapter or two of *Jerusalem*. *Dodgem Logic* is me trying to do something intelligent yet accessible. *Jerusalem*—I don't care if anyone likes it or not. I am just trying to do the best possible piece of writing that I can. *Jerusalem* is between myself and the world. If nobody reads it, that's a problem for me, whereas *Dodgem Logic* is important in a different way. It is important in terms of the issues that it raises about the area, and those are issues I want people to hear about. They are both attempts to reinvigorate and reinvent that neighbourhood in different contexts. *Dodgem Logic* is attempting to literally and practically reinvigorate the area and give something back to its people. *Jerusalem* is more akin to what Iain Sinclair achieved with his wonderful book *Hackney, That Rose-Red Empire*. He captured the rich snow globe of the Hackney that was vanishing under his feet. He managed to get all of the broad characters and lost eras captured in that book before they are flattened and steam-rolled over to make way for the Olympic Village. With fiction, you have a means— perhaps the only true means—to either resurrect or preserve the places that are going to disappear if not today, then tomorrow.

The concept of preserving the past through fiction is one that you embrace in *The League of Extraor-

dinary Gentleman*. Every cell is crammed with tons of historical and cultural references.

With the *League*, which by the way I can tell you that I have just finished writing book three as of today, we are attempting to create, through fiction, a cultural Noah's Ark within which all of the great writers and the great fictions that Kevin and myself feel are worthy of preserving can be kept alive for a little bit longer before they sink in the depths of ignorance.

The *League* exists in a strange space between fiction and reality.

Absolutely. We have a very well-defined reality and it is something that gets stronger as the story goes on. It has probably got to be, by definition, the single biggest continuity in literature of all time because it has all of the characters' individual continuities subsumed within it.

There are so many fictional characters and their histories in the *League*, it's impressive that it's all kept cohesive.

We are trying to fit all of these fictional inspirations from certain eras into our final continuity, so you have a world where the Nazis *did* invade and Fu Manchu *was* real, but at the same time it mirrors our own world and our own world's development. It may be a distorted glass, but it helps order our perception of our own world. It is like a dream glass. Our reality wasn't like that of the *League*'s, but it might have been what we were dreaming of in our fictions and in ourselves. It allows us to see what might have been and what we might have aspired to. It is the other half of the story.

Right.

And there is actual history in the series too, but that in itself is a kind of fiction. Then there is the kind of history presented in our art, books, and literature. Which, in a peculiar and psychological sense, is truer and more dependable than supposedly factual, conventional history, which might not in fact be true in any sense at all. Throughout the *League* we have established a sense that fiction is in fact the bedrock that mankind is standing upon and that our

303

real world is ultimately based upon fiction.

How do you continue to shove so many literary and cultural references into the *League*?

They are my interests and Kevin's interests and a result of the research that we did when we hit upon the concept. Then we started to think seriously about what would happen if this were a story in which everything from the world of fiction could be included. This meant that it would need its own geography, which we dealt with in the appendix to the second volume. It would also need its own history, which was dealt with in *The Black Dossier*. For example, we didn't have Adolf Hitler in our fictional reality, we had Adenoid Hynkel from Charlie Chaplin's *The Great Dictator*. In our reality, the M figure, who is the leader of MI5, turns out to be Harry Lime from *The Third Man*, which was written by Graham Greene, who based that character upon his lifelong friend and a real spy who defected to the Soviet Union, a man named Kim Philby. And then Harry Lime, we decided to just make that a pseudonym for Robert Sherry, who was one of the characters who attended Greyfriars School in the Billy Bunter books.

Crazy.

We then decided to make George Orwell's Big Brother into Harry Wharton, who was the leader of the gang at Greyfriars. We also turned Greyfriars into a British public school that was recruiting for the spy service, which in turn fades nicely into real history. What clinched it was discovering that there had been a brief spat between Frank Richards, who had written the Billy Bunter stories, and George Orwell, who had written an essay about how the Bunter books represented everything that was bad about the British Empire. Frank Richards disastrously attempted to write a riposte to Orwell, where he replied to the accusations that he portrayed foreigners as being in some way comical simply by saying: "They are." That link between reality, fiction, and the fiction being discussed in reality makes our uses all the more piquant.

The *League* and *V for Vendetta* both portray fascist dystopias. Do you ever fear that the fictional futures you have created may come to pass in your lifetime?

No. I could of course be completely wrong, and I do think that fascism is still set to cause us a lot of trouble, but I genuinely think that it comes from a place of such ignorance that it cannot adequately cope with the realities of the 21st century. It is too simple a concept and it lacks the complexity necessary to deal with the fairly chaotic daily realities of our current situation. It is only really effective on a thuggish street level, which can cause trouble for marginalised minority groups. That is a terrible reality for a lot of people, but as a political force, fascists cannot be taken seriously. I agree with [comedian] Reginald D. Hunter, who says, "You have to let the fascists talk." Allowing them to speak in public will do them no good at all since their voice is so shrill, unpleasant, and off-putting that I don't think it will in any way aid their electoral prospects. If you attempt to silence them, you allow them to claim oppression by the liberal elite.

What can we expect from *Jerusalem*? Will it pick up the themes dealt with in *Voice of the Fire*?

Jerusalem will certainly have elements in common with *Voice of the Fire* and there will still be elements of formal experimentation, but it will not be quite the same structurally. *Jerusalem* will be divided into three books. It will hopefully come in one volume with three parts. The first part will be reminiscent of *Voice of the Fire* in that it will jump about from character to character in different times in the third-person past tense. The second book involves a continuous linear narrative from chapter to chapter but does peculiar things with language and perspective, and it's certainly where some of the more fantastic elements of the novel take place. It is rather akin to a mad children's story due to the majority of the protagonists either being children or the ghosts of dead children. Part 2 also involves a working-class paradise with working-class angels who play billiards with human souls, which is an idea I am keen on. The third part, which is currently about nine chapters from completion, is the most experimental and demented piece of writing I have ever done. Thus far it is all in the present tense and each chapter is written in a wildly different style. The chapter that I have just finished is entitled "Round the Bend" and it deals with the St. Andrew's hospital, which is a marvellous place where my wife and I had our wedding. Its patients have included Spike Milligan; Dusty Springfield; Patrick Stewart; Sir Malcolm Arnold the composer; J.K. Stephen, the Jack the Ripper suspect; and Lucia Joyce.

For our readers who don't know, she was the daughter of James Joyce.

She spent 35 years there as a mental patient. The chapter I have just finished involves Lucia Joyce wandering around the grounds of the hospital while she is also wandering in her mind, where she is meeting other patients from other times who she could not possibly physically meet. It is a hallucinatory tour around the hospital grounds and around Lucia's mind, and it is all written in what I am sure is a lousy attempt at her father's language, which takes you through this angelic state that Lucia is in. William Blake is another figure that is of course hanging over *Jerusalem*, even though he doesn't directly appear in it, as well as John Bunyan, who does. They both helped inspire the visionary aspects of the novel. The Lucia Joyce chapter took me forever to write.

Is your book on magic still in the works?

It certainly is. Once I've finished the final book of the *League* and *Jerusalem* it will be time to tackle that.

What is it about magic that you find so interesting?

Magic to me offers a new perspective with which to look at the world, your life, and reality, as well as a new approach to your relationship with your own consciousness.

It kind of gets classified along with New Age stuff, so it's hard for a lot of people to even consider.

I was initially very skeptical about magic due to the enormous number of idiots associated with it. However, science cannot explain or rationalise the concept of consciousness because it cannot replicate it in a laboratory. That leaves the single biggest area of our experience of the world unexplained. With magic, all sorts of possibilities are offered as to what consciousness might be, what areas of consciousness might have strange qualities, and what might be practical applications for those qualities.

It used to be that intellectuals and philosophers could be openly interested in magic without getting ridiculed.

Magic is simply a way of exploring the world. It involves following concepts that certain individuals have been exploring since humanity's inception. Some of them were charlatans, some of them were deluded maniacs or attention seekers, but some of them are the pillars upon which our entire reality is based. Paracelsus basically put forward the concepts of modern medicine, as well as being the first person to explore the concept of the unconscious—centuries before Freud or Jung. He was also a magician. He wouldn't have used that term himself. He probably would have thought of himself as a natural philosopher—

Maybe we need to go back to that term. But please go on.

Many of the cornerstones of our culture have roots in the occult. The earliest writers and artists came from shamanic culture, and science comes from alchemy. Isaac Newton was an alchemist. Einstein apparently died with a copy of Madame Blavatsky's *The Secret Doctrine* on the corner of his desk, and there are certainly similarities between that work and Einstein's theory of general relativity. However, magic tends to be viewed as this deranged relation that we don't want to bring up this far along in the advancement of our culture.

What led you to write a book on magic?

The idea came about when I decided, along with my magic partner Steve Moore, that it was time to lay our cards on the table and explain what magic was, how to do it, and why you probably should learn about it from a book that wasn't hiding behind pseudo-creepy imagery or incomprehensible occult jargon.

MARTIN AMIS

INTERVIEW BY JAMES KNIGHT
PORTRAIT BY TARA SINN, WITH A PHOTO BY ALEX STURROCK

Published December 2008

Martin Amis is one of the great writers of contemporary fiction. Even if he'd given up putting pen to paper after his third novel, *Money*, this would be an irrefutable fact. Period. Sorry. He writes grippingly of ugly characters consuming for the sake of consumption, blind to their own greed. His hideous, and occasionally hilarious, creations have always been both of their own time and chillingly in line with whatever is going on outside your window on any given day.

Amis gives interviews rarely and has a reputation for being spiky and guarded. Having read all of his work and been more than a little bit into it, actually picking up the phone to talk to him had me shaking like a wee little leaf on a tree. Luckily, Amis ("Marty" to his buddies) was kind, willing, and open. He also has the most mesmerising way of emphasising words mid-sentence. Go watch him talk about his book *House of Meetings* on *Charlie Rose* on YouTube right now and you'll hear what I mean.

Vice: Having grown up with the towering novelist Kingsley Amis for a father, was there a point where you made a conscious decision to be "a writer", or was it always sort of a given?
Martin Amis: At around 13, a certain self-awareness came over me as I was writing prose and poems in notebooks and diaries. What you are doing at that age is communing with yourself in a new way and becoming articulate within yourself. I think that everyone goes through that state and the people who end up becoming writers are simply those who never grow out of it. I never did. I

also have to admit my father as an early influence. I read his stuff, but I also felt like it was an independent decision that I made to be a writer. I knew that it wasn't a case of just writing a single novel and thinking, "I've done that now," or that I'd impressed my father and purged the influence. I had the feeling that it would be a long-haul thing—in a good way.

What other novelists were early influences on your writing?

Well, I'd not read Bellow by the time I had written my first novel. I read a lot of Austen early on but I fail to see how anybody could be influenced by her, she's simply too *lucid*. I'd read some Nabokov too, but I suppose the biggest early influence was Dickens. His stuff was just nuts and wild, which is beguiling at that age. It's impossible to imitate Austen, as it is all understatement, whereas with Dickens the prose is so hairy and muscle-y; you can really gorge on it.

Early on you seemed preoccupied with the present—its excess and its vacuity—both in the rampant consumerism of *Money* and the Thatcherite capitalism of *London Fields*.

Certainly during the early period, yes, but there comes a point where you're not really *in* the culture any more. You become removed from it. My father put it well to me once. He said: "At a certain age you think it's not like that anymore—it's like *this*. But you are not quite sure what *this* is." I think it would be insane to harbour the idea that you can remain plugged in forever.

You've also spoken of being "addicted to the 20th century". Has the 21st proved not quite as compelling so far?

Possibly that was the point where, for me, *that* became *this*. The novel I am coming to the end of now is set in 1970, so perhaps I am clinging to the 20th century.

London has always had a looming presence in your novels. What was it about the city that fas-

cinated you?

I always felt grateful to be in one of the world's great cities. It would have been completely impossible to write anything like the novels I wrote if I were living somewhere like Cambridge. It was very much a case of being in it again—living, breathing, and swimming in it. And as we all know, the fish doesn't ask about the water. You just sit there, run your nerve endings up against it, and it all comes out of the other end of your pen.

At times you have written in forms outside of fiction to reflect on society in the same way you have within your novels.

Fiction utilises a different part of the mind and you can see it in action and see the difference when you produce nonfiction. I studied Stalinism and Russian history extensively when working on *Koba the Dread* [nonfiction] and then *House of Meetings* [fiction], and due to the formal differences, similar feelings were expressed in different ways. Fiction acts like a slow zoom lens, it allows you to go deeper in and say something else. It took three years to get from the brain to the back of my spine, and then I felt ready to say something.

Even when not dealing directly with politics, your novels exist in an atmosphere of political threat. Over time the threat has shifted from Soviet Cold War to the axis of evil, but always with a sense of potential Armageddon.

I was very apolitical as a young man. I was left of centre, but being surrounded by Trotskyites like Christopher Hitchens made me seem moderate in comparison. I was unattractively proud of not knowing a great deal about politics. Literature was what I had and it was my thing. Despite writing about nuclear weapons in *Einstein's Monsters* and the Holocaust in *Time's Arrow*, I only really gave myself a political education when I began to study Russia. Suddenly I could see the categories and the precedents. It all came alive to me. When September 11 came along, I wasn't prepared for anything as interesting as that to happen in my lifetime. If I had to explain what my novels were about in one word it would be masculinity, and here was masculinity in a whole new form. It takes the essence of what it is to be a man straight back to violence, and really the political history of man is the history of violence. The social history of man is simply sex. Those have always been the most interesting questions to me: what is it that makes man put himself about in such a way and what is it that makes him treat women in the way he does? When I have chosen to speak out about topics in nonfictional form it is with these concerns in mind.

Are you talking about *The Second Plane*, your collection of pieces about Islam?

Yes. I felt I had something to say and nonfiction was a very immediate way of saying it. So I did.

The plot devices that you became infamous for using came to be classified as postmodern. Were they conscious, formal decisions or were they subconsciously demanded by the story?

Postmodernism wasn't really this grand bandwagon that it may have seemed at the time. It was in the air and if you were of your time you saw the point of it. In the end it proved not the rich vein some had hoped and something of a dead end, but it was very predictive in terms of life itself becoming very postmodern, what with buildings having their piping on the outside and politicians talking openly about "the plumbing". There was a whole new level of self-consciousness that developed, as well as an interest in one's own age that would have been unknown in, say, the 18th century. History is still speeding up and I want to reflect that, so when I sit down to write I want to push the form of the novel and play so that there is a conscious and deliberate sense of pushing the form. If anything, though, I am now returning to realism with a modernist sensibility without that tricksiness of postmodernism.

How do you feel about the current state of fiction?

It will always be produced; I worry more about it being read. Poetry is already dead in those terms. Poetry requires that you stop the clock. When you read a poem the writer is saying, "Let's stop and examine this writing." People don't like solitary reflection anymore, so poetry no longer has a place in the culture. This will eventually seep out to include the novel. The day of the long, reflective, discursive novel, such as the great Saul Bellow novels, which were eight-month best sellers in their time, are over. The novel now is streamlined and sped up. It is a reflection of the age.

Are there any young novelists working now who you admire?

The truth is that I don't read my youngers. It seems a terribly uneconomical way to organise your reading, by studying those unproved by time. I read my friends, so I take in Will Self and Zadie Smith with great interest. It all seems healthy out there but I can't make any broad statements about "where" the novel is now. Sorry.

In conversation with Self you have said that "the middle classes are underrepresented in my novels". You also seem to have a recurring preoccupation with the lower classes.

I like extremes. There is a certain latitude necessary to be a character, often in a repulsive way in the case of the upper classes, but it gives you the freedom to be a little more extreme and extravagant at either end of the social scale. The pressures at the lower end of the spectrum are very intense and that leads to characters becoming interestingly twisted into strange shapes. The middle classes are written about by everyone. They shan't whimper with neglect because I am not writing about them. All fiction is essentially kitchen-sink. It is just that some kitchen sinks are more expensive than others.

You mentioned a novel that you are working on now. Can you tell us any more about that or will you get in trouble?

I hope not. It is a novel set in the social revolution, and the main character is 20 years old. Its title is *The Pregnant Widow*, which comes from a remark by the wonderful Russian thinker Alexander Herzen. He said that when political or social orders change by revolution one should be pleased that the old is giving way to the new, but the trouble is that you get the death of the new order and no heir apparent. You are left not with a child but a pregnant widow, and much grief and tribulation will take place between the death and the birth. I would say that even now the baby of the social revolution is yet to be born 30 years on.

Like London, America figures often in your novels. In *Money* you portray the country as the unbridled consumerist paradigm that London strived to be, but lacking that British inhibition.
America is a wild place, an awesome place, and like Henry James I very much believe it to be a world rather than a country. As a place it is very difficult to generalise. Having watched the last eight years with horror I am of course thrilled about the election because the potential to go wrong in America is so huge and here at last is someone genuinely impressive as well as someone who can help heal that great wound in American life. I think we could be entering a great era.

Perhaps an era in which we see the baby of the social revolution born?
Perhaps.

There was talk at one point of David Cronenberg making a film of *London Fields*. Was there any truth to that?
There was. I met him a couple of times and he rewrote the script a little but he would only have got a sliver of the novel and not the whole book, so it was left. The project is still alive, though. They did *The Rachel Papers*, which was fun, and *Dead Babies*, which was sort of fun. They are making my novels in order—just at 20-year intervals. I have never had a great time with writing for cinema, though. I did a terrific script for an adaptation of *Northanger Abbey*, which was picked up by Miramax and then sat on. I'm not sure what happened to it. I should probably check on that, actually. Cinema is a won-

derful form, though, and a young form. As Bellow said, film is about exteriors whereas the novel is concerned with interiors. So there are many possibilities yet to explore.

What caused you to move to Uruguay for two years?
My wife is half Uruguayan and half New York Jew—a heady mixture. She has about 25 first cousins out there. We visited it for a winter and liked it very much so we stayed. We eventually left as our girls outgrew it and needed better schools. The landscape is fantastic but it was too quiet politically to have any impact on my writing. It is a real anomaly in terms of how gentle and sane it is in the context of South America.

Recently you began teaching at Manchester University. Why, of all places, Manchester?
Quite simply: they asked me. My father taught and by all accounts was fairly good at it and I felt that I might do all right at it as well. I enjoy it very much and I like my colleagues, which is rare for a job. All I do is teach novels. What could be more agreeable than that? I don't guide my students' elbows while they write. In fact I don't even see what they write. We talk about it a little and I talk a lot about Nabokov, Kafka, and Dostoyevsky, all of whom are the people I like to talk about anyway. So I'm rather happy with myself.

Is it true that you were a mod and then a hippie during the 60s and 70s?
I was a mod but that all ended after my fifth scooter crash. And then, yes, I was a rather opportunistic hippie. All that free love and music sounded fun, but I was never particularly pious. Mod was more about having the right pink socks on the right day anyway. The hippie thing was a coherent idea, but there was a very dark side to it. Like John Updike said, it was a "fascinating dark carnival". All this optimism with a dark underbelly where, if you rooted around in it long enough, you'd find Charles Manson.

GLENN DANZIG

INTERVIEW BY SAM MCPHEETERS | PHOTOS BY JEANEEN LUND

Published May 2010

Most performers have to span a gap between their public image and their private life, but Glenn Danzig has to jump between two distinct public versions of himself. Think of the disconnect between the cheesy camp of his "Mother" video and the lurid power of the song itself. Occult Glenn earns public ridicule to almost the same degree that Songwriter Glenn earns praise, like an actor who wins a Razzie and an Oscar in the same week. When I mentioned this interview in an email to a friend, the friend wrote, "You don't really think of Danzig as someone you get to ask actual questions of."

Because I'd been scheduled for an interview, and not a jam session, I'd steeled myself for all variety of Occult Danzig worst-case scenarios. This was needless worry. Glenn met me at his Los Angeles office with a friendly nod and a handshake. No hooded Metalocalypse minions guarded the periphery. In person, that legendary voice was a shade smokier than I'd expected, still marked with traces of a Jersey accent, like an off-duty James Gandolfini. He led me into his dimly lit inner sanctum, turned down Fox News on a TV in the corner, and motioned for me to take a chair. Only at that moment did it occur to me that I'd just stepped into a dark room with Glenn Danzig.

Vice: Thanks for doing this interview in person. It gives me a strong incentive to not be a smartass.
Glenn Danzig: Yeah, my day's slammed, but I got here early to try and accommodate.

I've always been curious how a band like Danzig works. You're the figurehead, the front man, the namesake, and the songwriter...
That started after Samhain, when I hooked up with Rick [Rubin], because we were courting lots of major labels at the time. It was his idea to change the name to Danzig. I said, "Well, I was gonna do that after the Misfits. I just thought it sounded too much like Billy Idol or something." But by the time Samhain had run its course and was becoming Danzig, people knew what to expect from me, from Danzig. The original idea was to have a different lineup every record.

What changed that?
We got into touring mode. But it should have been done sooner.

It seems like that would deny you any lasting chemistry with your bandmates. There are basically term limits on your musicians.
No, you just work with a lot of different people. You get to experience lots of different stuff and do a lot of different things. I like that freedom a lot better. It's like, "Maybe I can work with this guy." I still like

that kind of rebellious punk thing where you change it up all the time. If you get bored, change it. When it's stale, fix it.

I guess I'm curious about this because it kind of puts you in the position of being the employer. How do practices work if you're like the boss of the band?
I don't like to look at it like that.

I'm not saying you are the boss, like you have laminated posters with Employee Rights and Grievance Number Hotlines on the wall of the practice space, but...
At the end of the day you have to make sure you do pay attention to the business end. But it should still be that everyone's having a good time. If you're not having a good time, there's the door. If you come in and you're like [makes whining noise]—goodbye. I don't have time for that fucking shit. There's not a lot of money in music these days; I do it because I enjoy it. I could get a lot more money doing other shit. Am I going to tour forever? Probably not. But I enjoy doing it still, and anyone who puts a damper on that, I don't need you. You really should be doing music because you love playing music. And if you're going out on the road, you've got to enjoy playing live. If you don't like playing live, you shouldn't be on the road, because people are paying to see you and they don't want you up there all bored. That's bullshit.

So how do practices work when you're the primary songwriter?
I'm the only songwriter.

Do you show up with prewritten parts? Do you say, "Hey, Tommy, here's the new part"?
This is the same question you would ask Bowie or somebody.

Yeah, but I'm never going to get to meet Bowie. You're it.
You've never been able to ask this question before?

I've never spoken with anybody who's reached this point in their career.
Oh, OK. Well, basically I write the songs, I bring them down, show everybody their part, and then we play it until it sounds good.

So if at any point one of your musicians says, "I've got a way this could sound better," does that constitute employee insubordination?
If it's just a way to play the riff or the chord pattern, no. But if you're trying to change the actual makeup of the song, yeah, that won't fly.

For most musicians, that's an alien concept. Every band I've ever known has operated on a level far below this, hashing out competing musical visions in cramped practice spaces. What's your process for writing songs?
Sometimes I get the guitar lines, sometimes I write on the piano, sometimes I'll write the lyrics first and then figure out the chord patterns on guitar, and sometimes I write the drum pattern first. It's all different.

Is it all up here [points to head] or do you keep stuff on a tape recorder?
When I first started working with Rick, he made me buy not one but a couple of microcassette recorders, because I would come to rehearsal and I would go, "Man, I had this great song on the way here." I wrote a lot of songs when I was banging on my steering wheel, driving and screaming "Fuck you!" to really bad drivers, but I would forget the songs by the time I got to rehearsal. Rick was like, "You gotta get a microcassette recorder! That could have been a hit song!"

I would think that after the first time that happened you'd be banging your head on the dashboard.
I don't stress on that shit. But now, unless I'm at my pad or whatever and a song comes to me and I just pick up my guitar and write it and lay it down on something, then yeah, I usually hum it into a microcassette recorder and then I transpose it when I get home and work it out on guitar or piano.

I've read that you're going to slow down on touring some because you don't want to deal with the downtime that comes on the road.
After the 2005 Blackest of the Black tour, I stopped touring. Then I said, "Well, I'll do local shows, because I don't have to sit on a bus for fucking three days between shows, doing nothing." I'm a workaholic, and so I've always got to be doing stuff. When you're on the bus, you can't do shit. You're not at home, you don't have all your shit.

But I guess you then got tired of not touring...
I love playing live, so I started out again with a couple local shows. Then we put together a West Coast run and I flew home after every two or three shows. And then we tried this thing where we flew out to the East Coast, did four shows, I flew home, and then we started a West Coast run that went out to Denver for two and a half weeks, and every two or three days I flew home. It worked out OK, so in 2008 we did a Blackest run where I flew home every few days. That didn't bug me, so we'll try a full tour this time. I'm going to try the flying-home thing and see how it works.

That implies that you had decades of not doing that, of being on tour and dealing with the constraints of Tour Time. I've known so many touring musicians who surrendered to the downtime, who would let their natural rhythms go to hell and sleep until three, not exercise, not read, not do any of the things they'd do at home...
I try to work out, but a lot of hotels don't have gyms anymore, so I always try to find a local gym where there's not a ton of 'roid-heads, 'cause I can't stand them. It's tough. I read a lot, so that helps.

Are you able to read on tour? Meaning, can you concentrate even with other people's noise?
I get my own back area where people stay away from me. [laughs] I'm always reading or going to bookstores. When everyone else is farting around in the daytime, I'm at bookstores.

But you must have had years before that where

you were staying at people's houses, in the early days. In the 80s, you weren't staying at hotels and you didn't have a bus.
We would sleep in the van sometimes.

Everybody?
Yeah.

Dude, I've tried that. It's like a jigsaw puzzle.
In Samhain, I carpeted everything but I built a thing so the amps would never hit you, and it was also a bunk. So it had doors on the top, and when you opened them you could get to the amps or you could climb up to the top bunk. The top bunk could have two people sleeping up there. It was all plush carpet. You could fit another four people below there, plus three people in the front.

Feasible, but not posh.
It was comfortable. It was better than the Misfits, I'll tell you that. In those days you could still have the cab connected to the back of the truck, so you didn't have to get out of the truck to change drivers. I would be like, "Here, switch off," and while I was driving, I would jump out of the seat and hold the wheel until another person jumped in and grabbed it. Real touring, motherfucker!

I've always assumed "Mother '93" was kind of the dividing line when you started to get a lot more public recognition. Is that correct?
MTV didn't want to play the "Mother" video, but it was being played five times an hour on the Music Box. The original was banned when it came out. MTV told Rick they needed the censored version. He thought he sent them censored version, but he sent them the uncensored one. They played it, and they got all these religious people—who can go fuck themselves anyway [holds up middle finger to empty space]—freaking out, and MTV banned us almost forever.

Am I right in thinking that when you go out now, to the supermarket or wherever, you get a certain amount of gawkers?

Yeah. I have to sign autographs wherever I go.

Here's a question I've always had. Have you heard of Jerusalem syndrome? That's the thing where normal tourists go to the Holy Land, freak out, and convince themselves they're John the Baptist or Jesus.
I've never heard of that.

It's a recognised psychological phenomenon.
I've never heard of it.

I guess it's not that well known. I didn't make it up, though.
All right. 'Cause I read a lot.

Well, I'm wondering if there is a Danzig syndrome? Do you have a thing where your persona or physical presence inspires people to flip out?
I don't know, you'd have to ask them.

What I mean is, have people freaked out on you? Has anyone come up to you in public and acted unhinged at the sight of you in person?
I don't know about that. I think people are just like, "Wow," and are really happy that they saw me. "Oh, will you sign something for me or take a picture for me?" Most of my fans are pretty cool.

I'm talking about 1 percent of 1 percent. The person who comes up to you and says, "I sacrificed my dog in the name of Kramdar. Here's the body, Lord Danzig."
No.

I saw John Carpenter speak in 2002. He was 54 then, but he looked ten years older, and he talked for a while about his sagging energy levels. You're the same age now, right?
Give or take.

Well, you look my age and it's kind of weirding me out. Do you ever have problems with your energy levels?
No.

What's your secret?
I don't know. I don't eat shit food. I don't do drugs. I don't know what else to tell you.

I'm 40. I don't do any of those things. I eat salad for lunch. And I wake up almost every day feeling like a wet bag of sand.
Salad is terrible if you put creamy crap on it.

It's low-fat creamy crap!
There's no such thing.

So you have nothing to share, nothing to impart to those of us who are rapidly turning into jiggly piles of goo? It seems like it happens quick.
Uh, do you work out at all?

Not every day.
You don't need to do it every day. Diet is really important and I think vitamins are really important also. Maybe you want to go to a nutritionist and find out what your body is lacking and what it's not lacking. And I don't mean a fucking quack, chemo, murdering doctor. I mean a nutritionist, who evaluates your blood and tells you what you're deficient in and what you're not deficient in.

Those are all good things to know, but they're no surprise. You don't have any one thing that...
If I can help it, I don't go to modern doctors.

How come?
They're full of shit.

Across the board? All of Western medicine?
Pretty much. If you had cancer would you get chemo? You'd be dead in a week.

I wouldn't be dead in a week!
Bet you. [laughs]

What would you bet me? Let's make this interesting.
I wouldn't bet you anything, because in a week, even if you live, you're not going to live that much longer! Chemo radiation will kill you, and it's not the way to heal your body from cancer. You need to make your body stronger. Your body has natural things that fight off diseases. Cancer is just cells deteriorating more rapidly than your body can heal and fight it. So you have to find out what that imbalance is. Doctors are too busy writing scrips that they get kickbacks on and charging you hundreds of thousands of dollars for chemo.

I think what I was looking for here was something that would help me to not look like Elmer Fudd every time I look in the mirror. But you're not going to give it up, and I respect that.
Well, you gotta work out. Do you work out? You said no. [laughs]

I said no in italics. There's some wiggle room there. I go to the gym once or twice a week. [laughs unconvincingly] Here's something else: This morning there were reports—false ones—that the guy from the Twilight movies was set to play Kurt Cobain in a biopic. At some point, someone's going to play you in a movie, whether it's about stuff that you've done, or at least peripheral to stuff you've done.
I've never even thought about that. [laughs]

It's inevitable. Who plays you?
That will never happen.

Here's where the bet comes in. There's gotta be some money in this for me.
First off, that's never gonna happen. And I couldn't even tell you who I think should play me because by the time a movie like that is ever done, whoever I would pick now would be too old. [laughs] And also, you know Hollywood doesn't ever pick the right people to play those parts.

That's kind of what I'm getting at here.
Hopefully I'll be dead and I won't have to know about it.

A WOMAN WHO MADE
A DOCUMENTARY
ABOUT VAGINOPLASTY

INTERVIEW BY ANDY CAPPER | PORTRAIT BY ALEX STURROCK

Published October 2008

Heather Leach is a filmmaker from Rochdale, which is most famous for being the birthplace of 80s "soul" singer Lisa Stansfield. Recently, Heather plunged herself headfirst into the murky world of vaginoplasty, or "voluntarily having a plastic surgeon chop off your labia". We talked to her about what she found, and it was quite revealing, if not something you should read if you're eating lunch right now (especially anything with roast beef or pastrami in it).

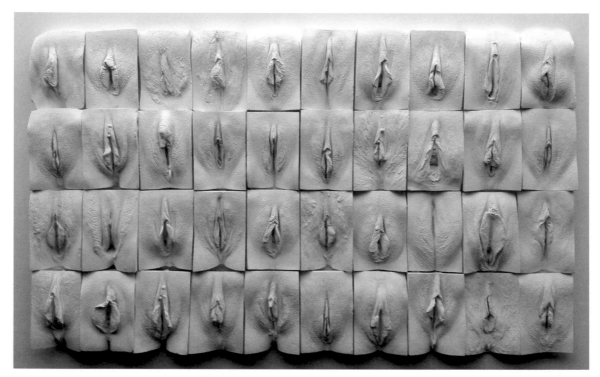

This sculpture/cast is called "Design a Vagina" and is by British artist James McCartney. Some of the girls in Heather's film had their vaginas cast especially for this piece.

Vice: Hi Heather. Why did you make this movie?
Heather Leach: Well, Channel 4 asked me to. After that, I researched it and found out that, in the UK at least, the number of women getting surgery on their labia has doubled in five years. More shockingly, the number of women getting the procedure has gone up by 300 percent in the last two years. Even girls as young as 16 are having these labiaplasties.

Crikey.
I would hear girls complain of awful comments being made to them all the time. Things like "Your vagina is fucking disgusting" or "Going down on you is like going down on the Mersey Tunnel". Then there was one girl who was bullied by her sister and she'd say stuff like, "It looks like hanging ham down there."

That's not a very nice thing to say.
There are different physical and psychological rea-

sons for operating on vaginas and there are differing methods, but the majority of doctors reshape the vulva by amputating and trimming. They do this by slicing the inner labia off so they don't hang below the outer labia.

I'm wincing.
Yeah, they slice it all off with a scalpel. But some surgeons cut open the labia and tie up the nerve endings so they will still have sensation. Then they fold it over in and restitch it all together. One thing people don't realise is that the nerve endings in the labia are connected to the clitoris, so they stand a chance of permanently hampering their sex lives. But I guess teenage girls don't think about this because they just want a "perfect fanny".

We should say for our readers in the States that over here "fanny" means "cunt" and "bottom" means "ass". "Fanny" doesn't mean "ass" here

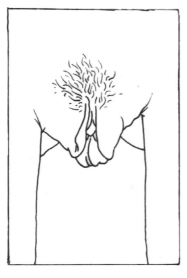

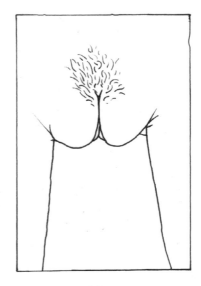

Before   *After*

like it does there.

Yeah, well, anyway, people used to think that if you had a tit job it meant having "perfect tits" back in, say, 1985. And now they think having a stranger hack away at your fanny is going to mean the same thing: perfect flaps. They're also going in for things like vaginal liposuction.

Oh come on.

They suck fat out of the pubic bone area to make it flatter. They're also doing a Botox injection that goes into where your G-spot is supposed to be. It's a called "G-Shot". You have to keep going back every three months to have it refilled with Botox. It's about £1,000 a session and you have to get it through private cosmetic surgeons.

To what do you attribute this sudden increase in teenage girls getting their labia sliced?

There are the things like the big advertisements in women's magazines from large cosmetic surgical corporations. Then you blend that with peer pressure from teenage peers, particularly boys.

How so?

It's teenage boys who are watching pornography all the time. As far as I've seen, you don't see any kind of modern pornographic imagery that contains what I would consider to be a normal vagina. People start to think that the perfect fanny should not have the inner labia protruding and that it should be completely hairless.

Right.

Bikini waxing has a role to play in all this. When Bill Clinton reduced the laws regarding porn, the porn producers pushed for total waxing so that viewers could see the whole vagina for the first time, close up. Now these images are everywhere and making young girls think that it's some kind of natural ideal, to have a hair-free tiny-lipped fanny.

It's becoming like, "I'm going to have somebody cut my fucking labia off. No biggie."

Yeah, but what people don't realise is how harrowing it can be to have the operation. The recovery period can take up to six months. I filmed a surgery and it was horrendous. Once they're chopped off, the pieces are flung straight in the bin and thrown away with the rubbish.

Self-portrait by Karl Lagerfeld

KARL LAGERFELD

INTERVIEW BY BRUCE LABRUCE

Published March 2010

When *Vice* called me last month with an out-of-the-blue offer to fly to Paris and interview the Kaiser himself, Karl Lagerfeld—creative director of the $10 billion Chanel empire, the house of Fendi, and his own eponymous line—I jumped at the chance. I have to confess that I wasn't an expert about the fabled fashion kingpin prior to *Vice*'s proposition, but I did know that for a faggot it was tantamount to an audience with the Pope! I was duly excited to meet the Man Behind the Fan (which, I would soon discover, has long since been replaced by the Collar), the guru behind the dark glasses, and to try to separate the myth from the reality.

But having now met and spent time with Mr. Lagerfeld, it seems that, as close as I can figure out, the man really is the myth. It's not that there isn't any *there* there; it's that somehow, by some strange alchemy, the person who descends the stairway of his fashion house, infinitely multiplied by mirrors, has transcended this mortal coil to become a pure creature of creativity. Lagerfeld is a study in perpetual motion, tirelessly darting between creative endeavours while devouring both history and the ephemeral present, the zeitgeist. A voracious reader and observer of life through books and popular culture, he filters the world into his couture and other creative outlets like a sort of supercomputer. When I suggest to him in the following interview that he may have Asperger syndrome, a rare form of autism characterised by an obsessive-compulsive "disorder" manifested as a kind of genius, he concurs.

What struck me most about Lagerfeld when I was doing my research was how closely aligned many of my beliefs were with his. Despite owning a private jet and multiple luxury homes, he is anti-materialistic and remains detached from his possessions, particularly as he has become more mature. He has a healthy appreciation for what some people might consider the "low life"—prostitution, promiscuity, what have you—and he is decidedly antibourgeois, which encompasses his distaste for the idea of gay marriage.

On meeting, I presented him with a list of ten beliefs that we have in common, which acted as a nice icebreaker. From the outset, he was warm and convivial. However, I must admit he cast a spell on me. For the hour and a half that I sat with him, I felt almost as if I were in a dream or under hypnosis—relaxed but entranced, and even slightly blissed out. La Lagerfeld is a guru, all right, and not just one of the fashion variety.

Vice: So, you're very busy as usual.
Karl Lagerfeld: I'm always busy, but this is a really busy time. I like really busy times.

I do too. I've been watching various documentaries about you. I've been kind of surprised, as I've learned more about you, by how your philosophy has become very distilled.
Down-to-earth.

Yes, very down-to-earth.
Sophisticated down-to-earth.

That's almost like a paradox, but I understand.
I love paradoxes.

Me too. I think it's all about paradoxes. People don't get it; they think you're being contradictory, but two things can exist simultaneously that are opposed. There's no mystery in that.
Truth is only a question of point of view.

I like that you make it clear that you don't want to be photographed or filmed without your sunglasses on. I don't either. Who would?

They're my burka.

Exactly. A burka for the eyes.
A burka for a man. I'm a little short-sighted, and people, when they're short-sighted, they remove their glasses and then they look like cute little dogs who want to be adopted.

I'm actually near-sighted in one eye and far-sighted in the other.
You can't operate at all with what you have?

No. They say I'll never need glasses because I only use one eye for distances and one eye for close up.
That's perfect, no? I want to stay short-sighted or else I will need glasses for reading. But I don't want them because I sketch, I do everything without glasses, except for speaking to strangers. Especially if they wear glasses, too.

I hate it when photographers are like, "Can we have one with your glasses off?" Why? You can see me just fine.
I had an interview once with some German journalist—some horrible, ugly woman. It was in the early days after the communists—maybe a week after—and she wore a yellow sweater that was kind of see-through. She had huge tits and a huge black bra, and she said to me, "It's impolite; remove your glasses." I said, "Do I ask you to remove your bra?"

You have to be careful what you ask for. Something that you do, which I also try to do in my art, is to treat all aspects of creativity equally. Fashion, photography, books, whatever—it all comes from the same place.
Yes, exactly. Everything comes from the same head. The three things I like best in life are fashion, photography, and books. There are a lot of other things I may like but that I'm not gifted for. I'm not gifted for music. I'm not gifted for singing. I don't like to act because my life is a pantomime anyway.

Well, the gifts that you do possess have certainly served you well.

I'm perfectly happy, and what makes things even better is that I can do things the way that I want to. I have no problems in terms of down-to-earth issues; I can do everything I'm doing in the best conditions. My fashion business, Chanel, is the biggest luxury ready-to-wear brand in the world. Fendi is a part of LVMH, which is very big, too.

You've been famous for quite some time, but the whole landscape of celebrity has changed so dramatically in recent years.
That's part of our life, our culture.

Do you think it's become kind of toxic?
Yes, but you cannot fight against it. There's a price you have to pay for fame, and people who don't want to pay that price can get in trouble. I accepted the idea of celebrity because of a French expression: "You cannot have the butter *and* the money for the butter."

I like that. You have to choose one or the other.
And now I cannot cross the street. I cannot go anywhere.

But you don't mind being alone and isolated?
I have bodyguards. I have big cars.

Do you travel with bodyguards?
Oh yes. But I don't travel commercially. Whenever I go around the world I go on private jets.

What if you went to a nightclub or something?
I don't. I never go anywhere, not even from here to the Quai Voltaire, where I live. Never ever. People wait in front of my house.

How long has it been that way for you, with fans outside your home?
For the past ten years. Before that, it was OK. And when I was younger, people didn't really know me. I had the time to be young and not to be troubled by this kind of thing.

We see these young stars being eaten up and de- stroyed now, and it's sad in a way. But to be honest, I'm not so worried about the stars. I'm worried about the average person who spends far too much time thinking about celebrities.
If I were pretentious I would say that I'm not an average person. But really, I know how that is.

Well, yes, I know that you care, because you are interested in both high and low culture.
That is because there is only culture.

As in, there is only one large culture and everything is a facet of it.
I like to know everything; I like to be informed. I am not pretentious. I can speak several languages. I can read in every language.

The word "pretentious" is most often used pejoratively, but I don't think it's necessarily bad to be pretentious. So, I know that you're a very hard worker. That's another thing that we have in common. I hate holidays. I can never go away and just lie on a beach.
I was a beach boy in my youth.

Those were your salad days. You've said that you learned about life in those times. What did you do then?
Everything one can do to see what kind of life one wants—what you like, what you don't like, what's OK for you. I understood quickly that there are a lot of things that are not for me but that I have nothing against. I have not one prejudice. I don't judge things.

Being the sort of hard worker that you are is like being a monk.
But hard work is like being politically correct. Be politically correct, but please don't bother other people with conversation about being politically correct, because that's the end of everything. You want to create boredom? Be politically correct in your conversation.

What does being politically correct mean to you?

It means people talking about charities. Do it, be charitable, but don't make a subject of conversation out of it because then you bore the world to death. It's very unpleasant. But I don't go out a lot so I'm not so exposed to people.

And being isolated is not a problem for you?
I have no problem. That's the miracle of my life. There are no problems, only solutions—good ones or bad ones.

You are against the idea of gay marriage. I totally agree with you on that.
Yes, I'm against it for a very simple reason: in the 60s they all said we had the right to the difference. And now, suddenly, they want a bourgeois life.

It's normalising.
For me it's difficult to imagine—one of the papas at work and the other at home with the baby. How would that be for the baby? I don't know. I see more lesbians married with babies than I see boys married with babies. And I also believe more in the relationship between mother and child than in that between father and child.

I take it you don't want children.
If I were interested in children, I would be a godfather—or a godmother. I don't like the idea of taking people out of their lives and their contexts. If there were a child I wanted to adopt, I would try to find the family of the child and give them the money for an education in his life and his context.

What about famous gay artists like Francis Bacon or Wilhelm von Gloeden? They both had important relationships that were almost like marriages.
I knew Francis Bacon; he was the sweetest man in the world, like a Middle English lady with the finger up drinking tea in Monte Carlo. My best friend, who is dead now, was very friendly with Bacon. They gambled and drank together.

Did Bacon have his protégé with him, or was it his lover?
I think that he was dead already—the famous one was dead.

Ah, George Dyer.
I only saw Bacon with my friend, drinking and gambling heavily.

Your best friend is…
He's dead, too.

What happened to him?
AIDS. That happened 20 years ago.

How did you cope with that whole period? I'm sure you knew so many great people who died of AIDS.
I don't want to go back through that age. In those days it was a hopeless case.

It was a death sentence.
You may be a bit young to remember. It was horrible. Beyond horrible.

It decimated the fashion world.
It killed a whole generation of people.

You know, Fran Lebowitz said that AIDS killed all the cool people.
Yes, exactly.

Which I quite agree with, because it was usually the people who were living really hard and experimenting who got hit with it.
Perhaps things went too far then. But now they want to be too bourgeois.

Exactly. It's swung back the other way. This bourgeois idea of gays wanting to take on a traditional family life—I just don't understand it. It's like the oppressed are becoming the oppressors.
In a way, yes. Exactly.

They want to be the type of people who have al-

Karl and Bruce at Karl's studio in Paris. Photo by Olivier Saillant

ways despised them.
When I was a child I asked my mother what homosexuality was about and she said—and this was 100 years ago in Germany and she was very open-minded—"It's like hair colour. It's nothing. Some people are blond and some people have dark hair. It's not a subject." This was a very healthy attitude.

You were lucky in that regard.
Some people make drama out of it. I don't even understand. It's not a problem. It doesn't exist. It's not a subject. For me it never was.

What were you like as a child?
I was very much like a grown-up. I have photos of me as a child wearing a tie, and it's the same as I am today. And of course I was very successful with

paedophilia. I knew about it when I was ten.

So you used it consciously?
Well, I wouldn't go that far. It was impossible to touch me. I would run away and I would tell my mother about people she knew, like the brother of one of my sister's husbands. Nothing happened, but my mother said, "You know, darling, it's your fault. You see how you behave."

Did you ever actually have sex with somebody older?
No. It never went that far.

The comedian Chris Rock once said that whenever he was at a family picnic or something and one of his cousins or uncles would try to diddle him,

he would go to his mother and his mother would say, "Walk it off."
This is a less sophisticated version of my mother. That's why in a modern world these things shouldn't be subjects. Children should be informed.

What about your relationship to the whole political gay movement?
I have nothing to do with it. This is just a part of normal life. I mean, the 20 percent or so who are like this, made by God or by whoever, they are as they are supposed to be. So where's the problem?

The argument would be that the more organised and political they are, the more they are able to fight against things like homophobic violence.
I never met anything like this in my life. I had an overprotected life. What can I fight about? I don't know what to do. It never happened to me, and it never happened to people I know.

It's like Marianne Faithfull says, "What are you fighting for? It's not my reality."
Exactly. And I'm mad for her. She's great.

I'm wondering if gay political groups have tried to enlist you.
Yes, but I've never voted in my life—for any kind of politics.

Me neither.
I'm a stranger here; I'm a stranger in Germany. I'm just passing by.

Politics is just so business-oriented.
I'm in fashion. Politics is not my job. I don't vote in France even though foreigners here can. I will never vote in my life.

I'm the exact same way.
Good. I could vote for myself because I know everything about myself. And I can lie to everybody, but I cannot lie to myself. My mother used to say, "If you're really honest and you have a certain kind of

education, you will know the question and the answer."

Did you work with Carla Bruni, the French president's wife, when she was a model?
Oh yes. She was one of the ten supermodels.

I was kind of obsessed with her. I pulled photos of her out of magazines, and when I was editing a film in the early 90s I would stare at her picture on my wall. I don't know why. She had something.
She has a great education and speaks many languages. She's perfect for the job of first lady. I even photographed her naked.

Did they dig those up after she became first lady?
Yes, but they were elegant and she had nothing against it. She couldn't care less. She's very cool like that. The photo is beautiful. I can show you the nude of her. I did it for *Visionaire* in 1998. Everybody knows how a man or a girl is built, and everybody goes to the beach. So where's the problem?

And you have no problem with porn, either.
No. I admire porn.

This is another thing that we have in common.
And I personally only like high-class escorts. I don't like sleeping with people I really love. I don't want to sleep with them because sex cannot last, but affection can last forever. I think this is healthy. And for the way the rich live, this is possible. But the other world, I think they need porn. I also think it's much more difficult to perform in porn than to fake some emotion on the face as an actor.

Yes, there's a quote from you about how giving a blowjob on film is more difficult than acting out grand emotions, which can be feigned. I totally agree. I think people don't give porn actors credit. It's not easy what they do.
I admire porn actors.

Me too, and prostitutes as well. There's a real art to it.

Frustration is the mother of crime, and so there would be much more crime without prostitutes and without porn movies.

You got in trouble when you used a porn star in one of your shows in the early 90s.
But who cared?

Anna Wintour cared.
Yeah, but I'm still on the best terms with her.

There is so much hypocrisy against porn. So many people watch it and then look down their noses at people who are in it or who make it.
And those movie theatres don't exist anymore, not like they did in the 70s.

There's one left in Toronto, where I'm from.
I never went to one because I think it's a quite sleazy situation.

It has its charm.
I'm not sure I want to be charmed.

Concerning the female form: Beth Ditto from the Gossip? What do you think of her image?
She is very good. I know her very well. She's genius. She doesn't end up in what we use for shows, but she has real personality.

I just saw the Gossip in Berlin and she's amazing. There's so much criticism about fashion and the emaciated body, but you obviously love the voluptuous as well.
Yes, totally.

Let's talk about fur. I grew up on a farm. My father was a trapper and a hunter.
Me too. My father was not really a farmer, but I spent my time around the country so I know everything about country life.

Mine used to trap wild mink and muskrats and beavers.
There's nothing else to trap in those areas.

It was part of his income.
That's why I always say, when people talk about not using fur: "Are you rich enough to make an income for the people in the north who live from hunting? What do you want them to live off of when there's nothing else to do?"

That's why I've always found the anti-fur thing kind of strange. It was part of the way that my family made a living.
It is farmers who are nice to the cows and the pigs and then kill them. It's even more hypocritical than hunters. At least the hunters don't flatter the animals. I remember when they killed the pigs when I was a child. I still hear the noise in my ears.

Are you a vegetarian?
Not really. I have to eat meat once a week because my doctor wants me to, but I prefer fish. I don't like that people butcher animals, but I don't like them to butcher humans either, which is apparently very popular in the world.

You're sort of irreverent about fur.
If you cannot afford it, just forget about it. Don't use it as an investment piece to show people how rich you are. Use it like a cheap knitted thing. It's like a big stone. Lucky you that you can have a big stone, but if it troubles you financially to have the stone, don't have the stone.

This is another paradox that I like about you. There's nothing conspicuous about the way you use things.
If you can afford it, OK. But if you think it's an investment, then forget about it.

Your relationship to technology is kind of interesting.
Well, I hate telephones. I prefer faxes because I like to write.

Who are you faxing? Nobody faxes anymore. You're like the only person with a fax machine.
People I'm really friendly with have faxes. Anna

Wintour has one. We speak via fax. And in Paris I send letters to people.

That's a lost art.
I have somebody to deliver letters all over every day.

You send a note over.
Yes, I send notes.

That's very Victorian.
Yes, but there's not one bit bad about the Victorian. Civilised living for me is like this. I'm not a chambermaid whom you can ring at every moment. Today, you know, most people act like they work at a switchboard in a hotel.

The whole culture of cell phones, texting, and instant messaging is very impersonal and also very distracting.
I'm not working at a switchboard. I have to concentrate on what I'm doing. The few people I have in my telephone are already too much. When I'm on the phone I talk, but I really want to be alone to sketch, to work, and to read. I am reading like a madman because I want to know everything.

I think that you might have Asperger syndrome. Do you know what that is? It's a kind of autism. It's like an idiot savant.
That's exactly what I am. As a child I wanted to be a grown-up. I wanted to know everything—not that I like to talk about it. I hate intellectual conversation with intellectuals because I only care about my opinion, but I like to read very abstract constructions of the mind. It's very strange.

That's quite Asperger's. There's a boy who's 20 years old; you can see him on YouTube. He'd never seen Paris from the air before and they flew him over Paris in a helicopter. Then they took him to a studio and he drew the entire city. Building by building, street by street.
I can do that with the antique Greek world.

That's what I've heard.
If I had to make another choice I would have studied languages and antique civilisations.

Did you study Latin at all?
Yes, but for someone who speaks German it's easy. It's the same grammar and it's pronounced the same way. For French speakers it's much more difficult. When I was 10 or 12 years old I could speak Latin like I speak English. But I cannot speak Latin with French people. I don't understand the way they pronounce it. For me, they don't pronounce it right. But I love dead languages. Homer was one of the first books I read when I was starting to read. I think the *Iliad* is still one of the greatest books in the world.

You've said that possessions are a burden and one mustn't get attached to things, that owning things victimises and imprisons you.
It's nice when you can afford something, but the minute you become a victim of it you shouldn't keep it.

Coming from you, some would think that's quite a contradiction.
It's exactly like people who say they don't like money. Be rich first, and then you will know. If you have never touched money, you don't know what money is. If you're rich, get rid of it. It's very easy.

It's lightness.
Yes, for me the most important thing is light. Nothing overweight, anywhere. Not on the body, not on the brain.

And a certain detachment, too.
Yes, totally. I was brought up to be detached. You can take nothing with you. There are very few important things, and they are not possessions.

Yoga is such a trend. There are all these rich people who study yoga now. I heard a story about a famous yoga master who was working with this woman who had a lot of wealth and money. He was in her mansion and he walked over to the mantle

and took a Ming vase from it and he dropped it on the floor, smashing it. She was freaking out. That was the first lesson for her about not being attached to the material world.
That's the best lesson there, because I don't believe too much in yoga. It's another culture; it's not my culture.

People treat it like it's exercise. There's no spiritual dimension to it.
Yes, I know. One of my best friends does it all the time. It's not my culture because I have not got much time.

Which brings us back, I think, to trying to avoid distraction in the digital age.
I don't know how people can concentrate today when they have their cell phones ringing and all that. I like to be with music, books, and paper and to sketch and think everything over. To brainwash my own head and to write letters. I never have the feeling of being alone. For me loneliness is when you are old, sick, have no money, and nobody's around. But if you are vaguely known and vaguely not poor, to say it nicely, then it's the top of luxury.

Is it hard for you to find time for yourself?
I have to fight to be alone, but I need time to recharge my batteries. Daydreaming is the most important thing for me. It would be a nightmare not to daydream.

Music is so important to you, and I was trying to convince your assistant that you should start DJing at clubs.
I did it once with the DJ Michel Gaubert.

Did you like it?
Yes, but it's not really my job. I prefer to listen. For me it's too much work.

You can get someone to do that for you. It's about selecting the songs.
I'm inclined to have CDs. I like to buy CDs and then make my selection, and then I have my iPod.

That's all DJing is. Just making an iPod playlist. But there's something about playing live to an audience and getting them to dance.
For me that is also difficult, and not because I'm against it, but I don't drink, I don't take drugs, I've never smoked in my life.

Did you used to?
No.

You never experimented with drugs at all?
Never.

Ever?
I saw others doing it and I didn't think it was such a success.

You didn't even have a curiosity?
No. There was a famous man who had written about flies and insects, and I'm like the one who watches the insects. I prefer to see how drugs work on others. And I cannot smoke cigarettes. I need my hands for something else. When I was 14 I wanted to smoke because my mother smoked like mad. I wanted to smoke to look grown-up. But my mother said, "You shouldn't smoke. Your hands are not that beautiful and that shows when you smoke."

Which made a long-lasting impression.
Yes, I never smoked, so thank God. I should thank her. She smoked like mad, and when there were no cigarettes around she was in such a bad mood. I can tell you, we did everything to give her cigarettes. Sometimes she tried for three days not to smoke.

What was the relationship like between your mother and father?
It was neither of their first marriages. They fought a lot. My mother had left several times; my father was a very sweet man but a little boring. He was older and my mother was a very difficult, very funny person so she spent her life making jokes out of him. I was born when my father was 60 and my mother

Karl in the film L'Amour, *1973.*
Photo from The Films of Paul Morrissey *by Maurice Yacowar, Cambridge University Press, 1993*

42. But I don't think I know anything about my parents' lives. I'm not sure one should.

Another form of detachment.
Yes, but I knew they loved me. Their private lives weren't my business.

I don't understand people who spend their lives seeking the approval of their parents. It's the same with the gays seeking the approval of society.
I never had the feeling that there was no approval. I couldn't even imagine. My father used to say, "Ask me what you want, but not in front of your mother because she'd make a joke," and my father said yes to everything I wanted. He gave me sports cars when I was 20 and things like that, so he spoiled me. If I asked my mother for something she'd say, "Ask your father."

Let's talk about sex. I don't know if you read it, but there was recently this interesting article about Andy Warhol in the *New Yorker* by Louis Menand.
Yes, I liked that article.

It was good. It talked about Warhol's sex life. It was kind of shocking to me that they said he was really good in bed in the early 60s.
No one should remember that.

And that his voyeurism wasn't about asexuality. It was more that he was interested in public sex.
It was something new then. What he did could be considered porn, but it's art now, because the world thinks it's erotic art. I don't know where the borderline between pornography and erotic art is. Look at the attributes; you have to be very intellectual to see any borderline there. You know, I was in a Warhol

330

movie. It was called *L'Amour*. I knew him and I knew all the people around him. It was a trendy, funny thing to do then.

Who else was in it?
Patti D'Arbanville, Jane Forth, Coral Labrie, Donna Jordan, me, and Paul Morrissey. I remember the girls better.

What did you do with the girls?
I had to kiss Patti D'Arbanville.

That's it?
No, I did lots of other things.

Were they topless?
Yes, the girls in that scene were topless. Maybe wearing less.

Were you naked?
Sometimes. Not overdressed, let's say.

We have to get ahold of that film.
I can imagine myself as this creature with long hair.

Do you have a copy of it yourself?
No.

I don't think you can rent it or anything.
It was fun to do it then. For a fashion person, I am not a prude.

What was your relationship with Warhol like? Were you friends?
I don't think anybody was really friendly with Andy. He was very sweet, very nice. But I was not living that kind of life; I was not taking drugs and all that.

He didn't really, either.
No, but he pushed others to. I was, in a way, a little too sophisticated for that, and I was more of an outsider inside. I never wanted to have my portrait done by Andy Warhol because I don't care about portraits. I have enough, from Helmut Newton to Irving Penn. I have them all but I only keep cartoons of myself.

I think that's much more fun. But Andy was very nice and so was Fred Hughes, who died in a horrible way. The drama is that Andy was an OK illustrator who became a great artist. Antonio Lopez, who was a much better craftsmen and master artist, tried to chip into the art world and couldn't do it.

When Warhol did the Brillo boxes he was actually copying the work of James Harvey, an artist who was doing commercial illustration.
But James Harvey was not good at PR. Andy was perfect at PR. The movie that I am in was by Paul Morrissey, who is very sick and old now. People say it's not a Warhol movie, it's a Paul Morrissey movie. But it wouldn't exist without Andy. They were both there.

Well, the thing about Paul Morrissey's movies...
What are his movies without Andy?

He made *Beethoven's Nephew*.
I didn't think it was that great. I like him because I like to talk about silent movies with him. I'm a specialist in German silent movies, and he knows quite a lot. We can share that subject.

He made *Forty Deuce*, which is about a male prostitute. It was quite good. Kevin Bacon's in it.
Yes. These are not as famous as the ones he made with Andy. *Flesh* and *Trash* and all that.

It almost seemed like Morrissey was slumming in those movies, that he was kind of making fun of the transsexuals. But the transsexuals were so brilliant and so amusing and so witty.
I shouldn't say this, but physically he was quite repulsive.

Who was?
Andy.

That *New Yorker* article kind of suggested that he was maybe a little more sexually attractive when he was younger.
He was not handsome.

Since Karl likes comics of himself, we commissioned this one by Johnny Ryan.

He did OK. So I recently watched the movies *Lagerfeld Confidential* and *Karl Lagerfeld Is Never Happy Anyway*.
People like me in this vision of loneliness. There was another one called *Un Roi Seul* [*A Lonely King*]. It's a very good movie, though the title is stupid.

Your whole transformation fascinated me, like seeing you before you had lost the weight and you were always holding a fan.
In my youth I was very skinny.

You went up and down, right?
I started to go up when I was 35. Then I had to be careful and then I was bored.

You got tired of working out?
I worked out when I was very young and then one day I was bored to death by it. I did it before other people did it. I did it in the 60s and late 50s.

And when you finally lost the weight, what made you do it?
Well, there came this new line from Hedi Slimane at Dior, that you needed to be slim to wear. It said, "You

want this? Go back to your bones." And so I lost it all. I lost 88 pounds and never got them back.

It was a transformation in style for you as well.
Yes, but if you look at old photos of me as a child I was dressed like this. I never changed.

One documentary was in German and the other was in French. There's something interesting about the way you speak in French.
I'm another person. I am three. When I speak English I am one person, when I speak German I'm another, when I speak French I'm another. I'm happy that you got that message.

Your philosophy is more clear in French somehow.
I'm not Kierkegaard. Don't call it that way.

But everyone has a philosophy, that's my philosophy.
Yes, but I am more a pupil of Spinoza.

I like the fact that you quote Marcuse in *Lagerfeld Confidential*. It was something that he said along the lines of "Happiness and a comfortable life are

indecent".

In a way they are, if you display them too much.

What's your relationship to communism?

If you look at history, you see how many victims they had. The German Nazis, who were the worst thing in the world, are poor beginners next to the communists, who killed more than 30 million people.

You're talking about the Soviets.

Yes, the Soviets and other countries you don't mention because they're still around. North Korea and things like that. So what do you want me to think about it?

Communism has been in vogue in France at various times, often among intellectuals.

In France, after the war, communism became a kind of snobbishness of intellectual wealthy people who were not overly wealthy.

We call them Champagne Socialists.

No, this comes later. What I'm talking about is what the French call gauche caviar. It's softer.

It was something like a trend?

Yes, it was a trend. I'm very sorry, but none of their lives worked like their talk. There was only one philosopher like that before the war—Simone Weil. She was the daughter of a rich banker and she gave all her money away and lived like the poor communists she was defending. She died as a result, because she got tuberculosis from living in poor conditions. This I admire.

She was kind of a martyr.

Yes. Whereas bourgeois people having lunch and drinking hard and "changing the world"…

It's hypocrisy.

Yes. I'm very sorry. It doesn't work with me. You have to live the life.

If you're going to talk the talk, you've got to walk the walk.

Give your money away and live the life that you are fighting for. That's the way it should be. I hate rich people when they try to be communists or socialists. I think it's obscene.

The reason I brought up Bacon earlier in this conversation is because a male prostitute became his muse and his surrogate son.

And von Gloeden paid for those boys to have their photographs taken. It's outrageous.

He had a special assistant named Il Moro who was his lover.

But if you look at those photos they are not sexy. They have ugly teeth and I think they're dressed repulsively. It's the mood that may be interesting.

It was peasant boys that he was photographing.

People who were not groomed properly, who have big bellies and ugly teeth.

So you don't like von Gloeden's photography?

I understand the mood but I will never have a photo of his on my wall.

But he also sort of invented sex tourism in a certain way because everyone was visiting him in Taormina, where he lived in Sicily.

Have you been to Taormina? I think it's a depressing place.

It is. I think it's become too touristic.

I got the flu there and stayed in bed for two weeks at the hotel and then I never liked the place again.

Have you ever had the kind of relationship that Bacon had with someone who kind of becomes a muse?

Yes, but they were not prostitutes, they were professional models.

Right. You mentioned Spinoza. Which thoughts of his particularly resonate for you?

Spinoza said, and I have to translate it into English, "Every decision is a final refusal." I live with this.

CHRIS CUNNINGHAM

INTERVIEW BY ANDY CAPPER | ILLUSTRATION BY TED PEARCE

Published October 2008

Chris Cunningham is a dark, reclusive genius who lives in a cave beneath the Thames. He spends his days rocking back and forth in a creaky old chair while projecting binary code onto the wall and reading the Russian translation of *Dante's Inferno* while Squarepusher records play backwards at 78 rpm through speakers made out of space-shuttle rockets. And all the while, he's frowning and sighing.

Pretty much every article I'd ever read about Chris led me to believe that the above would be true. So I was quite relieved when I met him a few years ago that it wasn't. At all.

Instead, the reclusive-ish genius that made the darkest music videos and short films ever is actually one of the giggliest people I know. It's a giggle that reminds you of when you would sit at the back of class and be pissing yourself with laughter at the teacher's speech impediment or at the giant dicks you were drawing in your geography textbook.

For this issue we spoke to Chris about the new photography and films he's been working on and how they relate to two of his favourite topics: British soft porn from the late 1980s and videos of dogs wanking themselves off.

Vice: The main thing we had in common when we met was our appreciation of classic British "top-shelf jazz mags", aka softcore wank books.
Chris Cunningham: Ha ha, yeah. My favourites were always *Razzle* and *Men Only*.

Those were my favourites as well. What is it about them you liked?
I've often tried to figure it out. I think it's the photographic style. It was really unlit and plain. My photographic style is starting to get more and more overtaken by that look. I've just shot Grace Jones for a magazine and the way I shot her is kind of like the way they would shoot the girls in *Razzle*.

How? The girls in *Razzle* were usually flashing their tits while eating baked beans by the side of the road.
Ha ha ha, no, I mean I just shot her in a really plain way. I don't think sex should be lit in a complicated way. It should be really plain. The other mags of the time had a lot of expensive lighting but *Razzle* was the opposite.

A lot of other British soft porn was like big-production lighting with girls wearing elaborate silk robes in four-star hotel rooms.
Yeah, I didn't like those ones. What were the posh ones called?

Well, posh is the wrong word really.
Ha ha ha. But things like *Playboy* and *Penthouse*, at the time, made *Razzle* seem like snuff.

Playboy and Penthouse would have girls shot through soft focus lenses on long exposure with log fires in the background.
The *Razzle* stuff was meat-and-two-veg porn. It was girls next door and secretaries, shot really simply.

And that style of porn is what's come back around again. You have Sasha Grey wearing no makeup and being shot with Contax cameras. And that's how Penthouse is doing things now.
Yeah, well, something must have happened to me in the last seven years because it's not something I pay much attention to anymore. And seven years ago I would have felt a lot more comfortable talking to you about it!

There's no thrill in acquiring porno anymore. The days of going to the newsagent, really nervous, aged 14, and pleading with the guy in there to sell it to you are gone.
Absolutely. Actually when I think about it I reckon the things that shocked me most when I was a teenager are the things that were most important in influencing my work.

Like what?

I remember the Readers' Wives section of *Razzle* and it was so shocking to see these horrible-looking women, with their bodies all mashed up, shot in this plain style. And I took that style of photography to shoot unusual things that you wouldn't ever see in real life. I'm talking about stuff like the *Rubber Johnny* book or the shots I just did of Grace Jones, for example. Actually I guess that style of photography is like what *Vice* has sometimes. Most of the imagery for my photography book is of that style.

What's the book?

It's a book of my own photography and stills from films, all taken by me over the last ten years really.

Wow. When's it coming out?

I think I've got to get a couple of feature films finished first. There's one I'm working on now that you could loosely describe as a horror. Actually talking about this reminds me of that scene in *American Werewolf in London* when he changes into the werewolf in the front room. That really shocked me. I think it was because it was shot in a brightly lit, stark front room and he's naked and although there's something really shocking happening in it there's a sexual element to it.

I can definitely remember sexual experiences that have involved brightly lit English front rooms and something really shocking happening in them.

Ha ha ha. I mean it's usually quite shocking for me, the whole experience. I don't know about you. That's just reminded me about one of the most shocking things I saw in my teenage years. It was finding a copy of *Whitehouse* magazine behind the scout hut.

Yeah. *Whitehouse* was really gynaecological. It was like the first hardcore porn you could get in Britain. I remember walking across a park near my home and finding a bunch of issues that somebody had thrown away in a fit of guilt or something. The images were made more shocking by the way they were all drenched by the rain in this public place. They had slugs and stuff crawling in between the pages.

When I first moved to London my front room flooded and it drenched my stack of old *Razzles*. Ha ha, that reminds me—an old flatmate of mine had a huge stack of porn mags and his tastes were a lot more gynaecological than mine. They were almost like snuff. I mean, I didn't like to look at them. Anyway, one day he asked me if I could look after them for him because his girlfriend was coming around. He had a pile of 100 or so and I didn't know where to hide them so I had to spread them out in piles of around 15 all around my room. Well, my own girlfriend came around later but I went out to the shops for a while and when I was gone she accidentally found a stack underneath the phone table or something.

What happened?

When I got back from the shops she was gone.

No way.

Ha ha ha. She'd totally left. I couldn't get hold of her for days and then when I did I found out what had happened. She'd dropped something on the floor, then gone to pick it up and her hand brushed against a big wodge of these magazines. I told her what the story was and I actually said to her that if she had found the porn mags that had belonged to me then I would have been in less trouble because his were like something that Fred West would have had.

Ha ha ha. Ugh.

They were a bit too wrong for me. I always thought her being there and finding them would have been like that scene in *The Shining* where she's going through his papers.

And she's walking out of your front door with terror in her eyes, bawling.

And I'm walking the other way back from the shop, all nonchalant with no idea of what's happening.

Amazing.

Yeah, well, I got dumped over that. I got chucked for a couple of weeks at least but we got back together.

Tell me that story again about the cokehead guy who came around your flat once.

Ha ha ha, well, the only problem with that story is trying to think of a way of saying it without incriminating the guy. OK, well, this guy came round my house and me and my friend were there. This guy had been doing coke. He'd got the coke horn and after a while of being there he asked me if I had any porn mags.

So creepy.

Ha ha. So I gave some to him, and me and my friend were talking but we were kind of looking at the guy and he was staring at the mags really serious—like he was trying to work out how to do a really difficult equation. Then after about ten minutes he looked at me all serious and asked if me and my mate could go upstairs for a while because he wanted to have a wank.

And you actually went upstairs.

Ha ha ha, I know. We did. We were so shocked that he'd asked us that we just went. And so we were upstairs trying to not think about it and we looked at the clock and realised he'd been down there for more than ten minutes. And it dawned on us that he was maybe taking the piss a bit.

Maybe...

And the thing is that the longer you leave it the harder it is to go downstairs and ask him what's going on.

I suppose it's harder and harder to be shocked by anything you could label as "porn" these days because of the way it's so omnipresent. What was the last thing you saw that made an impression on you? Is it that film of the dog wanking itself off that you're always showing people on your phone?

That dog wanking itself off is literally my favourite thing I've seen in the last decade. You wouldn't believe how many times I've watched it. To me, it's like when the monkey throws the bone up in the air in *2001*.... In that movie, it symbolises the monkey moving onto the next stage of evolution or something. I feel the same way about the dog wanking itself off.

What do you like about it so much?

I love the fact that the person filming it is having the same reaction as I do when I watch it.

Which is what?

Ha ha ha. "I can't believe this is happening." I love the way animals have absolutely no dignity about things. The wanking dog is an organism that's completely out of control.

When did you last watch it?

I watched it again last week. I'm hoping people will forget about it actually because I've based a scene in my new film on it.

SAME OLD BULLSHIT

**RAEKWON KEEPS US WAITING FOR TWO DAYS, THEN TALKS ABOUT CAKES
WORDS BY ANDY CAPPER | INTERVIEW BY JAIMIE HODGSON
PHOTO BY BEN RAYNER**

Published June 2009

This magazine used to be well known for interviews with big-name American rappers. Back when Dave 1 from Chromeo was still writing for us every month we had scoops like Eminem's first ever interview, Ol' Dirty's last ever interview, Lil' Kim shot by Terry Richardson, and Fat Joe walking us around the Bronx. 50 Cent talked to us about "How to Rob" three years before most people had heard of him, Benzino threatened to kill us, Young Jeezy made us an exquisite corpse, we reunited the Hot Boys, and we broke the story that Cappadonna was broke and working as a cab driver.

Our most recent rap piece involved Bradford Cox from Deerhunter interviewing Soulja Boy, which was OK, but most new rappers are so conservative and dull that it's a waste of time talking to them.

This month, though, we were offered an interview with Raekwon and thought, "Well, why not?" It's the Conversations With Distinguished Gentlemen Issue and he certainly fits that description, right?

As well as being the hardest member of the Wu next to Masta Killa, he and Ghostface made the finest albums about selling crack ever, in the form of *Only Built 4 Cuban Linx* and *Ironman*. Lex Diamonds also made Tommy Hilfiger and Lexus cars fashionable, but we'll forgive him for that.

But guess what? The whole process of interviewing him turned into a total ball ache and reminded us why we don't do rap interviews anymore. After keeping our photographer waiting for nearly two days while Raewkon watched WWF and got stoned in his hotel, his management refused to send us even a streamed link of the album so we can't even tell you how it sounds. On the basis of the couple of tracks we've heard leaked, it sounds like, well, pretty good to mildly OK. So what could we talk about? See below.

Vice: So, you're 39 years of age and a family man, many times over. How's the home life?
Raekwon: I'm still infatuated with this art I do. I make it my business to do my business, you know? But I'm a father, and I make the most of that. I want to be the best family man I can be.

What keeps you busiest at home?
I love to cook more and more, every day. That's part of growing up and becoming a man. I come from a long line of people who know how to cook. So yeah, maybe I was destined to be "The Chef" in multiple ways, you know?

What's your signature dish?
I do a really good baked salmon, and baked chicken with the crispy skin. We all be on that. It's good to be able to relax with your friends and family and make some good food.

Who would win a Wu edition of *Come Dine With Me*?
I don't know. There's some good cooks in Wu. GZA be on some baking shit. He does like a strawberry cake and, like, a lemon one, like that lemon glazed shit.

A lemon drizzle?
Yeah, that's the one.

Jack Walls and Ryan McGinley at Patti Smith's house, Michigan, 1999.

DICK FACE

**WHY IS JACK WALLS THE COOLEST MOTHERFUCKER ON EARTH?
INTERVIEW BY RYAN MCGINLEY**

Published November 2007

I spent two weeks making 500 hand-drawn balloons for Jack Walls's 50th birthday party. It was my present to him. With a black Sharpie, I drew all of his classic expressions on 500 silver balloons. He's well known for these sayings and everyone who knows him has their own Jack Walls imitation.

Jack is an artist, writer, muse, and infamous man-about-town. He was Robert Mapplethorpe's boyfriend for many years, up until his death. Jack grew up as a gangbanger in the ghetto of Chicago. He joined the Navy for a few years and then moved to New York and met Robert in the early 80s. Jack is in many of Robert's most famous photographs.

I met Jack in the late 90s, right around the time I started making my own photographs. He's been like a big brother to me. After his birthday party was over I couldn't part with the balloons. I deflated them all and took them back to my studio and made a book out of them. Jack claims he didn't say half the things we say he did, but if you've ever heard him talk, you know that everything he says is instantly quotable.

Vice: You have these sayings that all your friends know you for. Everyone tries to imitate you.
Jack Walls: Some of this stuff I never said. People tell me I said stuff and I know I didn't say it and they argue with me! Like I never said, "Spaghetti is straight until you boil it". What is that? Dash Snow made that one up. He is the main culprit. I'm not even lying. Look, out of all the shit I say, do I ever make reference to food? That's a dead giveaway. I cannot equate food with talking shit. I don't operate like that.

I'm calling this article "Why Is Jack Walls the Coolest Motherfucker on Earth?" and that's my question for you. Why does everyone want to be your friend?
Bad judgment.

Come on, you're a celebrity in certain circles.
Yeah, a very limited circle. The circle's about an inch.

People want to know you. You've lived like ten exciting lives. You've been in the Navy and in a gang, you've been a notorious downtown New York junkie, you've been the boyfriend to basically the most famous photographer of the later part of the 20th century...
I don't know, I don't think that's nothing. I think I'm a late bloomer and for the first time in my life I've decided to really pay attention to art and writing, so I really do believe that I'm just starting out.

Shit, I guess that gives hope to all of us.
Hey, it ain't over till it's over.

Where are you from?
I was born in Chicago, 1957. I lived there until I went into the Navy in 1978.

You were a gangbanger, right?
I participated in gang activities, yes. I tell you one

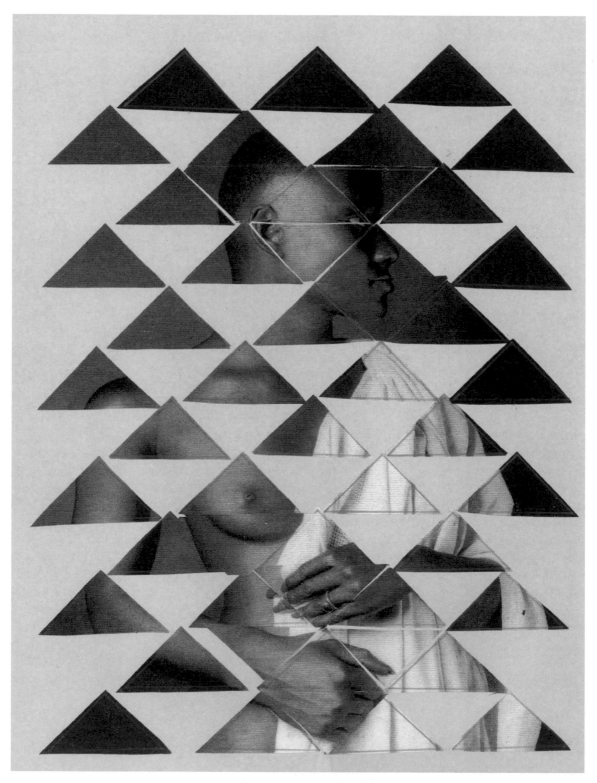

Ada (b), 2007, by Jack Walls

thing, being in a gang is like being gay. Anything that's all guys is gay, that's why I knew the Navy would be perfect for me. Psychologically, I already knew, even at a young age, that being in a gang or the military or being an athlete, it's all homoerotic. Plus I was a big Jean Genet fan. Being in a gang was romantic. Everything I do has a sense of romance to it, everything.

Tell me about your gang.
The gang I was in was called the Morgan Deuces, in the Chicago area called Pilsen, and I was in the gang from the age of 14 to 17. I got arrested all the time. My brother was killed from gangbanging. He was shot and killed.

Me and you both have two sisters and six brothers, one of whom died. It's such a weird coincidence, isn't it? What was it like growing up with such a big family? What were you like?
I don't know, I'm pretty much the same. People don't change. I've known you for ten years and you're exactly the same, except maybe you got a little bit worse.

I thought I got better.
Well, think again.

Do you remember how we met?
I can tell you exactly. We met in June 1998. I had just come back from LA and the day I got back the actor Dwight Ewell said, "You have to meet these kids, they're the best." And I told him, "Look, I don't want to meet anyone, I just want to go to Cherry Tavern." Somehow he tricked me into going to this party and the first time I saw you, you were sitting there getting your hair cut. I was so pissed off that Dwight had set me up, I went out and sat in the hallway. Later that night some people were hanging out at my place on 29th Street and you showed up at 4 AM. We talked about photography.

That was our initial bond. You had Mapplethorpe prints and Patti Smith drawings, and it was a clutter of art books and weird art objects and postcards everywhere. It was 20 years of collecting stuff. All I could think was, this was the coolest place I'd ever been to. I've styled my own place based on how yours was. You knew so much and you taught me so much.
But at that point in my life I had turned my back on the art world. I definitely didn't think of you in terms of being an artist. I remember one night, you were about to drop out of college, and you said, "Jack, I don't know what I'm going to do now. I'm not gonna get a job and I'm not gonna bartend." And I remember thinking, OK, he's on the right track, because that's exactly how anyone I've ever known who ever did anything with themselves did it—they never developed another skill. That's the trick. I'm gonna be an artist and nothing else. And that's when I decided I would help you. And I helped get you that show at 420 West Broadway.

That was my first photo show. You also helped me get my first internship. You always helped me out. Yet I never took your advice, and you were always right. You're always like, "You're so stupid. I told you two years ago not to do that!" So tell me about this new art project of yours.
Well, last winter I started making collages and I'm going to have a show of them at Fuse Gallery this February.

What inspired the collages?
Last year around this time I quit smoking. And every time I wanted to smoke a cigarette I did a collage instead. And the next thing you know I had 66 of them! That's the truth. I'm not gonna make it seem like Robert came to me in a dream and said I should make collages from one of his images.

The image in your collages is a Mapplethorpe photo of a girl named Ada. Tell me about her.
I met Ada in the summer of 1982. She was walking down 8th Street with an old friend of mine from Chicago, this Puerto Rican girl named Margie. She yelled out, "Hi-Fi!" which was my old nickname from back home, and I turned around and said, "Margie!" And she said, "Oh, it's Cita now, as in mamacita." She had a blonde mohawk and Ada was bald and rail

"The Only Thing Between
Us Is Air and Opportunity"
That means ain't nothing
stopping us. It means
all systems are GO. Like
somebody comes up to me
and says, "Hey, Jack, we
should hang out sometime,"
and I say, "Yeah, that's cool,
'cause ain't nothing between
us but air and opportunity."
It's like, yeah, right on.

"Trade Alarm"
That's when you look at
someone and you just know
they have a huge cock.
Instinctively, bells go off.
That's also what you call a
"dick face". When you see
somebody and you go, "Oh,
they got a big one."

"Don't Make Me Put My
Baby Down"
That's a ghetto thing. By the
time girls are 15 years old
they got babies, so they're
walking around the hood
with a baby on their hip
and they're getting into
fights and that's the ultimate
threat: "Don't make me put
my baby down!"

"Clock the Basket"
Again, look at the basket.
There's a lot of basket sayings. And packages. Every
day is like Christmas for me,
darling!

"Features Balls"
That's when you look at
somebody's basket and you
can tell it's mostly balls.

"Ghetto Deluxe"
That's when you go to
someone's dinner party and
you just know all the food
on the table is gotten with
food stamps. Like, a cheese
truck used to roll up in the
hood and people would run
out to it and they would
give you these big pieces of
government cheese. Every
party you went to had
grilled-cheese platters and
speakers turned outside
the window but locked safe
inside the house. That's
ghetto deluxe!

"Even People in Hell Need
Ice Water"
No, no, you got it phrased
wrong. It's like when people
go, "Hey, Jack, I want this, I
want that," and you just tell
them, "Yeah, people in hell
want ice water"—you ain't
getting it!

"Motherfucker I Will Slap
the Shit Out of You Right
Now"
Because sometimes you
have to represent. Because
before I slap the shit out of
a person I'm gonna let them
know that that's what I'm
about to do. I don't like to
get physical but I can.

"No Bitches Just Niggas"
All cats, no hos.

"What Did My Pussy Ever
Do to You?"
That's from a Bobby Garcia
porno. A marine is fucking
him and the guy is screaming, "Oh my pussy, you're
destroying my pussy! What
did my pussy ever do to you,
you treat it so bad!"

"Smile Now Cry Later"
That's an old song by Sunny
and the Sunliners. We call
them gangbanging songs
because that's what we
listened to when we were
teenagers and in gangs. I
stopped listening to all that
old music until I told Ryan
about it and he became
obsessed with the whole
genre and went and found
each and every song. That's
one thing I love about him.
I'll just mention the stupid-
est thing in passing and
suddenly a week later he'll
know everything about it.

"Stinkyfoot Junkie"
Most junkies have notori-
ously stinky feet because
they're always walking
around looking for dope.
Especially back in the day,
the drug spots were always
moving. You had to do a
lot of walking around for
heroin if the main spot was
closed. That hallway on 2nd
Street between Avenues A
and B, that was the spot.
New York was paradise for
a junkie back then.

"Sacrifice the Relationship"
Say you know a cat, and
you're good friends, and
it gets to the point where
you go, he's my friend, but
I think he's hot, now do
I wanna make this thing
sexual and end the friendship if he's not a fag? Are
you gonna sacrifice the relationship because you're a
horny fag or are you gonna
respect this individual?

"Potential Dick Flow"
That's like, what are the
chances you're gonna get
laid or not. You dig?

"Basket Picnic"
Hahaha, that means you
see somebody with a big
package—it's a basket
picnic! You get it, don't you?
Listen, I'm drunk half the
time. These things I say,
I don't even know I say. I
can't think about it, I just
talk.

thin. I thought, "What a look!" I was headed over to Robert's and I invited them to come along. He photographed both of them that day. Later that summer, the girls were living in Queens and I heard that both of them got pregnant at the same time. They disappeared. That day is a special memory for me and I've always loved that image. Robert did too.

How did you meet Robert Mapplethorpe?
Oh, everyone knows that story. It's old and grey and dusty.

I love that story and I want to hear it again.
Fine, we met in 1982 because I had just gotten out of the Navy and was living in the West Village, the hub of gay activity. Christopher Street was the centre of the universe if you were a fag. I would see Robert around and check him out because he was a good-looking cat.

Who cruised who first?
We cruised each other. We would look at each other and finally one day he gave me his number. I called him up that night and he invited me out for dinner. We met at the Pink Teacup and then we never stopped seeing each other.

Wait, I thought you told me that you met in an ice-cream parlour.
Well, I saw him around for a while before we actually met. Eventually he came up to me and handed me his business card, which just said "Robert Mapplethorpe, photographer".

I love that story because you told me that it was the middle of summer and he was wearing full leather and getting ice cream.
Yeah, it was 99 degrees out and he had on those motorcycle boots that go all the way up your leg. Eating a big waffle cone. I'll tell you he had a great look. He was the most amazing-looking fucking beautiful boyfriend I've ever had. The best boyfriend ever. Let me tell you something, I loved Robert. Still to this very day.

When I look at pictures of Robert, I think, Oh my God, if I saw that guy on the street I would have sex with him in a minute.
He was something else, darling. Who would have thought when I met him in 1981 that he would be dead by 1989?

Tell me about the early days of AIDS.
There's nothing to talk about. It was just sad.

Well, I like talking about it because it's been a big part of both our lives. Robert and my older brother Michael both got HIV at around the same time. For all we know they could have fucked each other.
Probably not... Maybe they both fucked the same person.

Yeah, my brother was into black guys too, so it is possible. How come Robert never did heroin?
He did it once. But, you know, Robert was bourgeois. Robert was piss-elegant. He didn't want to hang out with a bunch of junkies.

In 1985 Basquiat painted your portrait for a series he was doing of all the downtown black kids on the scene at the time. What was it like being painted by him? Was it interesting seeing his process?
Nah, we were just smashed on heroin. But I tell you one thing, I had done so much heroin that day that when I left there I got amnesia. It's the only time that's ever happened in my life. I was walking around Manhattan and it was snowing and for about four hours I could not remember who or where I was.

Can I ask you about your sex life?
You know what? Honestly, I don't have a sex life.

You are such a liar.
But see, if I talked about my sex life I would incriminate people.

Well, you don't have to use their names.
Yeah, but it's not even that important. I mean, you suck a dick, you suck a dick.

POGUE MAHONE MEANS KISS MY ARSE

**AN INTERVIEW WITH SHANE MACGOWAN | INTERVIEW BY ANDY CAPPER
PHOTOS BY BEN RAYNER**

Published May 2008

We won't go too much into who Shane MacGowan is here because, for God's sake, you should know. He's got our vote for best lyricist of the 20th century, and he's a singer who can bring grown men to tears with just one well-turned phrase. Is he a drunk and a now-and-then junkie? Sure. But the fans that find amusement in that, the ones who hold him up as some kind of mascot of Irish debauchery, are missing the point entirely. That's a simpleton's way of looking at Shane. That's how fucking Walt Disney probably saw the Irish. The only thing we want to say about his boozing is that it's a shame it will probably kill him before his time. Or who knows, maybe it will kill him right at his time. Who are we to guess how long Shane MacGowan will live? He turns 51 this year. We hope he lives forever.

We interviewed Shane on March 1, 2008 in his kitchen in Dublin's Donnybrook area. Donnybrook is historically one of the unruliest parts of Ireland thanks to the reputation of the Donnybrook Fair, which was notorious for its drinking, fighting, carousing, and banshee-like shrieking. It was banned in 1855, and Donnybrook is now one of the city's most respectable areas, but the legend remains.

During our time in his kitchen, Shane was projecting images from a DVD of traditional Irish folk music from the 60s and 70s onto the wall of his living room while singing along to the music. He drank white wine and gin from a mug with "Morphine" written on the side and chain-smoked hash. He punctuated almost every sentence with "Know what I mean, yeah," and then made his trademark laugh, which is indescribable but can best be transcribed as, "Eeeeshshshsh".

PS: We never put "celebrities" on our cover, but we couldn't do the History Issue without this man on the front of it.

Vice: Hi, Shane. We came to take your photo and maybe talk a bit about history.
Shane MacGowan: OK, you better sit down then. Some people would say that these cameras were worse than guns because they could steal your souls. Know what I mean, yeah? Eeeeshshshsh.

Which Irish historical figure do you most admire?
Gerry O'Boyle.

But he's your friend, so let's say anyone apart from Gerry.
Eamon de Valera. He was the Irish prime minster, president, and, like, the main author of the Constitution of Ireland. He had an American passport because his mother was an immigrant who went over to America, right? She got married to a Hispanic American. So they got their American passports and they came back.

He was president of Ireland all through the 60s, right?
Yeah. He was a politician but he was a crack shot as well. He was tasty. He took it up with the Brits in the civil war.

What else was special about him?
He did what Stalin did, but he did it without killing all the people, know what I mean, yeah? He was a great figurehead for Ireland. When World War II came

around, the English asked him for their support and he said, "Fuck you, Churchill, you bastard!"

Excellent.
Churchill kept saying, "We want to use your ports," but Valera pointed out that he already had the main ports across the world. Eeeeshshshsh.

What do you think about Churchill?
A lot of people nowadays complain about Mad Bomber Harris and what he did, but really all he was doing was carrying out the orders of Churchill, who was a mad, fascist, racist nutter. And the fucking Americans were as well. They completely destroyed Dresden and they had to rebuild it, stone by stone, over 15 or 20 years. The Germans were keeping all their most valuable treasures underground, know what I mean?

You've been a big supporter of Irish independence your whole life. How do you think the ceasefire and the withdrawal of troops from Northern Ireland have changed the country?
Well, there have been less bank robberies, you know what I mean, yeah? Eeeeshshshsh. There's generally been less paramilitary activity.

Right. What else has changed?
Well there have been a few things like girl-napping and child-napping and child killing and girl killing and girl and boy abuse and that's led to a lot of people getting kicked out of their jobs in the priesthood. Eeeeshshshsh. That was a joke, that was a joke. I didn't mean that.

It's funny because it's true. But what have been the actual benefits of the ceasefire?
For a start, we got rid of the Brits, you know? And now Ireland's, like, the biggest growing economy in the world. Ireland was like a child at school that was bullied. Then one day it says, "No fucking more, right?" This country's been growing at something like 3.7 per cent per year. Ireland leads the way in education in the world. This didn't hap-

pen overnight but it's happened and it's growing all the time.

So Ireland is in a good place now, in your opinion.
Look, when you get to the point where people are complaining about the price of a pint you know that you're out of the real shit, yeah?

How much is a pint here anyway?
I couldn't tell you. Thirty years ago I could have told you what a pint cost. It was about ten pence.

When the British were in Ireland, what were the darkest times?
Things like Bloody Sunday and when they were bringing in the SAS. Know what I mean? It wasn't looking good.

And now in Belfast, the ex-loyalist paramilitaries are entrenched in criminal activity because there's nothing else for them to do.
When you've been in full-time active service for years and then suddenly it's done, you've got to do something, right? Whenever there's change in society there's criminality, you know what I mean? The English had their highwaymen. They would rob from everybody.

During our time in Shane's kitchen, we mentioned that the following day we were going to see Nick

Cave play with Spiritualized in London. Knowing that the two were old friends, we asked Shane if he had a message for Nick. He made a drawing for us to pass along. We still haven't given Nick the drawing because we kind of want to frame it and keep it.

Vice: When did you become friends with Nick Cave?

Shane MacGowan: It was at Filthy McNasty's for an *NME* thing with him and Mark E Smith. We were all talking. I thought Mark E Smith was an idiot. He's not very nice. He was going on about the IRA and he didn't know what he was talking about.

Is there a time during the Troubles that you remember fondly?

There was a ceasefire in '64, and then in '66 there was a celebration of the Easter Rising, which was the rebellion attempted by the Republicans to win independence from the Brits. The celebration wasn't in any way threatening to the English. It was just a year of people getting pissed and it started at Easter with Nelson getting his first blowjob. Know what I mean, yeah?

Right, when the IRA blew up Nelson's Pillar. That was an unpopular monument to the British admiral Lord Nelson that was on O'Connell Street in Dublin.

Ireland is like Vietnam, right? The forces had to leave. They were flushed out of Vietnam, just like here.

Wasn't Irish hero John F. Kennedy president of the United States when Vietnam began, though?

Yeah, but Kennedy was going to pull out. He probably would have pulled out and that's probably why they shot him. He was sick of getting shafted by the army and the navy telling him what to do all the time. Then Bobby Kennedy was carrying it on and he got plugged before he even got time to do anything. Bobby also got shot because he was an Irish Catholic immigrant.

History hasn't been kind to the Irish.

On the whole, history has been absolutely, stupendously stupid. But the thing is that Ireland has got faith and hope. We have that more in abundance than any other country. We live in the moment.

I guess we should talk a bit about music too. How've you seen the music industry change?

I remember times when I first started dealing with labels and things, there were people like Chris Blackwell at Island who were good. When I was first around there was like a huge musical and cultural revival going on. There was no generation gap really in music and now there is. And I remember MTV starting as well, and that was meant to stir things up and be good but then it just turned into Dire Straits and Van Halen and then Michael Jackson and then all the rest. You know what I mean, yeah?

Are you still making music?

Of course. But I don't really write music. I just play and the song comes out, you know what I mean? And I still listen to the old Irish music because it's incredibly powerful, you know?

Are there moments in your life that you don't care to remember?

No! I remember all of it. And I liked all of it—even all the bad stuff that happened. That was all OK as well.

That's a good way of looking at it.

It's like evolution, yeah? I think all Darwin really proved is that some things are better looking than others. Life is like a Groucho Marx movie. It's good to create your own world, yeah? You know what I mean? From the bad to the good, you've just got to live with it all. There are humans and monkeys and there are differences between some of them sometimes. But I think generally there's not much difference really. Eeeeshshshsh.

Special thanks to Gerry O'Boyle and Lisa Moorish.

ACKNOWLEDGEMENTS

Thanks to Jamie Byng, Dan Franklin, all the folk at Canongate
and Jon Elek for being kindred spirits.

VICE International
Eddy Moretti
Amy Kellner
Chris Cechin
Thomas Morton
Rocco Castoro
Matt Elek
Ben Rayner
Jonnie Craig
Old Man Sturrock
Dylan Hughes
Aldene Johnson
Tim Small, Milene Larsson, Tom Littlewood, Mathieu Berenholc
and all the cats from Europe, Asia, Australia and Japan.

H.M.S.I Forever